1-2-3® Command Language

Darien Fenn

Que™ Corporation
Indianapolis, Indiana

1-2-3® Command Language

Copyright © 1986 by Que™ Corporation

Library of Congress Catalog No.: 86-61155
ISBN 0-88022-268-9

90 89 88 87 86   8 7 6 5 4 3 2

Interpretation of the printing code: the rightmost double-digit number is the year of the book's printing; the rightmost single-digit number, the number of the book's printing. For example, a printing code of 87-4 shows that the fourth printing of the book occurred in 1987.

Dedication

To Dessa

Daddy's rugrat and World's Greatest Child

Product Director
David P. Ewing

Editorial Director
David F. Noble, Ph.D.

Managing Editor
Gregory Croy

Editors
Kathie-Jo Arnoff
Pamela Fullerton

Technical Editor
Terri L. Thompson

Composed in Garamond and Que Digital
by Que Corporation

Cover designed by
Listenberger Design Associates

About the Author

Darien Fenn

Darien Fenn received his B.A. in psychology from the University of
Arkansas at Little Rock, an M.S. in psychology from the University of
Oregon, and is currently an *nth-year* graduate student at the University of
Oregon. He will be completing his Ph.D. in Clinical Psychology "any day
now," and has taken computer science as his cognate for that degree.
Darien Fenn has 16 years of experience working with computers,
beginning in 1970 when he worked for Texas Instruments and designed
computer-controlled machinery that made integrated circuits. Since that
time he has been unable to avoid computers; he has learned numerous
programming languages and countless commercial programs, and has
written programs for psychological research, data analysis, and simulation.
He has published numerous articles in *Absolute Reference*, has written for
PC World magazine, and is the author of *Symphony Macros and the
Command Language*, published by Que Corporation. Darien Fenn works
as a consultant for the Coast Consulting Group in Portland, Oregon, where
he lives with his 10-year-old daughter, Dessa.

Table of Contents

4   Automatic and Hybrid Macros 63

5 Macro Library 85

7   Introducing the Command Language . . 173

8   Functions 191

Foreword

"So it will run the keyboard for me. Big deal."
—Darien Fenn (August, 1983)

Sometime in the summer of 1983, I went to work for a management consulting firm, ostensibly to do some data analysis. I had an extensive background in statistics, was familiar with microcomputers, and could program in a half-dozen languages. I was ready for anything. However, because the data involved was largely financial, I was told that we were going to use a new integrated spreadsheet program called 1-2-3. It was supposed to have some really nifty database functions, generate super graphics, do lickety-split calculations, and be easy to use. "It's the current rage," I was told.

Fine, except for one thing. The entirety of my experience using spreadsheet software consisted of a 15-minute session with VisiCalc on an Apple® II. I had no exposure to a spreadsheet's underlying concepts, nor did I know what it was used for. I remember ending that first session with less knowledge than when I started. There's an old joke that spreadsheet was a service offered by fertilizer companies. At that point, I couldn't have told you why the joke was funny.

Well, okay, if we were going to do the data analysis with 1-2-3, I was going to have to learn 1-2-3. So with a large sigh, I settled down with the even larger manual, opened it to page one, and began reading. The experience was recent enough that I can clearly remember how overwhelming the task seemed. Although I don't think I actually voiced the sentiments expressed in the opening quote, I remember thinking them when I came across the section on macros. Frankly, I couldn't imagine how a function that pushed keys for me could possibly be of any use. How would it know which keys to push? I made the natural mistake of assuming that my brain was going to be needed to decide which key was going to be pushed, each and every time it needed pushing.

Fate, however, had decreed that I was to learn macros early on. Although I started reading the manual a week before I actually started the data analysis job, I of course was nowhere near proficient with the software when the time came for me to start entering the data and analyzing it. Because of my lack of proficiency, my primary mode of learning consisted of launching myself into one abyss of ignorance after another, looking up commands in the manual and correcting the damage as I went along—a form of learning that could aptly be called "error and retrial."

The moment of truth came when I actually had to start making some sense out of the 180-column-by-80-row database I had spent several weeks creating. When I began the first sort on the data, I discovered that I should have been building an 80-column-by-180-row database. That's right folks; I had built my database *sideways*. I read through the "/Data Commands" section of the manual several times before I finally convinced myself that I had indeed committed a Monumental Mistake. I could not sort, select, or otherwise utilize the powerful 1-2-3 /Data commands and functions on a sideways database.

A Conversion Experience—of Sorts

At that point I had two choices. I could (gasp) start over, or I could (groan) go through the tedious process of moving and copying the data until it was rearranged correctly. Of the two alternatives, the former seemed to be the least threatening to my continued sanity, and I actually almost did start over.

Fortunately, I remembered having seen (and skipped over) a section in the manual that began: "Do you sincerely want to become a programmer?"—or something to that effect. At the time, I very much wanted to become a programmer, and I opened to that section of the manual with an enthusiasm usually reserved for a weekend at the coast or on the ski slopes of Mt. Bachelor.

Thus began The Macro Era in the course of my 1-2-3 development. My first attempt at a transposition macro rearranged the rows and columns of my database at the rate of one cell every 5 seconds. I realized that this process might take a while. But it took no effort whatsoever on my part, so I simply left the macro running at the end of the day and went home. When I returned in the morning, the macro was not only still running, but not very far along (180 columns * 80 rows * 5 seconds = 72,000 seconds = 20 hours). I realized that perhaps some refinement was in order. The second-generation macro took me about 2 hours to develop, but finished the rearranging job in another 2 hours. My experience with this first macro proves the old adage that there is indeed more than one way to skin a catastrophe. But that is a topic about which I will have more to say later.

The transposition was a success, including, much to my surprise, every formula in the database. There were also a couple of fringe benefits: one, while all these automated operations were taking place, I got to take a little break; and two, such operations look impressive. Macros that generate a lot of screen activity almost never fail to draw comments such as "Aren't these computers amazing?" I was so pleased that I began to look for new ways to use my newfound knowledge.

Reaching Macro Maturity

A number of factors combined to further my macro education. First, the carpeting in the office where I worked generated so much static electricity that when people walked into the room, they often were surrounded by a faint blue glow that would cause papers to leap up off the desk and stick to their clothing. Those of you who have experienced this phenomenon are also likely to be acquainted with the effect that static electricity has on a computer (*not* a good effect) and know why the phrase PARITY CHECK 2 can strike fear into the hearts of IBM PC users. I found myself on many occasions repeating the same portion of work, keystroke for keystroke, that I had just completed an hour earlier and had *almost* saved to disk. I came to value highly any technique that would enable me to streamline work.

The second factor has to do with my line of work. Being in the consulting business means that virtually everything you do is, if not unusual in itself, at least different from anything else you have ever done. I was constantly stretching 1-2-3 to do something new, or more frequently, something that it was clearly not intended to do (such as exploded pie graphs or form-oriented data entry). I admittedly derived some sort of perverse pleasure in making 1-2-3 do the impossible.

The third force in my macro education involves a quote from one of my former employers, who contended that lazy people made the most creative employees. Being an essentially lazy person myself, I have always felt this to be a particularly insightful pearl of wisdom. At any rate, since then, I have always endeavored to enhance my creative potential wherever possible. And macros were often just the ticket to make that happen.

The final factor, as it relates to this book, is my experience developing training materials for seminars on 1-2-3 and, later, Symphony. Having to teach material to someone else always forces you to learn it well first. More important, teaching has given me an excuse to sit and play with the system, both to see what it could do and to experiment with alternate methods and optimization.

What This Means to You

As a result of my experiences, I have become a macro fan (fanatic). I now use some form of macro or command language program in literally every worksheet that I construct—either during its actual construction or its operation. Macros and command language programs save me great amounts of time and have increased my spreadsheet productivity tremendously. The most important facet of having a programmable spreadsheet is that the automation can dramatically reduce the tedium that can sometimes accompany computer work. Now, whenever a task is tedious, I automate it.

In this book, I hope to give you the benefit of my experience: the tricks, the tips, and the disasters to avoid. Most important, I hope to share some of the enthusiasm I have for the usefulness and virtually unlimited potential of what I consider to be the most powerful component of the most powerful software on the market today.

Acknowledgments

Thanks to Craig Stack for a couple of macros.

Thanks also to Dave Bills for the inspiration for the goal-seeking program.

Thanks to the folks at Coast Consulting for letting me take on this project and for providing an endless stream of insoluble problems that have forced me to learn all the details and tricks presented in this book.

Finally, thanks to my parents for their endless patience and support.

Trademark Acknowledgments

Conventions Used in This Book

A number of conventions are used in *1-2-3 Command Language* to help you learn the program. One example is provided of each convention to help you distinguish among the different elements of 1-2-3.

References to keys are as they appear on the keyboard of the IBM Personal Computer. Direct quotations of words that appear on the screen are spelled as they appear on the screen and are printed in a `special typeface`. Information you are asked to type is printed in *italic*.

The first letter of each command from 1-2-3's menu system appears in boldface: **/R**ange **F**ormat **C**urrency. Abbreviated commands appear as in the following example: /rfc. **/R**ange **F**ormat **C**urrency indicates that you type /rfc to select this command if you were entering it manually. The first letter of menu choices also appears in boldface: **C**opy.

Words printed in uppercase include range names (SALES), functions (@PMT), modes (READY), and cell references (A1..G5).

Conventions that pertain to macros deserve special mention here:

1. Macro names (Alt-character combinations) appear with the backslash (\\) and single character name in lowercase: \\a. In this macro command example, the \\ indicates that you press the Alt key and hold it down while you press also the A key.

2. All /x macro commands, such as /xm or /xn, appear in lowercase, but commands from the command language within braces are uppercase: {WAIT}.

3. 1-2-3 menu keystrokes in a macro line are lowercase: /rnc.

4. Range names within macros are uppercase: /rncTEST.

5. In macros, representations of cursor keys, such as {DOWN}; function keys, such as {CALC}; and editing keys, such as {DEL}, appear in uppercase letters and are surrounded by braces.

6. Enter is represented by the tilde (~). (Note that throughout the text, Enter is used instead of Return.)

The function keys, F1 through F10, are used for special situations in 1-2-3. In the text, the function key name is usually followed by the number in parentheses: Graph (F10).

Ctrl-Break indicates that you press the Ctrl key and hold it down while you press also the Break key. Other hyphenated key combinations, such as Alt-F10, are performed in the same manner.

Key sequences, such as End+Home, are performed by pressing and releasing each key in turn.

Because the number of characters on a single typeset line is limited, some characters that actually appear on a single line of the screen are carried over to another line and indented in this text.

Introduction

1-2-3® Command Language gives you the skills you need to begin using 1-2-3's most powerful new tool: the command language. The book teaches you how to use the command language in an evolutionary fashion, beginning with simple macros and moving gradually into the command language and the more complex considerations of programming. Along the way, you learn how to use 1-2-3's @ functions as powerful programming tools. Whether you intend to use 1-2-3 in your own work or apply yourself to writing complex application packages for use by other people, this book provides many valuable ideas, techniques, and insights that can speed learning.

1-2-3 Command Language contains beginning to advanced material. Whether you are a new computer user, a battle-scarred 1-2-3 veteran upgrading to Release 2, or a former Symphony® user, you will find material here that you can use.

As a 1-2-3 user, you probably already know a fair amount about how to use the worksheet commands. Therefore, the book begins by showing you how to use macros to automate your commands. Initially, what you will create are macros that are simple sequences of steps. These macros, easy to write and follow, will help you learn the basic elements of macro writing and "get a feel" for the system.

After being introduced to the basics in Chapters 1 through 3, you will study in Chapter 4 a program that will write your macros for you. Using the macros created with this program, Chapter 4 explains how you can modify the simple sequences of keystrokes so that the macros will stop to allow you to respond manually and will loop to create automatically repeating operations. Chapters 5 and 6 describe numerous examples of how you can apply even these basic operations to a large number of worksheet tasks.

Chapter 7 introduces the command language and the concepts associated with programming. At this point, *1-2-3 Command Language* begins to address 1-2-3 not as a spreadsheet, but as a complete programming environment. As you move beyond simple macros, the level of complexity, power of the system, and potential for problems all are magnified immensely. The second half of the book, therefore, addresses some important issues that arise when you write programs, along with some special considerations involved in programming in 1-2-3.

Chapter 7 explains how @ functions and commands in 1-2-3 are, in a sense, a form of computer programming. Chapter 8 describes in some detail how to use @ functions, especially the string functions that are new to Release 2, as essential elements of command language programming.

Chapter 9 discusses the differences between the new command language and the old /x commands of 1-2-3's Release 1A. This chapter also shows you how to use Release 2's string-handling capabilities to enhance the command language's performance.

In Chapter 10 you will learn how to construct a program "from the ground up," including testing and debugging of the final product. This chapter also provides numerous guidelines for writing good programs, including how to optimize your programs so that they run faster.

Chapter 11 contains a number of examples of command language programming, ranging from enhancements to worksheet utility macros to complicated programs. These programs demonstrate a variety of programming techniques that can be applied with the command language and can help inspire ideas for your own applications.

Chapter 12, which describes the command language itself, is organized alphabetically so that you can use the chapter as a reference when you write your own programs. Each command language instruction is illustrated with a demonstration program, which not only illustrates that instruction's function, but also performs some useful programming task. You should find many routines here that you can incorporate directly into your own programs.

Command language programming terms are defined in a glossary at the end of the book.

Although the basics of spreadsheet operation are not part of what this book is about, I have provided some information that isn't, strictly speaking, command language oriented. Included are some undocumented features, tricks, and traps (see "Biases and Tips") that I have discovered while learning Release 2 of 1-2-3, as well as some detailed information about "the basics" that will become relevant when you are trying to get a macro or program to run correctly. When you enter @SUM into a worksheet cell, you are programming 1-2-3, although in a form somewhat different from command language programming. As you will see, however, making effective use of Release 2's programming power involves integrating the command language into the powerful environment of the spreadsheet.

Beyond Descriptions of Instructions

1-2-3 Command Language goes beyond descriptions of instructions. You will learn how to put instructions together, integrate them with functions to perform complex operations elegantly, and construct command language programs that are easy to write and modify. The book also shows you how to plan and organize your programs, how to avoid common pitfalls, how to avoid problems arising from quirks in 1-2-3's operation, and how to debug programs quickly.

A Guide to Good Programming Practice

This book provides guidelines for designing programs. If you approach writing programs in the same way you design a spreadsheet model, pitfalls await you. Program writing differs, in several ways that aren't intuitively obvious, from spreadsheet assembly. I don't attempt to teach you everything about programming, but I do hope to keep you from committing the most common of programming atrocities and thereby spare you much grief down the road.

Although command language programs are generally simple compared to the large system programs written for mainframes, many issues involved in writing programs for mainframes also apply to command language programming. These issues apply to a greater degree as the complexity and power of an application program increase. If you follow good programming practices, your programs will be simple, but elegant and powerful. You will be able to make most changes in a matter of minutes, debug your programs quickly, and create new programs by modifying old programs. You also will have a library of useful routines that you can use to assemble powerful programs quickly.

To make the process of building programs as easy as possible for those of you with no prior programming experience, Chapter 10 of *1-2-3 Command Language* includes a comprehensive programming example that traces program development from its conceptual stage through development, testing, debugging, and modification.

How This Book Is Organized

This book is designed to be both a tutorial and reference manual. Much of the material presented builds on, or refers to, material presented earlier. In addition, as each topic is covered, it is covered in depth, from simple basics to quirks of operation that occur only under unusual circumstances. This type of organization lends itself best to several readings. Go over the material lightly, work the examples that interest you, and give yourself an overview of all the topics covered. When you get into a complex application, run into problems on your own, or feel ready to move up a notch in expertise, go back and delve into the exotic and unusual.

The material in this book is presented in an evolutionary fashion, covering four major topics: macros, the command language, program design, and application examples. The book starts with simple macros, moves to a form of macro that you create by having 1-2-3 record your keystrokes, and then shows you how to make those recorded macros more powerful by modifying them. Gradually, *1-2-3 Command Language* works toward developing procedures so complicated that they are truly programs, in the same sense that procedures written in FORTRAN, BASIC, COBOL, and other languages, are programs.

Macros

I define *macro* in a very restrictive sense to mean only those commands that replicate procedures you can do on the keyboard. The command language instructions used in macros are nothing more than names of keys. Therefore, except when important tricks or traps should be considered, the macro section of *1-2-3 Command Language* focuses on how to apply the macros rather than on the macros themselves. Although this information just scratches the surface of the 1-2-3 command language potential, you can gain light years in productivity just by becoming proficient with macros.

The Command Language

The command language is the second focus of this book. Each instruction is examined, with many cross-referenced examples provided. The description of @ functions is mandatory for anyone who is anything less than a whiz at string functions and who expects to become adept at using the command language. Even more than the macro section of this book, the command language section is application focused. In the command language section, however, a great deal of attention is also devoted to the program's internal structure, with concentration on learning to develop programs that are, in some sense, optimal.

Program Design

Program design is the third topic. In this section of *1-2-3 Command Language*, you will find basic guidelines for creating complex, but structured, command language programs. Research into computer science revealed long ago that wrong ways and right ways exist to write programs. But this book is not a text on programming theory. This book does, however, recognize that the command language is a toolbox much like any other toolbox: it gives you enough material to be dangerous. Therefore, the rudiments of some programming theory are covered in the hope that you need not learn old lessons the hard way. If you have never been exposed to the concepts of structured programming, or if you have never created a program so complex that you couldn't follow it yourself, you may think a lot of fuss is being made about something trivial. A properly designed program, however, can save much time and effort in the long run.

Also featured in this section of the book is a rather complicated program developed from the ground up. Step-by-step explanations are provided of the program development process. If you work through this example, you will get an idea of how to develop programs. This program is included for the insight it can give you. Watching the development process unfold can be more valuable than looking at finished (and, admittedly, purified) examples. This example also contains deliberate errors and debugging procedures that should prove helpful if you ever (heaven forbid) make a misteak.

Macro and Program Libraries

Application examples are the fourth subject of this book. Chapters 5 and 6 comprise a library of macro applications. In Chapter 12, each of the command language instructions is illustrated with one or more short example programs, many of which can be used as modular routines in larger programs. Chapter 11 contains a listing of several larger programs that shows some of the variety of applications you can generate with the command language.

Biases and Tips

In the course of teaching people (including myself) how to use this complex software, I developed some biases about the best way to learn the material. I try to be candid about those biases throughout the book. If you disagree with an observation, keep in mind my first bias: there is no "best" way to do anything with software. In 1-2-3's rich computational environment, many ways are available to implement almost any task. Some ways are better than others, depending on circumstances and application.

You will find, scattered throughout the book, TIPS, TRICKS, TRAPS, and GUIDELINES. These brief statements summarize what I believe are important aspects of creating command language programs.

TIPS help point out the easiest way to accomplish a specific task. As is true for programming in any language, the command language provides more than one way to get from point A to point B. This is perhaps even more true with 1-2-3 than with standard programming languages because you are programming in a spreadsheet environment. You therefore have at your disposal, in addition to the programming language statements, all the power and flexibility of the spreadsheet functions and commands. Frequently, some unusual combination of spreadsheet function and command language instruction can yield a simple solution to a complex problem. TIPS help point out these laborsaving opportunities.

TRICKS point out ways to use spreadsheet functions, commands, command language instructions, or combinations of these in unusual (but helpful) ways. TRICKS also explain how you can perform tasks that would otherwise be impossible—impress-your-friends and power-user stuff.

Some TRAPS point out the pitfalls that await the unwary user. Most of these involve things that you naturally think would work, but that don't. Other TRAPS identify instances where instructions perform differently under different conditions. Still other TRAPS point out what appear to be bugs in the 1-2-3 system.

GUIDELINES are something like TIPS, but with a bit more emphasis. TIPS are things you would probably want to do (because they make your task easier), whereas GUIDELINES are things you *should* do because they will make life easier for you in the long run. Think of the GUIDELINES as advice.

Whatever your level of expertise, pay attention to the TIPS, TRICKS, TRAPS, and GUIDELINES sprinkled throughout the book. I do not think they are gospel or even represent the best way to do things. Frequently, however, they embody assumptions that I make and incorporate into the rest of the material in the book.

References and Index

When you construct a program, you must know each instruction's syntax, options, and usage restrictions. You also need to know how to combine the instructions into routines that perform program functions. To facilitate the book's use as a reference for these tasks, *1-2-3 Command Language* contains an alphabetical listing of all the command language instructions, complete with an in-depth discussion of usage considerations. Also included with each instruction is a short command language routine that illustrates the instruction's use. Because these sample programs usually contain many different instructions, you will find the index at the back of the book useful. The index lists each instruction and all the examples in which the instruction appears. By using the index as a reference, you can see most of the instructions in several examples.

In addition, the examples provided to illustrate the operation of the instructions often perform useful programming tasks, such as controlling user input, screening for input errors, and printing multiple ranges. You can copy many of these routines directly into your own programs and use them as subroutines. To help you use the examples in your programs, the index lists the program routines by name as well as groups the routines by the functions they perform.

Information for New Users

Many new users of 1-2-3 avoid macros. New users often think that because they are not programmers, the topic is over their heads. This may be true (at first) for advanced programming applications, but is *not* true for the beginning steps of macro use. Using 1-2-3 without macros is like trying to get by without the Copy command. Think of macros as just another part of 1-2-3—no harder to learn than any other part and just as useful.

If you have never used macros before, start at the beginning of the book, type all the examples into the worksheet, and execute them. Seeing the system work conveys much more information about what is going on than any reading can, no matter how obvious the examples may seem at first. As the book progresses, the routines presented build on previous examples and become more complicated, powerful, and elegant. Multiple ways of accomplishing the same task are provided. Routines vary one from another in how easy they are to program, how quickly they can be typed, and how fast they run. Try all the routines to see how they work. Then pick the version that best suits your current needs.

Information for Expert Users

Even if you are a veteran 1-2-3 user, an old hand at macros, and you are upgrading to Release 2, you will still find virtually all the information in this book to be new. The original /x commands of Release 1A remain intact, but largely for purposes of compatibility with macros you may have written before.

The new command language is a true programming language, not simply an enhancement to keyboard macros. In addition to learning the 53 new command language instructions, a 1-2-3 programmer must now contend with the problems inherent in this much programming power. Program design, structure, documentation, and logic are all addressed in this book, as are the unique aspects of programming in a spreadsheet environment.

How To Become an Expert

1-2-3 has dozens of commands, functions, and command language instructions—a fact that can discourage new users. Don't feel overwhelmed. Each attribute is just another tool in a powerful toolbox. This book describes many ways to use those tools. It shows you how to combine the tools to accomplish specific tasks and how to combine tasks into applications.

If you work through the whole book, you should have a good idea of how to use the command language for a wide variety of problems, from simple laborsaving tasks to sophisticated applications. The real secret to becoming a 1-2-3 expert, however, is to know intimately everything the program can do. You should know all the program's commands, functions, limitations, and quirks.

Think of learning 1-2-3 as learning a new spoken language. You may be able to get your point across to a Frenchman even if you speak only a dozen words of French, but you will expend a great deal of effort and be limited in your eloquence. Such is the case with the language of 1-2-3. The more familiar you are with the details of 1-2-3's operation, the more sophisticated and eloquent your programs will be. Here is a suggestion for improving your expertise:

HEAR AND FORGET

SEE AND REMEMBER

DO AND UNDERSTAND

I found these words of wisdom (covered with cobwebs) somewhere in the dark reaches of my brain. People have told me repeatedly that when they first read the 1-2-3 manuals, they seemed complete gibberish. Later, after some practice with the program, the manuals begin to make sense. I have therefore developed the following tip for becoming a 1-2-3 expert.

TIP: 1. Read the manuals.

2. Try everything once.

3. Read the manuals.

4. Read the manuals.

You may notice a certain theme to this tip. Although it may look humorous, the advice is serious and derived from experience. The more of 1-2-3's powerful features you are aware of, the more tools you can use when the need arises.

Reading the manuals in one sitting can turn your brain into oatmeal, a phenomenon called "information overload." After a while, you just can't assimilate any more material. Skimming the manuals once gives you a broad picture that you can apply to specific needs. Trying everything gives you more in-depth knowledge. Frequently, after I try using a specific command, function, or command language instruction, and I see it in action, the explanation in the manuals suddenly becomes clear. ("So that's what the writers meant!") When you read the manuals a second time, you probably will be surprised at how much clearer they are, and the points you missed on the first reading will stand out. Discovering that the program does tasks you wished it did but thought it did not can be a lot of fun.

When you read the manuals for the third time, which will probably occur several months after the second reading, the details that will stand out will be the subtleties of using commands and functions—subtleties you missed the first two times around. Knowing these subtleties is what differentiates the true experts from the merely good users. You are also likely to find that this level of knowledge of 1-2-3, compared to the basic information you learned previously, saves you more time and enables you to create more complex and elegant applications.

1

An Overview

This book is about a special and unique programming language: the command language of 1-2-3 (Release 2). The command language represents the latest step in the evolution of programming languages, in a progression that brings ever more power and flexibility to personal computer users. Programming languages enable you to code your applications into a form the computer can understand. The computer, in turn, provides solutions to those applications in a form you can understand.

During the short history of the computer, a major advance in this person-machine interface has occurred every 10 years. The latest of these major advances was the original spreadsheet program, VisiCalc®. That program, in computer science circles, is considered to be a very advanced form of programming language.

While the basic concept embodied in VisiCalc was revolutionary, spreadsheets have continued to improve dramatically with time. The original 1-2-3 improved tremendously on its predecessor and added macros, or automated keystrokes. Release 1A of 1-2-3 also went a little beyond keystroke automation and included the /x commands, which are rudiments of a programming language. With 1-2-3's success came demands from its users for even more of this power, which is provided in Release 2 as the command language.

In Release 2, programming power is now available to you in three forms: the spreadsheet itself, the ability to automate keystrokes (macros), and the command language. Each level builds on the previous level, giving you more power and enabling you to handle more complex applications in the process. The structure of this book reflects this progression, moving from spreadsheets to macros to programming.

The Programming Environment: 1-2-3 Release 2

Release 2 of 1-2-3 is an update of Lotus® Development Corporation's phenomenally successful 1-2-3 integrated software program. Actually, Release 2 incorporates most of the features originally found in the spreadsheet portion of Release 1A's immediate successor, Symphony. Therefore, Release 2 represents the third generation of Lotus spreadsheet.

Release 2 of 1-2-3 is much more powerful than Release 1A. The size of the spreadsheet has been extended to more than 8,000 rows. Memory management is more efficient. Support is now present for a math coprocessor and memory beyond 640K. Dozens of new functions have been added. And the original 1-2-3 macro facility has matured into a full-featured programming language.

Compared to Symphony, Release 2 of 1-2-3 is "lean and mean." Whereas Release 2 has virtually all the spreadsheet and graphics enhancements of Symphony, the database functions resemble Release 1A more than they do Symphony. And Symphony's powerful word-processing, communications, and windowing facilities are not a part of Release 2.

The result is a program that, with its help file, still fits on one floppy disk and has room in RAM for almost 400K of spreadsheet data. A high-powered, no-nonsense spreadsheet, Release 2 is remarkably small and fast, given the features and power that have been added since Release 1A.

1-2-3's command language contains most of the features common to other computer programming languages. But the fact that the command language is embedded in a spreadsheet creates special programming considerations. From a programmer's point of view, all the commands and functions of the spreadsheet serve as extensions and enhancements to the command language rather than the other way around.

The Language: Macros and Programs

Because the command language's power and flexibility are on a par with traditional programming languages, I believe that continuing to refer to command language procedures as "macros" is misleading. At some point, the complexity of what you are doing demands that you give its development the same kind of attention and concern you would give a program in a conventional language such as Pascal.

To help clarify this point, let me make my definitions explicit. For macros, the phrase "typing alternative" is apt; you can use macros to make Release 2 (or Release 1A) type for you. Macros are powerful because you can use them to automate sequences of commands you use frequently. Creating and activating a macro generally takes less time and effort than repeatedly issuing a sequence of commands.

Automation, however, involves more than combining sequences of operations into a single command. The command language derives much of its power from the capability to (1) perform controlled repetitions and (2) to select alternative sequences, based on the results of some test. If you have had any formal exposure to computer science, you may recognize the key terms in these descriptions: *sequence, repetition,* and *selection.*

One of computer science's central theorems, developed decades before the advent of the first digital computer, is that these three concepts are all that's required to perform *any* computational task. However, computer languages with these capabilities vary greatly in power and sophistication. The earliest implementations of sequence, selection, and repetition used cogs and gears as basic mechanisms. Some of these mechanical marvels could perform complex computing tasks, but only with great effort on the part of programmers.

The macro facility in Release 1A of 1-2-3 contained the rudiments of programming but, as a programming language, was as primitive as cogs and gears. That facility lacked any form of repetition control, had a virtually unreadable syntax, and encouraged development of programs that were difficult to follow and maintain. These limitations, of course, didn't keep many 1-2-3 users from developing complicated and powerful applications. But just because creating artificial intelligence with Tinkertoys is possible doesn't mean that it's a good idea.

From a programmer's point of view, the shortcomings of the Release 1A macro language have been remedied in the command language of Release 2. 1-2-3 users now have at their disposal a true programming language. As such, distinguishing between the simple sequences of macro commands and the more complex gyrations of a command language program makes sense.

Developing and maintaining a macro that executes only a simple sequence of steps is a fairly straightforward task. The macro's operation and function can be divined from a simple step-by-step reading of the contents. Developing programs that include selection and repetition, however, is a more complex task. The design of the program and how it is documented become critical issues. What the program is designed to do can't be determined simply by examining the program instructions. The same series of program instructions will perform different actions under different conditions. In addition, the simple clerical task of locating the program code that is to be executed when control is transferred to another part of the program can become unbelievably difficult in large, poorly written programs.

Whereas a casual approach to the construction of macros that repeat sequences of commands is appropriate, extending that attitude into the creation of more complex programs is not. Therefore, keeping in mind the level of complexity of the intended application is important. Recorded sequences of keystrokes require an adequate level of documentation, but more complex procedures require *thorough* documentation and careful step-by-step development.

To help emphasize this distinction, the term *macro* as used in this book refers only to *sequences* of operations that can be performed on the keyboard. Conversely, the term *program* is used if *selection* or *repetition* is involved. One gray area exists, into which falls what I call hybrids. A *hybrid* is a modified macro that is a little more than a macro but a little less than a program.

The organization of the material in this book, building from the simple to the complex, also takes advantage of the natural distinction between macros and programs. Macros, the easiest to learn and follow, are covered first, with hybrid programs providing a transition to the more complex aspects of programming with the command language.

Applications: When To Use Macros or the Command Language

Macros and command language programs can be applied to an endless variety of tasks, ranging from *utility* macros that speed everyday work to stand-alone data processing systems that completely isolate the user from the worksheet. After you are familiar with how the system operates, you should begin with the simple macros and move gradually into the more complex programs. Even if you are a Release 1A macro expert, you should review the material that follows. You will find some subtle, but important improvements in Release 2. The following examples will give you some idea of the range of applications to which macros and programs can be applied.

Simple Macros

During the construction of a spreadsheet model, a number of common operations must be performed repeatedly. Figure 1.1 shows an example of such a situation. With the cell pointer in its present location, do the following:

1. Draw a line under the last number in column B.

2. Enter the @SUM formula in the cell below the line.

3. Copy both the line and the formula across in order to sum the series of adjacent columns.

These keystrokes can be placed into a macro, reducing their execution to a single keystroke.

	A	B	C	D	E	F
		Jan	Feb	Mar	Apr	May
1						
2						
3	Office supplies	210	217	172	151	177
4	Telephone	385	514	376	445	551
5	Rent	1800	1800	1800	1800	1800
6	Electricity	410	313	200	262	252
7	Pizza	125	141	99	120	153
8	Insurance	88	88	88	88	88
9	Water & Gas	35	40	58	65	43
10	Automobiles	800	800	800	800	800
11	Secretary	1200	1200	1200	1200	1200
12	Payroll Tax	156	156	156	156	156
13						
14						

B13:   READY

Fig. 1.1. A common worksheet task.

If you use 1-2-3 to write memos, or you do other word-processing tasks, you can simplify your work by storing frequently used words and phrases in macros that are executed with easy-to-remember Alt-[letter] combinations.

The concept just described can be extended. With single keystrokes, you can make 1-2-3 type the headings for a business letter, your company name and address, and even an automatically updated copy of today's date. Or you can instruct 1-2-3 to automatically enter the names and addresses of people or companies you write to frequently.

A simple looping macro can more than double the speed of entering a column of data. The macro controls the downward movement of the cell pointer, thus enabling you to turn on Num Lock and use the numeric keypad for data entry. If you modify this procedure, you can avoid typing decimal points by letting the macro divide each entry by 100 before entering it into the spreadsheet.

For applications in which multiple reports will be printed from a single spreadsheet, macros can handle all the setup work. They can specify the range to be printed, margins, and Init-String codes, and scroll the page to the tear-off point after printing is completed.

Combining a menu macro with a number of the print macros (as described in the preceding paragraph) not only speeds the process of printing one or many reports, but uses the menu prompts as reminders of the contents of each of the specific reports.

A simple looping macro with a timed delay can turn Release 2 of 1-2-3 into a slide show by calling up a series of stored graphs.

Command Language Programs

In a worksheet, you can include a command language program that executes automatically whenever you load the worksheet. For instance, the program could import ranges from other files before releasing control to you.

By combining an auto-execute command language program with menu macros, you can create user-friendly systems that can perform virtually any function entirely on a menu-driven basis.

A simple command language program can create a table of stored settings for use in printing, database queries and sorts, data tables, or any other application where you would usually enter multiple settings and change them later.

A program only 5 lines long can add goal-seeking capabilities to your spreadsheet. *Goal seeking* describes the process whereby one value in the worksheet is systematically changed until some other calculated value reaches a desired state (the goal). With goal seeking, you can, for example, use a model that shows the return on the investment in an office building and answers such questions as "What rate of occupancy growth must be achieved in order to return 20% annually on the investment over 5 years?"

Have you ever created a worksheet so large and complex that you had trouble keeping track of what was where, what portions were obsolete, and what portions were currently being used? With the command language, you can construct a simple program that creates a map of your worksheet and identifies which cells contain formulas, which cells contain labels, and which cells are blank.

Advanced Applications

A command language program can turn 1-2-3's rudimentary text-handling capabilities into a system that closely resembles a full-featured word processor. A word processor that you develop has the advantage of including only those features you want. And if you want to add features, such as decimal tabs, you can do so at any time simply by adding to the program.

You can enhance 1-2-3's somewhat limited database capabilities by expanding on the strategy embodied in the last example. You can create forms that guide user input, prompt for specific responses, and screen for errors. On the output side of the database, you can create programs that at the touch of a button produce multiple sorts of your data and print on separate pages sorted sections of the data, complete with separate headings and subtotals. You can also overcome 1-2-3's two-sort-key limitation.

What Are the Limits?

I am tempted to say that the limits to using the command language are those of your imagination, but that statement would not only be trite but incorrect. Instead, I will give you a general rule: The question is not "can it be done?" but "are you willing to pay for it?"

This rule acknowledges the tradeoff that accompanies all systems development. Whereas the theoretical limitations of command language programming are few, a number of practical limitations emerge when time and expense factors are taken into account. These limitations fall roughly into the following categories: implementation time, execution time, memory, and limits inherent in the command language itself.

Implementation Time

Release 2 of 1-2-3 can act as a database manager, accounting system, word-processing system, and more. Someone, however, has to program all that automation. For significantly less than the cost of paying a programmer, you can purchase the most extravagant and powerful of commercially available software packages designed for specific use.

Implementing such programs in 1-2-3 has several advantages. The system can be customized to your exact specifications and can be altered if necessary. Also, users don't have to learn multiple systems. And because you can use all of 1-2-3's built-in functions as part of the system, writing a program in the command language is much quicker than implementing an identical system in a traditional programming language, such as BASIC.

Execution Time

In program execution time, Release 2's command language could qualify as The World's Slowest Programming Language. Even when compared to notoriously slow interpreted languages such as BASIC, Release 2 is a snail. Consider the results of the following unscientifically conducted benchmark experiment. A program that incremented a variable from 1 to 10,000 was constructed in Turbo Pascal®, BASIC, and Release 2's command language. Here are the program listings and their corresponding execution times.

Turbo Pascal

```
Program Benchmark;

  var
    i, counter : integer;

  begin {main}
    for i := 1 to 10000 do counter := counter + 1;
  end.
```

Execution time: 0.35 seconds

BASIC

```
10 FOR I = 1 TO 10000
20 COUNTER = COUNTER + 1
30 NEXT
```

Execution Time: 2.8 Seconds

1-2-3 Command Language

Figure 1.2 shows the command language equivalent for the Turbo Pascal and BASIC programs.

1-2-3's execution time for the program shown in figure 1.2 was 5 minutes and 27 seconds. According to these results, 1-2-3 is 117 times slower than BASIC and 934 times slower than Turbo Pascal. If this ratio held true, a program that takes 5 minutes to execute in Turbo Pascal would take 3.2 days in 1-2-3's command language. Of the 3 programs, the 1-2-3 version also took the most time to type. Obviously, applications exist for which 1-2-3 would be a ridiculous choice of programming languages.

The comparison is unfair, of course. *Given the right application*, 1-2-3 has features that can make it more powerful than BASIC or Turbo Pascal. But a

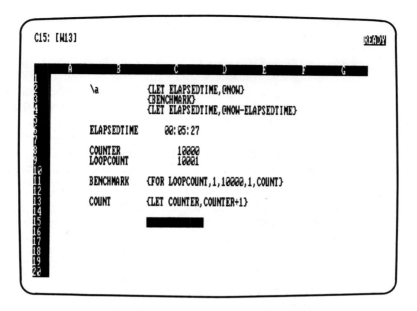

Fig. 1.2. A command language program that counts to 10,000.

lesson can be learned from the preceding comparison of execution times: Do not expect 1-2-3 to fulfill every programming need. In some applications, the program is unbeatable. In other applications, 1-2-3 is totally unsuitable.

Memory

One of 1-2-3's greatest strengths, especially when compared to other spreadsheet programs, is its overall speed. Those of us who cut our spreadsheet teeth on 1-2-3 take this speed for granted; indeed, it is one of the hallmarks of the program. Speed is such an important part of 1-2-3's reputation that representatives for Lotus Development Corporation have stated publicly that speed was one aspect of product quality they would never compromise. The implication of the focus on speed, however, is that any necessary compromising would be done at the expense of memory usage.

Although 1-2-3 is not as large as its big brother, Symphony (which is truly monstrous), 1-2-3 is, at 175K, still a large program (almost twice as large as its predecessor, Release 1A). With a minimum configuration of DOS 3.0 in a computer with 256K of RAM, only 50K is left for worksheet memory. If you put in your computer the maximum usable memory of 655,360 bytes (640K), a potential worksheet space of about 443K remains. However, you might want to do still other things with the available RAM.

For example, if you have full-time access to a computer, literally hundreds of wonderful timesaving programs are available to help you with any number of your daily activities. The most useful of these programs are the so-called TSR (Terminate and Stay Resident) programs, also known as pop-up programs. This breed of software loads into your computer before you load your main programs and "pops up" right in the middle of whatever you are doing with your current program. Pop-up programs feature such amenities as appointment calendars, on-screen calculators, notepads, outline generators, spelling checkers, and keyboard enhancers.

The real advantage of these programs is that they are available instantaneously. If you had to take 30 seconds or a minute to load them into your computer, you would probably do without them. The real disadvantage to pop-up programs is that while they are in your computer awaiting the keystroke that calls them into operation, the programs are also occupying your precious, limited RAM.

For an extreme, real-life example, look at figures 1.3 and 1.4, which show the memory usage in my computer before and after I have loaded the TSR goodies I like to keep on hand. Among the TSR programs loaded are DOMUS's PRINT SCREEN®, Borland's SuperKey®, Borland's Turbo Lightning™, and Living Videotext's Ready!™. Even with 2 megabytes of additional RAM on an INTEL Above Board™, my usable worksheet space has shrunk from 443K to 155K.

A working memory of 155,000 bytes may seem like a large amount, but not for 1-2-3. The problem is not that 1-2-3 uses memory inefficiently, but rather that the program is so powerful that it *invites* large applications. You may be familiar with the computing axiom that states that your applications always expand to fit your hardware capacity. With 2,000,000+ cells available in the spreadsheet, plenty of *area* exists to lay out databases, tables, projection calculations, and whatever. Unfortunately, even with expanded memory, everything you enter into a cell uses some of your computer's conventional RAM, which will be exhausted long before your model has occupied more than a fraction of available cells.

The addition of the command language to the system can, on one hand, circumvent memory limitations by allowing you to write programs that dynamically link models contained in different files. On the other hand, the power of the command language has a way of encouraging even larger applications than would otherwise be possible. So the blessing is decidedly mixed.

Furthermore, as soon as you go beyond single-worksheet applications and start using the command language to combine files, the complexity of the required

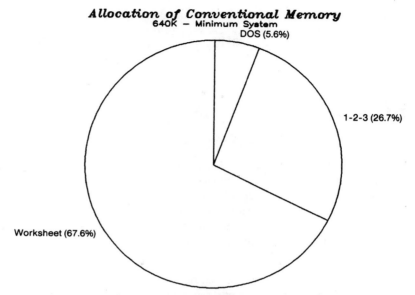

Fig. 1.3. Worksheet space with only 1-2-3 and DOS in a 640K computer.

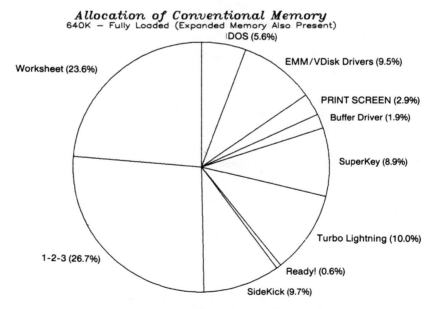

Fig. 1.4. Allocation of conventional 640K of memory with a fully loaded system, including software to run expanded memory applications.

software skyrockets. Complex programs take more time to write than simple programs. Therefore, although you may find ways to avoid the memory limitations, you may be trading them for "time is money" limitations.

Limitations of the Command Language

If you have used 1-2-3's macro language or spreadsheets with no language at all, you will find the command language such a significant step forward that you probably will overlook its relative lack of sophistication. However, the command language lacks many constructs considered essential in most advanced languages: local variables, recursion, strong data typing, in-line machine code, multiple-file access, programmable graphics capabilities, user-definable data types, and program code indentation.

One of the language's most frustrating limitations is that you can't access 1-2-3's internal settings, such as current range specifications and margin settings for printing. Although proper programming strategy can overcome the problems this limitation creates, the fact remains that this limitation encumbers a program development system, which is already somewhat constrained.

In the final assessment, the command language is a remarkable addition to the power already inherent in a spreadsheet program, but has room to mature. Lotus Development Corporation's approach to the command language has been, to date, to view it as a spreadsheet adjunct, not as a programming language in its own right. I think that this approach is probably good, in the sense that many people who use 1-2-3's command language have no formal training in programming or experience with the intricacies of machine-language interrupt handling. On the other hand, I find myself wishing that the program did things it does not. Given 1-2-3's add-in capability, however, I would not be surprised if an advanced programming package incorporating many such features becomes available.

Until then, 1-2-3 remains the world's greatest spreadsheet with an adequate, but not wonderful programming language—a little like a Maserati with wooden wagon wheels. But I'm not complaining. I believe that users will need years to discover what they can do with this program, and 1-2-3 will undoubtedly improve and develop with time.

2

Getting Started with Macros

You don't have to be a 1-2-3 expert to use macros. In fact, you can use macros as learning aids; by using macros *with* the basic commands, you can speed up the learning process. You can look up a command you've never used before, turn it into a macro, and forget about that command. I don't, however, recommend that you use macros to learn commands you might need to use regularly. Commands such as Copy or Move are essential to master in order to carry out normal spreadsheet work.

As mentioned in the introduction, *1-2-3 Command Language* is not a beginner's book on 1-2-3. I assume that you know how to use 1-2-3 to perform most basic spreadsheet operations and that you are comfortable with the commonly used commands. Brief explanations of seldom-used commands are provided when those are used in the macros discussed here. If you find unfamiliar material in the text, I recommend that you look up the item in question in the 1-2-3 manuals or in an introductory text such as the second edition of *Using 1-2-3*.

Learning To "Think Macro"

As you read, you will probably notice that I tend to advocate using macros or command language programs as a solution to virtually every problem. I don't believe that the enthusiasm is misplaced. 1-2-3's macro and command language facilities are very powerful. You can use them to customize 1-2-3 to do things your way if you don't like the way the program operates. Or you can use these facilities to extend 1-2-3's capabilities when you want to move beyond its built-in functions.

23

While writing this book, I deliberately looked for ways to use macros in my regular work applications—ways that I might otherwise have overlooked. I discovered two things. First, I realized that virtually unlimited opportunities exist for using macros to get my work done faster and easier. Second, although I had assumed that many macro applications would take more time to implement than they would save, my conjecture rarely turned out to be true. The more you use macros, the easier constructing them becomes. You can start with very simple macros that are easy to create, then move to more complex macros as you become more expert.

Automating Commands

TIP: If you find yourself performing the same task more than twice, consider creating a macro to do the job for you.

You will probably do some small tasks, such as putting @SUM at the bottom of a column of numbers, hundreds of times. *Not* putting these operations into macros is a waste of your time. Chapters 5 and 6 contain a library of such macros, which are based on my experience with spreadsheet tasks. The type of work you do with 1-2-3 will bring unique opportunities for you to use macros and create customized macro libraries of your own.

Automating Repetitive Tasks

If tasks are repetitive in nature—even if those tasks are linked only to one job—you should consider turning them into macros. For example, as part of an analysis of a large database, I had to generate 48 graphs and graph files for PrintGraph printing. After generating the second graph and graph file, I decided to see whether a macro could automate the process. Ten minutes later, I had a command language program that completed the entire task in another 10 minutes. The program was just 3 lines long.

The importance of this experience lies in the fact that until I sat down to create the program, I didn't know how easy it would be to generate. A few minutes of contemplation saved me a great many more minutes of key pressing, to say nothing of boredom and perhaps even accuracy. The moral of the story should be obvious: Think macro. It's easier than you imagine.

What Is a Macro?

A *macro*, in its most restricted sense, is a series of keystrokes placed in a worksheet cell. These keystrokes are a label, like any other label that appears in the worksheet. 1-2-3 can also execute string formulas or string functions—a more advanced topic that will be explained in Chapters 8 and 9. The general rule is that anything that appears as a label in the worksheet can be executed as part of a macro.

What Can a Macro Do?

A macro can replicate anything you can do on the keyboard, including the execution of commands. The advantage of putting commands into a macro is that a macro can execute entire *sequences* of commands, which you can invoke by pressing only one key.

No limit exists to the number of commands a single macro can execute. A macro can contain a /File Combine command that loads other macros from another worksheet. Once loaded, these new macros could be invoked automatically and could load more macros. If you use such a technique, no limit, not even that of computer memory, applies to the length and power of macros.

How To Execute a Macro

Simply entering a label into a worksheet cell does not a macro make. You must also tell 1-2-3 that you want it to take control of your computer and execute the macro you have written. Macros can be executed using the Alt key, or you can have 1-2-3 execute a macro automatically.

Using the Alt Key

Before you can execute a macro, you must give it a special kind of range name: one alphabetic character preceded by a backslash (\ ). This naming system gives you a total of 26 macros (A–Z) that you can call from the keyboard. When naming macros, you can use either uppercase or lowercase letters.

To execute a macro, all you have to do is hold down the Alt key (called the Macro key in the 1-2-3 manuals) and press A. Think of Alt as a kind of shift key. To type an uppercase A, you hold down the Shift key and press A. To type Alt-a, you hold down another shift key—Alt—and press A.

As the macro begins executing, CMD appears in the bottom center of the screen (see fig. 2.1). This indicator is helpful because it tells you that the system is busy "thinking" (during a long recalculation, for example) and not "dead" or otherwise in need of intervention.

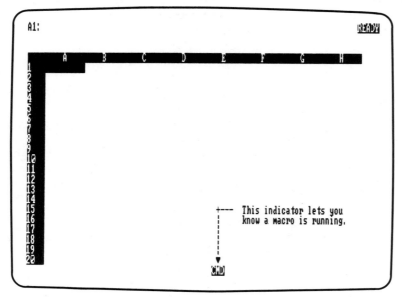

Fig. 2.1. The CMD indicator.

Autoexecute Macros

Another method exists for executing a macro: you can use a range name that begins with a backslash. If you assign a macro the name \0 (a zero, not the letter O), that macro is executed automatically when the worksheet containing the macro is loaded. This macro can't be executed from the keyboard by pressing Alt-0. If you want to execute the \0 macro from within a worksheet, you can assign the macro a second name, one of the 26 Alt-[letter] range names.

Starting Your Good Macro Habits Now

As you learn to use macros and, later, command language programs, you are acquiring knowledge that can be dangerous. Creating macros will affect the way you use your worksheet. Now, when you are first starting to use macros, is the time to develop some good habits that will save you trouble later on.

Macro Readability

GUIDELINE: In a worksheet, put all your macro names where you can see them.

After you have more than a couple of macros in a worksheet, you can easily lose track of the macros' names. If you don't keep some kind of record of what range names you've assigned to what macros, you can find youself with a spreadsheet full of macros that you don't know how to execute.

A related problem can arise if you erase a macro—for example, a \a macro—and lose track of the location of the cell named \a. Accidentally pushing the Alt key (instead of the Shift key, for example) can make unusual things happen if you activate a macro when you didn't intend to do so.

You can live with these problems. To identify names already assigned and their corresponding locations, you can use the /Range Name Create command, /Range Name Table command, or the GoTo (F5) and Name (F3) keys. 1-2-3 then lists the range names in current use. This process, however, is cumbersome and unnecessary. An easier method is available.

Using the /Range Name
Labels Right Command

GUIDELINE: Use the /Range Name Labels Right command to name your macros.

Using the /Range Name Labels Right command to name your macros is easy and requires only one more keystroke than conventional range naming. For instance, figure 2.2 demonstrates what to do to name a macro \n.

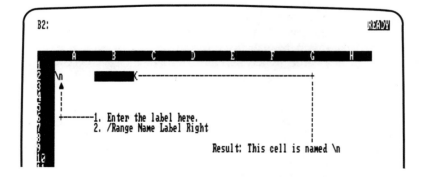

Fig. 2.2. Using the /Range Name Labels Right command to name a macro.

1. Position the cell pointer in the column directly to the left of where you want to put your macro.

2. Type the macro name. Remember that the backslash is a repeating label prefix, and label prefixes are not considered part of the cell contents. For example, if you enter \a in a cell, *aaaaaaaa* appears in the worksheet, but the cell's contents will be simply *a*. To avoid this problem, type a label prefix in front of the backslash. Use '\a instead.

3. With the cell pointer on the name you typed, give the /Range Name Labels Right command. 1-2-3 then assigns that name to the cell on the right of your typed name.

When you use the /Range Name Labels command, you have four options: Up, Down, Left, and Right. You use these options to assign names to cells that lie in the specified direction from the cell that holds the name.

/Range Name Labels Right is probably the most useful option. /Range Name Labels Up doesn't work; the macro tries to execute the name you just entered (see the explanation of multiline macros in Chapter 3). /Range Name Labels Left can obscure the macro's contents if the macro has more characters than the cell width permits. Remember that long labels extend beyond cell boundaries unless the cell to the right is not empty. /Range Name Labels Down works just fine and, when space is at a premium, can help conserve that precious commodity. Using that option, however, can easily confuse the macro's name with the macro itself.

Advantages of Using /Range Name Labels Right

Using the /Range Name Labels Right command as shown in figure 2.2 required 10 keystrokes. In contrast, the /Range Name Create command would have required 8 keystrokes. Although the /Range Name Labels Right command requires 2 extra keystrokes, this is a small price to pay for the benefit of having a visible record of the macro name. When several macros are close together, you can use the /Range Name Labels Right command to name them all at once. In those cases, using this command is also the easiest way to assign range names.

This method has one other advantage: you can use /Range Name Labels to reassign the range name somewhere other than its original location. If you use /Range Name Create to reset a range name, the name first appears where you originally assigned it, because 1-2-3 remembers the original range assignment. To reassign that range name to a new cell, you must cancel the name in its original location before assigning the name to a new location.

Why All the Fuss about Macro Names?

I may seem to have gone on excessively about macro names, but my arguments are based on experience with people's habits as well as on considerations for the more complex command language programs to come in this book. Keeping track of the little details mentally isn't a problem if you have only a couple of simple macros in a worksheet. Therefore, forcing yourself to develop good housekeeping habits that require extra work at the outset is difficult. But after you've been using macros for several months, or even years, you will have hundreds of macros in hundreds of worksheets. Six months after you create a macro, you are unlikely to remember all the details of its operation. If you haven't documented the macro well, you will find yourself spending a great deal of time either interpreting what you did or starting over and redoing the whole macro.

With the command language, you can create programs of any complexity you desire. They can easily get so complicated that you can't recall all their internal details the next day, let alone six months later. You can keep details in your head up to a certain point. But then things become too complex to keep track of mentally. By the time you realize that a problem exists, it's too late. You can avoid learning the lesson the hard way later by starting your good habits now.

Your First Macro

Now that you've covered the essentials of macro construction, you should sit down at your computer and try out the system. You can do an infinite number of things with macros, but, for now, you can start with a simple operation. After you see how easy it is to construct and execute macros, you will be ready to move on to more complex applications.

Typing Your Name

To construct your first macro, start with an empty worksheet. In cell A1, enter the macro's name: \a. Remember to type the label prefix character before the backslash.

Use the /Range Name Labels Right command to assign that name to cell B1. Move the cell pointer to cell B1 and type your name there. Then move the cell pointer to C1. Your worksheet should now look like the example in figure 2.3, except that B1 contains your name instead of mine.

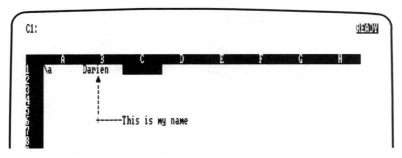

Fig. 2.3. A macro that types your name.

To activate the macro, hold down Alt and press A. Remember that Alt works like a shift key on a typewriter. You hold down Alt as if you were going to capitalize a letter, then press the appropriate letter key.

Your name appears on the command line above the window border (see fig. 2.4). Notice that although your macro, which is in cell B1, contains a label prefix, 1-2-3 doesn't type the label prefix when you execute the macro. A macro doesn't execute any of the five label prefixes.

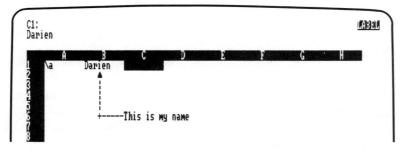

Fig. 2.4. The macro activated.

Press Alt-a a few more times. Figure 2.5 shows what appears on the screen.

Press Enter. 1-2-3 enters what you just created into the worksheet (see fig. 2.6).

You can call on this automated typist anytime. For instance, suppose that you type

My name is [Alt-a].

The following appears on the screen.

My name is Darien.

Fig. 2.5. The macro duplicated by repeated keystrokes.

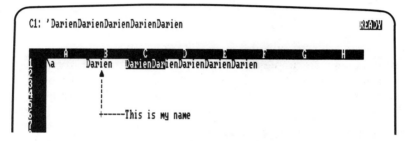

Fig. 2.6. The results of the macro entered in the worksheet.

A Practical Example: Avoiding Division-by-Zero Errors

A macro that automatically types the contents of one cell is more useful than you might think.

TRICK: To prevent division-by-zero errors, use a macro to alter a formula.

If you have a formula that contains a cell reference as the denominator in a division, you can sometimes run into trouble when that reference cell unexpectedly assumes a value of zero. The standard solution to this problem is to include in the formula a test for the error condition. If the error condition occurs, the formula returns a zero instead of the ERR value (see fig. 2.7).

In figure 2.7, the formula in cell A10 returns ERR if the denominator (A2) is zero. In the modified formula shown in row 12, an @IF function is used with the @ISERR function to detect the error condition. @IF substitutes a zero for the formula if an error occurs. If no error occurs, @IF uses the formula itself.

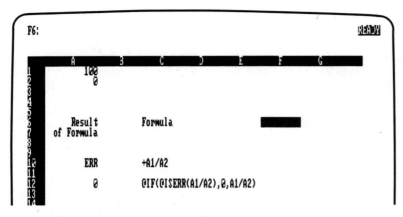

Fig. 2.7. Formula for trapping a division-by-zero error.

This example is, of course, so simple that the formula benefits little from a macro and is presented only to demonstrate the concept. In the "real world," the formula in question is never that simple. Your formula would more likely look like the following:

(((@SUM(B1..B121)^2 – (@SUM(C1..C121) / K1)) *
((@SUM(D1..D121)^2 – (@SUM(E1..E121) / K1)) /
@SQRT(@SUM(F1..F121)^2)

To automate the process of copying the formula, do the following:

1. Create an Alt-[letter] macro name for the cell containing the formula. With your cell pointer in that cell, press

   /Range Name Create \a ↵

2. Turn your formula into a label by pressing the following keys:

   Edit Home ' ↵

   Don't forget to type the apostrophe.

3. Enter your new formula by typing

   @IF(@ISERR(Alt-a), 0, Alt-a) ↵

That's all there is to creating a new formula. In the third step, the two Alt-a's cause 1-2-3 to enter your formula in both locations. You may never need this trick; but keep in mind that a macro can type anything for you, even formulas.

Macro Keywords

All the examples so far have used only the regular typewriter keys. 1-2-3 was designed to use *all* the IBM® PC's keys. Therefore, you need to be able to tell 1-2-3 to use special keys (such as the cursor-arrow keys) in a macro. The keys, however, have no special symbols. To specify a *macro keyword*, you enclose the key's name in braces, as in the following:

{DOWN}

When 1-2-3 encounters this keyword in a macro, the program "pushes" the down-arrow key (↓). You can use macro keywords to press virtually every key on the keyboard. You do, however, have to know the names that 1-2-3 uses for each key. Table 2.1 lists the keywords, and the section immediately following the list describes some of the finer points of the keys' uses. If you aren't familiar with all of 1-2-3's special keys, reviewing these sections should be helpful. Knowing these keys and the nuances of their operation is as important as being familiar with all 1-2-3's commands and functions.

Table 2.1
1-2-3 Keywords

Key Name	Macro Keyword	IBM PC Key
Abs	{ABS}	F4
Backspace	{BACKSPACE} or {BS}	←
Big Left	{BIGLEFT}	Ctrl-←
Big Right	{BIGRIGHT}	Ctrl-→
Break		Ctrl-Break
Calc	{CALC}	F9
Caps Lock		
Ctrl		
Del	{DELETE} or {DEL}	
Down	{DOWN}	↓
Edit	{EDIT}	F2
End	{END}	
Escape	{ESCAPE} or {ESC}	
GoTo	{GOTO}	F5
Graph	{GRAPH}	F10
Help		F1

Home	{HOME}	
Ins	{INSERT}	
Left	{LEFT}	←
Macro	\ (with A..Z)	Alt
Menu	{MENU}	/
	/	/
	<	<
Name	{NAME}	F3
Num Lock		
Page Down	{PGDN} or {BIGDOWN}	PgDn
Page Up	{PGUP} or {BIGUP}	PgUp
Query	{QUERY}	F7
Enter (Return)	~	↵
Right	{RIGHT}	→
Scroll Lock		
Shift		
Step		Alt-F2
Tab	{BIGRIGHT}	|←⁻ ⁻→
Table	{TABLE}	F8
Backtab	{BIGLEFT}	Shift-Tab
Up	{UP}	↑
Window	{WINDOW}	F6
Left Brace	{{}	{
Right Brace	{}}	}
Tilde	{~}	~

Some Qualifications to the Keyword Listing

For the most part, all the keys, when used as keywords in a macro, work the same way they do when you press them. You should, however, be aware of a few restrictions.

Keys You Cannot Use

Some keys you can't use in macros. You get an error message if you try to use these keys:

1. The three "lock" keys: Caps Lock, Num Lock, and Scroll Lock

2. The three "shift" keys: Alt (Macro), Shift, and Ctrl

3. Four special-function keys: Help, Compose, Step, and Break (Ctrl-Break)

4. The Tab and Backtab keys

These restrictions should cause few problems. Although you can't use these keys in a macro, a macro can still duplicate the functions that the keys perform. For example, instead of using the Shift key, you can enter uppercase letters directly into your macro. Then uppercase letters will be used when the macro executes. The Step key (Alt-F2) is the only exception; for more details, see the section on debugging macros in Chapter 10.

In the 1-2-3 documentation, Lotus refers to the Alt key as "the Macro key." In fact, you will probably see the word *MACRO* from time to time in braces, just like any other keyword. {MACRO}, however, is not a legal keyword in 1-2-3. If you want to call a macro from within a macro (a slightly more advanced topic that will be explained in Chapter 9), you refer to the external macro by preceding its letter name with a backslash, as in {\a}.

Compose Key Sequences

You can't initiate the Compose key (Alt-F1) sequences (used to generate print codes and special characters) from within a macro. But Compose key sequences are probably unnecessary. You can specify any of the special characters, including print attributes, simply by typing them into the macro.

The Cursor-Movement Keys

Before you start using keywords, you should be aware of some of the special key names that 1-2-3 uses.

{BIGUP} *and* {BIGDOWN}

1-2-3 uses some odd-sounding names for the cursor-movement keys that control big cursor jumps. {BIGUP} and {BIGDOWN}, for instance, are the same as {PGUP} and {PGDN}.

{BIGRIGHT} *and* {BIGLEFT}

{BIGRIGHT} and {BIGLEFT} represent the Ctrl-right arrow and Ctrl-left arrow combinations. These keys have different effects, depending on whether they are used in EDIT mode or in the usual worksheet environment.

Tab and Backtab

The Tab key and its shifted form, Backtab, can't be called from a macro by these names. They are, however, functionally equivalent to {BIGRIGHT} and {BIGLEFT}, respectively.

Using the Tilde To Specify the Enter Key

To designate the Enter (or Return) key, you must use a special abbreviation: the tilde (~). This symbol is convenient because Enter is used so often.

Don't use {RETURN}. That is a special command language instruction and has a different meaning from ~ when used in a macro.

Entering Braces or the Tilde from a Macro

The right and left brace characters have a special role in delimiting keywords in a macro. You can use the right brace (}) as a character in a macro, but you can't use the left brace ({). 1-2-3 interprets the left brace as the beginning of a keyword or command language instruction. Likewise, because it is interpreted as Enter, the tilde character can't be typed directly from a macro. However, you can include the two illegal characters in macros by placing them in braces, as in the following:

　　{{} types {

and

　　{~} types ~

Also, for the sake of consistency, you can specify the right brace as {}}, which types }.

Activating the Command Menu

Usually, the slash key (/) activates the command menu in 1-2-3. In Release 2, two additional methods are available. The first of these is the Less-Than key (<), which is the character above the comma. To call the command menu, you can use this key instead of the slash.

The other way to activate the command menu from within a macro is to use the special {MENU} keyword. When used from within a macro, {MENU} is functionally equivalent to the slash.

Keys for Future Use

At the time this book was written, add-in applications for 1-2-3 had been announced but not formally released. An add-in application, a concept originally pioneered with Symphony, enables you to "attach" other programs to 1-2-3 in order to add more features to the program. Lotus has reserved four function keys—Alt-F7, Alt-F8, Alt-F9, and Alt-F10—for use with these add-ins. These keys have been designated as {APP1}, {APP2}, {APP3}, and {APP4}, respectively, for use in macros.

3

Creating More Complex Macros

Chapter 2 described the basics of macro definition and construction. This chapter explains in detail the rest of what you need to know to get the most out of macros, including the rules for creating long, multiple-line macros, and guidelines for layout and documentation. Also discussed are the ways to make a macro stop executing, issue worksheet commands, and execute another macro. Finally, this chapter traces in detail the development of macros, from simple initial form to refined final form, including the testing and debugging process that is an inevitable part of any programming.

Creating Multiline Macros

In the examples you've seen so far, the macro has been in a single cell. As you read descriptions of some of the more advanced macro applications, you will realize that such complexity could not possibly be crammed into a single cell. When executing macros that occupy more than one cell, 1-2-3 executes the instructions in the beginning cell, then moves down to the next cell and executes any instructions found there. 1-2-3 continues processing downward until it comes to a cell that is either blank or contains a number or numeric formula. Macro execution then stops, and control of 1-2-3 returns to you.

1-2-3 is tolerant of how instructions flow from one cell to the next. In figure 3.1, for instance, all the macros perform the same task: they type my name and press the Enter key.

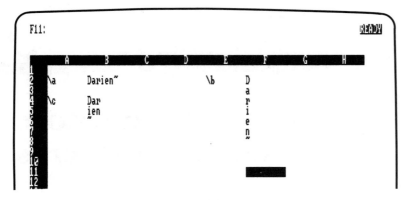

Fig. 3.1. Three macros that do the same thing.

Where To Break a Line

As soon as 1-2-3 finishes executing the contents of a cell, the program moves to the next cell and continues uninterrupted. The only limitation to this procedure is that you can't split keywords (or command language instructions) enclosed in braces. The following construction is therefore illegal.

    {INS
    ERT}

If you try to break a keyword in this way, 1-2-3 returns a syntax error. On the other hand, even when keywords perform a single operation, you can place them on separate lines. For example, the following two-line construction is legal, even though it represents only one command (move to the lower right corner of the active area of the worksheet).

    {END}
    {HOME}

Maximum Line Length

The length of a single line of macro instructions is limited only by the 240-character constraint for entries in a cell. Although long macro lines are possible, you would not want to make a practice of using them. Lines that extend beyond the limits of the screen are hard to read, hard to edit, and prone to errors. The most important macro habit you can develop is to make your macros (including explanatory comments) readable as you enter them in the worksheet.

Macro Organization

The importance of good documentation is a recurring theme in this book. This theme bears repeating both because it is important and because it is one of the hardest programming habits to establish. Adding documentation to a program is never as much fun as writing the program itself. Although the documentation does not *do* anything, in the sense that a program animates your computer, documentation is a very important part of computer work.

Most programmers—and using macros and the command language makes you a programmer—go through three distinct stages of documentation thoroughness. In the first stage, as a new user, forcing yourself to add some comments to your macros is easy. Until you're familiar with the function of each keyword and how macros operate, the comments help you monitor the progress of your program development.

The new-user stage quickly gives way to the power-user stage. As you learn to speak the language of macros, the comments become redundant; you can read the keywords and understand their functions immediately. The importance of documenting your macros won't become evident until some time has passed, and you have to modify or debug a huge macro written months earlier.

At this point, with a well-documented macro, you can quickly refamiliarize yourself with its function and get on with the work at hand. With an undocumented macro, you would have to track each step in detail and reconstruct its intended function. To understand how painful this process can be, you have to experience it, and you have to compare it with that of working on a well-documented macro. Only then will you be able to appreciate the difference that documentation can make. Some programmers reestablish their good documentation habits at this point, but a more traumatic programming experience becomes the turning point for others.

With expertise in macros and command language programming comes the ability to construct tremendously complex programs and to create powerful systems based on 1-2-3. A level of complexity exists, however, that exceeds the grasp of ordinary human minds; the volume of detail is beyond anyone's capacity to remember and follow. For such applications, documentation becomes essential. Without documentation, the programming process virtually grinds to a halt. Those programmers who learn to document can readily expand the scope of their applications to almost any size. Those who don't document usually give up large-scale programming and go back to macros.

To give up large-scale programming is to unnecessarily give up some of the best features of the system. After good documentation becomes an ingrained habit, it becomes self rewarding. I learned to document my programs the hard way. I watched experienced programmers laboriously adding hundreds of comments to large programs, thought I was above all that, and threw away a number of good programs that got too complex to follow. Now, when I write a complex program, it is always well documented. On many occasions, I have been glad that I went through the effort, because documentation made simple what could have been a difficult task. I've even gone back to some of those programs I gave up on, reorganized and documented them, and made them work.

As you begin to write macros, adding line-by-line comments will enhance both your learning process and the macros you develop. Some guidelines for such documentation are offered here. As you write more complex applications, you will need to also add comments that explain the function of program modules. This second level of documentation is covered in Chapter 10.

Three-Column Format

GUIDELINE: Use a three-column format to organize your macros.

As explained previously, organizing your macros into two columns—that is, putting the macro names into the first column and the macros into the second column—documents the names assigned to macro cells. You should also use a third column in which you write explanations of what the macro does at each moment. By *column*, I don't mean the spreadsheet column (A, B, . . . IV), but the way your work is grouped on the screen. Figure 3.2 is an example of macro organization with documenting comments. Thanks to the comments, the macro's function is obvious at first glance.

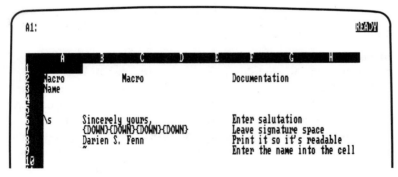

Fig. 3.2. Comments added to a macro.

This arrangement, of course, has some effect on how many macro keywords you can put on one line. Ultimately, you're limited by the width of the screen, which accommodates 78 characters. If you have one column (about 9 characters) for macro names and 3 columns (about 27 characters) for comments, approximately 40 characters are left for macro keywords—plus room for a 1-character space between columns. This method, however, isn't necessarily the best for organizing your macros.

GUIDELINE: The ultimate goal is readability.

One way to organize your macros is to put keywords on individual lines and explanations of the keywords in the third column. An advantage of this arrangement is that you can use the comment column to document all the macro's actions. The chances are slight, however, that you will go to the trouble of documenting each {DOWN} or {END} in a macro—at least not for very long. Even if you don't document every line, putting each keyword on one line has another disadvantage: you generate very long, thin macros that are hard to follow because you can't see much of them at once (20 keywords maximum). The following sections offer some solutions.

Documentation

To help you arive at a compromise between too few keywords on a line and too many, keep in mind the following general rules for organizing macros.

1. Leave the far left column for names, the middle four columns for the macro, and the three rightmost columns for comments.

2. Group keywords on a line, according to the function they perform. In the example in figure 3.2, the four {DOWN} statements performed one function: they left signature space. You can therefore use one comment to describe these keywords. If you decide later that you need five spaces instead of four (suppose that the signature were large), you can add those spaces without changing the comment line.

3. "Start thin." As mentioned, you may want to add something to the middle of a macro. In fact, if the macros are simple to begin with, you may expand virtually every macro you make. If, on the other hand, your macro starts extending beyond the screen's limits, try condensing the macro somewhat. If you think this advice contradicts what is written in some of the preceding paragraphs, you're right. Establishing a rule—one that works on every occasion—about how many keywords to put on a single line is difficult. You have to learn to balance the readability that comes with width against the expandability that comes with narrowness.

4. Write comments liberally. You may be saving yourself a great deal of work later on if you easily can go back to a macro and understand what it does. Macros do get obscure after the passage of time.

5. If you're going to create macros other people may have to interpret or modify, write more comments than you would otherwise. If you have any doubts, comment. What is obvious to you can be a complete mystery to someone else.

6. Don't make the documenting process painful. Keep your efforts reasonable, or you will burn yourself out and lose your good habits. Just keep in mind that writing comments for your macros *is* important.

Organizing Macros in Your Worksheet

Whether you use macros to construct or to use a worksheet, you will probably begin with several macros and add more as you develop the worksheet. When you organize your worksheet, keep your needs in mind: you need space for your macros; you must have regular access to them; and you may want to modify them from time to time. The best way to take care of these requirements is to have a standard location for macros.

GUIDELINE: Select a remote worksheet location as your standard macro location.

Because of the way Release 1A of 1-2-3 allocated memory, worksheet layout was restricted to a tight rectangle in order to avoid wasting a limited amount of space. Approximately four bytes of memory were reserved for every cell in the active area of the worksheet. The active area was a rectangle that extended as far right as the rightmost occupied cell and as far down as the lowest occupied cell.

With Release 1A, putting macros in an out-of-the-way location could waste a lot of memory. In figure 3.3, the shaded area represents memory reserved by 1-2-3. As you can see, the area between the worksheet data and the macro area uses up memory even though the cells are unoccupied. Because this amount of wasted memory was a luxury that few could afford, macros were placed close to the worksheet data.

Release 2 uses a different memory management scheme, sometimes referred to as a *semi-sparse matrix* technique. Instead of reserving memory for the cells in the active area, memory is allocated on a column-by-column basis. In true sparse matrix memory management, memory would be allocated only to cells that contained data. With semi-sparse matrix memory management, memory is reserved between the highest and lowest points in a single column. If you place the number 1 in cell A1 and in cell B8000, only about 8 bytes of memory are used. (The figure is actually higher than that, because 1-2-3 allocates memory to 4 cell groups; but the average is 4 bytes per cell.) On the other hand, if you

Fig. 3.3. Memory allocation in Release 1A of 1-2-3.

put your numbers in cells A1 and *A8000*, you use up 32,000 bytes of memory, because 1-2-3 reserves 4 bytes for each cell between A1 and A8000.

Figure 3.4 shows how memory would be allocated in Release 2 for the same worksheet as shown in figure 3.3. As you can see, much less memory space is wasted. This change in memory management gives Release 2 users much more flexibility in macro placement. As long as you place your macros in columns that are not used by other entries, you can place the macros anywhere in the worksheet without "memory penalty."

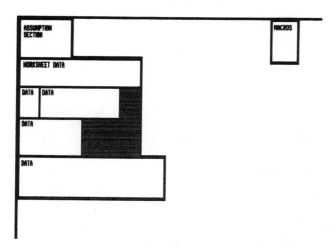

Fig. 3.4. Memory allocation in Release 2 of 1-2-3.

Selecting a worksheet area for macros involves another consideration: the effect of inserting and deleting columns and rows. The process of inserting and deleting rows is common to worksheet development. If you place your macros directly to the side of your worksheet data, inserting a row into your data can insert an unwanted row into your macro as well (see fig. 3.5). Worse yet, deleting a row can delete part of your macro. If your macros are above or below your work area, the same danger exists for column insertions and deletions.

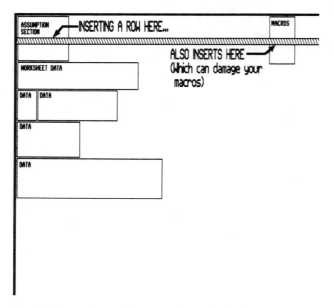

Fig. 3.5. A row inserted in a worksheet, which also inserts an unwanted row in a macro.

One solution that resolves most of these problems is to place your macros very far to the right—for example, in column HA—and down a lot of rows, perhaps row 1000. This arrangement allows your work area to be 208 columns wide before it interferes with your macro area or starts gobbling up memory. Because of the columnar memory allocation used in Release 2, your worksheet can extend past row 1000 and not affect memory usage. (But you still should be careful about inserting and deleting rows.)

If you adopt this macro placement strategy, the End+Home keystroke combination will have a new function. Instead of taking you to the lower right corner of your worksheet data, this keystroke sequence takes you to the lower right corner of your macro area. This feature could be an advantage or a disadvantage, depending on how you're used to using End+Home.

TIP: Use a window to work on macros and to retain your place in the worksheet.

When using macros, you will find that you often need to go from your macro area to your worksheet area and back again. Sometimes you pop into your macro area to create a quick macro. Other times you alternate between worksheet and macro to refine, alter, or debug an existing macro. Bouncing back and forth between two areas of the worksheet can waste a lot of time if you can't go directly to your point of interest. Because the cell pointers can be independent in unsynchronized 1-2-3 windows, creating a window for developing macros lets you work on macros without leaving your place in the worksheet area (see fig. 3.6). By pressing the Window key (F6), you can move back and forth between the two areas and keep your place in each. Always use the newly created window for macros; when you're through working on your macros, clearing the window leaves you in your worksheet area.

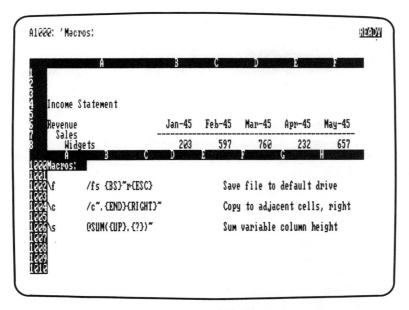

Fig. 3.6. A window used to work on macros while keeping your place in the worksheet.

TIP: Use a range name to mark your macro area.

Whether or not you use the lower right corner of your worksheet for macros, assigning a range name to the macro area can speed up the process of moving there for macro work. Name the area MACROS, and you probably won't forget what name you assigned.

TIP: To locate your macro area, use the Name key (F3) with the GoTo key (F5).

After you assign a range name to your macro area, you can specify that name in response to the Address to go to: prompt that appears when you press the GoTo key (F5). Easier still, if you press the Name key (F3) in response to that prompt, the screen displays a list of existing range names. Point to the name for your macro area, press Enter, and you're there.

TRICK: Use a space or control character as the first character in your range name.

When you use the Name key (F3), 1-2-3 presents the list of range names in alphabetical order. If you use the right name, you can cause your macro name to always appear first on the list. This arrangement makes the GoTo process that much easier; the name you want is always first, and you can select it merely by pressing Enter.

If you use a space as the first character of the name, you can virtually guarantee that your macro range name will be at the top of the alphabetical list. 1-2-3 uses ASCII/LICS codes to determine alphabetical order. The space character has a code number of 32, the letter A is 64, and numbers and characters come in between. Therefore, the space character comes before A in a computer alphabet.

Creating a range name that begins with a space can be a little tricky, especially if other names are already assigned. When other names exist, 1-2-3 interprets the pressing of a space bar as the pressing of the right-arrow key and moves the menu pointer. To force the space to become the first character, you type the range name, press the Home key, then the space bar, and then Enter. 1-2-3 then adds a space in front of the name you typed.

If you want to guarantee your macro range name the top billing in the range name list, use a control character as the first character in the name. Control characters have codes lower than 32 and will therefore come before of any character you can type on the keyboard. Because you can't enter these characters from the keyboard, using them in a range name is trickier than using a space. Here's how to do it:

1. Go to the cell to which you have assigned the range name and move one cell to the left.

2. Enter the control character by using the @CHAR function and add your range name as a string formula. The control character will appear

to be a space. For example, if you want to use the first control character and name your range MACROS, you type

    @CHAR(1)&"MACROS"

3. Convert the formula to a string by using the /Range Value command (/Range Value Enter Enter).

4. Use the /Range Name Label Right command to assign this name to your selected cell.

When you use the Name key (F3), you will see your new range name at the top of the list, preceded by a funny character that looks like the upper left corner of a square. (The control character has this appearance.)

Using Macros on a Regular Basis

GUIDELINE: Develop consistent macro habits.

Develop some consistency as to where you put macros in your worksheet, what you name your macro area, and what you name your macros. Consistency is most important for the macros you use regularly. The keystrokes for activating these macros will become as familiar to you as 1-2-3's command structure. Whereas the command structure never changes, however, your macros can. If you don't develop some consistent habits regarding macro names, it is just a matter of time until you begin using a macro and find that the one you wanted to use is not in that particular worksheet. If you're lucky, the macro that *is* there won't do much damage before you get it stopped.

To reduce the likelihood of such a problem occurring, you can reserve certain keys for use by a specific set of macros. This procedure leaves the remaining keys for macros that change from worksheet to worksheet.

Terminating Macro Execution

As mentioned previously, a macro will continue executing as long as succeeding cells contain labels. Specific worksheet conditions, however, can make determining the point at which a macro stops executing a little more complex than you might think.

Blank Cells

You may recall from the description of multiline macros that a macro stops executing when it encounters a blank cell. A little ambiguity exists, however, as to what a blank cell is. For instance, a macro stops executing when it encounters a cell that contains *only* a label prefix even though such a cell is not truly *blank*. When you use the End key to move the cursor, 1-2-3 considers the cell containing the label prefix to be nonblank, and the @CELL("type") function returns *l* (label) for that cell. This distinction is subtle but just the kind of thing that can create a horrible debugging problem in a complex macro or command language program.

String Formulas

Macro execution halts when 1-2-3 encounters either a blank cell or cell containing a number or numeric formula. What this statement implies is that a macro executes a string formula as if it were a label. This statement is indeed correct and is a powerful aspect of advanced programming in 1-2-3. To give you a hint of what will be explained in Chapter 9, imagine a macro that alters something in the worksheet, causing a string formula that is part of that macro to change and display a different result. That's right: a macro can alter itself!

Ambiguous Formulas

Some formulas can display a string sometimes and a number or blank at other times. Can you tell which formulas in figure 3.7 would cause a macro to stop executing? The only formula that would *not* do so is the formula in A4. This formula is the only one listed that returns a string value as a result. The formula in A2 returns a number, and the formulas in A6 and A8 return empty cells. Notice that if the contents of B2 were changed to a string, the formulas in both A2 and A8 would change to strings, which macros can execute.

The Effect of Recalculation

Whether a string in a formula cell is considered executable depends on the cell's *current* contents. If a worksheet hasn't been recalculated, the cell in question *and* the operation of the macro containing that cell are determined by information that may not be up-to-date. This situation can be a problem for macros or command language programs intended to change so that they reflect current data. However, with care, this situation can also be used to advantage.

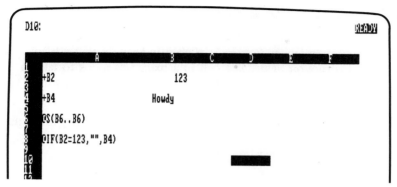

Fig. 3.7. Formulas with ambiguous result "types."

Some 1-2-3 functions recalculate *only* when you press the Calc key (F9), regardless of the current recalculation setting. In addition, some functions that are usually recalculated in an automatic recalculation are not updated if they're part of an executing macro or command language program. This important topic is discussed further in Chapter 9.

The Appearance of the Screen

1-2-3's screen does not always display the current values of cells after a recalculation. This situation occurs with specific functions in specific circumstances that are too variable to describe fully. Most of the time, this situation arises when the calculations are updated from within a macro or command language program. As far as macro execution is concerned, the *internal* values govern what the macro does. If you have any doubts about a recalculation's status, you can update the screen by pressing the Calc key (F9).

The Effect of Cell Format

Cell format has no effect on whether the cell contains an executable string value. Cells formatted to either Hidden or Text work just as they would if formatted to any other specification. In other words, although a hidden cell may appear blank, it is executable if it contains a label or string formula.

In contrast, although a Text formatted cell appears to contain a string (the formula itself), the cell is not executable unless it returns a string result. If the cell returns a string value, the macro executes the hidden result of the formula, not the text version of the formula. Before you can execute a formula, you must convert it to a string, as described in the "Ambiguous Formulas" section.

A Common Macro Error

1-2-3 continues to execute macro instructions as long as the program encounters cells that contain labels. You must therefore be sure that a blank cell follows your last instruction. If the last cell in a macro happens to fall on the last line of the screen, you might not see something executable in the following cell because it's off the screen.

When checking for executable cells that follow your macro, watch out for cells with a Hidden format. Also be on the lookout for cells containing spaces only or formulas that return a string consisting only of spaces.

Using Macros To Issue Commands

Having macros perform typing tasks sometimes can be helpful; but the real power of macros is their capability to issue commands. In most applications, you will perform sequences of commands repeatedly. Putting these sequences into a macro can streamline operations a great deal.

A File-Save Macro

Saving a file to disk is one task that all 1-2-3 users perform repeatedly. Using a macro to save a file to disk doesn't save you much time as far as keystrokes are concerned. However, this File-Save macro turns out to be marvelously handy because of the number of times you perform this operation. Making this macro a one-keystroke operation facilitates backing up your files more frequently. In its most basic form, the macro looks like the following.

    /fsMYFILE~

The command operations appear as the first characters of the command—in this case, the / that calls the command menu, the *f* from File, and the *s* from Save. Commands are always entered this way, first letter only. Think of the macro as replicating your typing, keystroke for keystroke, as you issue each command. The following command performs the same task.

    /f{RIGHT}~MYFILE~

Why? Look at the menu in figure 3.8. The figure shows the menu as it appears after File has been selected on the command menu. You can select any command on this menu by pressing the key that corresponds to the first character in the command's name. You can also select a command by pointing to it and pressing Enter. The second option on the File menu is the Save command. By moving the pointer one place to the right and pressing Enter, you select Save. The preceding modified form of the macro uses the keyword {RIGHT} to move the pointer and a tilde (~) to press Enter, thereby selecting the Save command.

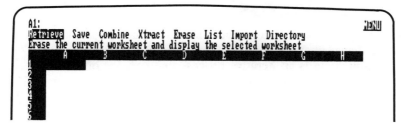

Fig. 3.8. The File command menu.

GUIDELINE: Avoid using the point-and-select method in macros.

Even if you are accustomed to using the point-and-select method to choose some commands, you shouldn't use this method in a macro. The macro becomes harder to "translate" when you go back to it later. When you select things other than commands, such as file or range names, you have no guarantee that the file and range name lists will be the same when you execute the macro as when you constructed it.

Macro Readability

Returning to the examination of the File-Save macro, notice that the name of the file to be saved, MYFILE (followed by a ~ to complete the name entry process), appears in uppercase, whereas the command strings themselves are in lowercase. This convention makes macros more readable. When your macros get complex, this convention can help you sort commands from names.

GUIDELINE: Differentiate your commands from your file names by using lowercase characters for one and uppercase characters for the other.

You can establish this convention either way: commands in lowercase and files in uppercase, or vice versa. The important thing is to differentiate. Macros can easily become obscure.

In the next chapter, you will use a special macro that records your keystrokes. With that macro, you can create macros just by performing the operation manually. That special macro records keywords in capital letters. Using uppercase for keywords will make your macro conventions consistent with the output of the "learning" macro and with a range-naming convention that is discussed in Chapter 9.

Developing Macros

In general, whether you're constructing simple macros or complicated programs, you will rarely find that your first effort produces exactly the desired results. Typically, most programming is an iterative process that consists of an initial attempt, testing, debugging, refining, and perhaps one or more repetitions of this cycle.

Starting Simple

When you create a macro, you may want to start out by constructing it in its most basic form. With more complex macros, this procedure helps confirm the design of their basic operations. You will then want to polish your macro, adding to it the "whistles and bells"—the little extras that make the macro easier to use or more helpful than the basic version. You will also want to *test and debug* your macro—that is, make sure that it operates as you intended it to *under all conditions*. The following examples help demonstrate the debugging process.

Debugging Macros

The logic underlying the macro development process is important. When you develop your own macros, the problems you want to solve will be completely different from those addressed here; nonetheless, the following procedures should help you over the hurdle. Focusing on logic rather than on content becomes especially important when you begin programming in the command language.

The First Tests

When you use the File-Save macro for the first time, it performs a complete File Save operation. After the first use, 1-2-3 notices that a file with the name you are using already exists on the disk (from your first use of the macro). Because 1-2-3 was designed to help you avoid disastrous data-destroying errors, the program stops before overwriting the existing file with the version you're currently trying to save and gives you one last chance to change your mind. Instead of performing a complete file-change operation, the macro displays the "last chance" menu (see fig. 3.9).

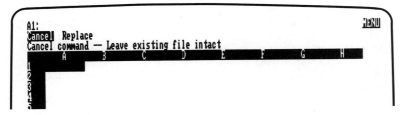

Fig. 3.9. The "last chance" menu.

You now have a design choice to make. If you want to have the opportunity to make this decision manually, you can leave the macro as it is, and it will stop when the last chance menu appears. You will always be able to make the final decision.

If, however, you assume that the conditions under which you will save your file will always require an *r* response at this point, then you could modify the listing:

/fsMYFILE~r

Now the macro *always* replaces the existing file. All you have to decide is whether to replace the existing file *before* you execute the macro.

More Refinements: A Universal File-Save Macro

The preceding macro will now perform a complete file save, making it a one-keystroke operation. The macro, however, does have a few limitations. Because the name of the file is part of the macro, this macro works only for one particular file. This is not a great problem; editing a new file name into such a short macro is actually a rather trivial task. Notice that the macro automatically bypasses a safety feature. Therefore, before you implement any changes, you should consider the operation of the macro under all possible conditions.

How To Damage Your File

As constructed, this macro could cause problems under certain conditions. Variations on a worksheet are easy to create by starting with an existing file, entering the necessary modifications, and saving the file under a new name. If your original file contains the last version of the macro, and you create a similar file by modifying the original but *fail to modify the macro to reflect the new file name*, then using the macro in your modified file causes the modified file to overwrite the original file.

A Partial Solution

The solution to this problem is to remove the file name, leaving the macro looking like the following:

    /fs~r

When you select the File-Save macro *after you've saved the file at least once*, 1-2-3 supplies a file name in the prompt as a default. At this point, pressing Enter instead of entering a new file name causes the file to be saved under the default name, which is the same name used the last time the file was saved. This macro can now be used *as is* for any file.

How To Destroy Your File

The solution just described has one serious limitation. If you try to use this macro *before you specify a file name* in the file-save operation, 1-2-3 can destroy a file on your disk. When you ask 1-2-3 to save a new file for the first time, pressing Enter instead of typing a file name causes the program to use the first file name it finds—one that already exists on the disk. The placement of the tilde (~) in this macro produces exactly that result, and the *r* following the tilde replaces the existing file with the current file.

A Final Solution

What you need to do is to modify the existing macro so that it will cause neither of the two preceding problems. The macro that will do the job is

    /fs {BACKSPACE}~r

A space has been added after the *s*, and the space is followed by the keyword {BACKSPACE}. When a file name exists because the file has been saved, these changes merely enter a space after the file name and then remove the space. When the tilde is executed, the file is saved normally.

If a file name doesn't exist in the file-save prompt, this macro acts somewhat unusually. When a list of file names appears on the screen, the space bar acts as an alternative to {RIGHT}, moving the pointer to the next entry in the list. The space isn't entered into the file name. When the subsequent {BACKSPACE} is executed, it becomes an illegal keystroke because no file name exists over which to backspace. 1-2-3 beeps, the menu of file names disappears, and 1-2-3 enters EDIT mode. The tilde puts an Enter into the system. This calls back the menu of file names but *doesn't select any of the names.* The final *r* in the macro is interpreted to be the first character in a new file name, and the macro stops, leaving the screen as shown in figure 3.10.

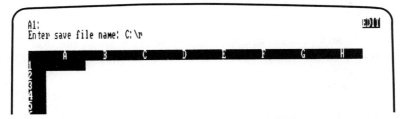

Fig. 3.10. The appearance of the screen after the File-Save macro has been used, where no file name specification exists.

To recap, if a file has been saved and given a file name, the macro operates as a one-keystroke save operation. If no file name has been assigned to the current file, the macro doesn't save the file, but neither does the macro overwrite any other files. In fact, the beep helps alert you that something is amiss, as does the appearance of the screen (see fig. 3.10).

Note to Hard Disk Users

When the current file directory includes a subdirectory, the Backspace key is a valid keystroke, serving to remove the last subdirectory from the file-save prompt. Suppose that you have your file directory set to

   C:\123\

The {BACKSPACE} keyword in the latest version of the macro causes the prompt to change to

   C:\

Because this keystroke is valid, it doesn't cause 1-2-3 to beep and enter EDIT mode. Therefore, you run the risk of overwriting a file in your root directory. To avoid this problem, add an additional space and another {BACKSPACE} keyword to your macro.

   /fs {BACKSPACE}{BACKSPACE}~r

The macro will then perform as intended. For each additional level of subdirectory used, you will need to add another space and another {BACKSPACE}. Suppose that your files are stored in

C:\123\DATA\

You will have to change your macro to

/fs   {BACKSPACE}{BACKSPACE}{BACKSPACE}~r

Further Debugging

The File-Save macro doesn't perform as expected if you use it when the disk doesn't contain the file of which you want to save a new version. In this situation, the *r* at the end of the macro becomes superfluous and is typed into your worksheet. This no-file situation can arise in two ways: if you change disks intentionally to make another copy of your file on a separate disk or if you accidentally leave the wrong disk in the drive. (The latter situation occurs when the file gets too large to fit on your current disk. 1-2-3 displays a Disk Full error message, and the file disappears from the disk.) In both cases, the superfluous *r* doesn't damage anything; it is, at worst, a minor annoyance. If you remain aware of this limitation of the macro's operation, you can simply delete the extra *r* by pressing Esc when *r* appears.

GUIDELINE: Don't live with minor annoyances when you don't have to.

Macros that perform in an annoying fashion soon become unused macros, which defeats the whole purpose of having them. Although some minor annoyances that crop up in macro development are unavoidable, the no-file and disk-full situations are avoidable. You can modify the macro to include {ESCAPE}, a keyword that clears the extra *r*. Pressing the Esc key after a file operation does nothing but clear the control panel of whatever characters appear there. Therefore, adding that {ESCAPE} can't hurt. The macro now looks like

/fs {BACKSPACE}~r{ESCAPE}

This is the final form of this simple macro. The addition of {ESCAPE} produces an interesting effect when the macro is used without a file specification (as described previously). Instead of leaving the screen looking like figure 3.10, {ESCAPE} clears the file specification entirely, leaving the prompt

Enter save file name:

With {ESCAPE}, the macro either performs as intended or prompts you for a file name if one is needed.

This macro was chosen as an example because it illustrates the debugging process. Most macros this simple aren't so complicated to debug. In fact, with a little practice, you can easily create fairly complex macros that work perfectly the first time. What is important, however, is considering potential problems that can arise when you automate portions of your work, especially when that automation bypasses any of 1-2-3's safety features. Much of the debugging can be handled in the form of a thought experiment; you don't always have to try out every possibility. The best method for debugging, however, is to put the macro through its paces. If the macro can result in data loss, use dummy data and see what happens. Some subtleties in 1-2-3's internal operation can fool you.

A Conceptual Sequence for Creating Simple Macros

What you've done so far can be summarized in the following steps. This is not a formal procedure for debugging, but rather a conceptual sequence for generating simple macros. When you start creating complex macros and command language programs, you will have to be more systematic about program design *and* testing.

1. Create the basic macro and test it.
2. Consider all possible conditions that could affect the macro's operation.
3. Modify the macro as necessary.
4. Test the final version of the macro.

One Last Refinement: Shortening the Macro

If you use abbreviations for the keywords in this macro, you can shorten the macro to

/fs {BS}~r{ESC}

This macro is not only more readable, but easier to type.

Executing Macros Automatically

You can execute macros automatically when you load a worksheet. This capability becomes more important when you begin designing command language programs, but has a few uses at the macro level.

To identify an autoexecute macro, you name the starting cell \0. This macro can't be executed from the keyboard. Pressing Alt-0 types an @ but doesn't execute the macro. Figure 3.11 shows an autoexecute macro. This example keeps a record of the date and time that a worksheet is loaded. Chapter 5 describes the macro in detail.

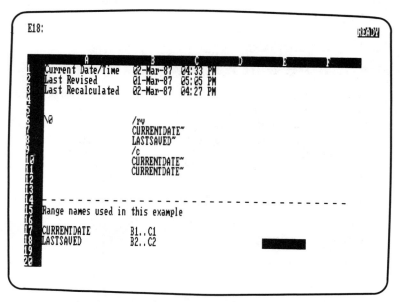

Fig. 3.11. A macro that executes automatically when you load the worksheet.

After you name the \0 macro, that information becomes part of the worksheet and is saved with the rest of the worksheet information when you save the file. The macro swings into action whenever you load the worksheet.

Executing a Macro
from Inside Another Macro

You may sometimes want to combine the operations of two or more macros. Look at the two simple macros in figure 3.12. You will undoubtedly develop many such single-task macros.

The first macro, \s, creates a @SUM formula for a column of numbers directly above the cell in which the cell pointer is located and copies the resulting formula across the five columns immediately to the right. The second macro, \f, formats a specific cell to Fixed format with two decimal places.

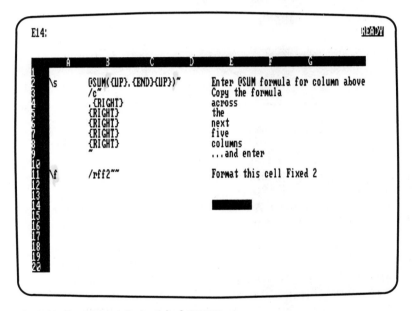

Fig. 3.12. Two separately developed macros.

Suppose that you have an application in which you want to combine two functions and format the newly created @SUM cell *before* it's copied to the other columns. 1-2-3 makes this task simple by enabling you to "call" one macro from within another (see fig. 3.13).

All you have to do is treat the macro you want to reference as another keyword by putting braces around the name. When 1-2-3 encounters this name in a macro, the program locates the specified macro, executes it, then returns to the first macro and continues executing it.

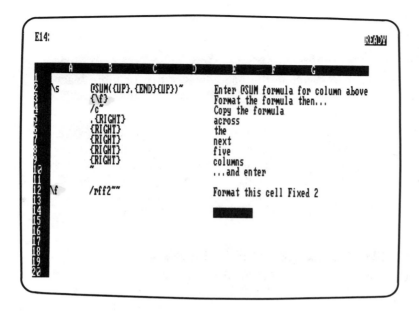

Fig. 3.13. A macro called from inside another macro.

In programming parlance, a macro within a macro is called a *nested subroutine*. A nested macro can contain another nested macro. Each successive call to a new macro is called a *level of nesting*. A macro within a macro within a macro is *nested two levels deep*. You can nest up to 32 levels before 1-2-3 "gets lost" and quits.

Combining macros is a convenient way to save yourself a little work, which is what this book is all about. However, combining macros is *more* than just convenient. It's a powerful technique that will become an essential part of program development when you start writing more complex command language programs. Writing short macro modules is easier than developing longer macro modules, and following the execution of a long macro is easier when it comprises a series of smaller units, each of which performs a specific task.

4

Automatic and Hybrid Macros

Despite the power and flexibility that macros bring to 1-2-3, they have one major limitation: they are tedious to write. One reason is the way you must specify keys as macro keywords. For example, to create a macro that executes the {EDIT}{HOME}{RIGHT} sequence, you have to type 19 keystrokes plus 9 more to enter a range name. You do all this in order to save only 3 keystrokes.

Another reason involves the debugging process. Even the simplest macro is susceptible to typographical error. With Release 1A of 1-2-3, the recommended method for constructing a complex macro involved performing the operation you wanted to automate manually, writing down each keystroke as it was executed. After completing this process, you would take your handwritten list of keystrokes and translate those into the actual macro. The effort involved in writing a macro this way always had to be weighed carefully against the benefits of using the macro. Because of this trade-off, effective uses of 1-2-3 macros were usually limited to very complex or frequently performed operations, and many potential uses for automating keystrokes were ignored.

How do you decide when a macro will save you work and when a macro will be more trouble to create than it is worth? With the addition of the command language to Release 2, this question is no longer of great significance. You can create a short command language program (described in the following section) that will write your macros for you. All you have to do to use this Automatic Macro program is start it and manually perform the operation that you want to code into a macro. The command language program captures your keystrokes and places them into the worksheet.

This program makes possible a new class of "quick and dirty" macros that may only be used once, then discarded, like notes made on scratch paper. These "scratch-pad" macros and other kinds of automatic macros are the topics of this chapter.

This chapter also provides a transition into the command language. Two command language instructions are discussed that can add power and flexibility to "learned" and handwritten macros, without getting you into the more complicated aspects of programming. By mastering these "hybrid" macros, the automatic macros, and the scratch-pad macros, you will have a good foundation on which to build your command language programming skills.

Automatic Macros

The inner workings of the Automatic Macro program involve advanced concepts that won't be addressed until later chapters. The Automatic Macro program, however, is an excellent tool for beginning macro students.

To use the program, you need only to enter it into the worksheet, exactly as the program appears in figure 4.1. Don't forget to use the **/Range Name Labels Right** command to assign all the range names that appear in the left column of the listing to the cells to their immediate right. After you enter the macro and assign the range names, you can let the program write your macros, forget about typographical errors, and concentrate on learning how and when to use macros.

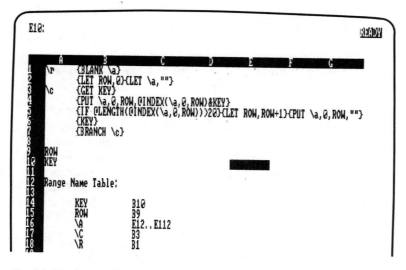

Fig. 4.1. The Automatic Macro program.

A Sample Data Transformation Task

The Automatic Macro program can be applied to simplify worksheet tasks that would otherwise be complex or tedious. In the following example, creating the result that you want involves performing operations on every other column of the data. Although 1-2-3's Move and Copy commands enable you to manipulate large areas of the worksheet with just a few keystrokes, these standard worksheet commands can't be applied easily when alternating columns require different modifications. The Automatic Macro program, however, allows you to create a temporary macro that can handle such a problem with ease.

Suppose, for example, that you wanted to present the sales volumes for various segments of a company. You most likely want to display a column of volume figures; a total beneath the column; and a second column, alongside the first, indicating the percent of the total each sales number represents.

The starting point for generating such a worksheet usually looks something like figure 4.2. Although only 5 columns of data are shown, monthly sales figures could easily extend 24, 36, or even 60 columns. No room is available for percentage columns, and no command exists that will insert new columns in between existing data columns.

```
J4:                                              READY

            I         J       K        L        M       N
1
2
3   Cost Center      Jan     Feb      Mar      Apr     May
4                  ███████
5   Aloha           12,556  13,880   15,320   13,672  12,893
6   Beaverton      101,252 136,582   99,830   72,640  61,631
7   Bend            45,828  23,372   13,869   19,604  13,068
8   Eugene         145,223  97,762  108,898   71,310  42,394
9   Grants Pass     63,200  70,299   75,565   83,385  45,893
10  Gresham         13,551  16,098   15,502    9,706   7,649
11  Newport         32,181  17,240   19,068   12,602  16,322
12  North Portland 201,520 272,502  335,389  288,969 381,695
13  Tillamook        8,923  10,558   11,834    7,942   6,185
14  Vancouver      325,102 476,778  530,597  750,244 421,698
15
```

Fig. 4.2. Sales data in its premodified form.

No matter how you approach the problem, putting the data into its final format will require a great deal of tedious work. A macro would be helpful. However, because of the number of steps involved in creating just one of the percentage columns, the macro would also be tedious to write and probably would require some debugging.

Another disadvantage exists to using a manually written macro to do this task: you are unlikely to need a macro exactly like this one again. Writing such a macro is much like writing yourself a note on scratch paper; the note is useful for a short time only. Scratch-pad macros can be very useful. The problem posed in this example is only one of dozens of similar spreadsheet tasks.

Automating the creation of scratch-pad macros enables you to use them on a regular basis. You simply invoke the Automatic Macro program and perform your spreadsheet task (such as creating the column of percentages in the preceding example). 1-2-3 automatically writes the macro for you. Not only does this process make creating scratch-pad macros easy, but because 1-2-3 does the writing for you, no typographical errors occur.

The Recording Range

In addition to typing the Automatic Macro program into the worksheet, you must predefine the range that will store the macro keywords you create when you perform the operation. The name for this range must match the range name used in the Automatic Macro program. The program listed in figure 4.1 uses the range name \a. The range need only be a single column, but must contain enough rows to store all the recorded keystrokes. Most scratch-pad macros will occupy about 10 to 20 rows. However, if the code for the task is particularly involved, a scratch-pad macro could conceivably occupy 100 or more rows.

Creating a Scratch-Pad Macro

In this section, the process of creating a scratch-pad macro is described in detail, using the example described previously and the data in figure 4.2.

1. To begin, as described in the preceding paragraphs, you will need to enter the Automatic Macro program into your worksheet. If you have created a file for your program, you will need to /File Combine it into the worksheet.

2. Go to the sample data and place your cell pointer in cell J4, the cell just below the date and above the top number in the first column of data.

3. Start the Automatic Macro program. The beginning point in the program has been named \r (for record). Therefore, you start the program by pressing Alt-r. The CMD indicator appears at the bottom of the screen, indicating that a macro is in progress.

4. Begin typing. For this example, use the keystrokes that follow. The keys you should press appear in macro format. That is, if a keyword appears in braces—{RIGHT}, for example—you press the right-arrow key. Don't type the braces or keywords themselves.

You may notice that 1-2-3 is a little sluggish while the Automatic Macro program is recording. The program is writing the macro into the worksheet as well as performing the operations you are specifying. Therefore, a pause occurs each time 1-2-3 updates the worksheet. The number of times the program updates the worksheet varies according to the operations selected. If you find the lag in response bothersome, you may have to type slower.

Keystrokes	*Explanation*
^($)~	Enter a centered label ($) above the dollar amounts.
/wcs{RIGHT}{RIGHT}~	Set the column width a little wider.
{RIGHT}	Move right by one cell.
/wic~	Insert a new column.
^(%){LEFT} {END} {DOWN} {DOWN}	Enter a centered label (%) above where the percentages will be. Then move left and down to the cell just below the column of numbers. Notice that you enter the label by moving left instead of using the ~.
\-{DOWN}	Draw a line under the numbers and move down one.
@SUM({UP}.{END}{UP} {DOWN}{DOWN})~	Enter an @SUM formula.
{RIGHT}	Move right by one cell.
+{LEFT}/{LEFT}{ABS}~	Enter the percentage formula. Notice that you need to divide this number by itself, but make the second reference absolute. The result of this operation is equal to 1; or, because the number referenced by the formula just created is the total, 100 percent. When this formula is copied, the cell to the left of the new copy is divided by the total.
/rfp0~~	Format the result to %0.

/c~{UP}{UP}.{END} {UP}{DOWN}~	Copy the formula to the column.
/wcs{LEFT}{LEFT}{LEFT}~	Set the column width narrower.
{UP}	Move up by one cell.
\-{END} {UP} {RIGHT}	Put the underline in this column, move up, and stop where the next column operation will start.

5. After you enter the last keystroke in the preceding list, stop the Automatic Macro program by pressing Ctrl-Break. This action generates a Break error, which you will have to clear by pressing Esc. Although using Ctrl-Break to stop the recording process isn't the most elegant way to halt a program, other methods result in a longer and more complicated program. Compare your result to figure 4.3.

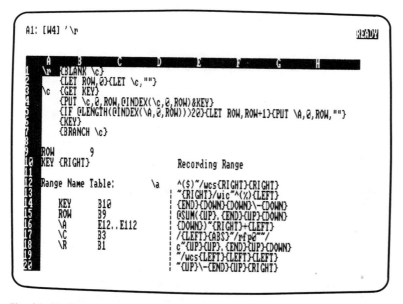

Fig. 4.3. The \a macro, created with the Automatic Macro program.

6. Make sure that your cell pointer is in L4 when you stop creating your scratch-pad macro. If your cell pointer is somewhere else, press Alt-c and move the cell pointer to L4. Alt-c restarts the Automatic Macro program but *doesn't erase the contents of the recording range.* After you position the cell pointer in L4, stop the Automatic Macro program

as before by pressing Ctrl-Break, then Esc. These steps add to your macro the additional keystrokes necessary to permit *chaining*, which is the repeated execution of the macro without intervening keystrokes.

How To Use Your Scratch-Pad Macro

After you execute the macro, your cell pointer is positioned so that the macro can be activated a second time. To process the next column of data, all you have to do is press Alt-a. 1-2-3 immediately begins duplicating your activities, keystroke for keystroke, except—this time—one column to the right.

If you copied the example in figure 4.2 correctly, you now have two columns of modified data and three columns of unmodified data (see fig. 4.4). To finish modifying the data, press Alt-a three more times. You can press Alt-a three times quickly because the keyboard buffer stores your keystrokes until 1-2-3 can catch up. Now all you have to do is sit back, wait, and watch.

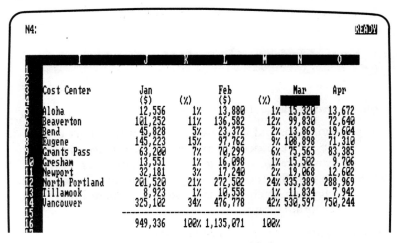

Fig. 4.4. Sales data with the first two columns modified.

The Longer Method Is Often Shorter

An alternative to the creation of alternating columns of data and percentages is the construction of a parallel table of percentages below or to the side of the original data. If you were going to perform the entire operation manually, the parallel table method would probably be the better of the two. It would certainly entail fewer keystrokes. If you had created a parallel table, then constructed a macro to insert columns and to move the percentage data to its final location, the macro would probably have been shorter.

However, when you can create a scratch-pad macro, the simplest method is often that used in the example. Essentially, you perform the modifications as if you had to modify only one column. Be careful to arrange the beginning and ending points so that when the macro executes repeatedly, it operates on successive areas of the worksheet.

How To Recycle a Scratch-Pad Macro

After you modify all the columns of data that require change, you are unlikely to need this scratch-pad macro again. When you need to create another scratch-pad macro, simply follow the steps provided for using the Automatic Macro program. Starting the Automatic Macro program by using Alt-r automatically erases the recording range and the current scratch-pad macro. If you want to save the current scratch-pad macro, copy the keystrokes in the recording range to a new location and give the first cell in the listing a new Alt-[letter] range name.

Guidelines for Using the Automatic Macro Program

GUIDELINE: Make your recording range 100 rows long or longer.

The Automatic Macro program stops and generates an error if you don't create a range large enough to store the recorded keystrokes. Because recovering from such an error is difficult, having a range that is too large is better than having one that is too small. Be sure that the recording range doesn't include any areas of your worksheet that contain data. Each time the Automatic Macro program is started, it erases the *entire* recording range.

TIP: Place a column of labels next to your recording range.

Because the recording range is erased automatically, you need to take some extra precautions to ensure that you don't enter important data in the recording range cells. Most of the time, the lowest rows in the recording range will be blank. Nothing alerts you to the fact that anything placed in those cells will be erased the next time you use your Automatic Macro program. To call attention to the recording range, you can place a column of labels into the cells immediately adjacent to the recording range (see fig. 4.5).

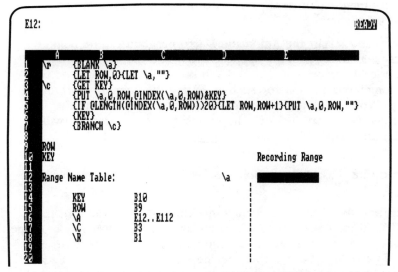

```
E12:                                                        READY

        A       B              C              D              E
 1  \r      {BLANK \a}
 2          {LET ROW,0}{LET \a,""}
 3  \c      {GET KEY}
 4          {PUT \a,0,ROW,@INDEX(\a,0,ROW)&KEY}
 5          {IF @LENGTH(@INDEX(\a,0,ROW))>20}{LET ROW,ROW+1}{PUT \a,0,ROW,""}
 6          {KEY}
 7          {BRANCH \c}
 8
 9  ROW
10  KEY                                                Recording Range
11
12  Range Name Table:                    \a
13
14          KEY            B10
15          ROW            B9
16          \A             E12..E112
17          \C             B3
18          \R             B1
19
20
```

Fig. 4.5. Worksheet layout for the Automatic Macro program and the recording range; labels entered next to the blank recording range.

GUIDELINE: In scratch-pad macros, select your beginning and ending cell pointer positions carefully.

Where your scratch-pad macro begins and ends is important. When you use a scratch-pad macro to perform a repetitive operation, such as modifying several columns of data, perform the task on the first column (using the Automatic Macro program to record your keystrokes) and stop the recording process with your cell pointer exactly where you plan to begin that task on the second column. In this way, when you use the macro that has been created by your Automatic Macro program, the macro will end in the location where the macro's next use should begin. This strategy allows you to link multiple executions of the macro, a process known as *chaining*. This procedure is illustrated further in the material that follows.

TIP: Save the Automatic Macro program and recording range in a separate disk file.

The Automatic Macro program is one you will probably have use for in many worksheets. To save you the trouble of typing the entire program in each worksheet, type the program and the recording range into a blank worksheet and save that worksheet to disk. When you want to use automatic macros in another worksheet, just /File Combine the Automatic Macro program file into your current worksheet, name the cells by using /Range Name Labels Right, and you're ready to roll.

TIP: While you are building a macro, you can turn the Automatic Macro program on and off anytime.

Being able to stop and restart the Automatic Macro program can be helpful during the macro-generating process. Suppose that you are doing something with the Automatic Macro program on, and you see something you need to change before completing the macro (such as setting the column width or erasing an entry). You can stop the Automatic Macro program, make the change, and resume where you left off. The Automatic Macro program will resume recording the macro in the recording range, below the last cell containing an entry.

GUIDELINE: To create reusable operations, use POINT mode in scratch-pad macros.

Whether you created the preceding example macro or simply examined the listing, notice that all modifications to the data occurred in POINT mode. Range names or cell addresses weren't used at all. Most operations you perform in a scratch-pad macro shouldn't be tied to a specific range or cell. This is because while you are modifying data in one column, you are simultaneously creating a macro that will work on the subsequent columns.

Like a relative reference in a Copy command, the macro operates on data in relation to the cell pointer's starting position rather than in relation to the overall worksheet. This procedure is generally the most useful for constructing scratch-pad macros.

GUIDELINE: Use a range name when you need an absolute reference in a scratch-pad macro.

When your scratch-pad macro needs to reference a specific cell in your worksheet, specify a range name instead of pointing to the cell. For example, use a range name to reference such constants as interest rates in an amortization calculation. This method resembles the way in which the Copy command works with absolute references. Before invoking the Automatic Macro program, you must plan ahead and be sure that a range name that will be specified exists. Although a little extra effort is involved in this procedure, it has its advantages (see the following GUIDELINE).

GUIDELINE: Avoid using cell addresses in macros.

The problem with using cell addresses in a macro is that macro instructions, whether entered directly or through the automatic macro program, are simply worksheet labels. If you alter the worksheet in such a way as to affect the cell addresses in a formula—by using a Copy or an Insert command, for instance— 1-2-3 automatically adjusts the formulas to reflect the new cell addresses that changed as a result of the operation you performed. With labels, however, 1-2-3 makes no attempt to interpret the contents or to determine which parts of the label might be cell addresses.

If you alter the worksheet, and your macro contains a cell address, your macro may no longer refer to the correct cells. Range names, on the other hand, serve as intermediaries in the alteration process. 1-2-3 automatically alters the range name's address specifications if the change affects that name, whereas the name, of course, remains the same. If you're in the habit of using in formulas cell addresses for {GOTO} commands, range specifications, and so on, you would be well advised to change your habit.

TRAP: Running out of room in your recording range causes an error to occur.

Be sure to specify plenty of room in your recording range before starting to create your automatic macro. If you run out of room, 1-2-3 displays an Illegal offset in PUT error message, and the operation stops. You can recover from the error by doing the following:

1. With the /Range Name Create command, increase the size of the recording range.

2. Return to the exact place where your macro stopped.

3. Turn the Automatic Macro program back on by using Alt-c (to "continue" the recording). Using Alt-c restarts the Automatic Macro program at a point past the instructions that erase the recording range. Be sure not to restart the Automatic Macro program with Alt-r. This erases your scratch-pad macro.

4. Resume "training" your macro.

TRAP: When 1-2-3 stops the macro creation process because the program runs out of room, you lose a few of your last macro keystrokes.

Be sure to check your recording range after causing an Illegal offset in PUT error. You may have lost a few of the last keystrokes. If you intend to go back and continue your macro, you may have to restart at a point prior to where the error occurred.

Hybrid Macros

One of the obvious advantages of using the Automatic Macro program is that you can easily create long macros. Macros that reproduce keystrokes are, however, somewhat inflexible. If an identifier is included, such as a range name, the macro will always include that name and that name only. If you wanted to use the macro with a different identifier, you would have to make a copy of the macro and use EDIT mode to change the names. Then you would have two macros—one for each set of conditions.

Another alternative would be to use one of the 1-2-3 command language instructions to modify the original macro so that it stops, waits for you to supply the variable information, and then continues executing. A macro created with the Automatic Macro program and modified with a command language instruction is called a *hybrid macro*. A little more than a macro because of the command language instruction, this macro is less than a program—hence the term *hybrid*. Hybrid macros are very powerful and can save you a great deal of time in creating macros or modules for use in programs.

The {?} Instruction

The {?} instruction is a special kind of macro keyword that you either type into a macro or enter using EDIT mode. As is the case with all 1-2-3 command language instructions, {?} has no keystroke equivalent.

When a macro encounters a {?} instruction, the macro stops executing, and you receive control of 1-2-3. You can then type characters or numbers, or use the cursor-arrow or function keys; you can do anything but press Enter. As soon as an Enter is detected, macro control resumes. The Enter that causes the macro to resume executing is *not* entered into the system. If your macro requires that you press Enter after you use the {?} instruction to input something, you must program the Enter as a tilde (~) directly into the macro.

TRAP: One of the most common macro errors is an omitted tilde (~) after a {?} instruction.

One of the differences between an experienced macro programmer and a novice is that when a macro doesn't work as expected, the experienced person immediately looks for an omitted tilde (~). Everyone omits tildes occasionally. These errors are described in more detail in the section on debugging in Chapter 10. For now, just keep in mind that the Enter you type in a {?} instruction doesn't flow through to the system.

Creating a Hybrid Macro

The process of constructing a hybrid macro is quite simple. You use the Automatic Macro program to create the macro, using names of specifiers that might apply. You then delete the names, replacing each with a {?}. When you run the macro, it stops and enables you to enter new names.

Consider a moderately complex operation: executing the /Data Sort command. If you are performing the sort for the first time, or if you want to sort a different range of data, you must specify as many as three settings (Data-Range, Primary-Key, and Secondary-Key) before you can actually execute the command.

Figure 4.6 shows a typical sorting application. In this example, the entire block of data is being sorted, using the first column as the Primary-Key and sorting in Ascending order. By using the Automatic Macro program, you can create a macro that automatically sorts any contiguous block of data, using the first column of the range as the primary sort key.

```
I3: [W13] 'Blade                                           READY

          H        I           J        K        L       M        N
          Description  Part Number  On Hand   Added    Sold    Current
 1
 2
 3        Blade        NK2565-27    3800     3400     2580    4620
 4        Blade        EV5601-98    4200      700     4080      820
 5        Blade        RU7316-92    7700     3800     4980    6520
 6        Blade        JA4764-36    5200     4050     2820    6430
 7        Blade        DI8889-65    6600     4500      360   10740
 8        Blade        WH7144-14    1600     4650     2640    3610
 9        Blade        CA9835-14    9600     3250     2940    9910
10        Hub          BG1127-88    1000     3650     2760    1890
11        Hub          DV6730-78    7200      750     5220    2730
12        Hub          AH4417-57    1700      300     1440      560
13        Hub          OD3066-80    3200      200     2820      580
14        Hub          CR6068-29    6500      450     2760    4190
15        Hub          Z04697-32    3500     1250     4200      550
16        Hub          LR4535-76    3300     4000     4200    3100
17        Hub          HV2850-31    8500     3050     3240    8310
18        Hub          UJ6940-95    8400      550     1980    6970
19        Insert       AO1636-19    4900     3150     2160    5890
20        Insert       SF7145-76    9900     1600      420   11080
```

Fig. 4.6. A typical /Data Sort application.

Figure 4.7 shows two versions of a macro that enters all the necessary settings and executes the command. The \b macro was created with the Automatic Macro program, simply by executing the /Data Sort command manually with the Automatic Macro program on. The other macro, \c, is the same macro in its modified, hybrid form.

The following description "stretches out" the Automatic Macro program version of the macro so that you can examine each step in turn.

Keystrokes	*Explanation*
Automatic macro	Macro description
/ds	Invoke **/Data Sort** command.
r	Reset to clear any existing settings.
d	Select **Data-Range** from menu.
{END}{DOWN} {END}{RIGHT}~	Specify range. This method assumes that the data is in a contiguous block and that the cell pointer was located at the upper left corner of the block when the **Sort** command was invoked.
p	Select **Primary-Key** from menu.
~	Select current column as **Primary-Key**.
a~	Select **Ascending** sort order.
g	Select **G**o; invoke command.

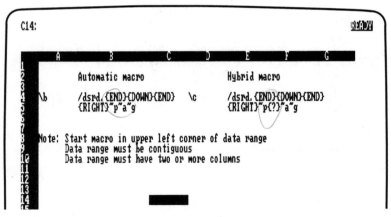

Fig. 4.7. *Automatic and hybrid /Data Sort macros.*

In the hybrid macro version, shown in column E of figure 4.7, a {?} instruction has been placed between the *p* that selects the **Primary-Key** menu option and the tilde (~) that enters the sort key into 1-2-3. In the preceding listing, the {?} instruction would appear after the *p*. Notice that the ~ after the *p* has *not* been replaced; the ~ is needed to complete the sort key specification. Using the modified "hybrid" macro, you can specify any column in the data range as the primary sort key.

Using the Hybrid Macro

To use the hybrid macro, you press Alt-c (if you used that range name). The macro stops when the sort key is called for by the /Data Sort command. The macro waits for you to move the cell pointer to the sort column you want specified as the Primary-Key and to press Enter. As the macro operates, you may not see the usual set of prompts and menus. The macro operates too quickly to follow. However, you will see the CMD indicator highlighted at the bottom of the screen. This indicator lets you know that the macro is running.

After you press Enter, the macro continues. It sorts the data range according to the sort key you specified. When the macro is finished, the CMD indicator goes off, and system control returns to you.

Using More {?} Instructions
for Greater Control

To make the macro even more flexible, you can add more {?} instructions. For example, the modified macro in figure 4.8 enables you to specify both the Primary- and Secondary-Keys.

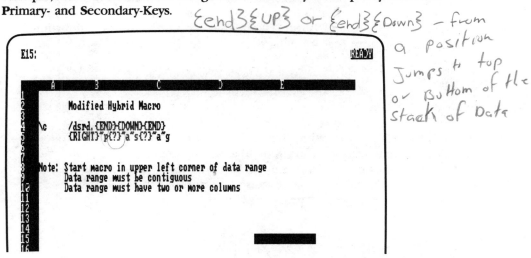

Fig. 4.8. More flexibility added to a hybrid macro.

GUIDELINE: Include in the macro comments any restrictions about the form of input the macro requires.

As a reminder to yourself, you should include with the macro a note that describes any unusual features or any hidden assumptions regarding the macro's operation. For example, the macro in figure 4.8 won't work properly under any of the following conditions:

1. The cell pointer is not in the upper left corner of the data range when the macro is invoked.

2. The data range is only one column wide.

3. Other worksheet information is immediately adjacent to the data range, either on the bottom or on the right.

4. The leftmost column or the lowest row contains a blank cell.

All these restrictions apply because of the

{END}{DOWN}{END}{RIGHT}

sequence used to define the data range. Although spelling out potential problems in this much detail is probably unnecessary, you should at least make some reference to the fact that the macro will not operate as desired in all circumstances, as in figure 4.8.

You could add still more {?} instructions to the sample macro. You could place a {?} instruction at the point where the data range is defined or at either of the points where *a* or *d* is specified for determining sort order. Of course, with the flexibility gained by using {?} instructions, you lose some level of automation, which defeats the purpose of having the macro in the first place.

TRAP: You can't type a left brace ({) or tilde (~) in the Automatic Macro program.

Because of the method used to execute keystrokes in the Automatic Macro program (see the section on the {GET} instruction in Chapter 12), you shouldn't attempt to type either the left brace character or the tilde while recording a macro with the Automatic Macro program. Typing the left brace causes the Automatic Macro program to halt and display an error message. Typing the tilde doesn't necessarily cause an error, but the tilde will be executed as an Enter when your program runs.

The {BRANCH} Instruction

You can use one other command language instruction to create hybrid macros: the {BRANCH} instruction. Although its function is simple, to understand this instruction fully, you need to know a little computer terminology.

A computer, even at the machine-language level of operation, uses an *instruction pointer* to keep track of program execution. The instruction pointer contains the location of the next instruction to be executed. In a lower-level computer language, this location is a memory address. In 1-2-3, the location is a cell address.

When you invoke a macro, 1-2-3 loads an internal instruction pointer with the address of the range name you assigned to the macro. Using that address as a starting location, 1-2-3 begins executing the cell's labels as macro instructions. When 1-2-3 detects the end of a label, the program automatically moves the instruction pointer to the next lowest cell and starts the execution process over again. The automatic reassignment of the instruction pointer continues until a blank or numeric cell is encountered, or the program is otherwise interrupted.

Although the instruction pointer is internal, and you therefore can't see which cell the instruction pointer is referring to, you can control the cell assignment by using the {BRANCH} instruction. The {BRANCH} instruction consists of the word BRANCH and a cell address or range name, enclosed in braces and separated by a space. As soon as the {BRANCH} instruction is encountered, the instruction pointer is assigned to the address included in the braces. This procedure causes the macro to begin executing in the cell specified by that address. For instance, all the following examples are valid {BRANCH} instructions.

{BRANCH NEWCELL}

{BRANCH \a}

{BRANCH E203}

The first two examples transfer the instruction pointer to the ranges called NEWCELL and \a, respectively. When a range has more than one cell, 1-2-3 assigns the instruction pointer to the upper left cell in the range. The third example transfers the instruction pointer to cell E203.

Two {BRANCH} instructions appear in the macros in figure 4.9. In the \a macro, the {BRANCH} instruction at the end of the macro causes the instruction pointer to move to cell B6, where macro execution continues. Therefore, when you invoke the \a macro, 1-2-3 executes *both* the \a and \b macros.

In the \c macro, {BRANCH} is in the middle. When 1-2-3 encounters this instruction, the program makes the instruction pointer point to the cell specified by the range name SKIP. The instructions in cells F10 and F11—which are, in effect, dead cells—are never executed.

TRAP: Don't confuse {BRANCH} with {GOTO}.

A {BRANCH} instruction is very much like the {GOTO} instruction, except that {GOTO} controls the movement of the cell pointer in the worksheet, and {BRANCH} controls the instruction pointer. Confusing these two instructions is

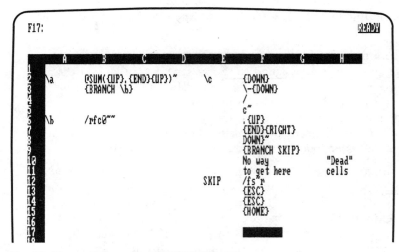

Fig. 4.9. Macros that use the {BRANCH} instruction.

easy, because when you are controlling macro flow, you can think in terms of having macro execution "go to" a new location. Keep in mind that {BRANCH} controls a macro's internal operation, not anything visible in a worksheet.

A Useful Application of {BRANCH}

The most useful application for a {BRANCH} instruction is to create a macro that branches to itself, otherwise known as a *looping macro*. You can then perform an operation repeatedly without invoking the macro each time.

Figure 4.10 is an example of what is probably the most useful looping macro. This extremely simple macro pauses for you to enter some data, moves down one cell, and loops. The macro is useful because it enables you to press Num Lock (for those using IBM PCs or similarly configured machines) and then type a column of numbers. When you press Enter, the {DOWN} instruction in the macro enters the data you just typed and simultaneously moves the cell pointer to the next cell. This capability allows you both to enter numbers and to move the cell pointer without turning Num Lock off and on (or without using the Shift key for the same purpose).

Other examples appear in figure 4.11. The \a macro, a modified version of the macro in figure 4.10, double-spaces entries. The \b macro enters data in a row, moving to the right instead of down. The \c macro enters data in two columns, alternating between one column and the other. You can include any sequence of movements and any number of {?} instructions in such a macro and automate data entry in any configuration imaginable. Notice that you aren't limited to simply typing numbers with such a macro. You can enter formulas or labels too.

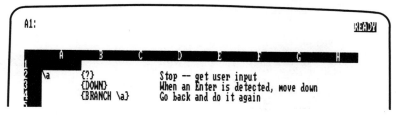

Fig. 4.10. A looping macro.

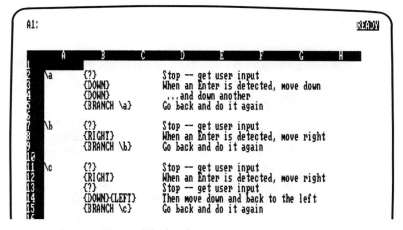

Fig. 4.11. Alternate forms of the looping macro.

How To Stop a Looping Macro

The macro continues to loop back on itself and will continue executing forever. To stop it, you press Ctrl-Break. A Break error then is displayed. To return to normal operation, you press Esc.

Further Enhancements

One handy way to save a lot of drudgery in the data entry process is to include some data transformation operations in the macro. Figure 4.12 shows several examples.

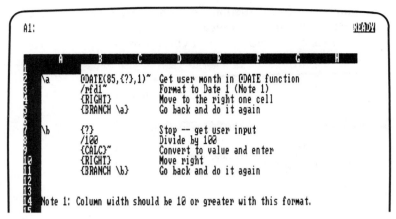

Fig. 4.12. Data modifications made in looping macros.

The \a macro creates a row of dates, each specified as the first day of the month for the year 1985. The macro pauses for you to enter the month number, then formats the cell to **Date 1** (such as 01-Jan-85) before moving to the next column and repeating the process.

The \b macro is useful for entering currency data. This macro is the same as the basic looping macro, except that before placing the number in the cell, the \b macro divides by 100 the number you enter. All data you enter is therefore assumed to represent pennies. To avoid entering the divide-by-zero formula into the cell, the macro contains a {CALC}, which converts the formula to a number before entry. This conversion also saves memory. You can use this kind of macro to create any kind of transformation. For instance, you can make the macro multiply the numbers by 1,000 before putting the numbers in cells.

TRICK: To divide by 100, put percent signs after data you enter.

If you put a percent sign (%) after a number, 1-2-3 divides the number by 100—a little-used, but convenient feature. By including the percent sign in your macro, as shown in figure 4.13, you achieve the same results as the \b macro in figure 4.12. The macro in figure 4.13 is a little easier to create and runs slightly faster.

TIP: To move to a new location for data entry, use the cursor-arrow keys instead of ending the macro.

Remember that during the pause that the {?} instruction generates, you can use the cursor-arrow keys to move around the worksheet as well as to enter information into the worksheet. If you are entering columns of data and want to

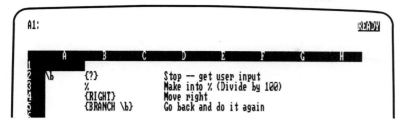

Fig. 4.13. A data transformation macro trick.

start a new column, simply turn off Num Lock (or hold down the Shift key) and press

```
{UP}
{END}{UP}
{RIGHT}
```

You will find the cell pointer at the top of the original column of data and over one column to the right. You can now enter a new column of data.

TIP: To make corrections, use the technique described in the preceding TIP.

If you make a mistake when executing a looping macro, release Num Lock, move to the offending cell, make the correction, and continue.

TIP: To skip a row in a data entry macro, press Enter without entering any data.

If you want to skip a row (leave a cell blank), press Enter. In addition, if you want to return to your previous location after making a correction, press Enter. The macro issues a {DOWN} instruction each time you press the Enter key. The data in the current cell isn't affected.

5

Macro Library

This chapter and Chapter 6 contain a library of many useful macros, examples of things other people have done to make life at the keyboard a little easier. Some macros simply automate basic operations; other macros are more complicated. A few are even tricky. Hopefully, they will inspire you with ideas for macros of your own and make you start "thinking macro."

The library is divided into two sections: worksheet maintenance macros and worksheet data macros. The divisions were made roughly according to where you would use the macro described. (Some overlap does occur.) Each macro listing contains a general description of the macro and its uses, some suggestions on mnemonics for naming the macro, and comments on using it. Because only 26 macro names are possible, some mnemonics overlap. The names are included more to get you started in making them up than as specific suggestions. The comments explain any conditions for using the macros—that is, problems that may arise if you use the macros incorrectly. The macros illustrate techniques of macro instruction as much as uses of macros *per se*. A number of the listings contain more than one version of a macro. Each alternate listing also illustrates possible variations in the construction or application of macros.

Taken as a whole, this library provides a model for the flexibility and power of macros. Notice that despite the complexity of some of the functions, all listings are simply macros; they contain none of the powerful command language instructions that are covered in the second part of the book. If you are not ready to tackle command language programming, the macros in this library provide examples of how much can be accomplished by simple sequences of commands. If you really want to become a programmer, mastering the macro techniques illustrated in this library will provide you with a good foundation on which to build your programming skills.

The macro listings are separated to allow for the detailed comments included with each significant operation. In practice, you may want to write the macros in a more compact form in order to conserve space.

How To Create a Macro Library

I keep handy and use frequently most of the macros in this book. I have so many macros, however, that putting them all in every worksheet would take up a significant amount of space. Keeping track of them would also be a problem. To make accessing your macros easier and to avoid having to enter them into your worksheet over and over again, you can put them in a library file. If you don't have a fixed disk, putting your library file on one of your 1-2-3 system disks makes the file more accessible.

GUIDELINE: Put your macro library on a disk, such as your system disk or help disk, where you can easily access the library.

As you accumulate macros in your library, you will need to organize them. You want to be able to keep track of the macros you have and transfer them easily into a worksheet. Following are several ideas that will help you keep your macro library organized.

Naming Macros

GUIDELINE: Choose macro names that help you remember the macros' functions.

Although you can arbitrarily assign any one of the 26 Alt-[letter] names to a macro, you should choose the names carefully. If you adopt naming conventions, you will have less trouble remembering your macros' functions. The technical term for something that helps you remember is *mnemonics*. If you have a macro that performs a copy operation, for example, \c is a mnemonic because that letter reminds you of copy. Similarly, \f would be a logical choice for a file-save macro.

GUIDELINE: Reserve Alt-[letter] names for the macro's starting address.

Sometimes you may have more than one name assigned to a macro. For instance, a looping macro may perform some preliminary setup operations before a second section of the macro is executed, and that second section is the only one that is repeated. The macro shown in figure 5.1 is constructed in this way. The first line of the macro sets the column width wide enough to accommodate the **Date 1** format used in the succeeding macro section. Lines 2 through 5 are the looping part of the macro. Notice that only the starting point in the macro requires an Alt-[letter] name. A second range name, LOOP, is assigned to the top of the loop. The {BRANCH} instruction then contains this name instead of the \d that starts the macro.

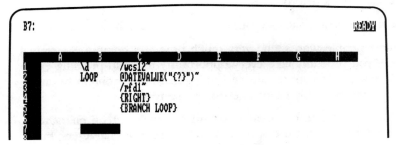

Fig. 5.1. A looping date entry macro.

TRAP: Beware of assigning a range name that is also a valid cell address.

If you use range names other than the Alt-[letter] type in a macro, be careful not to create a name that is also a valid cell address. For example, you might be tempted to use *d1* as a secondary name in the macro just described, because the cell named is the second name used in the Alt-d macro. Although 1-2-3 will allow you to assign the name d2, the {BRANCH} instruction will transfer the instruction pointer to *cell* D2 instead of *range* d2. When this mix-up occurs, 1-2-3 gives you no indication that an error has occurred; things just don't work properly.

Using two-letter combinations is not always safe either. 1-2-3 has so many columns that *im1* as a name for your number-one *insert macro* conflicts with a cell address. Using such combinations is alright if the first character comes after *I*, but you would be better off not using such combinations at all.

TRAP: Don't give macros the single-character names l, r, u, or d, or any range names that duplicate a macro keyword.

As described in Chapter 3, 1-2-3 enables you to call a macro from within a macro. You simply specify in braces the external macro's name. This feature places some restrictions on the range names that you can assign for use in a macro.

If you use the single-character range names l, r, u, or d, 1-2-3 interprets {L}, {R}, {U}, or {D} as an attempt to invoke those macros rather than as the {LEFT}, {RIGHT}, {UP}, or {DOWN} abbreviations the names also represent. Using these four letters as range names, either within or outside a macro will cause problems if you attempt to use those letters later as abbreviations for cell pointer movement keywords in a macro. In fact, whenever a range name in a worksheet conflicts with a macro keyword, 1-2-3 assumes that your substitution was deliberate and overrides the keyword's usual function. This rule applies to *any* occurrence of a range name that conflicts with a keyword, whether or not that range is the name of a macro.

GUIDELINE: Make your range names descriptive rather than short.

If you are like most people who spend very much time at a computer terminal (myself included), you probably take every opportunity to avoid pressing even one more key. A tendency to abbreviate everything can be a problem because the names you use will probably be of interest or use to only you.

Whenever possible, you should use long, descriptive names. Fifteen characters are available; use them. You can use spaces as well as special characters, but you should avoid using mathematical symbols. 1-2-3 accepts the symbols in range names and, unlike Release 1A, doesn't confuse them with mathematical operators. Your names, however, will look like formulas, which could be confusing.

Organizing Macros in Your Library File

When you create a macro library file, being organized in your approach is very important. As you accumulate more and more macros in your library, they will steadily become harder to keep track of and more difficult to maintain. You can minimize problems, however, if you thoroughly document the macros' functions. If you set up your library file according to the following guidelines, you should have no trouble maintaining a library of 100 or more macros. Taking advantage of some of Release 2's advanced features, these guidelines create a system that is easy to use and maintain.

The Macro Range

GUIDELINE: Create a macro area.

Figure 5.2 shows how to set up the ranges for your macro library file. The macro listing begins in row 101. The area above is reserved for the library's table of contents, which is described later in this section. The first line of the macro area is a simple header. It is included in order to remind you to include all the documentation when you add macros to your file. With the /Worksheet Titles command, you can fix this line on the screen so that it is displayed even when you enter macros below the first macro library screen.

Elements of the Macro Range

Header Line

Description Line

Name of
Macro Range

	A	B	C	D	E	F
100						
101	Macros:	Keys	Codes			Comments:
102						
103	LABELRIGHT					
104		ENTER LABEL AND NAME CELL TO RIGHT				
105		\l	'{?}~			
106			/rnlr~			
107			{RIGHT}			
108						
109	SETTITLES	SET OR CLEAR WORKSHEET TITLES				
110						
111		\v	/wtv			Set vertical titles
112						
113		\h	/wth			Set horizontal titles
114						
115		\b	/wtb			Set vert and horiz
116						
117		\c	/wtc			Clear all titles

Macro
Range

Three-Column Format

Fig. 5.2. Arrangement of ranges in the macro library file.

To combine the macros from your library into your active worksheet, you will need to give each macro a range name. This range name should encompass the entire macro, not just the starting cell. You can't use the **/Range Name Labels Right** command to assign these range names because that command creates only single-cell range names. After you assign the name to your macro range, place the name in column A. The name you place in column A will provide a visual reference for the ranges, will keep you from duplicating names, and will help you locate the macro when you are editing your library.

GUIDELINE: Create a description line for each macro or set of macros.

The upper left corner of your macro range should contain a description of the macro's function. This description is different than the comments usually included line by line with the macro instructions. Rather than a detailed description of each step in the macro's operation, this description is "global." Placing it in the upper left corner of the macro range will enable you to include the description easily in the table of contents.

TIP: Unprotect the description line.

If you use the **/Range Unprotect** command on the cell containing the description line, 1-2-3 displays that cell either in a different color (if you have a color monitor) or in high-intensity lettering (if you have a monochrome monitor). This arrangement creates an effective visual separator for the macro listing.

GUIDELINE: Enter your macros in the standard three-column format.

You've seen this guideline before, but it bears repeating here. The macro included with the table of contents also assumes that the range names needed will be in the first column of the macro.

GUIDELINE: Don't actually assign the range names to the macros in your library.

Two major reasons exist why you shouldn't assign the range names used by your macros in your library file. The first is that those names will interfere with the table of contents, as described in the next section. The second is that your library will eventually contain several macros that use the same Alt-[letter] names and, possibly, some other internal range names as well. If you use your library as a testing ground for macro development, you will have to assign the associated range names; but be sure to delete those names after you complete the development process. The only range names in your library should be those assigned to the macro ranges.

GUIDELINE: Include a note in your macro range if any range names can't be created correctly with /Range Name Labels Right.

One assumption made in assembling this library is that all the range names needed to run you macro appear in the leftmost column of the macro range, as described previously. Some macros, however, may contain ranges that can't be assigned this way. The Automatic Macro program is one example. Because the program contains more than one row, the \a range name used by the Automatic Macro program must be assigned with the /Range Name Create command, In general, any multirow or multicolumn ranges will need to be noted.

The Table of Contents Range

GUIDELINE: Put a Table of Contents range in your library.

Figure 5.3 is an example of a Table of Contents range for the macro library. In the left column are all the range names of the macros in the library. To the right of each name is the corresponding range address. The next two columns show the number of rows and columns in each range. And on the right are short descriptions of the macros.

The purpose of the Table of Contents range is to help you use your library. If you have only a few macros in the library, you can probably keep track of them all by memory alone. After you have accumulated a sizable number of macros, however, remembering them all can become a bit difficult. This is where the table of contents comes in. When you're ready to combine macros from the library into a worksheet, you can start by combining appropriate items from the

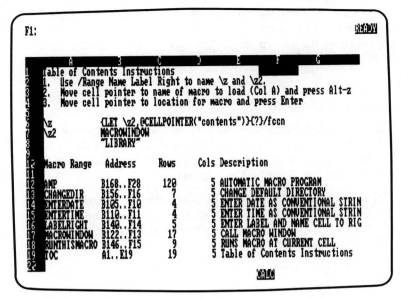

Fig. 5.3. The macro library table of contents.

table of contents. The table of contents holds a listing of (1) all the macros in the library, complete with short descriptions; (2) the range name to use in your file-combine operation; (3) the number of rows and columns needed in your current worksheet for the macros; and (4) a macro to automate most of the combining operations.

Creating the Table of Contents

If you've set up your macro range as described in the preceding sections, you can construct the Table of Contents range with little effort. Here's how.

1. Position your cell pointer in cell A6 and issue the **/Range Name Table** command. This creates the first two columns of your table of contents automatically. To make sure that your table of contents lists your macros correctly, your library worksheet should contain only the range names assigned to the macro ranges. Remember that these are the ranges that contain the entire macro—description and all—rather than the range names used by the macro itself.

2. In cells C12 and D12, enter the following formulas:

   C12: @ROWS(@@(A12))

   D12: @COLS(@@(A12))

These two formulas will list the number of rows and columns assigned to the macro ranges. Both formulas use the special @@ function as an indirect reference to the macro range. The @@ function is described in Chapter 8.

3. In cell E12, type the following formula:

     E12: @@(@LEFT(B12,@FIND(".",B12,0)))

This somewhat bizarre-looking formula uses part of the address listing from the /Range Name Table command to create a copy of the description line from each of your macro ranges. The various functions used by this formula are described in Chapter 8.

4. Copy the formulas in C12, D12, and E12 down the full length of your table of contents. The table of contents should now be complete. You will need to repeat this copy operation when you add to your library, and the table becomes longer.

5. Enter the \z macro as shown in figure 5.3, but don't assign the range names to the macro.

6. Assign the name TOC to the range from cell A1 to column E in the last row of your table of contents.

7. Save the file under the name LIBRARY.

The Library Combine Macro

Lines 6 through 8 of figure 5.3 show a macro that is part of the Table of Contents range. This macro will be combined into your worksheet with the table of contents and can be used to facilitate loading macros from the library.

The operation of the \z macro is quite simple. The macro uses the command language instruction {LET} (discussed in Chapter 12) and the @CELLPOINTER function, which is new to Release 2. The {LET} instruction with @CELLPOINTER("contents") takes a copy of what appears in the cell pointer when the macro is started and uses that string as a range name in a /File Combine command. The {?} instruction that appears after the {LET} instruction enables you to position the cell pointer before the file-combine operation copies the macro into the worksheet.

Inserting a Macro in Your Worksheet

After combining frequently used macros into your worksheet a number of times, you will probably remember the macro range names and know how much room to allot for the macros in your worksheet. For these macros, you may be able to skip the intermediate step of using the table of contents.

If you want to use some less familiar macros or if you need to see a reference list of what is available, you can begin loading macros by first combining the TOC range from your library into your worksheet. To be sure that you don't accidentally overwrite any data in your worksheet, choose an out-of-the way location for the table of contents. Be sure, however, that you choose a location that is near where you want to load your macros. You will be referring to the table of contents frequently as you load macros. The command string required to combine the table of contents is

   /wgrm/fccTOC~LIBRARY~

TIP: Set /Worksheet Recalculation to Manual before combining the table of contents.

Because the Table of Contents range contains formulas, you will need to turn off 1-2-3's automatic recalculation before bringing that range into the worksheet. If you don't turn off automatic recalculation, the data in the last three columns of the table will appear as ERR or Ø. After you load the range into the worksheet, be careful not to press Calc (F9), or you will get the same result.

If you want a more fumble-proof solution, use the /Range Value command to copy the table of contents to itself. This procedure replaces the formulas in the table of contents with their contents.

If you do press Calc (F9), recovery is easy. Simply perform the file-combine operation for the table of contents again. Another alternative is to leave things just as they are, with the ERRs and Øs showing. All that is missing is the descriptive information. The library macros can still be loaded with the \z macro in the usual fashion.

After you load your table of contents, and before you can use the \z macro to bring macros into the worksheet, you must assign the range names to the \z macro. All the macros in the library, including the \z macro, will be combined unnamed into the worksheet.

After you name the \z macro and the \z2 cell, loading library macros requires only two steps. First, you position the cell pointer on the macro name you want to combine (in the first column of the table of contents) and press Alt-z. The CMD indicator will appear at the bottom of the screen. The indicator tells you that the name of the macro has been loaded and that 1-2-3 is waiting for you to indicate where you want the library macro positioned in your current worksheet. Use the cursor-arrow keys to position the cell pointer; then press Enter. The \z macro will complete the loading process for you.

To load more macros, simply repeat the operation. You point to the name of the macro that you want to load and press Alt-z. Then you point to the location for the macro and press Enter.

After you load your macros, don't forget to establish all the range names required for the macros to operate. If you line up all your macros in the same column, you should be able to use the /Range Name Labels Right command to name all the macros at once. Be on the lookout, however, for range names that must be set with /Range Name Create. If you've followed the documentation guidelines outlined throughout the book (particularly those in Chapter 3), any such range name requirements should appear as notes in your macro range.

If you want to simplify the loading process even further, you can substitute for the \z macro shown in figure 5.3 the more elaborate version in Chapter 11. Before loading, the more powerful macro checks the range that the loaded macro will occupy and aborts the operation if any cells aren't empty. The macro then assigns the range names for the loaded macro.

TRAP: Be sure that none of your loaded macros share range names.

If you have a large library of macros, some will inevitably share the same Alt-[letter] range name. When you load macros into your worksheet, check for duplicates and assign new names as necessary. As a final step, after you finish loading macros, you can /Range Erase the table of contents.

Worksheet Maintenance Macros

These macros are some that you may want to make permanent parts of all your worksheets. As opposed to data and editing macros, which are useful primarily during worksheet construction, this group of macros helps you speed up the operations associated with file management, printing, and viewing a completed worksheet.

Macro 1: Change Directory

The Change Directory macros change the directory currently specified. You can use them to access files on a disk other than the one currently specified as the default. This procedure is handy for listing files, retrieving library macros, or getting files out of a noncurrent subdirectory on a fixed disk drive.

Suggested Mnemonics

Range Name   *Mnemonic*

Floppy disk drives:

\a	Change to drive A:
\b	Change to drive B:

For fixed disk subdirectories, use the first character in the subdirectory name:

\f	Change to C:\FIN_DATA\
\w	Change to C:\WORKFILE\

Comments

You can have as many Change Directory macros as you have directories to track. These macros can be especially handy if you have a fixed disk and segregate your data files on different directories. If you have more than one or two such directories, you might want to use the list-processing module given in Chapter 10's "Programming for Speed" section, or incorporate the list into a user menu (see Chapter 12—{MENUBRANCH} and {MENUCALL}).

TRAP: Don't forget when you have changed directories.

If the file name that appears in the supplied prompt doesn't include a directory entry, keep in mind whether you have changed directories. You may save a file to the wrong disk and lose track of that file. Most likely, forgetting that you've changed directories will cause you some inconvenience. You will have to delete such erroneously saved files and perform the /File Save operation twice: once on the wrong directory and once on the correct one.

Listing

Version 1

1.	\a	/fd	/File Directory command
2.		a:\~	Change to drive A:.

Version 2

1.	\b	/fd	/File Directory command
2.		b:\~	Change to drive B:.

Version 3

1. \f   /fd   **/File Directory** command
2.   c:\FIN_DATA\~   Change to directory C:\FIN_DATA on the fixed
                           disk drive.

Macro 2: File Save

This macro automatically saves a file in the current directory.

Suggested Mnemonics

Range Name   *Mnemonic*

\s   Save
\f   File save

Comments

TRAP: File-save macros written for Release 1A may not work with Release 2 of
1-2-3.

Subtle differences exist between the ways in which Releases 1A and 2 of 1-2-3
handle the file name prompt (the prompt that appears when you execute the
file-save operation). When you retrieve a file with Release 1A, the disk drive
identifier does not become part of the file name prompt unless explicitly typed
as part of the file name. In addition, any DOS path must be specified in the file
directory default. Paths can't be entered as part of the file name.

With Release 2, the disk drive identifier and path are automatically incorporated
into the subsequent file name prompt, even when the file is retrieved by the
pointing method. This difference makes it impossible in Release 2 to change the
destination drive for the save operation simply by changing the file directory
entry. You can't do this because the drive and path specifications in the file
name take precedence over those specified in the file directory entry. If you
have written file-save macros for Release 1A and have upgraded to Release 2,
you should test your macros to make sure that they're working as you intended.

The first version of the File Save macro is simple and works most of the time.
However, the macro can destroy data files if used to save either a file that hasn't
been saved before (and therefore has no specific file name assigned) or a file

that is a modification of an existing file and hasn't been assigned a new file name.

The second version of the macro prevents loss of data. Note that if you want to use this version with fixed disk subdirectories, you will have to make some modifications to the macro. See Chapter 3 for a description of the problems and solutions associated with this seemingly innocent little macro.

The third version incorporates the file name into the macro itself. This procedure helps prevent overwriting a file unintentionally. Be sure, however, that you change the file name in the macro if you change the name of the file. The macro is listed without the name of the file. To use the macro, you type the file name in line 2. Don't type the drive or path as part of this file name.

The final version, like version 3, also incorporates the file name as part of the macro. Unlike version 3, this version removes the drive path and specifications from the file name prompt. Without the drive and path specifications in the file name, 1-2-3 uses the drive and path specified by the file directory entry. This feature makes this version of the macro useful with macros that change the file directory (see the alternate form of Macro 3).

Cursor-Key Representation in Macros

1-2-3 Release 2 allows you to represent the repetition of cursor-key movement in macros in two ways:

1. You can enter a keyword to represent every repetition of pressing a cursor key. The following macro, for example, repeats {DOWN} three times.

   Version 1

   \a   {DOWN}
               {DOWN}
               {DOWN}

2. You also can represent the repetition of cursor movement by entering the keyword once and including a number that indicates how many times the cursor key should be repeated. The following macro, like Version 1, repeats {DOWN} three times.

   Version 2

   \a   {DOWN 3}

To illlustrate that macros are simply sequences of keystrokes, macros in this chapter use the first method for representing keystrokes.

Listing

Version 1

1. \s	/fs~	Save the file under current name.
2.	r	Confirm replacement of existing file.
3.	{ESC}	Remove the extra R.

Version 2

1. \s	/fs	Save the file under current name.
2.	{BS}	Space, then backspace
3.	~	Use current name or force error.
4.	r	Replace if name exists.
5.	{ESC}	Remove the extra R.

Note: When using a fixed disk, add one space and one {BS} for every level of subdirectory. For example, if the default directory is C:\123\, then version 2 should read

1. \s	/fs	Save the file under current name.
2.	{BS}{BS}	Two spaces, then two backspaces
3.	~	Use current name or force error.
4.	r	Replace if name exists.
5.	{ESC}	Remove the extra R.

Version 3

1. \s	/fs	/File Save command
2.	←———	File name goes here.
3.	~r	Confirm replacement of existing file.
4.	{ESC}	Remove the extra R.

Version 4

1.	\s	/fs	/File Save command
2.		{ESC}{ESC}{ESC}	Delete path and drive.
3.		◄———————	File name goes here.
4.		~r	Confirm replacement of existing file.
5.		{ESC}	Remove the extra R.

Macro 3: Double Save

The Double Save macro saves a file on two disks (or directories). This macro can prevent a real disaster by making two copies of a file every time you save the file. This method is better than backing up a file (copying it onto a backup disk) at the end of the day. The Double Save macro preserves all the work you've done since the last time you used the macro to save a file.

Suggested Mnemonics

Range Name	*Mnemonic*
\b	Backup
\d	Double save

Comments

The macros shown here assume that you're using a floppy disk system with B: as the default drive. The macro first sets the file directory to the nondefault disk drive so that when the double-save operation is complete, the system will be in its usual configuration.

Two versions of the macro are shown. In the first, the file name is entered directly into the macro for the first file-save operation but not for the second. This is because, once changed, the prompt doesn't revert back to its original form. To use this macro to save to other drives or paths, you change the drive and path identifiers wherever they appear. The first version of the macro is followed by an alternate form of the macro, which uses other macros as modules and combines them into a larger macro.

The second version saves on two disk drives without changing the file directory. This version works by modifying the drive letter that appears in the file name in the file save prompt. Usually, 1-2-3 doesn't let you edit the file name in this prompt. If you press the Home key when the prompt appears, 1-2-3 beeps to protest your "illegal" keystroke. If, however, you press the space bar first, 1-2-3 enters EDIT mode and allows you to edit the file name just as you would edit a cell entry. The {BACKSPACE} that follows the space must be added in order to delete the space; otherwise, an Illegal character in filename error occurs.

Listing

Version 1

1. \b	/fda:\~	Change to directory A:.
2.	/fs	/File Save command
3.	{ESC}{ESC}{ESC}	Delete path and drive.
4.	←———————	File name goes here.
5.	~r	Confirm replacement of existing file.
6.	{ESC}	Remove the extra R.
7.	/fdb:\~	Change to directory B:.
8.	/fs~r{ESC}	/File Save command

Alternate Form

This macro is a combination of the Change Directory and File Save macros. If both those macros were in the worksheet, you could use them to build this alternate macro. Suppose that the macro to change the directory to drive A is \a, the macro to change to drive B is \b, and the macro to save the file is \s. The Double Save macro would then become

1. \d	{\a}
2.	{\s}
3.	{\b}
4.	{\s}

This example is the first that illustrates *modular construction*, a method that can greatly simplify the work involved in creating complex macros. A complex function is constructed easily by assembling a set of modules—in this case, previously constructed macros. Modular construction allows you to create and test the parts of a complicated routine separately. The final routine is a simple series of subroutines.

Version 2

1. \b	/fs	/File Save command
2.	{BACKSPACE}	Enter EDIT mode and delete added space.
3.	{HOME}A	Change to alternate drive letter.
4.	{DELETE}	Delete previous drive letter.
5.	~	Execute command.
6.	r{ESCAPE}	Replace; delete *r* if necessary.
7.	/fs	/File Save command
8.	{BACKSPACE}	Enter EDIT mode and delete added space.
9.	{HOME}B	Change to original drive letter.
10.	{DELETE}	Delete alternate drive letter.
11.	~	Execute command.
12.	r{ESCAPE}	Replace; delete *r* if necessary.

Macro 4: Macro Window

Chapter 3 discussed various strategies for macro placement and recommended placing macros far to the right and below the active worksheet area. This placement keeps your macros safe from column and row insertions and deletions, and provides a standard location for macros.

If you create such a macro area, you can easily move to that area for editing and macro development by pressing End+Home. However, you can't readily return to your original worksheet location. The macro described in this section makes movement between the worksheet and macro areas easier by splitting the screen into two windows. You can then use the lower window to develop macros. When the lower window is cleared, the cell pointer is left in its original worksheet location.

Suggested Mnemonics

Range Name	Mnemonic
\w	Window
\m	Macro window
\e	Edit macros.
\s	Split screen.

Comments

This macro begins by moving the cell pointer down 20 rows, then up 10 rows. This movement positions the cell pointer at the 10th screen row and leaves approximately equal-sized windows for worksheet and macros. An equal-sized window arrangement makes developing macros easier because most development work involves both editing in the macro area and testing in the worksheet area. If you want more room for the macro screen, increase the number of {UP} instructions in lines 6 and 7 and reduce the same number in lines 11 and 12.

The macro takes advantage of 1-2-3's capability to set independent column widths and titles in each of its active windows. The /Worksheet Titles Both command sets titles in the macro window and enables you to move to the top of that window by pressing Home.

The macro also uses a command new with Release 2: /Worksheet Column Hide. This command is used to maximize the amount of usable space in the macro window. Conventional use of the /Worksheet Titles command freezes a column or row on the screen, but leaves the title column or row inaccessible to the cell pointer.

After the titles are set, the macro hides the title column, effectively removing it from the screen. The hidden title column still restricts cell pointer movement to the titles area within the macro window. However, an extra column is freed for usable space in that window.

This macro assumes that the upper left corner of the macro area is assigned the range name MACROS. See Chapter 3 for a further description of the macro window and figure 3.6 for an example of the window's appearance.

Listing

1.	\w	{DOWN}{DOWN}{DOWN}{DOWN}	Move down 20 rows.
2.		{DOWN}{DOWN}{DOWN}{DOWN}	
3.		{DOWN}{DOWN}{DOWN}{DOWN}	
4.		{DOWN}{DOWN}{DOWN}{DOWN}	
5.		{DOWN}{DOWN}{DOWN}{DOWN}	
6.		{UP}{UP}{UP}{UP}{UP}	Move back up 10 rows.
7.		{UP}{UP}{UP}{UP}{UP}	
8.		/wwu	Unsynchronize windows.
9.		/wwh	Split windows horizontally.
10.		{WINDOW}	Change back to original window.
11.		{UP}{UP}{UP}{UP}{UP}	Move cell pointer back to . . .
12.		{UP}{UP}{UP}{UP}	. . . original location.
13.		{WINDOW}	Switch to macro window.
14.		{GOTO}MACROS~	Move to macro area.
15.		{DOWN}{RIGHT}	New+Home location
16.		/wtb	Set titles.
17.		/wch{LEFT}~	Hide the titles column.

Macro 5: Formula Transpose

Release 2 of 1-2-3 contains a command that was often missed in Release 1A: /Range Transpose. It operates just like the Copy command, except that this operation results in a range in which all the rows are rearranged into columns, or vice versa.

When you use /Range Transpose, the result of transposing a range with formulas in it is exactly the same result you would get if you used the Copy command on each cell in the range individually. Unfortunately, for most transpose applications, the "copy" effect produces formulas that no longer refer to the intended cells. What you needed is a transpose command that operates like a Move command so that formulas in the transposed range still refer to the original cells. The Formula Transpose macro enables you to perform that task.

Suggested Mnemonics

Range Name	Mnemonic
\t	Transpose
\r	Rearrange
\s	Swap

Comments

Like the preceding macro, this macro uses a split-window arrangement to take advantage of the independent cell pointers that 1-2-3 assigns to each window. Three versions of the macro are provided, each with slightly different operating methods. All three macros require that you use the /Worksheet Window Horizontal command to split the screen manually before beginning the transpose operation. In most cases, you will also want to unsynchronize the windows before beginning—although whether the split is vertical or horizontal doesn't matter.

All three macros have two assumptions. First, the cell pointer in the window with the source range is in the upper left cell in the range. Second, the cell pointer in the destination window is *one cell above* the point where the upper left corner of the transposed range is to be located.

The first version of the macro transposes only a single cell at a time. After you finish transposing one row of your source range, you have to reposition the cell pointers in both windows before processing the next row.

The second version is a little more automated than the first, but requires more setup time. This version combines several copies of the first version—one for each column in the source range—with the keystrokes necessary to reposition the cell pointer in the appropriate location for processing the next source row. Getting this macro ready to use requires that you make an accurate count of the columns in the source range and make the required number of copies of the movement portion of the macro.

The third version requires less setup time than the second version, but doesn't run as elegantly. Version 3 is simply version 1 with a {BRANCH} instruction tacked onto the end. The macro will loop endlessly in order to transpose a row of data. This macro requires that you stop the execution of the loop with Ctrl-Break, reposition the cell pointers, and start again on the next row. Although this method may seem a little crude, it is well suited to transposing large ranges when you want to minimize the amount of setup time.

A more sophisticated version of this macro is included in the program library in Chapter 12 (see the {PUT} instruction).

Listing

Version 1

1. \t	/m~	/Move command: FROM current cell . . .
2.	{WINDOW}	. . . TO other window . . .
3.	{DOWN}	. . . and down one row
4.	~	Complete move (also change windows).
5.	{RIGHT}	Move to next starting point.

Note: Before using this macro, do the following:

1. Split the window (horizontally or vertically).

2. Unsynchronize the windows.

3. Place the cell pointer on the row above the range location in the destination window.

4. Position the cell pointer on the upper left corner of the range in the source window.

5. Start in the source window.

Version 2

1. \t	/m~{WINDOW}{DOWN}~{RIGHT}	Move one cell to next window.
2.	/m~{WINDOW}{DOWN}~{RIGHT}	Include one copy of this command string for each *column* in the source range.
	. . .	
n.	/m~{WINDOW}{DOWN}~{RIGHT}	
n.	/m~{WINDOW}{DOWN}~{RIGHT}	
n.	{DOWN}{LEFT}{END}{LEFT}	To beginning of next source row

| n. | {WINDOW}{END}{UP}{UP}{RIGHT} | To beginning of next destination column |
| n. | {WINDOW} | Back to source window |

Version 3

| 1. \t | /m~{WINDOW}{DOWN}~{RIGHT} | Move one cell to next window. |
| 2. | {BRANCH \t} | Loop and do it again. |

Macro 6: Set Titles

This simple set of macros, like the File Save macros described earlier in the chapter, doesn't save a lot of keystrokes. These macros, however, are very convenient because of the frequency with which you can use them.

Four in all, the Set Titles macros set the /Worksheet Titles to Vertical, Horizontal, or Both, or Clear the titles. To set titles, you press the appropriate macro key when your cell pointer is in the desired position. Having titles available as a single-keystroke operation encourages their use, which, in turn, makes the macros all the more useful.

Suggested Mnemonics

Range Name	Mnemonic
\v	Set **Vertical** titles.
\h	Set **Horizontal** titles.
\b	Set **Both** titles.
\c	**Clear** titles.

Comments

The only restrictions that apply to using these macros are those that apply to using the /Worksheet Titles commands manually. To set Vertical titles, make certain that at least one column is between the cell pointer and the left edge of the screen. To set Horizontal titles, make sure that one row is between the cell pointer and the top edge of the screen. Before you use the Both option, both these conditions must be met. Titles can be cleared with the Clear option from anywhere on the screen.

Listing

1. \v	/wtv	Set **Vertical** titles.
1. \h	/wth	Set **Horizontal** titles.
1. \b	/wtb	Set titles to **Both**.
1. \c	/wtc	**Clear** titles.

Macro 7: Print Settings Table

This macro creates a table of print settings. The macro serves the dual purpose of entering a set of print options and documenting those settings in a way that allows them to be easily read and modified. Perhaps one of the least friendly aspects of 1-2-3 is that the program can't store and recall a set of print settings, as the program can do with graph settings. If you want to print various parts of your worksheet in different type fonts (such as condensed, pica, or elite), to print sections of your worksheet out of order, or to print multiple sections of a worksheet separately, you must enter a new passel of settings each time you make a change.

One solution to this problem is to encode into a macro all the keystrokes required to set up a print range. You would need to create one macro for each separate print range. Using the Automatic Macro program to record the settings makes generating the macro a trivial task. The only disadvantage to creating the macro with the Automatic Macro program is that the resulting macro looks like the one in figure 5.4. It's hard to read and would be harder still to modify.

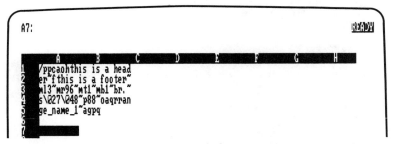

Fig. 5.4. A print setting macro created with the Automatic Macro program.

An alternative solution is presented here. This Print Settings Table macro lays out all possible print options next to a column of labels that describe those options. In its initial form, the macro steps through each option but leaves it unchanged. By making modifications to the macro at the appropriate point, you cause the macro to enter the settings you specify into 1-2-3's print system. Because all these settings fit into a single-column macro, you can group a number of these macros side by side. In this way, the macros can share the identifying labels and thus form a table of print settings. Each column in the table contains both the documentation for the settings and the macro that enters the settings.

Figure 5.5 shows the layout of a worksheet with multiple print areas. Four ranges are to be printed: an introduction entered as text, a set of assumption values, a table from the worksheet, and a listing of the raw data in a database.

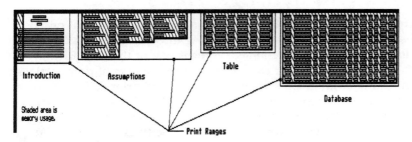

Fig. 5.5. A worksheet showing several ranges to print in one report.

Advantages of Print Macros

You can arrange your worksheet so that the introduction, assumptions, table, and database all appear in successively lower rows in the worksheet, as shown in figure 5.6. However, keeping the ranges separate, as shown in figure 5.5, and combining them at print time has several advantages.

Subsection Printing

When the sections of a worksheet are assigned their own print macros, you can easily print only part of a worksheet. This is handy, for instance, for printing only the table or database sections of the worksheet.

Memory Management

If the various pieces of the worksheet occupied columns as shown in figure 5.6, a substantial amount of memory would be wasted—even with 1-2-3's semi-sparse matrix memory management scheme. The shaded area in figure 5.6

represents unused memory allocated by 1-2-3. Compare the shaded area with that shown in figure 5.5, where the database area has been relocated in a way that saves a significant amount of memory.

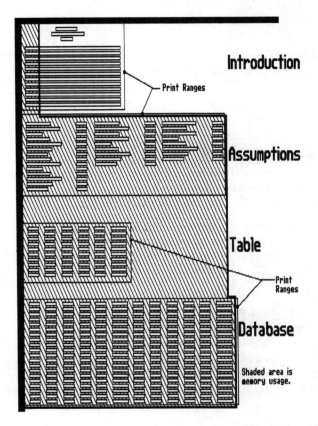

Fig. 5.6. Worksheet areas in the standard, sequential arrangement; shaded area represents wasted memory allocation.

Printing with Different Column Widths

Another advantage to placing the database as shown in figure 5.5 is that the table and database don't need to share the same column widths. This arrangement creates reports that look much better, and, because you can optimize the screen for each area, working with the data is a little easier.

Suggested Mnemonics

Range Name	*Mnemonic*
\i	Print introduction only.
\a	Print assumptions only.
\t	Print table only.
\d	Print database only.
\e	Print everything.

Comments

Print macros are prime candidates for modular construction. This example shows how to set up your macros in modular fashion so that you can use one master macro to print either all sections or any individual subsections. The macro actually comprises four macros, one for each printed subsection.

Although the table arrangement violates the standard three-column layout for macros, the benefits of the table arrangement outweigh the costs for this application. In fact, all the usual documentation for the macro—name, code, and description—is still present. It's just presented in a form more suitable for sets of repeated items.

By assigning the macros separate range names, you can activate each macro separately. You can still use the /Range Name Labels command to assign the Alt-[letter] names to the macros. With the table arrangement, the macro names appear at the top of the columns; therefore, you will have to use /Range Name Labels Down (instead of the usual Right) to name the macros. After you assign the names, pressing the corresponding Alt-[letter] enters the settings and prints only the designated area.

After you assign the individual range names, printing all the areas in the desired order is easy. You may recall from the discussion in Chapter 3 that macros can contain other macros. For example, to include a macro called \a in another macro, you enclose the macro name in braces:

   {\a}

The master macro in the listing, \e, uses the preceding technique to call four other macros—\i, \a, \t, and \d—and executes each in turn. Notice that you could easily rearrange the order of the printed output by rearranging the order of the macro calls in \e.

The master table macro is constructed so that each of the print options is selected and then canceled, leaving the option unchanged from its default configuration. To be sure that previous settings don't interfere with the current settings, the first step the macro takes is to Clear All the previous settings and return to the defaults as specified under /Worksheet Global Default. When you actually want to change one of the settings, you alter the entry in the macro in one of four ways, depending on how the option is usually specified:

1. Making alterations to most of the option entries requires that you add characters in front of the tilde, which appears by itself in the macro. For this type of option, 1-2-3 usually displays a supplied prompt that you can either change by typing a new entry or accept by pressing Enter. Margins and headers fall into this supplied-prompt category. To change one of these entries, you enter ahead of the tilde a range name for the print range; text for a header or footer; or numbers for margin, page, and setup string entries.

2. Border columns and rows require special treatment. If you press Enter, you select the current cell pointer position as the border column or row rather than canceling the option selection. To avoid making a selection this way, the master macro contains an {ESC}, which undoes the command and causes it to back up. Two {ESC} instructions are required to leave the menu in exactly the condition the menu was in prior to your selecting the Borders option. To specify Borders Rows or Columns, you type range names in place of the {ESC}{ESC}. You will also have to add a tilde after the range name, as specified by the labels at the left of the table.

3. The Other options in the print menu—As-Displayed vs. Cell-Formulas and Formatted vs. Unformatted—could have been handled with a single {ESC}, but are easier to interpret if they are included as a definite table entry. To change one of these options, you enter the opposite letter choice.

4. The last two lines in the master macro start the printing process (G = Go) and exit the print menu system (Q = Quit). You can alter these entries by adding characters as specified by the margin labels. The three options for these lines are A (Align), P (Page advance), and L (Line advance). With the proper combinations of these letters, you can control when a section is printed on a new page and where on the page the section is printed.

In the macro, remember to use range names, not cell addresses, to specify print ranges and border settings. This guideline also applies to the use of the print table with dynamically specified ranges (where you put {?} in your macro and use POINT mode to select the range). Rather than try to put the dynamic specifications in the print table, write a separate macro that assigns a name to the range and use that name in the table.

TIP: Set 1-2-3's default print settings to the settings you use most often.

1-2-3 allows you to enter the default settings for margins, page length, and setup string so that you don't have to reset them every time you perform a print operation. Use the /Worksheet Global Default Printer menu to enter the settings, and be sure to update the configuration file to make the changes permanent. The default settings you specify will be entered automatically when the /Print Printer Clear All command is issued at the beginning of the macro.

The listing that follows is the master form of the macro. If run *as is*, the macro returns all the settings to their defaults, but does nothing else. Because of the {ESC} in place of the print range name entry, the macro has nothing to print. The print range specification is the only required entry besides the macro name. If only a print range is entered, it will be printed with all the default settings. To make a complete print table, make additional copies of the second column in the macro.

Figure 5.7 shows a print table macro setup for the four ranges in the current worksheet example. The first macro column contains the \i macro, which prints the Introduction range. The subsequent columns set up and print the Assumptions, Table, and Database sections, respectively. Notice that the header and footer entries are the same in all columns. Repeating the entries is necessary because the macro clears all settings whenever it's invoked. Because the entries are in table form, you can easily generate repeating entries by using the /Copy command.

By following the sequence of settings across the columns of macros, you can easily envision the state of the final printout. The \i macro prints the range named PART1 with all default settings (except for the addition of header and footer) and aligns the paper before starting. Because the \i macro doesn't end with a page feed, the next macro begins printing wherever the first print range leaves off.

The \a macro is identical to the first macro, except that that \a macro forces a page advance when it is finished. Subsequent printing then begins on a new page.

The \t macro prints the range SCHEDULE. This macro (showing EPSON codes) also sets condensed print, 88 lines per page, new margins, and borders (using range names). After printing, the macro issues a page advance.

The last macro uses condensed print with no borders and prints 88 lines per page. The macro prints in the unformatted mode, which results in printing without page breaks, headers, or footers. The last macro also issues an extra page advance so that the printout can be removed easily from the printer.

TIP: Write your macros so that specified names appear on a line by themselves.

The print table macro illustrates the usual form for storing and entering complex settings into 1-2-3. Figure 5.8 shows two additional table macros—one for **Data Sort** operations and one for **Data Regression** operations.

	\i	\a	\t	\d
Macro name:	/PPCAR	/PPCAR	/PPCAR	/PPCAR
Range to print (Add ~):	PART1~	PART2~	SCHEDULE~	LISTING_DB~
	OH	OH	OH	OH
Header:	Final Report~	Final Report~	Final Report~	~
	F	F	F	F
Footer:	|Page -#-|~	|Page -#-|~	|Page -#-|~	~
	ML	ML	ML	ML
Left Margin:	~	~	15~	~
	MR	MR	MR	MR
Right Margin:	~	~	132~	~
	MT	MT	MT	MT
Top Margin:	~	~	~	~
	MB	MB	MB	MB
Bottom Margin:	~	~	~	~
	BR	BR	BR	BR
Border Rows (Add ~):	{ESC}{ESC}	{ESC}{ESC}	TopRows~	{ESC}{ESC}
	BC	BC	BC	BC
Border Columns (Add ~):	{ESC}{ESC}	{ESC}{ESC}	LeftCols~	{ESC}{ESC}
	S	S	S	S
Setup String:	~	~	\015\027\048~	\015\027\048~
	P	P	P	P
Page Length:	~	~	88~	88~
	O	O	O	O
A=As-Displayed ⟶	A	A	A	A
C=Cell-Formulas	O	O	O	O
F=Formatted ⟶	F	F	F	U
U=Unformatted	Q	Q	Q	Q
Add: A=Align ⟶	AG	G	AG	AG
Add: P=Page ⟶	Q	PQ	PQ	PPQ
L=Line				

Fig. 5.7. The print table for the example in the text.

Similar macros can be constructed for any standard sequence of operations. Guidelines for constructing your own table macros are as follows:

1. Place a prompt in the left column, specifying what is to be entered.

2. Set up the initial form of the macro so that it calls each option but resets it to original form. The reset can be accomplished with {ESC}, ~, or a **Quit** menu option, depending on the application.

3. Construct the macro so that modifications to the settings occur one per line.

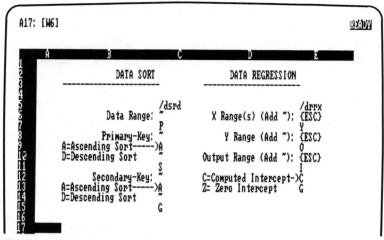

Fig. 5.8. Additional master table macros.

Listing

Master table macro (does nothing *as is*):

Macro name:	/PPCAR
Range to print (Add ~):	{ESC}
	OH
Header:	~
	F
Footer:	~
	ML
Left Margin:	~
	MR
Right Margin:	~
	MT
Top Margin:	~
	MB
Bottom Margin:	~
	BR
Border Rows (Add ~):	{ESC}{ESC}
	BC
Border Columns (Add ~):	{ESC}{ESC}
	S
Setup String:	~
	P
Page Length:	~
	O

```
A=As-Displayed ──────► A
C=Cell-Formulas        O
F=Formated ──────────► F
U=Unformatted          Q
Add: A=Align ────────► G
Add: P=Page ─────────► Q
```

Listing of the macro to print all the ranges:

1. \e   {\i}   Print the whole document.

2.   {\a}

3.   {\t}

4.   {\d}

Worksheet Data Macros

These macros are designed to help you construct a worksheet. They include macros that enter formulas, data, and labels or help with formatting and copying. You might want to put this group of macros in a separate library. You can combine the entire library into a new worksheet as you begin putting it together. As with the other macros discussed, pay as much attention to the techniques illustrated as to the macros themselves.

Macro 8: Prevent Equation ERR

Macro 8 is an extension of a macro described in the introductory section on macros in Chapter 2, "A Practical Example: Avoiding Division-by-Zero Errors." That macro simply typed one formula into another formula twice. The resulting formula prevented an ERR result by testing for the ERR value and substituting 0. The macro described in this section automates the entire replacement process. To alter a formula, you simply place the cell pointer on that cell and activate the macro.

This macro is most valuable when, in a formula, a cell in the denominator of a division unexpectedly takes on a zero value and generates an ERR condition. Other frequent ERR generators are failure to find a string match in a @VLOOKUP or @HLOOKUP function and inadvertent mixing of string and numeric data. Formulas that can produce ERR are easy to overlook and sometimes unavoidable. You should always guard against these formulas.

This macro also comes in handy when you construct formulas. You can enter the basic formula and then "zap" it with this macro. This macro is also an invaluable tool for fixing formulas that come down with a case of the ERRs when a change is made somewhere else in the worksheet.

Suggested Mnemonics

Range Name	*Mnemonic*
\z	Zero substitution
\e	Error fix

Comments

This macro will be most appreciated when applied to long formulas. However, be aware that using the macro can make you run into length limits quickly. The @IF part of the formula adds 16 characters to the formula, and because your formula appears twice, the upper limit for the original formula is 113 characters ((240–16)/2). If your formula contains range names, especially when these are absolute references, the limits may be even smaller.

Figure 5.9 shows an example of this last situation. The range name for the table range in a @VLOOKUP function is LU. Suppose that you want to copy the formula to another location. You would want to specify the range as an absolute reference: $LU. In this example, assume that the range in question refers to cell addresses AE112..AG121. When you first enter the formula, you type it as it appears in the top line of the control panel, specifying $LU as the range. When you activate the Zero-Fix macro, the internal representation of the range name—in cell-address form—becomes part of the formula. Your range name, specified as cell addresses, is as it appears in the edit line of the control panel. The range is specified as AE112..AG121—13 characters longer than the $LU that you typed. Because the formula must appear twice in the modified version, you've used up an extra 26 characters. An extra 26 characters will be added for each such range in your formula.

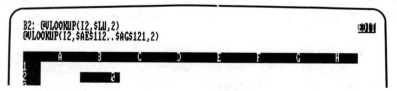

Fig. 5.9. An internal representation of a formula that is longer than what you type.

TRICK: Use range names rather than cell addresses to "shoehorn" a large formula into a cell.

The expansion of character count is a limitation because of the way the macro works. The macro begins with a formula and turns it into a label by entering EDIT mode and adding a label prefix. When the formula appears in the EDIT line of the control panel, the formula is in cell-address form, as in figure 5.9, and therefore the range names are expanded.

You can avoid this problem by initially entering the formula into the worksheet as a label. You can then modify the macro to appear as shown in version 2 of the listings. That version doesn't convert the formula to a label, because the formula is already a label. The number of characters is equal to that in the "label" formula. When the version 2 macro executes, it converts the referenced label to a formula.

TRAP: If you use range names to enter a formula longer than 240 characters, you can't edit that formula.

You can generate a formula that, when expanded to show cell addresses, is longer than 240 characters. Note that 1-2-3's internal representation of the formula is somewhat more compressed than what appears on the screen. EDIT mode, however, has a limitation of 240 characters as well. If you create such a formula and then try to edit it, 1-2-3 truncates the characters beyond the 240-character limit, and you lose them. In most instances, an error occurs from which you can recover by pressing Esc. If you need to edit the formula, you have to edit its abbreviated form (without the error trap) and reconstruct the formula. If you require a formula that long in one cell, you should probably keep a copy of the abbreviated version.

Notice that both versions of the macro automatically assign a range name to the cell being modified. Be sure that the name the macro is using is not one of the currently active names in your worksheet.

Listing

Version 1

This version converts a formula that is entered into the worksheet as a formula (as opposed to being entered as a label; see version 2).

1. \z	{EDIT}{HOME}'~	Convert the formula to a label.
2.	/rncXXX~	Use XXX as a range name.
3.	{BS}	Release any previous range.

4.	~	Assign name to this cell.
5.	@IF(@ISERR(	Begin formula entry.
6.	{XXX}	Use macro to type current formula.
*7.	),0,	If ERR, then enter a zero.
8.	{XXX}	Otherwise, use formula *as is*.
9.	)~	Complete the new formula.

*If you want the macro to enter something other than a zero on an error condition, substitute that "something" on this line between the two commas. For example, suppose that you put the following in the macro:

> 7.   ),"",

This substitutes the null string for the ERR value, causing the cell to appear blank under error conditions. You could also place message strings in the formula. If you were using this macro to trap the ERR produced by a VLOOKUP, you could use

> 7.   ),"Matching string not found",

or

> 7.   ),B13*A15,

That message would appear whenever the matching string was not contained in the VLOOKUP table.

Version 2

This version converts a formula that has been entered into the worksheet as a label (see preceding Comments).

1. \z	/rncXXX~	Use XXX as a range name.
2.	{BS}	Release any previous range.
3.	~	Assign name to this cell.
4.	@IF(@ISERR(	Begin formula entry.
5.	{XXX}	Use macro to type current formula.
*6.	),0,	If ERR, then enter a zero.
7.	{XXX}	Otherwise, use the formula *as is*.
8.	)~	Finish the new formula.

*See the note for version 1.

Macro 9: Round a Number

This macro takes the contents of a cell and makes them the argument of an @ROUND function. This macro can be useful when slight errors occur in 1-2-3's mathematics. Despite the fact that 1-2-3 is accurate internally to 15 digits, errors can occur. Errors usually happen because of the difficulty of representing the decimal numbers that humans use in the binary system that computers use. These errors crop up most frequently when many numbers—usually displayed in Currency format—are added both across and down, then (as "marginal" totals) added across and down for verification purposes. Rounding problems, however, can also occur when only a few numbers are involved.

Figure 5.10 shows an example of a rounding error. You can easily total in your head the three numbers shown and arrive at a result of zero. 1-2-3, however, produces something other than zero as an answer. This same result occurs with @SUM or a simple linking of the three cells with plus signs. Even though the error is very small, small discrepancies have a way of being magnified by large spreadsheets that are full of calculations.

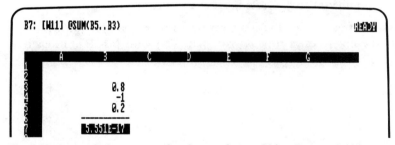

Fig. 5.10. A cumulative computational error that could be eliminated with @ROUND.

Suggested Mnemonics

Range Name	Mnemonic
\r	Round
\n	Numeric rounding

Comments

The most common use of this macro will probably be to round a large number of column or row totals in a standard crossfooting. This is where rounding errors are most likely to become evident. Entering the formulas without the @ROUND and using the macro later to modify the formulas frees you from concerns over 1-2-3's internal accuracies and enables you to concentrate on the construction of the worksheet. So that you can use the macro on a large number of formulas, the macro should move to the next cell automatically. You can then round a whole series of cells by repeatedly pressing Alt-r.

Version 2 of this macro is more automated. Lines 6 and 8 are the two instructions that increase the automation. Line 6 enables you to use the macro on blank cells and on cells containing labels. In both cases, adding @ROUND to the contents produces a formula that isn't valid. 1-2-3's syntax checking prevents entry of the invalid formula into the worksheet—entry that would normally occur at the ~ on line 5. The first {ESC} clears the invalid entry, but leaves the macro in EDIT mode. The second {ESC} exits EDIT mode.

The result of this addition to the macro is exactly what you want: the macro enters a formula only where it is valid. In all other cases, the macro doesn't disturb the original cell contents. The only price you pay is having to listen to the beeps the computer emits because of the error condition.

Line 8 makes the macro repeat indefinitely. To use the macro, you activate it by pressing Alt-r. To terminate the operation, press Ctrl-Break.

Both versions assume that you will use the macro to modify a column of numbers. To use the macro on a row, replace {DOWN} with {RIGHT} in each listing.

Listing

Version 1

1. \r	{EDIT}	Enter EDIT mode.
2.	,2)	Set to round to 2 decimals.
3.	{HOME}	Move to beginning of contents.
4.	@ROUND(	Enter first part of function.
5.	~	Enter formula into cell.
6.	{DOWN}	Move to next cell.

Version 2

1. \r	{EDIT}	Enter EDIT mode.
2.	,2)	Set to round to 2 decimals.

3.	{HOME}	Move to beginning of contents.
4.	@ROUND(	Enter first part of function.
5.	~	Enter formula into cell.
6.	{ESC}{ESC}	If error, cancel operation.
7.	{DOWN}	Move to next cell.
8.	{BRANCH \r}	Loop.

Macro 10: Negative of a Number

This macro, similar in construction to Macro 9, reverses the sign of a cell's contents. This macro is most useful when you are entering a series of numbers with varying signs. You can use the macro to reverse the sign of a number that was inadvertently entered with the wrong sign.

Suggested Mnemonics

Range Name	Mnemonic
\n	Negative of number

Comments

This macro wraps parentheses around the contents of the cell and places the minus sign before the opening parenthesis. Because the macro works in this way, it can serve some general functions. For example, the macro can reverse the sign of the result of a complex formula. The {ESC}{ESC} sequence at the end of the macro cancels its operation on blank and label cells, leaving them unchanged. If you repeatedly execute this macro on a single cell, the cell's contents alternate in sign. Although the construction that follows is legal, it makes the cell formula cluttered and difficult to read.

$$-(-(-(-(+A685*B686-2))))$$

Listing

1. \n	{EDIT}	Enter EDIT mode.
2.	)	Set closing parenthesis.
3.	{HOME}	Move to beginning of contents.
4.	–(	Enter opening parenthesis and sign.
5.	~	Enter the formula into cell.
6.	{ESC}{ESC}	If error, cancel operation.

Macro 11: Automatic and Semiautomatic @SUM

@SUM is one of the most frequently used functions. The two versions of the macro presented here use @SUM to speed the entry of formulas into the worksheet.

Suggested Mnemonics

Range Name	Mnemonic
\a	Add automatic sum
\s	Sum semiautomatic sum

Comments

Two versions of this macro are provided. Version 1 is fully automatic and probably works for the majority of situations in which @SUM is required. The numbers to be summed must be directly above the cell where the @SUM formula is to be entered, and the numbers must be in a continuous column with no blank cells. This arrangement is necessary because the macro uses {END}{UP} to find the top of the column of numbers. If the column of numbers contained blank cells, the range entered into the @SUM function would extend only to that first blank cell (see fig. 5.11).

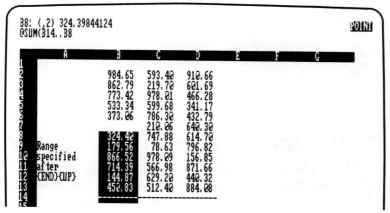

Fig. 5.11. The automatic @SUM macro used on only numbers that are in a continuous column.

TIP: To make changes easier, include an extra row in your @SUM range.

In line 4, notice the extra {UP}. This instruction extends the range summed by the function to one row beyond the start of the data. This extension enables you to insert extra rows into the range later. If you use the macro in a column of numbers that also contains a cell with a dashed line across the bottom, as shown in figure 5.11, then an extra row is included at the lower end of the range as well as at the upper end. Inserting rows in the field of numbers always results in an expanded range, and the formula remains accurate. The only limitation in this regard is that none of the cells in the range, including the extra rows, can contain a string formula. @SUM evaluates labels as zero, but a string formula causes @SUM to return an ERR condition.

Version 2 is a semiautomated macro that enables you to specify manually the range to be summed. You can use this version when the column of numbers has blank cells, when you want to sum rows, or when you want to sum an irregular range or a list.

Listing

Version 1: Automatic

1. \a @SUM(Begin entry of function.

2.   {UP}.   Move up and anchor range.

3.   {END}{UP}   Extend range to top of column.

4.   {UP}   Add an extra row.

5.   )~   Finish function and enter.

Version 2: Semiautomatic

1. \s	@SUM(	Begin entry of function.
2.	{?}	Stop for entry of range.
3.	)~	Finish function and enter.

Macro 12: Absolute Reference

This macro adds dollar signs to a cell address, converting a relative address to an absolute address. You will find this macro useful when you edit an existing formula in which the absolute references have been omitted.

Suggested Mnemonics

Range Name	Mnemonic
\a	Absolute reference
\s	$
\r	Absolute reference

Comments

This macro works only for cell addresses that reference columns A through Z. To use the macro, you invoke EDIT mode and place the cursor on the column letter identifier of the address. When activated, the macro adds two dollar signs to the address. This macro is ridiculously simple, but I find it surprisingly useful, most likely because the $ is an awkward character to type.

Listing

\a	${RIGHT}$	Convert cell address to absolute.

Macro 13: Copy a Cell Across an Existing Row

You will find this macro useful when you work with data that has already been entered and is configured as a series of columns, such as a monthly time series or projection. The macro copies a formula from the current column to the right across all the remaining cells in the row. You can modify the entire series of columns by changing the first column, then invoking the macro, which changes the rest of the columns.

Suggested Mnemonics

Range Name	Mnemonic
\c	Copy.
\r	Copy right.
\d	Copy down.

Comments

Version 1 copies a cell across a column of data. Use version 2 when your data is arranged vertically, such as in an amortization schedule.

One aspect of this macro's structure deserves comment. After you specify the current cell as the FROM range in the /Copy command, the logical way to proceed would be to move the cell pointer one column to the right, anchor the TO range, and use the {END}{RIGHT} sequence to expand the range. The first {RIGHT} of this sequence is omitted in the macro; therefore the FROM range is included as part of the TO range, and the cell is copied to itself. Copying a cell to itself does not cause any problems, and the omission of the extra {RIGHT} keystroke results in a macro that runs, under optimal conditions, up to 20 percent faster.

TIP: To limit the columns this macro alters, insert an extra blank column.

When editing or making changes to an existing spreadsheet, you will find the macro useful. Note, however, that this macro has one potential problem: completed spreadsheet models often have in adjacent columns data that isn't a part of the time series. Such is the case when monthly data has a yearly total at the right or when several columns of yearly data are next to each other, and the formulas from one year to the next aren't identical.

By inserting an extra blank column between the data you want to change and the data you want to preserve, you stop macro execution in the column before the blank column. To keep the worksheet identical (cosmetically) to the original worksheet, you can set the blank column's width to Hidden.

TRAP: If you use this macro incorrectly, you may lose more time than you save.

This macro is very much like a hammer, in the proverbial sense. It can be a great tool for driving nails, or you can hit yourself in the thumb. The {END}{RIGHT} key sequence, which finds the end of the existing data columns, is the potential troublemaker. If you use this macro when no data exists to the right of the current cell, the macro considers the right edge of the worksheet the rightmost limit for the copy operation. Unfortunately, making the mistake of using the macro in such a situation is easy to do, especially if the left columns are full of long labels and the column you are working with is the last visible column on the right side of the screen.

With Release 1A's memory management scheme, such a slip can be disastrous. The macro will make hundreds of copies of the formula, use up scads of memory (probably all of it), and tie up your computer for up to five minutes or more. With Release 2's sparse memory management, a slip still produces hundreds of unwanted formulas but few of the other side effects. When cleaning up from a boo-boo, be sure that you reset the format in the extraneous cells as well as erase the contents in order to avoid wasting memory unnecessarily.

If you are going to use this macro frequently, one way to protect yourself against the problem (it's just a matter of time until you run into it) is to arrange your worksheet like the one shown in figure 5.12. The trick is to place a column of something (it doesn't matter what; any character or number will do) just outside the columns in which you will be working. Then, if you do activate the macro accidentally, it runs into your "safety" column and stops. This method prevents the macro from trying to copy across the entire worksheet. This solution, however, is not complete. If you use the macro on a formula in a newly inserted row, the macro will still copy all the way across the worksheet because the insert creates a breach in the safety column.

Listing

Version 1: Copy across

1. \c	/c	Select /Copy command.
2.	~	Select current cell as FROM range.
3.	.{END}{RIGHT}	Anchor range and extend to right.
4.	~	Terminate copy sequence.

Version 2: Copy down

1.	\c /c	Select /Copy command.
2.	~	Select current cell as FROM range.
3.	.{END}{DOWN}	Anchor range and extend down.
4.	~	Terminate copy sequence.

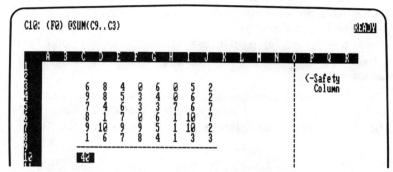

Fig. 5.12. Worksheet set up to trap a runaway \c macro.

Macro 14: Copy Across a Span of Blank Cells

This macro is an alternate form of Macro 13. Whereas Macro 13 alters an existing row or column of data, this macro adds a new row or column of data. This macro is most useful when you want to build a spreadsheet model based on a time series—that is, rows or columns of duplicate formulas and numbers (such as a monthly sales forecast or an amortization schedule). You will also find this macro useful when you have to add a new row or column to an existing model.

Suggested Mnemonics

Range Name	*Mnemonic*
\d	Duplicate

This macro is a kind of Copy macro that is often useful when used in combination with the \c macro (Macro 13). This choice of mnemonics allows both macros to exist in the worksheet simultaneously. Also, because the two forms of the Copy macro are similar in function, choosing letter names that are alphabetically sequential (and close to each other on the keyboard) serves as an additional mnemonic device.

Comments

The difference between this macro and Macro 13 is that this one contains a trick that enables you to copy a formula across a number of columns when the cells to the right of the cell just entered are all blank. The macro "grabs" the previous row of data and "slides" along that row to locate the end point for the copy operation. Following is a description of the steps required to make the macro operate as intended.

In figure 5.13, the copy process has been initiated, and the current cell has been selected as the FROM range. Even though the copy of the cell is to be made to the right, the first move the macro performs is to expand the TO range up.

In figure 5.14, {END}{RIGHT} expands the TO range to its rightmost limit, which in this case is the right edge of the previous row. This trick works because after the macro issues the {UP} keystroke (see fig. 5.13), the active cell of the TO range is in the previous row. The {END}{RIGHT} sequence then moves to the end of *that* row (see fig. 5.14).

If you were to complete the copy operation at this point, obviously you would copy your current cell over the previous row of data. However, as shown in figure 5.15, that is not what happens. {DOWN}, the last keystroke, reduces the TO range to a single row. Not incidentally, the TO range is now located where you want it.

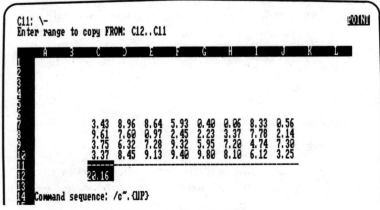

Fig. 5.13. The "grab and slide" technique after {UP}.

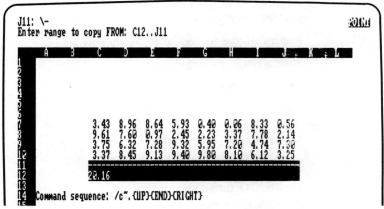

Fig. 5.14. The "grab and slide" technique after {END}{RIGHT}.

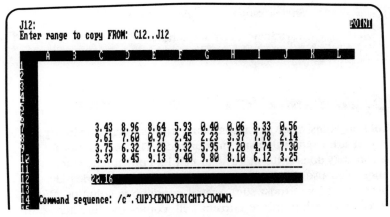

Fig. 5.15. The "grab and slide" technique after {DOWN}.

Version 2 of this macro copies downward.

Listing

Version 1: Copy across

1. \d	/c	Select /Copy command.
2.	~	Select current cell as FROM range.

3.	.{UP}	Anchor TO range and extend to previous row.
4.	{END}{RIGHT}	Expand range to end of previous row.
5.	{DOWN}	Shrink range to single row.
6.	~	Terminate copy sequence.

Version 2: Copy down

1. \d	/c	Select /Copy command.
2.	~	Select current cell as FROM range.
3.	.{LEFT}	Anchor TO range and extend to previous column.
4.	{END}{DOWN}	Expand range to end of previous column.
5.	{RIGHT}	Shrink range to single column.
6.	~	Terminate copy sequence.

Macro 15: Automatic Column Sums

The Automatic Column Sums macro is a combination of several previously described macros that are frequently used in sequence. The macro has a modular construction that does little more than call its constituent macros in the proper sequence. You use the macro when you have a time-series layout, such as a sales forecast, and you must sum several contiguous columns. When activated, the macro draws a line in the current cell, copies the line across the current span of columns, places an @SUM formula in the cell below, and finally copies the formula across the current span of columns.

Suggested Mnemonics

Range Name	Mnemonic
\s	Sum the columns.
\g	Go; sum the columns.
\b	Bottom formulas

Comments

When you activate this macro, be sure that the cell pointer is in the left column and in the first blank row below the columns of data. Otherwise, the macro may not work properly. Two blank rows should be below the columns of numbers.

This listing assumes that you have named the Duplicate macro (Macro 14) \d and the @SUM macro (Macro 11) \s. The listing uses \a to activate the macro, because \s is already used by one of its constituent macros.

Listing

1. \a	\-~	Enter repeating label to make a line.
2.	{\d}	Call duplicate macro to copy across.
3.	{DOWN}	Move to next row.
4.	{\s}	Call @SUM macro to enter @SUM formula.
5.	{\d}	Call duplicate macro to copy across.

Macro 16: Convert a Formula to a Label

This macro converts a formula into a label.

Suggested Mnemonics

Range Name	Mnemonic
\f	Formula modification

Comments

This simple macro often comes in handy. By turning a formula into a label, you can copy the formula to another location without having the relative cell addresses adjusted. This procedure enables you to do the following:

1. You can make an archive copy of a formula. You may want to do so when you are experimenting with the formula and want to be able to get back to a starting point. Making an archive copy is most useful

when you have a complex formula that isn't working. By turning the
formula into a label, you can make several identical copies (see fig.
5.16). Using the copy of the formula, you can then reduce each of the
operations in the master formula to an independent subformula by
deleting everything but that part. After you perform the deletions, you
can test each section of the original, more complex formula separately.
If a problem exists (such as an ERR condition) in the original formula,
the part of the formula generating that condition will be isolated.

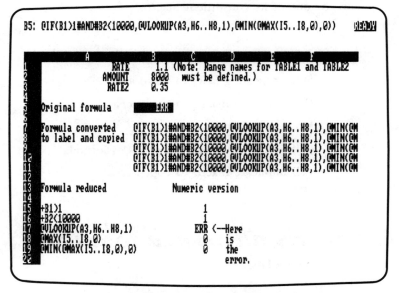

Fig. 5.16. A copy of a formula used to isolate an ERR condition.

2. You can remove one formula that is generating a circular reference
   from the series of circularly linked formulas. When you have a circular
   reference, more than one loop may be involved. This situation is most
   likely to arise when the circularity was generated by a copy operation
   that created many new formula cells at once. You can check for a
   circular reference by first identifying the offending cell (as indicated in
   the /Worksheet Status listing) and converting the cell to a label. If a
   single circularity exists, it disappears when the macro converts that
   cell to a label.

3. You can move a formula without generating an ERR condition. As you
   probably know, if you move a formula to a cell and the target cell was
   referenced in another formula, you generate an ERR condition. The

aftermath can be devastating, especially if the damaged cell was the corner of a range. In that situation, you lose the entire range.

On the other hand, when you copy new data to a cell, you don't generate the error conditions. However, if you copy a formula, any address not specified as an absolute reference is altered. This, of course, is the reason for using the /Move command in the first place. When you use /Move, you again have the ERR problem.

If you first convert the formula to a label, then use a /Copy command instead of a /Move command, you can have your cake and eat it too. To complete the operation, all you have to do is convert the label back into a formula (see Macro 17).

4. You can move a formula without moving any range name that may be assigned to the cell. This operation is just an alternate form of the preceding procedure. In this case, you are preserving the condition of the source cell rather than the target cell.

The procedure of converting a formula to a label, copying the label to a new location, and converting the label to a formula can be especially useful in command language programs that contain formulas. For details, see Chapters 9 and 12.

Listing

1. \f   {EDIT}   Enter EDIT mode.

2.   {HOME}   Move to beginning of contents.

3.   '   Insert label prefix.

4.   ~   Enter into cell.

Macro 17: Convert a Label Back to a Formula

This macro, the "companion" to the preceding macro, strips the label prefix character from the cell entry. The stripping process converts the modified formula back to its original form.

Suggested Mnemonics

Range Name	Mnemonic
\l	Label to formula
\g	Positional mnemonic

The mnemonics suggested for this macro are \l, which has an obvious mnemonic reference, and \g, which does not. I use the name \g in my worksheets primarily because I used the name \l for another macro. I also chose \g because G is next to F on the keyboard: an example of a *positional mnemonic*. Keep in mind that the goal is to devise a way to remember what macros have been assigned to what keys. The physical proximity of the keys and the logical relationship of their operation make this mnemonic device work well for me.

Comments

This macro has no effect on labels that begin with a nonnumeric character. Even though the macro strips the label prefix, 1-2-3 adds the label prefix right back when the label is reentered into the cell. If used on a formula, the macro deletes the first character of the formula, an action that will most likely result in the formula being converted to a label. If you use the macro on a number, you lose the first digit of the number.

Listing

1. \g	{EDIT}	Enter EDIT mode.
2.	{HOME}	Move to beginning of entry.
3.	{DELETE}	Delete label prefix.
4.	~	Enter results into the cell.

Macro 18: Label Formatting

Label-formatting macros arose from the need to take the tedium out of formatting multicolumn data. For several columns of data to be subsumed under one category label is not uncommon. Figure 5.17, which displays hierarchical relationships, shows several examples of such formatting.

Until you enter a label, you can't see exactly how it aligns with the information in the worksheet. If you are off by even one character, you must edit the label. With Label Formatting macros, you can see how the labels align as you modify them. The first two macros move the label one space to the right or left, respectively. The third macro creates the dashed lines surrounding the centered label, as shown in the top two lines of figure 5.17. The last macro, the inverse of the third macro, removes a character from each end of a label.

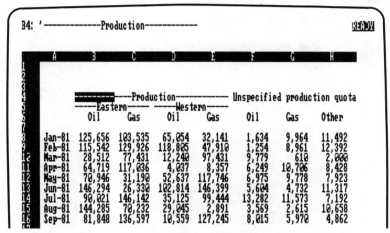

Fig. 5.17. Long labels used as multicolumn headers.

Suggested Mnemonics

Range Name	Mnemonic
\l	Move label left.
\r	Move label right.
\i	Looks like a dash
\o	Opposite of dash

For the second set of macros, I use \i and \o. I chose \i because it looks like a dash (albeit one that is vertical); \o, because it is next to the I key, which makes \o another example of a positional mnemonic.

Comments

These macros are very simple, but surprisingly useful. I keep finding more and more uses for them. A label-formatting macro is a good example of what you can produce when you find yourself repeating a sequence of keystrokes and decide to create a macro to simplify things.

You can easily construct all these macros with the Automatic Macro program.

Listing

Macro 1: Moves text right

1. \r	{EDIT}	Enter EDIT mode.
2.	{HOME}	Move to beginning of entry.
3.	{RIGHT}	Move past label prefix.
*4.	~	Add a space and enter into cell.

*Line 4 contains a space followed by a tilde.

Macro 2: Moves text left

1. \l	{EDIT}	Enter EDIT mode.
2.	{HOME}	Move to beginning of entry.
3.	{RIGHT}	Move past label prefix.
4.	{DELETE}	Remove a character.
5.	~	Enter into cell.

Macro 3: Adds dashes on either side of a label

1. \i	{EDIT}	Enter EDIT mode.
2.	–	Add a dash at the end.
3.	{HOME}	Move to beginning of entry.
4.	{RIGHT}	Move past label prefix.
5.	–	Add a dash at the beginning.
6.	~	Enter into cell.

Macro 4: Removes the dashes on either side of a label

1. \o	{EDIT}	Enter EDIT mode.
2.	{BS}	Remove a dash at the end.
3.	{HOME}	Move to beginning of entry.

4.	{RIGHT}	Move past label prefix.
5.	{DELETE}	Remove a dash at the beginning.
6.	~	Enter into cell.

Macro 19: Label Alignment

These macros are probably the most rudimentary in this chapter. All they do is duplicate the function of the /Range Label alignment commands. Furthermore, Label Alignment macros operate on only one cell; they can't change the label alignment of more than one cell at a time. Nevertheless, the macros are quite useful when you enter labels that require various alignments. The macros reduce a five-keystroke operation to one keystroke. The mnemonics make these macros easier to access than 1-2-3's standard label-alignment commands.

Suggested Mnemonics

Range Name	Mnemonic
\q	Positional mnemonic
\w	Positional mnemonic
\e	Positional mnemonic

If you've been implementing even a fraction of the macros listed in this chapter, you should be running out of keys that you can use as name-related mnemonics. Keyboard position can be an excellent mnemonic device for this set of macros. You can assign to them \q, \w, and \e, which represent left-, center-, and right-label alignment, respectively.

Comments

These macros don't use 1-2-3's /Range Label alignment commands. The macros change the label prefix directly by entering EDIT mode, deleting the old prefix, and inserting a new prefix. The macros are much longer than the standard commands, but run more than twice as fast.

Listing

Macro 1: Left Label Align

1. \q	{EDIT}	Enter EDIT mode.
2.	{HOME}	Move to beginning of entry.
3.	{DELETE}	Delete existing label prefix.
4.	'	Insert new prefix.
5.	~	Enter into cell.

Macro 2: Center Label Align

1. \w	{EDIT}	Enter EDIT mode.
2.	{HOME}	Move to beginning of entry.
3.	{DELETE}	Delete existing label prefix.
4.	^	Insert new prefix.
5.	~	Enter into cell.

Macro 3: Right Label Align

1. \e	{EDIT}	Enter EDIT mode.
2.	{HOME}	Move to beginning of entry.
3.	{DELETE}	Delete existing label prefix.
4.	"	Insert new prefix.
5.	~	Enter into cell.

Macro 20: Name Cell to Right

This macro automates the process of entering a label in the worksheet and using the /Range Name Labels Right command to assign the label as a range name to the cell to the right.

Suggested Mnemonics

Range Name	Mnemonic
\m	Macro name
\n	Name cells.
\l	Label cell to right.

Comments

This macro can be one of the most frequently used in your collection. The macro's primary purpose is to enter and name cells for use in constructing macros and command language programs. In addition, you can use the macro to great advantage when setting up a worksheet. You can use this macro to label and name all the constants entered into the assumptions section of the worksheet, or for range names to be used as reference cells for {GOTO} or other functions.

Listing

1. \m   {?}   Stop for name input.

2.   ~   Enter into the worksheet.

3.   /rnlr~   Name the cell to the right.

4.   {RIGHT}   Move to the named cell.

Macro 21: Data Entry

Data Entry macros are looping macros that stop and accept user input, move, and then repeat. Although they were described in Chapter 4, they are also included here for the sake of completeness.

The potential variations of looping macros are endless. You can configure them with any number of {?} instructions intermixed with any number of cursor-control instructions, in any order. A complex worksheet area with dozens of entries could use a macro that contained numerous {?} instructions and appropriate cursor-movement instructions in order to move to each entry point in a specified sequence.

Suggested Mnemonics

Range Name	*Mnemonic*
\d	Enter and move down.
\r	Enter and move right.

Comments

These macros are probably most useful in their simplest form, which is used to enter data in a straight line. The disadvantage of using Data Entry macros in complex arrangements is that recovering from a data entry error is difficult. If you move to a previously accessed cell and enter new data in that cell, you unsynchronize the macro.

The last macro listed contains a percent sign (%) after the {?} instruction. This sign, which causes 1-2-3 to divide the entry by 100, can be used for entering currency data.

Listing

Macro 1: Enter data down

1. \d	{?}	Stop and accept input.
2.	{DOWN}	Enter data and move down.
3.	{BRANCH \d}	Loop.

Macro 2: Enter data right

1. \r	{?}	Stop and accept input.
2.	{RIGHT}	Enter data and move right.
3.	{BRANCH \r}	Loop.

Macro 3: Enter currency data

1. \d	{?}	Stop and accept input.
2.	%	Cause numbers to be divided by 100.
3.	{DOWN}	Enter data and move down.
4.	{BRANCH \d}	Loop.

Note: To exit the loops in the preceding macros, you must execute a Ctrl-Break.

Macro 22: Date and Time Entry

These macros enable you to enter dates and times in more familiar formats than are required by 1-2-3's standard @DATE and @TIME functions. Both these macros take advantage of functions new to Release 2: @DATEVALUE and @TIMEVALUE. Both functions convert a string of characters entered in any of 1-2-3's standard date or time formats to 1-2-3's internal Julian date format.

Suggested Mnemonics

Range Name	Mnemonic
\d	Date
\t	Time

Comments

The macros enter a standard @DATEVALUE or @TIMEVALUE function, typing everything for you except the date or time string. The format of the string you enter can be any of 1-2-3's standard date or time formats. These include

Date	Time
04-Jul-86	12:15:05 PM
04-Jul	12:15 PM
Jul-86	

You can also use international formats, although which format you use depends on the current /Worksheet Global Default Other International Date and Time settings. 1-2-3 comes configured to use MM/DD/YY for the date format; HH:MM:SS with optional AM/PM, for the time format. Three other formats are available for both date and time settings.

Entering dates and times through the @DATEVALUE and @TIMEVALUE functions has the additional advantage of preserving the date or time format as you enter it. Because the output of this function is based on a string, that string will be visible whenever you view the cell contents in the command line. The format you use to enter the data is not, however, related to how the data is displayed in the worksheet. After you use one of these macros to enter the date or time, you must still format the cell to produce a date or time display. You are also free to choose any of the date and time formats available. Therefore, you can enter the date in one format and have it appear in another.

TRAP: Changing the international date or time formats can invalidate @DATEVALUE or @TIMEVALUE contents.

The one limitation to using @DATEVALUE and @TIMEVALUE with international formats is that these functions are restricted to the current setting of the /Worksheet Global Default. You can enter any string into the functions, but only a string conforming to the current international setting will be converted to date or time values. Likewise, if you change the international date or time settings, any formulas that contain one of the other date or time formats will be converted to ERR.

TIP: The @DATEVALUE and @TIMEVALUE functions accept many abbreviated forms of input.

You can speed up the data entry process macros by taking advantage of 1-2-3's tolerance for abbreviation with the @DATEVALUE and @TIMEVALUE functions. The following examples show the different forms of input and the associated output formatted to Date 1 or Time 1. Notice that 1-2-3 uses the year value from your computer's system clock to fill in any part of a date that is omitted. You can also omit the day argument, in which case 1-2-3 assumes the first of the month. With some of the alternate forms of input, 1-2-3 assumes a year value of zero. The last examples show illegal forms of input, all of which generate ERR.

Acceptable inputs for @DATEVALUE are the following:

@DATEVALUE("04–Jul–88")	04–Jul–88
@DATEVALUE("04–Jul")	04–Jul–86
@DATEVALUE("Jul–88")	01–Jul–88
@DATEVALUE("Jul–")	01–Jul–00
@DATEVALUE("7/4/88")	04–Jul–88
@DATEVALUE("7/4")	04–Jul–86
@DATEVALUE("7/")	01–Jul–86
@DATEVALUE("7//")	01–Jul–00
@DATEVALUE("7//88")	01–Jul–88

Following are acceptable inputs for @TIMEVALUE:

@TIMEVALUE("2:15:25 PM")	02:15:25 PM
@TIMEVALUE("2:15:25")	02:15:25 AM
@TIMEVALUE("2:15")	02:15:00 AM
@TIMEVALUE("2:")	02:00:00 AM
@TIMEVALUE("2: PM")	02:00:00 PM
@TIMEVALUE(":15")	12:15:00 AM
@TIMEVALUE("::25")	12:00:25 AM
@TIMEVALUE(":")	12:00:00 AM
@TIMEVALUE(": PM")	12:00:00 PM

Invalid inputs for @DATEVALUE and @TIMEVALUE are the following:

@DATEVALUE("Jul")	ERR
@DATEVALUE("Jul/88")	ERR
@DATEVALUE("88")	ERR
@DATEVALUE("7/88")	ERR
@DATEVALUE("/88")	ERR
@DATEVALUE("//88")	ERR
@DATEVALUE("/4/88")	ERR
@TIMEVALUE("2")	ERR

Listing

Date entry:

\d	@DATEVALUE("{?}")~	Enter date values.

Time entry:

\t	@TIMEVALUE("{?}")~	Enter time values.

Macro 23: Date Stamp

The Date Stamp macro automatically keeps a record within your worksheet of the last time you revised the worksheet. Recordkeeping can be especially important when you examine backup copies of files or old data containing multiple versions of a file.

For this macro to function properly, you must set recalculation to manual. The Date Stamp macro is assigned the range name \0, which causes the macro to execute automatically when you load the worksheet. The macro uses the @NOW function to keep a record of the current date and time. As long as recalculation is set to manual when you first load the worksheet, any cell containing the @NOW function displays the date or time from the last time you recalculated and saved the worksheet. The macro makes copies of the values of these cells before releasing control of the worksheet.

Suggested Mnemonics

No mnemonic is required. This macro executes automatically when you load the worksheet.

Comments

Because this macro identifies when the worksheet was last recalculated, you can use the macro to monitor when changes have been made. The macro does not, however, identify every change to the worksheet. Such an assessment is difficult to make. To detect all worksheet changes would require that every cell in the worksheet be compared with the contents of each cell at some previous time. Considering the magnitude of that task, you should find this macro a reasonable compromise.

TIP: Put a date- and time-stamp range in all your printouts.

If you are one of those wizards who can create an entire worksheet model without making intermediate printouts (or mistakes), then you can ignore this tip. The rest of us, however, may find that placing a date and time stamp on all the printouts we generate is very helpful in sorting out which printout goes with which version of what. If you are in a business that makes many "what if" analyses, you might want to format your time stamp to display seconds as well as minutes and hours. One easy way to include a date- and time-stamp range is to make it part of a top-labels specification in your print options.

When you load the worksheet, the macro automatically executes: the /Range Value command copies to the LASTREVISED range the CURRENTDATE range that contains the @NOW functions. The CURRENTDATE range is then copied to itself. The copy operation recalculates those cells so that they display the current date and time. (The 1-2-3 command language provides a more elegant method of recalculating portions of the worksheet, but copying a cell to itself works too.)

A third date and time range (LASTRECALC) contains a duplicate set of @NOW functions formatted as Date and Time as CURRENTDATE, the current date and time range (see fig. 5.18). This duplicate set serves as a display of the last recalculation of the worksheet. If you recalculate the worksheet before saving it, the LASTSAVED and LASTRECALC ranges will be identical when you next load the worksheet. On the other hand, if you load the worksheet and save it *without* a recalculation taking place, then all three date and time ranges will be different.

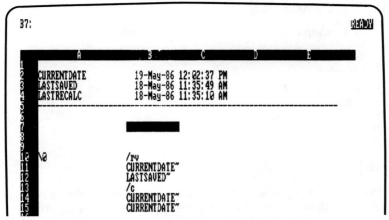

Fig. 5.18. Date- and time-stamp macro ranges and range names.

Listing

1. DATESTAMP	/rv	**/**Range Value command
2.	CURRENTDATE~	Specify CURRENTDATE as FROM range.
3.	LASTSAVED~	Specify LASTSAVED as TO range.
4.	/c	**/**Copy command
5.	CURRENTDATE~	Specify CURRENTDATE as FROM
6.	CURRENTDATE~	. . . and as TO range (forces recalculation).

Macro 24: Command Block Messages

This macro is actually more of a technique than a macro. It consists solely of {?}{ESC} added to a message that you want to appear in the control panel above the worksheet area. This trick can be useful for creating multiline messages in a macro.

Suggested Mnemonics

Range Name	Mnemonic
\m	Message
\o	Options
\t	Text
\h	Help

Comments

This macro has one potential drawback. If you press a cursor-movement key while the message is being displayed, the cell pointer moves and enters the message into the current cell. This process could overwrite data unintentionally. However, two ways exist to avoid that problem.

In some circumstances, entering the message into the worksheet could be an intentional part of the macro's function. By pressing the down-arrow key then pressing Enter for each line in the message, you can make a copy of the part of the message to be recorded. Pressing Enter without pressing the down-arrow key causes 1-2-3 to skip a particular line. For instance, you could create a macro that consists of a list of possible choices for entry into a database. To enter an item from the list into your database, you press Enter until the option you want appears in the command line. Then you press the down-arrow key, and the item is entered automatically. Pressing Enter repeatedly or Ctrl-Break ends the macro.

If you want to prevent any of the items from being entered into the worksheet, you just precede the text of the message with a character that forces 1-2-3 into VALUE mode. These characters are the following:

$+ - @ \# \$. (1 2 3 4 5 6 7 8 9 0$

In the macro, the message text will start with a label prefix and be followed by the value operator and then the text. When the macro executes, the text is typed into the system, starting with the value operator. This procedure creates a mixture of label and numeric operations, which is an invalid entry. If you press a key that would enter the text line into the worksheet, 1-2-3 detects the illegal syntax, beeps, and stops. You can proceed only by pressing Enter. Read-only lines can be mixed with lines that could be entered into the worksheet, as in version 2 of the macro.

Listing

The actual text of the listing depends on your application. The text shown here is arbitrary. Each line of the text must begin with a label prefix, although none are shown here.

Version 1: Read-only help text

1.	\h	To find out more about how to	(more . . . press Enter {?}{ESC}
2.		display messages the user can read,	(more . . .){?}{ESC}
3.		see the command language instructions	(more . . .){?}{ESC}
4.		LET, PUT, MENUBRANCH, MENUCALL, and DEFINE	End {?}{ESC}

Version 2: Options intended for worksheet entry

1. \o Press Enter to view options, down-arrow key to select, Break to quit

2.   Corporate Communications Department{?}{ESC}

3.   Data Processing Department{?}{ESC}

4.   Manufacturing and Maintenance{?}{ESC}

5.   Personnel and Training Department{?}{ESC}

6.   Sales and Promotions{?}{ESC}

More Macros

This chapter provides additional examples of how macros can be applied to your work. While all these macros are fairly straightforward, they illustrate the wide variety of techniques that can be applied to automating your worksheet and graphing operations. These macros also illustrate how to use some 1-2-3 commands and functions to make the macro construction process easier.

EDIT Macros

In this next group of macros are examples of utilities you can build to speed up the process of constructing or editing a worksheet. The first of these simply types some printer codes into the worksheet. It is mainly useful as a way to avoid memorizing obscure printer codes. The second macro demonstrates how you can automate a simple command and convert the command's function to a specific use, in this case, entering column headings. The third macro is a more complex application that can be adapted to many data input tasks.

Macro 25: Printer Line Control

The Printer Line Control macros save you a few keystrokes when you use control codes to add special effects to your worksheet printouts. Release 2 of 1-2-3 enables you to send control codes directly to your printer from the worksheet; the /Worksheet **Page** command is one example of this technique. In Release 2, a special label prefix, the vertical bar (|), identifies cells containing such print codes. A vertical bar followed by two colons is 1-2-3's special code for sending a page feed command to your printer. Other codes can be sent as well.

The syntax for the control codes is the same as that used in the setup string: a three-digit ASCII code beginning with a backslash. For instance, \015 represents ASCII 15. Other noncontrol characters can be included in the string in their usual form. To put the codes in your worksheet, you must precede the code string with *two* vertical bars. The first of these is the label prefix; only the second vertical bar appears when the entry is made into the worksheet.

Although this method enables you to control only one line at a time, you can create some attractive displays in your printed output. Figure 6.1 shows an example of the worksheet printout, and figure 6.2 shows the end result. The codes shown are for use with an IBM printer; consult your printer manual for the codes for your printer.

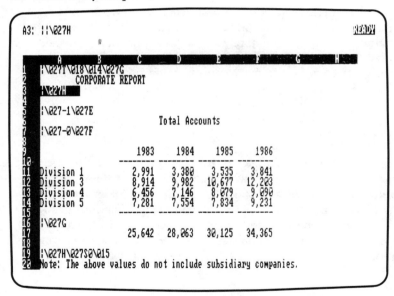

Fig. 6.1. Printer control codes entered into the worksheet.

The example shows five different type styles. The first line is expanded (double width) print; the second line is a combination of emphasized with underlined. The numbers are printed normally, except for the totals, which are in double-strike. The note printed in tiny type at the bottom is a combination of superscript and compressed print. Notice that for many print attributes, you must also send codes to turn off the feature. The codes shown in lines 3 and 7 in figure 6.1 are for that purpose.

```
CORPORATE  REPORT
```

Total Accounts

	1983	1984	1985	1986
Division 1	2,991	3,380	3,535	3,841
Division 3	8,914	9,982	10,677	12,203
Division 4	6,456	7,146	8,079	9,090
Division 5	7,281	7,554	7,834	9,231
	25,642	28,063	30,125	34,365

Note: The above values do not include subsidiary companies.

Fig. 6.2. Printed results.

These codes are, obviously, obscure and complex. If you have a laser printer, the problem is multiplied tenfold or more. (Most laser printers have control code sequences that contain 15 or 20 characters just to set one print style.) If you don't want to spend an inordinate amount of time looking up these codes each time you want to use them, the best solution is to code them into macros. Each of the following macros inserts one type of print code. Again, remember that these codes may not be correct for your printer.

Suggested Mnemonics

Range Name	*Mnemonic*
\b	Boldface
\u	Underscore
\e	Expanded print
\t	Tiny print

Comments

To help with formatting, the macros are set up to insert a line and enter the code. You can set up your worksheet with the formatting as you want it to be, then insert the control codes where you want special type styles. The control code lines aren't printed.

TRICK: A line that begins with a vertical bar doesn't print.

One of the characteristics of the vertical bar label prefix is that anything following it on a line doesn't print. This limitation applies only if the cell containing these codes is in the leftmost column of the printed range. You can use this aspect of 1-2-3 to your advantage by embedding in your worksheet comments that don't print. If you do this, however, be careful when you calculate the number of lines your output will contain.

TRAP: Printer control codes don't work when set in **Print Borders**.

If you are going to set your **Print Borders** (**Columns**), be sure that your printer control codes (including page feeds) are set in the leftmost column of your **Print Range**, not in your **Print Borders**.

The first macro sets boldface (double-strike) and stops. The second macro assumes that you want to set the underscore attribute for one line only. Therefore, the second macro inserts the underline code, moves down two lines, and inserts the code that turns off underlining. The third macro is set up to accept a variable number of lines in between start and end codes. The {?} instruction enables you to move the cell pointer to the line following the last line of the area you want to print in a special typestyle, then inserts the codes to turn off that feature.

Listing

Macro 1: Set boldface attribute

1. \b	/wir~	Insert a fresh row.
2.	||	Type special label prefixes.
3.	\027G	Enter double-strike code.
4.	~	

Macro 2: Set underscore attribute for one line

1. \u	/wir~	Insert a fresh row.
2.	||	Type special label prefixes.
3.	\027–1	Enter beginning underline code.
4.	~	
5.	{DOWN}{DOWN}	Skip the data line.
6.	/wir~	Insert a fresh row.
7.	||	Type special label prefixes.

| 8. | \027–0 | Enter ending underline code. |
| 9. | ~ | |

Macro 3: Set tiny print for variable line count

1. \u	/wir~	Insert a fresh row.
2.	‖	Type special label prefixes.
3.	\027S0\015	Enter superscript and compressed codes.
4.	~	
5.	{?}	Allow user to move cell pointer.
6.	/wir~	Insert a fresh row.
7.	‖	Type special label prefixes.
8.	\027T\018	Turn off superscript and compressed.
9.	~	

Macro 26: Heading Format

The Heading Format macro enables you to create quick, multiline column headers. To enter a heading over a column, you type the entire heading on one line, even if the heading is wider than the column. Then you invoke the macro. It uses the /Range Justify command to rearrange the entries within the column boundaries. Then the macro centers the label prefixes.

Suggested Mnemonics

Range Name	Mnemonic
\j	Justify labels
\h	Header

Comments

To avoid disturbing the alignment of data in your worksheet, the macro specifies a multirow justification range. If you use /Range Justify and specify a justification range that is only one row deep, 1-2-3 will move your worksheet data down (or up) to accommodate the changes the program makes while justifying. Figure 6.3 shows the outcome of this latter action.

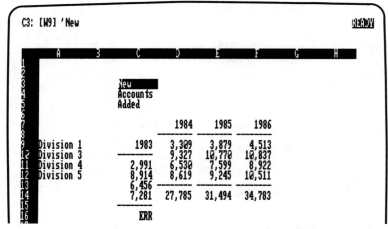

Fig. 6.3. Effect of the /Range Justify command on a worksheet layout.

If, on the other hand, you specify a multirow range to justify, 1-2-3 keeps all the changes within the specified range. To set the justification range, the macro uses the {END}{DOWN}{UP} sequence. This stretches the cell pointer down until it runs into a nonblank cell, then moves up one row to avoid including that cell. If the cell pointer encounters no nonblank cells, it moves to the bottom of the worksheet; this action has no ill effect on macro operation.

The only caveat for using this macro is that at least two blank rows must be below where you are using the macro. If only one blank row exists, then the {END}{DOWN}{UP} sequence returns the justification range to a single cell. Figures 6.4 and 6.5 show the "before" and "after" appearances of the worksheet in which this macro is used.

Listing

1. \j	/rj	Invoke **/Range Justify** command.
2.	{END}{DOWN}{UP}	Set justification range.
3.	~	Execute command.
4.	/rlc	Invoke **/Range Label Center** command.
5.	{END}{DOWN}~	Center the labels.

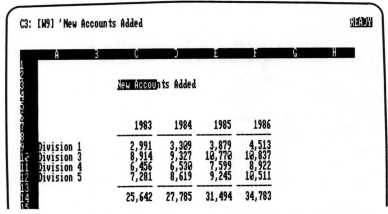

Fig. 6.4. Worksheet before Heading Format macro is invoked.

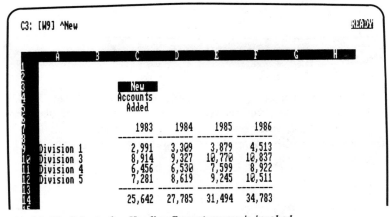

Fig. 6.5. Worksheet after Heading Format macro is invoked.

Macro 27: Selecting an Entry from a List

This macro, which is useful in a variety of situations, displays a list in a separate window. To select an item from the list, you use the cursor-control keys to point to the item; then you press Enter.

In the example shown in figure 6.6, the macro is used to select an accounting category name from a list of available categories. When an item is selected, it is copied into the location of the cell pointer at the time the macro was invoked. The macro ends by clearing the window and returning the worksheet to its appearance before you called the macro.

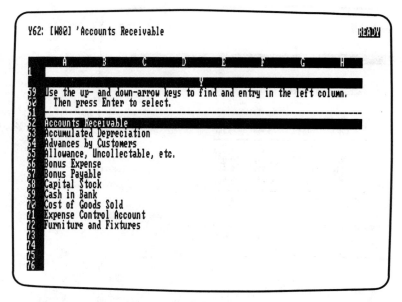

Fig. 6.6. The list setup.

If you are entering data into a database, two reasons exist for using this kind of macro to select default data. First, the macro serves as a reference by displaying the choices in a list. Therefore, you don't have to remember all the entries. Second, the macro eliminates the possibility of misspellings, which can play havoc with data analysis.

Suggested Mnemonics

Range Name	Mnemonic
\l	List of names
\a	Abbreviations

How To Prepare the List

This macro requires some worksheet preparation beyond the creation of the macro itself.

1. Find an area in your worksheet that is below and to the right of your working area. Assign the upper left corner of the area a range name (ABBLIST in the example).

2. Put a heading on the window, like the heading shown in lines 59 and 60 of figure 6.6. This kind of reminder is always helpful.

3. Type your list of data below the header that you just created. The data can be in more than one column and can extend beyond the lower edge of the screen. You can even include in an adjacent column a long prompt that explains something about each entry.

   In general, I've found that numbering or otherwise sequentially identifying the entries in the list isn't a good idea. This macro assumes that users will point to the entry and press Enter to select the entry. When numbers are present, users tend to try to select the entry by pressing the corresponding number, a procedure that doesn't work unless you construct the macro so that it allows such a selection method (see the "Comments" section).

Now you have finished preparing the list. When you access it, your message appears at the top of the window, as shown in figure 6.6. Because the macro sets Titles, you should be able to scroll through the entire list and still see the prompt lines, even if you move the cell pointer beyond line 76.

Comments

This macro is easy to use, but not foolproof. If you type anything except an Enter during the list selection process, the /Copy command will interpret your entry as a range name and will likely generate an error.

You can, however, use this limitation to your advantage. In figure 6.7, all the items in the list are numbered. Each item was given a range name consisting of the row number that appears to the left in the screen border. Therefore, you can select the listed item either by pointing or by entering a number. (Be sure, however, that these range names aren't used elsewhere in your worksheet.) The first item on the list was given the range name 4; the second item, 5; and so on. To select an item, you point to it and press Enter. The /Copy command then copies the cell's contents. You can also press the number key that corresponds to the item number. The /Copy command then interprets the number as a range name and the cell with that range name as the cell containing the item you want to enter.

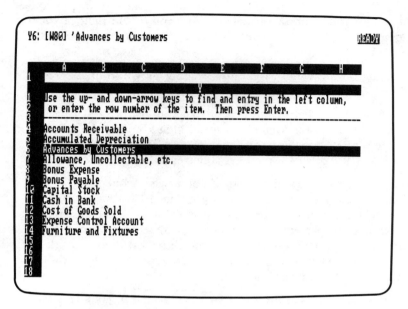

Fig. 6.7. List with items numbered.

Listing

1. \l	{DOWN 19}{UP 18}	Make space for list.
2.	/wwu/wwh	Unsynch and split window.
3.	{WINDOW}	Change windows.
4.	{GOTO}ABBLIST~	Go to the list.
5.	{DOWN 3}	Space for titles
6.	/wth	Set Titles.
7.	/wcs80~	Set column width to 80.
8.	/c{BS}	Start copy and release anchor.
9.	{?}~	Wait for user to press Enter.
10.	{WINDOW}~	Go back to starting point and copy.
11.	/wwc	Clear window.

GRAPH Macros

The following macros show how you can apply macro techniques to graphing as well as to worksheet operations. Macros can be especially useful in the graph operation process because of the number of keystrokes required to construct a graph.

Macro 28: Plot Regression Line

This macro calculates and plots a regression line for a set of X and Y variables. All you need to start the macro are a set of paired observations (the X and Y values) arranged in two columns and seven blank columns immediately to the right, as shown in figure 6.8. To use the macro, you place the cell pointer on the first X value and press the appropriate macro key (Alt-r in the example).

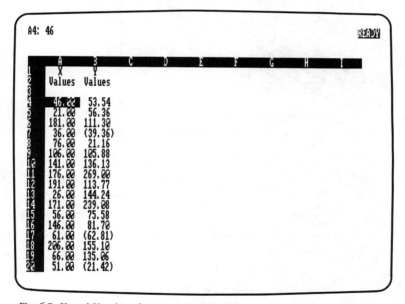

Fig. 6.8. X and Y values for regression calculation.

Suggested Mnemonics

Range Name	Mnemonic
\r	Regression
\p	Plot

Comments

The macro first uses the /Range Value command to make a copy of the original data. This step prevents loss of data should something go wrong with the macro operation and also "freezes" the data in its current state so that the calculated regression line isn't invalidated by changes made in the worksheet.

After making a copy, the macro uses the /Data Sort command to arrange the data in order, according to the values in the X range. This sorting is necessary for two reasons. First, regression graphs must be graph type XY in order to represent both X and Y variables as values. Second, unsorted XY graphs look like the meanderings of a mad housefly (see fig. 6.9).

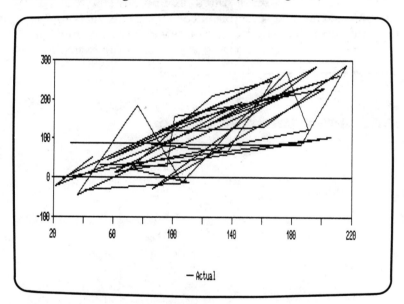

Fig. 6.9. XY graph using unsorted X range.

After the copy is made and sorted, the macro uses the /Data Regression command to calculate the necessary values and build the regression line equation. Using the three resulting columns of values, the macro creates a regression line graph. That graph represents the predicted values as a straight line plotted against the actual values. The format of ranges A and D are set to Symbols and Line, respectively, to create the final appearance of the graph (see fig. 6.10).

Although this macro has a simple construction with no tricks or unusual aspects, the macro is a good example of the way in which you can use macros

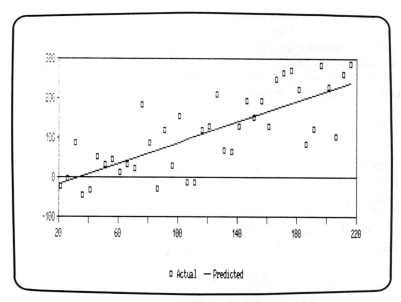

Fig. 6.10. Graph output from the Plot Regression Line macro.

to create miniature "utilities" for your worksheet. After constructing the macro, you don't have to remember all the steps involved in creating a regression line graph. You need to remember only where you stored the macro.

This macro illustrates techniques that you should remember when constructing macros you intend to use repeatedly. Many of the commands that macros use "remember" ranges assigned to them. This holds true for the /Data Regression command, the graph settings, and many others. To keep these remembered ranges from interfering with the intended operation of the macro, you should build into it some way of releasing these remembered settings so that the new ones are entered as required. Some commands, such as /Data Regression, offer a Reset option to accomplish this task; others, such as /Data Fill, don't.

This macro uses two alternatives to global resets. The first uses the {BS} keyword to "unhook" the remembered range. A second alternative is to use {ESC} here, but this does not yield the desired results. {ESC} leaves the cell pointer at the top left corner of the *old, remembered range*. What you want in this macro is for the cell pointer to end up in its original location. The {BS} technique is used to unanchor the ranges for /Data Sort, /Data Regression, and /Graph commands.

In some cases, a command remembers not a range, but a label of some kind. Such is the case for the legends applied to the graph in this example. {BS}, in this instance, doesn't delete the entire entry if one exists. {ESC} doesn't work either, but for a different reason. If an entry already exists, {ESC} works as intended. If no entry exists, however, {ESC} causes the command to "back up," destroying the sequence of the macro. The solution, as shown in lines 24 and 25, is to enter a space, then use {ESC}. The space ensures that an entry exists that {ESC} can erase, and thus the command sequence isn't altered.

Listing

1.	/rv {END}{DOWN} {RIGHT}~	/**R**ange **V**alue X and Y columns.
2.	{RIGHT}{RIGHT}~	Move to new location to the right.
3.	{RIGHT}{RIGHT}	Move to new copy.
4.	/dsd{BS}	Select /**D**ata **S**ort.
5.	.{END}{DOWN} {RIGHT}~	Sort range . . .
6.	p~a~g	. . . using X values as the Key.
7.	/dr	Use /**D**ata **R**egression command.
8.	x{BS}.{END}{DOWN}~	Set X range.
9.	{BS}{RIGHT}. {END}{DOWN}~	Set Y range.
10.	{BS}{RIGHT} {RIGHT}{RIGHT}~	Set **O**utput-Range.
11.	ic	Set **I**ntercept to **C**ompute . . .
12.	g	. . . and **G**o!
13.	{RIGHT}{RIGHT}	Move to blank column . . .
14.	+{LEFT}{LEFT}* {RIGHT} {RIGHT}{RIGHT}	. . . and construct . . .
15.	{END}{DOWN}{ABS}+ {RIGHT} {RIGHT}{RIGHT}	. . . the formula for . . .
16.	{RIGHT}{DOWN} {ABS}~	. . . the regression line.

17.	/c~{DOWN}.{LEFT} {END} {DOWN}{RIGHT}~	Copy to entire column.
18.	{LEFT}{LEFT}	Move to X range copy.
19.	/gtx	Set graph type to XY.
20.	x{BS}.{END}{DOWN}~	Set X range.
21.	a{BS}{RIGHT}. {END}{DOWN}~	Set A range.
22.	b{BS}{RIGHT} {RIGHT}. {END}{DOWN}~	Set B range.
23.	ofblasq	Set format of A to Symbols; B, to Line.
24.	la {ESC}Actual~	Set Legend of A.
25.	lb {ESC}Predicted~	Set Legend of B.
26.	qv	Quit and View.

Macro 29: Slide Show

This macro, the most basic of repeating macros, calls up graphs and displays them one at a time in the order you specify. Rather than use a program loop, this macro creates repetition by having a sequence of multiple copies of itself. To display all the graphs, make as many copies of the macro as you have graphs. The macro stops and exits after displaying all graphs.

Suggested Mnemonics

Range Name	Mnemonic
\g	Graph

Comments

This macro uses the /Graph Name Use command to view the graphs. Using this command is similar to invoking the Help function (F1), in that the macro temporarily loses control of the worksheet. In this case, /Graph Name Use causes the macro to halt and wait for you to press any key. Notice that no {?} instructions appear in the macro; the forced wait of /Graph Name Use performs that function.

TRICK: When looping isn't possible, use overlapping TO and FROM Copy ranges to create repetitive macros.

To create this macro, you must create multiple copies of some macro instructions—in this case, on every other line. If you are accustomed to using the /Copy command as it is usually used, the best you can do is create one double-spaced copy, copy it so that you have four copies, copy them to make eight copies, and so on.

You can, however, use the /Copy command to create in one operation as many double-spaced copies as you need. This use of the /Copy command is so handy that Lotus should probably include a description of the use in the 1-2-3 manuals. Because the procedure is a little tricky, some explanation is necessary.

You generally use the /Copy command as a unitary operation: /Copy THIS range to THERE. The copy, however, doesn't take place all at once, but in a sequence. By knowing what that sequence is, you can make the /Copy command do things it probably wasn't intended to do. The trick is to reverse (in a way) the ranges you usually specify as FROM and TO. In other words, you make the FROM range cover all the area (almost) where you want copies to appear, and you make the TO range a single cell.

Figures 6.11–6.13 show how the FROM and TO ranges are set up and the results. The FROM range is specified in figure 6.11. You want to copy what is in only the top cell of the range. Figure 6.12 shows the TO range, the location of which works as a spacing control. Move down two rows to get double-spacing; three, to get triple-spacing; and so on. Figure 6.13 shows the results of issuing the command as specified.

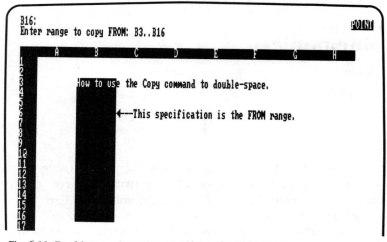

Fig. 6.11. Double-spaced copying: specifying the FROM range.

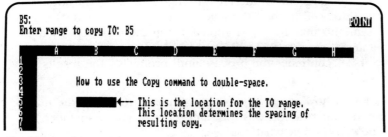

Fig. 6.12. Double-spaced copying: specifying the TO range.

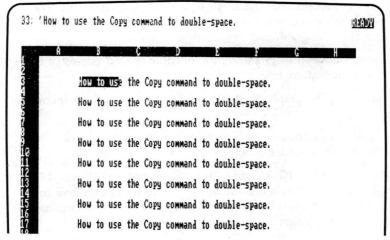

Fig. 6.13. Double-spaced copying: results.

Puzzled? Look again at figure 6.13. Following is a description of how the procedure works.

Remember that if you specify a large FROM range, 1-2-3 requires only the specification of a single cell as the TO range. 1-2-3 then copies the entire FROM range, using the specified cell as the upper left corner of the new copy. 1-2-3 is therefore ready to copy the entire range indicated in figure 6.11, which, at that point, is mostly blank.

When 1-2-3 begins to make the copy, the program moves to the top cell first and copies it. 1-2-3 then moves to the second cell and copies it, and so on. In this case, 1-2-3 copies the first cell in the FROM range, B3, to the first cell of the TO range, B5. The program then copies the second cell in the FROM range, B4, to the second cell in the TO range, B6.

Then 1-2-3 moves to the third cell in the FROM range. The program doesn't copy that cell to the third cell in the TO range because the third FROM cell is B5. This B5 is the same B5 that 1-2-3 just copied TO in the first step. By the time the /Copy command reaches this cell, it is no longer empty. Using this leap-frog sequence, 1-2-3 continues the process until producing the results shown in figure 6.13.

Here is an explanation of how to use the /Copy command to create the macro. Test this procedure. If your reaction was the same as most (mine included), you will probably be surprised at what you see.

1. Make one copy of the macro. Write the macro so that the graph name is isolated on the second line, but don't type the graph name yet. The third line of the macro contains the keystrokes needed to finish the operations on the first graph and exit to READY mode.

2. Use the /Copy command to create multiple, triple-spaced copies of the macro, including the blank line.

3. Fill in the names of the graphs in the order in which you want them to appear.

You can also use this kind of construction to print a series of ranges or other information specified by print settings sheets.

These macros perform the most basic kind of list processing. In Chapter 12 on the command language, you will see numerous, more elegant alternatives to these macros. Sometimes, however, these macros are quickest at performing repetitive tasks and are often easier to understand than other methods.

Listing

Initial macro:

1. \g   /gnu   Invoke /Graph Name Use command.

2.   Blank line for
         graph name

3.   ~q   Display and Quit.

Macro after copying:

1. \g   /gnu   Invoke /Graph Name Use command.

2.   Blank line for
         graph name

3.	~q	Display and **Quit**.
4.	gnu	Invoke **/Graph Name Use** command.
5.	Blank line for graph name	
6.	~q	Display and **Quit**.
7.	/gnu	Invoke **/Graph Name Use** command.
8.		Blank line for graph name
9.	~q	Display and **Quit**.

Final form of macro:

1. \g	/gnu	Invoke **/Graph Name Use** command.
2.	CASHFLOW	Graph name
3.	~q	Display and **Quit**.
4.	/gnu	Invoke **/Graph Name Use** command.
5.	INCOME	Graph name
6.	~q	Display and **Quit**.
7.	/gnu	Invoke **/Graph Name Use** command.
8.	SALES	Graph name
9.	~q	Display and **Quit**.

An Alternate Construction Method

You can also use 1-2-3's string-handling functions to construct repetitive macros. In figure 6.14, such functions are used to construct the macro you have just read about. Examine the formula's structure. In place of the graph name in the new macro, a reference appears in the cell immediately to the right of the current cell. When that reference cell contains the name of a graph, the macro appears as shown. By creating multiple copies of this formula and placing a list of graph names in column D, you construct the macro.

If you wanted a permanent macro, you could use the **/Range Value** command to copy the macro to itself or to another location. You could also leave the macro as string formulas; 1-2-3 executes these as well as ordinary label entries. An advantage to this procedure is that you could change the list of graph names

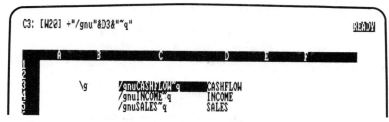

Fig. 6.14. String formulas used to construct repetitive macros.

anytime, and the macro would also change. (Don't forget to recalculate the macro formulas if you set **R**ecalculation to **M**anual.)

Try extending this process. To make the macro automatically adjust its own length and therefore the number of graphs displayed, you could use the following formula in place of the formula in figure 6.14.

@IF(@CELL("type",D3..D3)="b","","/gnu"&D3&"~q")

The @CELL function detects a blank cell in the list of macro names. If the cell is blank, the formula becomes "", which is a string zero characters long. When 1-2-3 encounters "" in a macro, execution stops. On the other hand, if the cell in column D contains an entry, the regular formula appears, with the graph name inserted in its usual place.

Macro 30: Selecting a Graph from a Menu

This macro selects a graph for display. The macro executes the graph commands to call up the list of graph names as a full-screen menu, then waits for you to select a graph.

Suggested Mnemonics

Range Name	*Mnemonic*
\g	Graph
\v	View

Comments

This macro uses the {NAME} keyword to convert 1-2-3's usual one-line display of graph names to a full-screen listing.

Listing

1.	\g	/gnu	Invoke /Graph Name Use command.
2.		{NAME}	Display all graph names, full screen.
3.		{?}	Wait for selection.
4.		~q	Display and Quit.

Macro 31: Graph Save

The Graph Save macro is an extension of the macro introduced as the alternate form of the Slide Show macro. In the Graph Save macro, the concept of a string formula macro is extended to include two items in each macro module.

To use the macro, you must create three columns of data. The first column contains the string formulas that comprise the macro itself. In the second column are the names of the graphs to be saved, as created with /Graph Name Create. The third column contains the name to be assigned to the .PIC file that corresponds to each graph. Figure 6.15 illustrates the macro's layout.

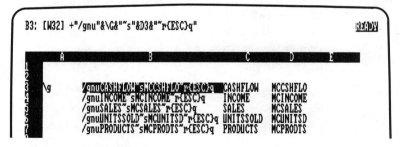

Fig. 6.15. Graph Save macro.

To save all the graphs listed, you need to "nursemaid" the macro through the forced wait imposed by the /Graph Name Use command. Pressing Enter a few times, however, is a lot easier than doing this procedure manually.

In addition to saving your work, the Graph Save macro is handy for record-keeping purposes. You can use as cross-references the two lists that specify the settings sheet and .PIC file names. If you generate many graph files, you may have difficulty making the names descriptive enough to identify the graphs' contents. Because the names are restricted by the eight-character limit DOS imposes on file names, your .PIC file names may be cryptic. If you must review a graph to determine what it contains, doing so in a worksheet is much easier than using the PrintGraph program's preview feature.

If you created this macro for record-keeping purposes, you can enhance the record-keeping function by adding a fourth column. In it, you can record detailed descriptive data on each graph.

Suggested Mnemonics

Range Name	Mnemonic
\s	Save graphs.
\p	Create .PIC files.

Comments

This macro assumes that you want to update graph .PIC files as well as save them initially. It answers *r* (for replace) when 1-2-3 asks whether you want to replace an existing file. This response automatically causes the existing file to be overwritten. If you want manual control over this aspect of graph image-saving, delete the *r* and {ESC} from the macro and insert {?}. If you use the macro where no file exists, the {ESC} cancels the extra *r*.

Listing

Basic Module

1.	\s	/gnu	Invoke /Graph Name Use command.
*2.		USER_GRAPH_1	Specify settings sheet name.

3.	~	Enter name specification.
4.	s	Invoke Save command.
*5.	USER1	Specify .PIC file name.
6.	~	Enter name specification and save.
7.	r	Replace if file already exists.
8.	{ESC}	Cancel r if file doesn't exist.
9.	q	Exit.

*These names are only examples; you use your own graph and .PIC file names in these lines.

7

Introducing the Command Language

If you have reached this point in the book by working your way through the macro section, congratulations! You will now move beyond the simple duplication of keystrokes and examine 1-2-3's potential as a programming environment. Because I assume that you are now fairly comfortable with both 1-2-3 and macros, the material in the rest of the book is presented at a slightly faster pace.

The rest of *1-2-3 Command Language* deals with programming at two levels: tools and techniques. Chapters 8, 9, and 12 describe the basic tools of 1-2-3 programming, functions, and command language instructions. The remaining chapters address the problems associated with writing programs: design, documentation, testing, debugging, and the special problems associated with programming a spreadsheet. Chapter 10 walks you through a fairly complex application—a form-oriented database—to illustrate program writing. And Chapter 11 contains a library of programs, ranging from elaborations of simple macros using command language techniques to some very complex applications.

This chapter is about how to get started as a programmer. Programming is both a science and an art, and through the rest of this book I address the topic from both perspectives. I also raise what I think are the most salient issues of using the command language to write programs, and I include guidelines that should help you avoid the most common programming pitfalls.

Do You Really Want To Be a Programmer?

Do you really want to be a programmer? This was the question posed by Lotus in the 1-2-3 Release 1A manuals. I assume that if you've purchased this book, you've at least considered the possibility. The question, however, is really moot. You already are a programmer. When you enter numbers into a spreadsheet, you are programming your computer.

So the question becomes "How advanced a programmer do you want to be?" The further you move beyond the basic structure of 1-2-3's spreadsheet commands, the more you venture into territory where you must become your own guide. If you stick to using spreadsheet commands, which include simple macros, then you are unlikely to encounter any major problems. The designers of 1-2-3 have done a marvelous job of anticipating your needs and the types of errors you are likely to make. However, if you choose to use the capabilities of 1-2-3 without the command language, be aware that you are using only a fraction of what is possible. All you need to move ahead is to learn a few programming language instructions and a few rules for their application.

How advanced a programmer you need to be depends in part on how complex your programs will be and who will use them. If you want to use the command language to create *smart macros* (decision-making macros that are limited to performing only one task), you will find that you don't need much more than a basic knowledge of the command language. As an enhancement to 1-2-3's macro facilities, the command language is wonderful. With a little practice, you will find that you can quickly create short, but powerful command language routines to solve some pretty knotty problems. In fact, the more you can use the command language with macros, the easier your life with 1-2-3 will be.

On the other hand, if you are going to use the command language to develop systems that extend 1-2-3's capabilities beyond its basic uses, such as creating an inventory or billing system, you must be very organized in your approach. You *can* sit down and just start creating such a system, using a trial-and-error approach to get the system into final form. As complexity increases, however, this method of program development becomes less satisfactory. An organized approach to programming can make small programs easier to develop and large programs *possible* to develop. This section of the book covers many of the issues that relate to organized program development.

If you intend to use 1-2-3 as a programming environment to set up data processing or accounting systems for clients or to sell as 1-2-3 templates, I hope you are a programmer or at least have one on your team. 1-2-3 can be a good tool for implementing such systems, but the number of potential problems grows exponentially according to system complexity, especially when the users aren't the system's creators.

The issues surrounding such systems go beyond the programs themselves and involve topics such as data interchangeability among systems, data integrity and security, provableness of program correctness, the ease with which the program can be modified, adequacy of documentation, and responsibility for maintenance and revision. The history of the software industry is replete with systems that took years to develop, cost literally hundreds of millions of dollars, and could not be made to work—and all this at the hands of experienced, knowledgeable people. I don't mean to seem an alarmist about such things, but I do suggest that you be realistic about your own limits. You should be sure that your levels of organization and caution are at least as high as your level of programming ambition. The command language gives you the opportunity to create powerful systems, but can also turn you into a sorcerer's apprentice in a swamp chock-full of alligators.

1-2-3 as a High-Level Programming Language

Some similarities exist between computer programs and the way we think, but these similarities tend to be overwhelmed by some very fundamental differences. Computers are obedient, but completely literal. Computers have to be given instructions in far greater detail than humans. Most beginning programmers have a difficult time bringing themselves down to the level of specificity demanded by the idiot mechanical intelligence that sits in the box on their desk.

When you have trouble turning your computational tasks into progr. .s, the problem is almost always that you have defined the task in human terms and left some aspect of the job vague or undefined. Novice programmers invariably suspect a hardware failure when a program doesn't run as expected. Experienced programmers know better: if the system doesn't fly right, it's due to pilot error. The right result depends on having the right program. Murphy's first law of computing sums up the overall situation: "Computers always do what you tell them to do, not what you want them to do."

Because no one yet knows how to make a computer think like a human, you are going to have to learn to think like a computer. Fortunately, learning how to think like a computer no longer requires that you learn the internal details of hardware functioning. Advances in computer programming languages, over the brief life of the modern digital computer, have enabled programmers to program using concepts that reflect thought patterns more and machine requirements less.

The more advanced programming languages are typically referred to as *high-level* languages, but they are still a long way from intelligent. What programming you do still needs to conform to the limitations of these languages. To better understand these limitations and how they will affect the way you write programs, you may find that starting at the beginning and tracing the historical development of programming languages is helpful.

Machine Language

Basically, a digital computer understands only *on* and *off.* The computer's memory is nothing more than millions of tiny transistor switches hooked together in such a way that they can be turned on and off individually. A computer's memory, in its most basic form, contains a group of binary numbers that might look like the following:

```
01000011
01101111
01110000 01111001
01110010 01101001
01100111
01101000
01110100 00100000
00101000 01000011 00101001
00100000 00110001
00111001 00111000
00110100 00100000
01000010
01001111
01100010
01001100
01000001
01001110
01000100
00100000 01001001 01101110
01100011
00000010 00000100
00000000 01110011 01001111
```

At the heart of the computer, the central processing unit (CPU) translates these coded instructions into operations it performs on its internal registers. The registers resemble the cells in a spreadsheet, except that all the numbers are in binary form. The instructions also tell the CPU to perform primitive input/ output tasks such as writing a character to memory or moving the bits in the register to the right by one space. These operations are primitive in the sense that a great many instructions are needed to perform even simple tasks. For instance, the routine that reads one character from the IBM keyboard is about 600 instructions long. These instructions are all the computer has to work with. Yet put enough instructions together in the right order, and you get 1-2-3!

Binary data might be okay for a computer, but humans have a hard time working with information in so rudimentary a form. This basic level of information must be grouped into higher-level forms in order to make it easier to understand. The 1s and 0s in the preceding listing represent the transistor switches in computer memory in their *on* (1) or *off* (0) states. These numbers are called *bits* and are grouped together into *bytes*, each of which contains 8 bits. Each byte, represented by a base-16 (hexadecimal) numbering system, can take on a value from 1 to 16. Each digit can be a number from 0 to 9 or a letter from A to F. A represents 10; B, 11; and so forth. If you convert the preceding binary representation into a hexadecimal representation, the result is as follows:

```
43
6F
70 79
72 69
67
68
74 20
28 43 29
20 31
39 38
34 20
42
4F
52
4C
41
4E
44
20 49 6E
63
02 04
00 73 4F
```

Assembly Language

The preceding arrangement may not seem like much of an improvement, but it *is* easier to follow *if* you must work at the machine-language level of programming. One of the first advances in programming languages was a set of mnemonic codes for the hexadecimal digits, much like the mnemonics that were made up for the macros. These mnemonic codes could be put together to create a string of instructions that, although still primitive, were more readable than hexadecimal or binary. The string of instructions could then be processed by a special program that "assembled" the list of mnemonic codes into their machine-language equivalents. This type of language is still in use today and is known as an *assembly* language. Following is the assembly language code for the hexadecimal listing:

```
INC     BX
DB      6F
JO      0184
JB      0176
DB      67
DB      68
JZ      0131
SUB     [BP+DI+29],AL
AND     [BX+DI],DH
CMP     [BX+SI],DI
XOR     AL,20
INC     DX
DEC     DI
PUSH    DX
DEC     SP
INC     CX
DEC     SI
INC     SP
AND     [BX+DI+6E],CL
DB      63
ADD     AL,[SI]
ADD     [BP+DI+4F],DH
```

The assembly language codes and their functions have a certain mnemonic relationship. INC means increment or add 1 to a register, which has the code name BX (column 2 of line 1). DB stands for data byte, which references a memory location used to store reference values that the program will use later. The instructions that begin with J are Jump instructions, the assembly language equivalent of 1-2-3's {BRANCH} instruction. The second character in the Jump instructions indicates the conditions under which a jump occurs. Transfer of program control takes place only when the conditions are met. Once you understand the mnemonics, the function of the program is traceable, although still not all that readable. As you can see, things are getting a little better.

Assembly language is a primitive way to communicate with a computer but has a few advantages. Most notably, assembly language programs (such as 1-2-3) run very fast. Unless you have an overwhelming need for speed, however, communicating with a computer in this way is tedious. Creating a program of any size also takes a great deal of effort. The only feasible way to write large programs in assembly language is to write subroutines that perform various tasks, and then group the subroutines to create programs. Typically, such subroutines perform functions such as getting a character from the keyboard, writing a list of data to a disk file, displaying a message on the screen, and so on.

High-Level Languages

To make your programming task even easier, you can write subroutines that conform to the way people think. After you write such subroutines, you can assign them names and collect a "library" of subroutines. You can then create entire programs by writing a list of subroutine names in the order in which you want them performed. A program known as a *compiler* can then take your list of subroutines and translate them into machine language.

Compared to lower-level programming, writing a program in this fashion is a vastly simplified process. This process is, in fact, the basic idea behind a programming language. The subroutines become the instructions for what can be called a high-level language, although exact definitions of what constitutes "high level" vary. For example, examine the following listing, which is written in Pascal. The listing contains the instructions that were compiled into the assembly language routine shown previously.

```
 1. program math;
 2.
 3. var
 4. type range: array[1..10] of integer;
 5. i,total: integer;
 6.
 7. procedure sum(values: range);
 8.
 9. begin
10. total:=0
11. for i:=1 to 10 do
```

12. begin
13. total:=total+values[i]
14. end;
15. end;

Even if you don't know anything about Pascal, you can look at the listing and get some idea of how it works. In line 10, a variable called *total* is given the value 0. The instruction in line 11 tells the program to take a variable called *i*, set its value to 1, perform the instructions that follow, increment the variable's value to 2, perform the instructions again, and so on—until the value of *i* reaches 10. The only instruction that manipulates data is in line 13. Each time that instruction is executed, another variable in the array, called *values*, is added into the current value of *total*. (An *array* is a set of numbers.) After this loop is executed 10 times, all the numbers in the *values* array have been added into the variable called *total*.

Ultra-High-Level Languages

Although primitive compared to the way people think about manipulating numbers, these individual operations make some sense to humans. Creating the preceding program is still somewhat complex, however, considering that all it does is add a few numbers. But the development of programming languages doesn't end at this level. To move closer to the way people think, you can use the same strategy that was used to move from assembly language to Pascal. In the Pascal program listing, the entire subroutine (or *procedure* in Pascalese) can be given a name that represents the subroutine's function. You can then use the procedure anywhere in a program by typing the procedure's name, just as if it were another kind of programming language instruction. For example, whenever you want to add all the numbers in an array (called a *range* in this program), you can type the following:

   sum(newrange);

(newrange) is an array of 10 numbers.

Looking back at the progression of program listings, the machine-language 1s and 0s that the computer requires to perform its task were reduced to a single statement that performs the task precisely in the manner people think about it. Until the point of the Pascal listing, the designers of the machinery and programming languages carried out the translation into higher levels of representation. Starting with the Pascal program, we, as programmers, took over and continued the process, essentially inventing our own programming language. You could keep extending your programming language, making up new instructions to perform tasks you carry out frequently. For example, you could write a procedure that found the average of *newrange* or counted the number of nonzero values in *newrange*, and so on.

What I'm doing should be obvious by now. 1-2-3 is, in a sense, just such a programming language extension. When you put @SUM(A1..A10) into a cell, you are telling 1-2-3 to execute a set of instructions that operates much like the previous subroutine. The process, however, can be carried even further than these high-level procedures. You can take the @SUM, @AVG, and other procedures available in 1-2-3 and use them to assemble an even higher-order representation, such as a financial model. Developing a five-year financial forecast would be extremely difficult if you had to program in 1s and 0s. By combining the operations into successively higher-order procedures, you can create very complex programs quickly and, more importantly, do so using terms that are closer to the way your brain thinks about things than 11001101.

To recapitulate, we've been creating increasingly higher-order constructs from primitive, lower-order operations by grouping the low-order operations into procedures that work as a unit. When you begin to use the command language to program 1-2-3, you will use this same strategy to turn macros and command language instructions into programs. Building complex modules from primitive operations is a good way to write programs and to think about programming. The advantages to this approach will be discussed when we look at the command language in more detail.

The Visible Data Set

The biggest advantage that 1-2-3, as a programming environment, has over other languages is the way 1-2-3 handles data. Computer users accustomed to using spreadsheets think nothing of the fact that the numbers they work with appear on the screen. This aspect of 1-2-3 seems unremarkable until compared to the data-handling capabilities of ordinary programming languages. For example, look at the following BASIC code:

```
10 dim var1(12),var2(12),var3(12)
20 for i=1 to 12
30 read var1(i),var2(i)
40 var3(i)=var1(i)+var2(i)
50 print var1(i),var2(i),var3(i)
60 next
70 data  17,15,3,4,4,4,4,4,4,4,4,4,3,12,3,5,5,12,3,5,5,2,5,6
```

This program performs a simple operation on a set of numbers. In line 10, the computer reserves space for 36 numbers: 12 numbers for each of the variables *var1*, *var2*, and *var3*. Lines 20–60 form a loop that is repeated 12 times. Line 30 reads into computer memory the variables *var1* and *var2* from the listing in line 70. Line 40 adds *var1* and *var2*, and line 50 prints the 2 input variables and their sum in 3 columns.

For purposes of comparison, look at figure 7.1, which shows the same numbers and operations as they would appear using 1-2-3.

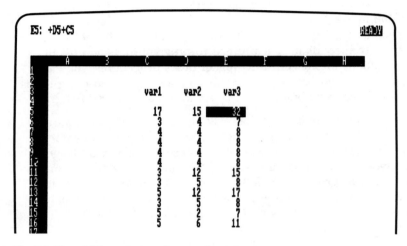

Fig. 7.1. The addition of two columns of numbers.

The 1-2-3 and BASIC programs perform the same function but, from a programmer's point of view, have several important differences:

1. The BASIC program operates on the numbers one set at a time. The program reads each number into memory separately and calculates each sum separately.

   With 1-2-3, the numbers are typed separately but remain on the screen. Twelve separate equations generate the sum of the columns. The data and results all are visible at once.

2. The numbers to be added appear in the BASIC listing. However, which number belongs to which variable is not clear until you run the program and print the results.

   With 1-2-3, the relationships between the numbers are clear as soon as the numbers are typed.

3. To maintain a permanent record of the results with BASIC, you must print the numbers on hard copy or send them to a file (operations

that may require additional instructions). The results of the program appear on screen when you run the program. But when the screen is cleared, the results disappear, and you can't reexamine them unless you rerun the program.

With 1-2-3, the results are part of the worksheet. You can look at the results later, even if they aren't visible on the screen for a time (when you move the window to another area of the worksheet).

4. If you want to change an input number in the BASIC program, you must change the number in the data in line 70. You then have to rerun the program.

   With 1-2-3, making the change in the input is the same as making the change in the output. You can rerun the program by recalculating the worksheet.

5. BASIC *does* have an advantage over 1-2-3: your computer uses more than 15 times the amount of memory to get these results with 1-2-3 than with BASIC, considering the memory used by the BASIC interpreter, 1-2-3's command processor, and the data.

All the previously mentioned differences, when considered together, constitute two large advantages that 1-2-3 has over BASIC and other similar programming languages: 1-2-3 programming brings the input closer to the output and the user closer to the data.

Simultaneous Input and Output

In the BASIC listing, the input (data entry) operations are separated from the output in both time and space. You type the data into the system when you write the program. The results, however, aren't available until later, at which time you can no longer see the original listing.

When you type numbers with 1-2-3, you generate the input (putting the numbers into the program) and output (creating a display of numbers) simultaneously. The very process of creating the input creates the output. Therefore, you immediately see the results of any equation you type into the system. The fact that you generate input and output together is most important when you make changes in the output format.

Notice that in figure 7.1, labels that were left out of the BASIC program output appear above the columns. This labeling process is a trivial problem for 1-2-3, but can be a major problem for ordinary programming languages. In those languages, the headings would have to be part of a separate program instruction, typed without the benefit of looking at the output for purposes of alignment and design.

In conventional procedural languages, creating complex output often involves creating elaborate mock-ups of output forms and carefully specifying the exact numbers of spaces and characters. If you are off by one space, you have to modify and rerun the program. Consider the magnitude of this problem when the program's output is dozens of pages long, when each label is potentially misaligned (or missing), and when the output is too large to be viewed on the screen. Then add to the time needed to revise the program an intermediate step—compiling the program, which many programming languages require to generate the program from the listing. That intermediate step can take several minutes.

Add all these factors together, and you have the reason why so many output forms generated by ordinary programs are crude and hard to read. Putting all the labels and numbers into an aesthetic arrangement is just too difficult and time-consuming.

Getting Closer to Your Data

Using the spreadsheet as a programming environment brings you closer to your data. In the BASIC listing, the relationships between the numbers in line 70 are not at all apparent. And this is more information than you would have were the data values not a part of the program listing.

Often, programmers don't type data into a program. They store the data in separate files that are read into the system when the program is run. When stored in external files in this manner, the data is invisible at input time. Keeping track of what data is contained in what file and in what format requires a significant amount of effort and organization. Situations even arise when the programmer inputs the data into the system when the program is running, much as numbers are entered into a calculator. In these cases, the programmer is quite divorced from the data.

The "User Illusion"

Having the input closer to the output and the user closer to the data makes working with the data much easier. This arrangement creates the "user illusion": the idea that you can work with the system without being aware of the system itself. You can concentrate instead on the numbers it contains and the operations you want to perform on those numbers. With 1-2-3, this illusion is so effective that you can easily forget you are programming a computer. You can work directly with the numbers, concepts, and relationships involved.

Most programmers developing complex programs keep charts and tables that describe all aspects of the data set the program will use. This descriptive information, sometimes referred to as a *data dictionary*, becomes a central document around which the programming project is structured and is usually quite dog-eared and coffee-stained by the time the program is up and running.

When the program modifies the data set during the program's operation, several versions of the data dictionary may be necessary. With a spreadsheet, the data dictionary is the worksheet, and the fact that you can see all the data is something you take for granted.

Having the data set visible makes creating, validating, modifying, and presenting information with a computer much easier than would otherwise be the case. That everything is visually oriented also makes the system fun to work with. You can see data relationships and the changes as they happen in those relationships. You can format your output one item at a time, adjusting as you go, and you can work more directly with the ideas your brain is generating about those numbers and what they mean. You can build a model a piece at a time to create a final result of immense complexity, and you can do so without having to go through the intermediate step of using a programming language.

When you compare BASIC and 1-2-3 closely, you can see more clearly how a spreadsheet is just another form of programming language. In technical terms, a *spreadsheet* is an object-oriented declarative programming language. The objects are the numbers, formulas, and labels you put in the cells. The fact that you perform operations on the spreadsheet as you develop your model, as opposed to writing the program first and running it later, makes the system declarative.

When you program a spreadsheet by entering information into it, the programming you do appears static. That is, after you type data in the worksheet, the data appears relatively stable. If you change a number or equation, the recalculation involved makes whatever changes are required. The system then becomes static again. Compare this process with ordinary types of computer programs, in which the emphasis is on the program's procedural aspects—that is, those operations that occur in a sequence.

Some aspects of a spreadsheet are procedural in nature: the commands you use to copy, format, or otherwise control the functioning of the worksheet program. You usually perform these operations manually. When Lotus introduced 1-2-3's macro capability, macros automated these operations somewhat. The enthusiasm with which users received macros led to the command language.

In combination, the object-oriented spreadsheet and the procedural command language create an extremely powerful programming system. The static programming enables you to create a highly structured data set and establish the relationships between its elements. The command language, which is procedural, allows you to change these relationships and examine the changes over time. Because you can use the command language to create subroutines that perform various operations, you can extend 1-2-3's capabilities into new areas and customize the program to fit your style and applications.

Labels as Data

Release 2 of 1-2-3 has one important improvement over Release 1A at the static-spreadsheet level: string manipulation. Labels in Release 1A are just that, labels. They are used primarily for formatting and labeling and for providing a connection between numbers and the concepts the numbers represent. 1-2-3's new string capabilities, on the other hand, are so powerful that words can now be considered data and treated with the same analytical processes previously reserved for numbers. This capability is important because string variables contain a great deal of information. In fact, virtually every command language program in this book uses string manipulations in one way or another, and many programs are devoted entirely to strings.

Implications

With the addition of the command language to the power of the static worksheet functions, 1-2-3 becomes a fairly complete programming system. 1-2-3 can perform virtually all the operations other programming languages support, but with certain differences. These differences are due to the division of 1-2-3 functions into static operations (with the worksheet) and procedural operations (with the command language).

Implications for Experienced Programmers

People who have experience with standard procedural languages will find the command language familiar territory. 1-2-3's other functions, however, make the programming process quite different from other languages. With all languages, you must fit the problem solution to the system. With 1-2-3, the system is a spreadsheet *with* all its functions. Developing a program in 1-2-3 includes adapting the program data to the spreadsheet layout. This adaptation process will often force on the data a structure, which will help the development process. As mentioned previously, the visible data set makes many operations that are problematic in other languages seem trivial in 1-2-3.

Experienced programmers will notice a certain disparity between the maturity of the spreadsheet functions, which are unsurpassed, and the command language instructions, which are rudimentary. Although the command language represents a real advance in spreadsheet capabilities, a few things are lacking, such as direct memory access, local variables, multiple file access, and recursion.

If you are an experienced programmer, your primary task will be to learn about all the rest of 1-2-3. The program is unbelievably slow where pure macro instructions are concerned, and it is fantastically fast where its built-in functions are concerned. The trick to writing good 1-2-3 programs is to put as much of the operation into built-in functions as possible. Doing this requires an intimate knowledge of some unusual functions that exist in no other programming language.

The command language contains almost everything you need for programming, although not necessarily in as powerful or convenient a form as might be desired. You *can* create good, modular, structured code, but the command language doesn't *force* you to create such code. With a little care, however, you can write compact, effective programs that are reasonably easy to test and maintain.

A New Breed of Programmers

Quite a few people reading this book are probably not experienced programmers. Some readers may have varying degrees of experience with Symphony, 1-2-3, or some other software, and those people may be ready to move beyond the programming limits imposed by static worksheet construction. Lack of programming experience has pluses and minuses.

The Good News

If you are using 1-2-3 and have no programming experience, chances are that you are an executive, engineer, or other businessperson using a personal computer to make your work easier or more effective. If you are such a person, you are also likely to be someone who will *use* the results of your programming efforts rather than produce results for someone else. You are therefore likely to focus on the problem that needs solving instead of on the programming required to solve the problem. This approach is called *top down*: you start at the conceptual level and work your way down to the mechanisms of implementation.

My experience with people using personal computers to solve problems for their own work is that such persons usually have a more complete understanding of the problem and of the effectiveness of the solution than a programmer who has only heard the problem described and isn't directly involved in the conceptual level of the problem or the use of the results. After you create a program, you are more likely to have addressed the problem thoroughly and less likely to have overlooked something important.

The Bad News

One of the things that makes 1-2-3 so popular is the degree to which the software tolerates casual methods of spreadsheet construction. With a visible data set and powerful /Move and /Copy commands, you can easily make a vague or misdirected beginning and eventually pull the spreadsheet into focus. When you begin using the command language, however, many of these advantages disappear. In the sense that many things must occur in a specific order, procedural programming is not as forgiving as static programming. You will have to be more organized and careful in command language programming than in simple spreadsheet construction.

The problems you are most likely to encounter are those that afflict novice programmers in other languages. Generating a program is in some ways like collecting string. If you have only a short piece of string, the way in which you store it isn't important. You can stuff the string into the corner of a box, and when you get the string out, you won't have much trouble untangling it. With larger amounts of string, the untangling process becomes time-consuming and tedious. Finally, you get to the point where there is so much string that untangling it becomes impossible. The more you try to untangle by pulling on an end, the more you end up tying knots somewhere else. The best way to collect a great deal of string is to divide it carefully into little balls and place them in a neat stack. This metaphor fits the procedures that apply to good programming practices.

If you follow the guidelines of creating large programs from single modules, you will find the process of generating large, complex, and workable programs manageable. A program that merely works, however, isn't sufficient. You must also be able to make the inevitable changes. For want of careful planning and execution, many a program has bitten the dust at this point. I have talked with people who routinely throw away old programs and start over, because that is less trouble than trying to figure out the mess of the original program. This practice is expensive and unnecessary, but you will have to learn a few techniques to avoid finding yourself in such a position.

Programming has one other pitfall. Many ways exist to write a program that performs a specific function, but not all the resulting programs are created equal. Converting your manual operations into programs—in a sense, creating supermacros—works, but not well compared to what you can accomplish with some special command language instructions and clever use of functions. The biggest difference usually lies in execution speed.

At the end of Chapter 10, I provide an example of performing one task in several ways. The first method is simply an automated version of manually performing the task on the keyboard. This approach, incidentally, duplicates the only way the function can be accomplished in Release 1A's macro language. Another method (the best), which uses both the command language and functions to achieve the same result, is more than 100 times faster and uses only 1 instruction. Writing programs that are short and fast is not only possible but highly desirable. 1-2-3's command language is slow; some programs in this book take more than an hour to run. Multiply that time by a factor of 100, and you have programs that are not worth running.

More Good News

Don't let any of the preceding text discourage you. 1-2-3 programs are, for the most part, easy to write. They're also fun. One of the best parts about writing this book was the excuse it gave me to play with 1-2-3. I encourage you to play with the program as well. Trying out things is the best way to learn, and you will reap the rewards later. You will have a better understanding of the system and be able to write programs more quickly. Experimenting is also a good way to discover the "tricks" of how to use 1-2-3 to carry out complicated tasks easily.

1-2-3 and the evolution it represents in programming are still new enough that much remains to be learned about what the program can do and how it can be made to work at peak level. When the command language made its debut with Release 1.0 of Symphony, the accompanying *Reference Manual* declared that no one really knows what can be done with the command language. That statement is still very much true today. Along with the command language, Release 2 places in the hands of thousands of enthusiastic users new /Data Parse, Regression, Matrix, and other commands. Given what 1-2-3 users accomplished with the crude and primitive /x commands, who can say what users will achieve with a real programming language? My favorite metaphor is that of an artist who has just been given a palette full of new, previously unknown colors. The possibilities may well be endless.

8

Functions

The Importance of Functions in Programming

For a program to work, it must accomplish two major tasks. First, it must manipulate data, including reading information from the keyboard or a disk file; evaluating formulas; and processing output to the screen, printer, or a disk file. Second, a program must control the sequence of operations, including executing instructions in order, calling subroutines, trapping errors, and branching conditionally. @Functions are equally important for both tasks.

Manipulating Worksheet Data

You may recall from the examples in the preceding chapter that functions are actually small programs. When used in worksheets, functions form the foundation of the static programming that makes the spreadsheet concept so powerful. When used in programs, functions have two distinct benefits. First, they comprise a set of subprograms that is part of the high-level language of 1-2-3. Therefore, for every function you use in a program, you write that much less program code (and make fewer errors). Second, functions manipulate data at assembly language speed (or nearly so), which is 50 to 500 faster than programming the same operations with the command language.

Controlling Program Flow

In the chapters on macros, you learned about the instruction pointer, which keeps track of the next instruction the macro executes. You were also introduced to the {BRANCH} instruction, which causes the instruction pointer to move to a specific cell so that macro execution can continue automatically. In programming terms, this transfer is called an *unconditional* branch. Whenever 1-2-3 encounters {BRANCH}, the instruction pointer transfers unconditionally to the location specified.

The capability to branch conditionally, that is, branch only when a specific condition exists, is what differentiates a macro from a program. 1-2-3 does not have a conditional branch instruction *per se*, but does have a generic conditional statement: the {IF} statement. {IF} uses a Boolean equation (such as B3>5) that is the same kind of equation used in the Criterion range in a database operation. This criterion equation appears within the braces of the {IF} instruction. If the result of the equation is anything other than zero, the equation is evaluated as TRUE, and the instruction pointer moves to the next instruction that appears on the same line as {IF}. If the result of the equation is zero or ERR, the test is FALSE, and the instruction pointer moves to the next cell, skipping whatever instructions might follow on the same line as {IF}.

The capability to execute statements conditionally is what gives the computer its appearance of "intelligence." These conditions are usually based on the current status of data or on the response of the person using the program. Functions play an important role in making such tests. Because they perform complex manipulations of data, functions enable you to use complex criteria for branching "decisions."

GUIDELINE: Whenever possible, use functions to minimize programming time and program execution time.

Consider an example of how functions simplify the programming process. In an interactive program, one of the most common kinds of branching decisions made is a test to determine whether the user's response is valid. In other words, the program must "guard" against the possibility of your accidentally pressing the Enter key, misspelling the response, leaning on the keyboard, and so forth. Figure 8.1 shows a short module that screens for a valid response.

In line 4, {GETLABEL "Enter your response (y/n): ", RESP} prints the displayed prompt in the control panel and accepts and places the user's response in the cell named RESP. In line 5, {IF RESP="y"#OR#RESP="n"} is the conditional test that is followed by the branch instruction: {BRANCH OKAY}. The prompt is for a Y/N response. If the user presses Y or N, the instruction pointer moves to the location OKAY, and the macro continues. If the user presses anything other than

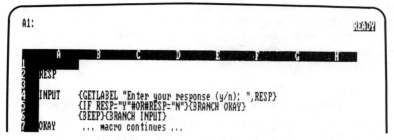

Fig. 8.1. A module that screens for a Y/N response.

Y or N, the conditional test is FALSE, and the branch to OKAY does not occur. Instead, the instruction pointer "falls through" to line 6, and the computer beeps to alert the user. The macro then loops back to the INPUT instruction so that the user can try again.

This procedure is simple to implement, but is not good programming practice. The test fails if the user types anything other than the characters specified—for example, if the person types *yes* or *no*. The level of specificity required in this response is intolerable to most users. If you want people to like your program, you will have to anticipate the various responses people could make and set up the system to accept any of those responses.

The most direct method for setting up the system with less specificity is to extend the test you have already created so that it includes additional possibilities (see fig. 8.2). Now, if the user types any of the specified responses, the program accepts the response. The tests listed show the responses a person can be expected to make. Because 1-2-3 considers uppercase and lowercase characters equivalent in this type of comparison, you can ignore the case of the responses. Notice, however, that even with the additional tests, some variations, such as including a space either before or after the characters, would still cause the test to fail.

Fig. 8.2. A more flexible input module.

Fortunately, you won't have to decide whether this setup is acceptable, because it isn't good programming practice either. A long sequence of similar statements (such as that shown in the example) is difficult to read. Moreover, although you can create such a sequence easily by copying and editing the original lines, it's more error prone than necessary.

Figure 8.3 shows a much-improved version of the module, in which functions make the test more powerful. @LEFT restricts the comparison to the first character in the response. Thus, any response beginning with either the uppercase or lowercase letters Y or N is acceptable. This version is much simpler and, although it does accept some illegal responses (anything beginning with the specified characters), is better than the previous module. You can still, however, make another improvement.

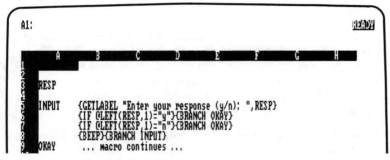

Fig. 8.3. Functions that improve the test.

The module in figure 8.4 has been improved in two ways. First, the @FIND function replaces the formulas in the previous examples. @FIND returns an ERR value if the string specified in the first of @FIND's arguments is not in the second argument. The test argument is specified as the @UPPER value of the user's response. Thus, any combination of upper- and lowercase characters that form the words *yes* or *no*, the initial characters *y* or *n*, or even partial words such as *ye*, is acceptable. The test is reduced to one line, which enables you to make the second improvement. The @ISERR function modifies the result that @FIND returns and thus reverses the nature of the test. Now, instead of screening for legal responses, the test screens for illegal responses. For any response that causes @FIND to return an ERR, @ISERR is TRUE, the computer beeps, and the module loops.

The final result of these modifications is a two-line module with one {BRANCH} statement. The module accepts all valid responses and, although it accepts some illegal responses as well, the module's programming is vastly improved.

Figure 8.5 shows one more version of the input module. This version uses the

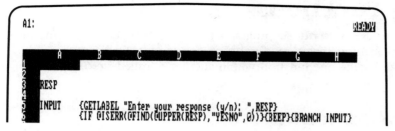

Fig. 8.4. A better method.

@VLOOKUP function to create a true screening module. Although this example requires the construction of an additional table, module design remains simple and does not accept any illegal responses. Because the table can be any length, any set of responses can be screened. The @VLOOKUP function is also case sensitive; therefore, exact responses can be screened.

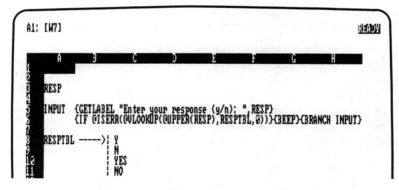

Fig. 8.5. @VLOOKUP response screening.

This example has what I like to refer to as *programming elegance*. The module performs the task desired, accepts all valid input, screens all invalid responses, and does all this with one instruction. The module is elegant both because it is correct and because it uses 1-2-3's built-in functions to accomplish the task with a minimum of programming.

The preceding examples illustrate two important points that have been made before but bear repeating. First, more than one way exists to write a program. The most direct methods, as illustrated by figures 8.1 and 8.2, are seldom the best; these methods work, but have limitations. The second point is that writing effective, elegant programs demands a thorough knowledge of 1-2-3. This chapter, which was written with this second point in mind, explains how to nest functions and how to use a special subset of functions to program.

Nesting Functions

Although functions are powerful subprograms in their own right, they come into their own when used together to perform with one instruction a very complicated task. Placing one function within another is called *nesting*.

Why Nest Functions?

Three reasons exist for nesting functions. The previous examples demonstrate one important reason: nesting increases the power of your test. For example, @UPPER by itself is of limited usefulness. When used with @FIND or @VLOOKUP, however, @UPPER greatly simplifies the task at hand. The second reason to nest functions is that you can perform more complex operations and functions than 1-2-3 otherwise provides, and you can conserve memory and worksheet space at the same time. The third reason for nesting functions is that some complex tests must be made in a single cell (inside an {IF} instruction, for instance) to ensure that all the important values have been recalculated.

You can obtain complex results without nesting simply by placing each operation of a complex function in a separate cell. Figure 8.5 could have included in a separate cell an @UPPER function that referred to the RESP cell. This arrangement would have created a *chain* of formulas, each of which performed a step in the required transformation. Such a version is functionally equivalent to the nested version, but uses more worksheet space and requires that the intermediate cells be recalculated before the final test is performed.

A Strategy for Nesting Functions

The following strategy for creating nested functions can help you generate complex nested statements with a minimum of effort.

1. Compare the input form of the data with the desired output.

2. Select a function to transform the data.

3. If the data is not in the form required by the function, apply Step 2 to the data that is input to the function.

4. If the result of the function is not the final form, apply Step 2 to the output from the function.

Example 1

The optimum development process proceeds both from the inside out and from the outside in. In other words, development moves from the general to the specific. You start with a general idea of how you want to accomplish a task. From that point, you may have to use more functions to modify either the arguments to your basic function or the function's output, or both. For example, you create the formula in figure 8.5 by doing the following:

Step 1: Compare the input form of the data with the desired output.

The input is any of the possible forms of response for a yes/no question. This input comprises the words *yes* and *no* or the first characters of each. If the input response is contained in a set of valid responses, the output is a 1; otherwise, the output is 0.

Step 2: Select a function to transform the data.

To compare the input data with a set of valid responses, you could use one of the following:

   a. Simple A=B tests

   b. @FIND

   c. @VLOOKUP or @HLOOKUP

As shown in the previous examples, *a* results in bulky programming, and *b* accepts invalid entries. Therefore, use *c*.

The formula is now

   @VLOOKUP(RESP,RESPTBL,0)

Step 3: If the data is not in the form the function requires, apply Step 2 to the data input to the function.

The @LOOKUP functions require exact matches. To create an exact match, you could either

   a. Include all possible exact matches in the table.

or

   b. Transform the input to the @LOOKUP function.

In this example, @UPPER restricts the number of comparisons required by ensuring that only all-uppercase comparisons are made.

The formula is now

@VLOOKUP(@UPPER(RESP),RESPTBL,0)

Step 4: If the result of the formula is not the final form, apply Step 2 to the formula's output.

The formula created by Step 3 returns either the position of the entry in the list or, if the entry is not in the list, ERR. @ISERR converts the formula into the form you want:

@ISERR(@VLOOKUP(@UPPER(RESP),RESPTBL,0))

Example 2

Suppose that you have imported a listing of names by using 1-2-3's /File Import command, and you want to sort the names by dividing them into first and last names. Figure 8.6 shows both the input and desired output forms.

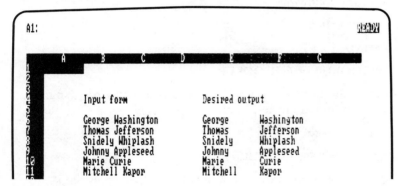

Fig. 8.6. Modified forms of names.

The same strategy for creating the desired formula can now be applied to this problem:

Step 1: Compare the input form of the data with the desired output.

The space between the first and last names is the key to transforming this data. The space appears at the exact spot where you want to divide each full name into two parts.

Step 2: Select a function to transform the data.

You must make two transformations: one to select everything to the left of the space and another to select everything to the right of the space. The formula you create also must contend with the variable length of the last names.

The @LEFT and @RIGHT functions are the obvious choices for transforming the data.

Step 3: If the data is not in the form the function requires, apply Step 2 to the data that is input to the function.

When you use @LEFT, you must specify the number of characters to be returned by the function. This number is the number of characters to the left of the space. You can find out what this number is by using @FIND:

@FIND(" ",B6,0) = 6

Because the solution to this function is 6, your formula for the first name portion of the desired output becomes

@LEFT(B6,@FIND(" ",B6,0))

Step 4: Another transformation step is required to make @RIGHT return the last name. The function must return a number corresponding to the number of characters remaining in the input string after the first name portion is removed. You don't want the space as part of your listing, so you must reduce by one the number you use as a length argument for @RIGHT.

@LENGTH(B6) – @FIND(" ",B6,0) – 1

The final formula for extracting the last name from the full name is

@RIGHT(B6,@LENGTH(B6) – @FIND(" ",B6,0) – 1)

Example 3

This example illustrates some of the problems that can arise when you create complex nested functions.

GUIDELINE: Create complex formulas a piece at a time.

As the following example demonstrates, you can create formulas of almost any complexity with the same four-step strategy described in the first two examples. At some level of complexity, however, a formula is more easily constructed in separate cells. Rather than try to "shoehorn" a long formula into one cell, you should place each separate function or expression in a separate cell and link the cells to form the final equation. An unmatched parenthesis or a syntax error in one of the formula's components can invalidate your result. If the formula is all in one cell, debugging is very difficult.

To make complex formulas work as intended, you must be sure that each level of nesting returns the desired result. This checking is especially important when you are screening user input and must contend with possible illegal values. By creating your formula in pieces, you can verify the results of each component or identify what segment is producing the ERR.

Describing the Input

Suppose that you are creating a program that processes items in an inventory. Your input instruction prompts the user to type a two-part inventory code, similar to the type of code used in most fixed asset management systems. The first part is a category code, which must correspond to existing category codes stored in a database. The category code can have two parts separated by a dash. The second part of the inventory code is a part number, which is separated from the inventory code by a dash. The number of digits in each of the three parts of the inventory code can vary.

The inventory code takes one of the following forms:

XXX–YYY–ZZZ
XXX–ZZZ

XXX represents the category code; YYY, an optional subcode; and ZZZ, the part number. Your task is to screen the input to make certain that the category code and subcode, if present, represent items already listed in the database.

Describing the Output

Although the desired output from this test is simply a TRUE or FALSE value, the conditions that determine the value are complex. You can break down the test into two major parts: (1) compare the category code with the database of category codes and (2) make sure that the valid category code is followed by a dash and at least one character. Your task is complicated by the fact that the category code may or may not contain a subcode.

The final output will therefore consist of two tests, both of which must be passed in order for the entry to be valid. To achieve this result, you can create two separate tests and join them with the Boolean operator AND.

First Steps

Select the basic operators for the first test. Because the database that contains the category code is a list of items, you can use @VLOOKUP to test for the presence of a specified category code in the list. To simplify the problem somewhat, assume that the category code is in the first field (the leftmost column) of the database. When the item to be tested is in the first column, you can use an @VLOOKUP function and specify the database range name as the *range* argument for @VLOOKUP. To create the *lookup* argument in the @VLOOKUP function, you must isolate the category code part of the code number. The left section of the inventory code is the category code. Therefore, you will probably need the @LEFT function.

Building the Formula

You could use the same strategy you used in the previous example to separate first and last names from a full name. However, a subcode may be between the category code and the part number. Because the full inventory number may contain two or three parts, the input may contain one or two dashes as separators. You want one formula that works under both conditions. Therefore, you may have to do a little testing as you go.

TIP: Use sample data to test each part of a complex formula as you construct it.

Complex formulas are more easily developed if you can see the results of each step in the development process. For this example, the formula must be able to process two separate forms of input. Setting up two parallel sets of formulas allows you to compare the results of each step and ensure that your formula is working under both conditions.

Figure 8.7 shows the test setup for this example. Cell D18 contains a mockup of a one-dash inventory number; B18, a two-dash number. In the cells above each of the inventory numbers are copies of the formula with the format set to Text. To the left of each of the text formulas is a cell reference to the formula (cell A15 contains +B15) so that the formula and its result can both be seen at once.

To use the test setup, you place in cell B15 the first part of the formula you want to construct. Use the /Copy command to place an identical copy of the formula in cell D15. The formulas in the B and D columns use different data as their sources, but should produce identical results if your final formula is constructed properly. Build your formula by creating additional formulas that refer to the cells immediately below. In this way, your final result will be the product of a series of formulas in a chain rather than of formulas nested within one another.

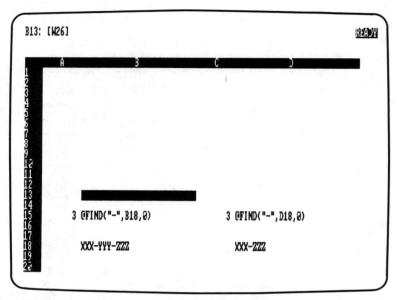

Fig. 8.7. Test setup for formula development.

Your strategy at this point is to keep every step as simple as possible and each part of the formula in a separate cell. After you find out whether the formula works, you can combine its parts into one cell.

As your first step, use @FIND to return the position of the first dash. Your screen at this point should resemble figure 8.7.

Both formulas return the value 3. If you used this formula as the argument for @LEFT, it would return the category code for the one-dash number but not for the two-dash number. As a starting point, you can find a second dash by using the location of the first dash plus one (see fig. 8.8).

Notice that you reference the result of the previous formula in your new formula. You don't have to do any nesting at this point. However, you have encountered a problem: the new formula works for the two-dash number but not for the one-dash number. For the latter, the formula returns an ERR value. You will therefore have to use the first formula for the one-dash number and the second formula for the two-dash number. How will you know when to use which formula? The ERR value decides for you. By using @ISERR to test for the ERR value inside an @IF function, you can automatically select one formula or the other. @ISERR has been added to figure 8.9.

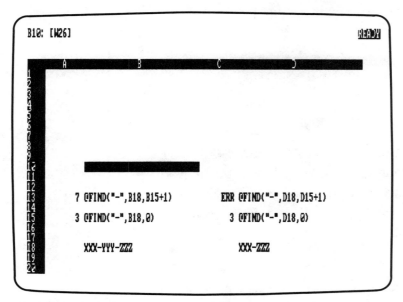

Fig. 8.8. Functions that find the second dash.

Also added to figure 8.9 is the @LEFT function and its result. This result is the argument for @VLOOKUP, which performs the test in which you are interested. Your original criterion calls for a 1 or 0 value, depending on whether the category code is in the database. Therefore, adding @ISERR to @VLOOKUP gives you the first part of the test.

The last modification you need to make is to invert the result of @ISERR so that it returns a TRUE value (1) when the category code is in the database. You accomplish this task by adding the NOT operator to the @ISERR function.

Figure 8.10 shows the final design for your nested function, minus the nesting. A dummy lookup table has been added so that you can test the final result.

At this point, the second part of your test is trivial. If the part-number portion of the entry is left off the input, the current formula interprets the last part of the category code as a part number. The formula also attempts to look up the remaining portion of the entry in the category code database. Because the remaining part of the entry is not the full category code, an error occurs. The formula *as is* guards against a category code entered without a part number. The only possibility that isn't covered is the failure to include a part number after entering a dash, in which case the inventory code input ends in a dash. The test for this possibility is shown as the final entry in the formula columns in figure 8.11.

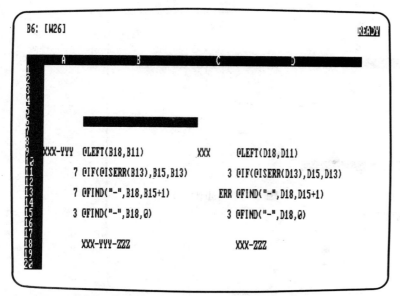

Fig. 8.9. *Formulas selected to suit the condition.*

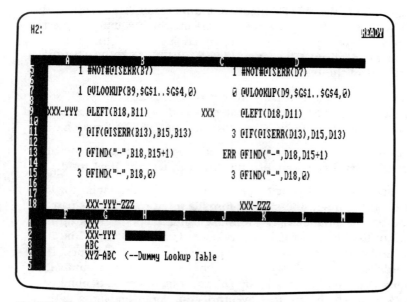

Fig. 8.10. *The first part of the unnested formula.*

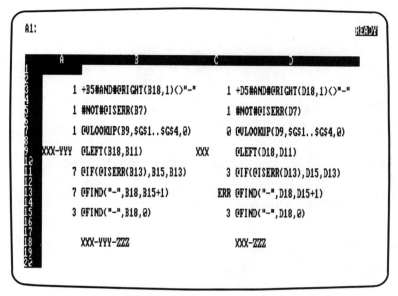

Fig. 8.11. The final unnested formula.

All you have to do now is create the final formula as a set of nested functions. By starting at the bottom and working your way up and eventually back down, you can type your formulas into a single, nested formula.

Using a Command Language Routine To Write the Formula

Figure 8.12 shows a short command language routine you can create to write the formula for you. This program can be helpful if you have as much trouble as I do keeping track of parentheses in a complex formula. The inner workings of the program are too complicated to be dealt with here, but a full description of how the program operates appears in Chapter 11.

To use the program, you must first place the word *stop* in row 17 (of fig. 8.11), in whichever column (B or D) you want to use. Then place the cell pointer in the topmost formula cell in column B or D and press \f. The program assembles the formula in the cell named SAVED.

Testing the Formula

TIP: Use the /Data Table command to test formulas.

To be sure that the formula works, use the /Data Table command to "feed" the formula a set of trial values. Figure 8.13 shows a test setup. Columns F and G show the valid values for this test. Column B includes a list of test values. The first five values are legal inputs and should evaluate to 1 (TRUE). The next

```
MACRO TO WRITE NESTED FORMULA FROM PARTS
-----------------------------------------------------------------------------------
SAVED
ADDR
MODIFIED
-----------------------------------------------------------------------------------
\f            {CHECKSTRING}
              {LET MODIFIED,@CELLPOINTER("contents")}
\f2           {DOWN 2}
              {CHECKSTRING}
              {LET SAVED,@CELLPOINTER("contents")}
              {LET ADDR,@CHAR(@CELLPOINTER("col")+64)&@STRING(@CELLPOINTER("row"),0)}
              {IF SAVED="stop"}{QUIT}
\f3           {LET MODIFIED,@REPLACE(MODIFIED,@FIND(ADDR,MODIFIED,0),@LENGTH(ADDR),SAVED)}
              {IF @FIND(ADDR,MODIFIED,0)+1}{BRANCH \f3}
              {BRANCH \f2}
-----------------------------------------------------------------------------------
CHECKSTRING  {IF @CELLPOINTER("type")<>"l"}{EDIT}{HOME}'~
```

Fig. 8.12. A command language routine to assemble nested formulas.

seven values are illegal and should evaluate to 0 (FALSE). The master formula is
moved to cell C3, and a /Data Table 1 command is issued, with B3..C15
specified as the table range and B18 indicated as the input cell.

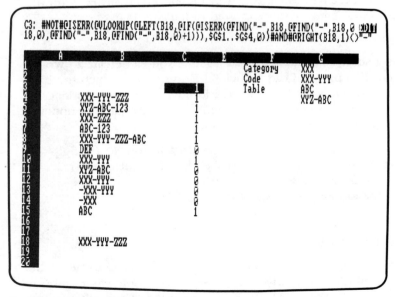

Fig. 8.13. A setup to test the formula.

The results shown in figure 8.13 indicate that the second test in the formula does not work perfectly. Recall that for the formula to evaluate as TRUE, the criteria required a part number to be present. The original formula didn't anticipate two kinds of entries: a category code with no dashes (ABC); and a category code with a dash and without a part number but with the first part of the category code itself a valid category code (XXX–YYY). Even though the latter may seem to be an unlikely occurrence in real life, you can use a simple test to fix both problems.

In both cases, the invalid entry appears in the lookup database in the listed form. You can screen these entries by adding a test to check the entry for an exact match in the database. If an exact match occurs, a category code must be missing a part number.

The Final Formula

The final formula, which is shown on four lines to make it fit the book margins, is

```
+#NOT#@ISERR(@VLOOKUP(@LEFT(B18,@IF(@ISERR(@FIND("–",B18,
@FIND("–",B18,0)+1)),@FIND("–",B18,0),@FIND("–",B18,
@FIND("–",B18,0)+1))),$G$1..$G$4,0))#AND#@RIGHT(B18,1)<>; "–"
#AND#@ISERR(@VLOOKUP(B18,$G$1..$G$4,0))
```

This formula looks intimidating, but its construction was quite straightforward. As with anything this complex, you should carefully document the formula's function. A good way to do so might be to save the formulas used in construction.

Example 4

Another use for nested functions is to create new 1-2-3 functions. This example—which uses two of 1-2-3's most unusual functions: @CELLPOINTER and @@—creates a function that returns the contents of the cell to the right of the cell pointer. Such a procedure can be useful for comparing items in a list. The primary reason for using this example, however, is to show you how you can use nested functions to convert data from one form to another—a process that enables you to perform operations that would otherwise be impossible.

Describing the Output

The final output should be the contents of the cell to the right of the cell pointer.

Describing the Input

To retrieve the contents of the cell below the cell pointer, you can use the @@ function. When given an address as an argument, the @@ function returns a cell's contents. To get that address, you can start with the @CELLPOINTER("row") and @CELLPOINTER("col") functions, which return the numeric equivalents of the cell pointer's current address. If you simply increment the column portion of the address that @CELLPOINTER returns and use the column portion as the argument for @@, you achieve the desired results.

Figure 8.14 shows the construction of the formula. It builds from bottom to top, as in the previous example. Column B contains the text version of the formula, whereas column A contains the results of each formula. A special test case is shown in columns C and D. When the cell pointer is in a column that contains a Z, such as Z, AZ, or DZ, you must convert the Z to an A. You must also increment the character preceding the Z.

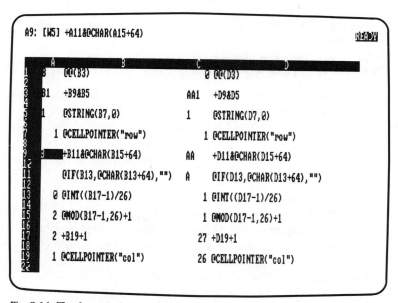

Fig. 8.14. The formula being constructed.

Describing the Formula

Following is a line-by-line description of the formula. Although this newly constructed 1-2-3 function may not have a great many uses, it illustrates how to use mathematical formulas to manipulate character data.

Line 19, @CELLPOINTER("col"), returns a number that represents the current column. This function converts the alphabetic columnlabeling scheme into a numeric scheme.

Line 17, +B19+1, increments the current column by 1.

Line 15, @MOD(B17-1, 26)+1, will always be in the range 1-26. The function is the numeric equivalent of the column or the second digit of the column heading.

Line 13, @INT((B17-1)/26), extracts the multiples of 26. When the column heading is a single character, the function returns a zero.

Line 11, @IF(B13, @CHAR(B13+64), ""), converts numbers into characters. If the number representing the leading column character is zero, the function returns a null string (""); otherwise, the function treats the number that forms its argument as an ordinal indicator and returns the equivalent character.

Line 9, +B11&@CHAR(B15+64), returns the alphabetic character for the second column character or for a single character.

Line 7, @CELLPOINTER("row"), returns the current row.

Line 5, @STRING(B7, 0), returns the string value of the current row.

Line 3, +B9&B5, ties the column and row strings together to form an address.

Line 1, @@(B3), returns the contents of the cell with the address specified in Line 3—in this case, the cell to the right of the cell pointer.

Caveat Programmer

One of the recurring themes in this book involves the problems associated with maintaining your work so that it will support later revision and modification. For programmers, complexity often seems to be its own reward. There is something satisfying about being able to put together something fantastically complicated and make it work. Unfortunately, 1-2-3 provides a fertile breeding ground for this kind of disease.

The generally recommended cure is to use generously the KISS method of programming: Keep It Simple, Stupid (no offense). And document, document, document. This whole section on nesting functions seems to fly in the face of such advice, and, indeed, potential trouble may be found here. Using the described methods to construct nested functions enables you to put together functions of such complexity that they are all but guaranteed uninterpretable after you enter them into a cell.

Cramming super-complex functions into a single cell may be necessary sometimes, but you can often avoid doing so. If you find yourself bumping into 1-2-3's 240-character formula limit, back up and see whether you can use a fresh, completely different approach to the problem—an approach that will be easier to sort out later on. If something has to be complicated, document what it does or how it works. You can use several techniques to help sort out programs after you construct them (see the section on debugging in Chapter 10).

Using Functions in Programs

A subset of the available functions is especially useful in programming. The argument could be made that all the functions are useful, but those listed here lend themselves especially well to controlling the flow of program execution. For a complete list of functions included in this chapter and their arguments, see table 8.1. These functions can be grouped into two general categories: functions that manipulate data for use with {IF} tests and functions that take some form of integer argument.

Table 8.1
Select 1-2-3 Functions

String

@EXACT(string1,string2)
@FIND(match string,source string,starting character)
@CLEAN(string)
@LEFT(string,length)
@LENGTH(string)
@LOWER(string)
@MID(source string,start position,length)
@PROPER(string)
@REPEAT(string,repeat number)
@REPLACE(source string,start position,length,insert string)
@RIGHT(string,length)
@STRING(number to convert,decimal places)
@TRIM(string)
@UPPER(string)
@CHAR(code number)
@CODE(character)
@VALUE(string)

Special

@@(cell reference)
@APP(application name,any function)
@CELL(string,range)
@CELLPOINTER(string)
@COLS(range)
@ROWS(range)

Error-Trapping

@ISERR(expression)
@ISNA(expression)
@ISNUMBER(expression)
@ISSTRING(expression)
@ERR
@NA

Logical

@IF(a,vtrue,vfalse)
@N(range)
@S(range)

Data Management

@VLOOKUP(test variable,range,column offset number)
@HLOOKUP(test variable,range,row offset number)
@CHOOSE(key,argument1,argument2, . . . , argument*n*)
@INDEX(range,column number,row number)

Statistical

@AVG(range)
@COUNT(range)
@SUM(range)

Database Statistical

@DAVG(Input range,Offset,Criterion range)
@DCOUNT(Input range,Offset,Criterion range)
@DSUM(Input range,Offset,Criterion range)

Mathematical

@INT(number or cell reference)
@SQRT(number or cell reference)

Special Mathematical

@MOD(number,divisor)

Trigonometric

@SIN(number or cell reference)

Date and Time

@DATEVALUE(date string)
@TIMEVALUE(time string)

Data Manipulation Functions

An important part of the "art" of programming in 1-2-3 is knowing how to use the functions that can test the condition of the worksheet and the data. Such tests give programs their appearance of intelligence, because the program changes its behavior according to the changing worksheet conditions. Especially important in this regard are @CELL, @CELLPOINTER, @VLOOKUP, and @HLOOKUP. The first two return information that is usually available only through visual inspection of the worksheet. The last two perform complex tests internally, provide positional information about items in a series (important for many database applications), and can perform arbitrary value conversions.

Integer Argument Functions

Most computer programming languages can perform controlled repetitions, usually in the form of a loop controlled by some kind of counter. In 1-2-3, the controlled-repetition mechanism is the {FOR} loop. Stored in a specified cell in the worksheet, a counter controls the loop and is incremented by some value every time the loop is executed. This simple concept is one of the aspects of programming that makes it powerful. By referencing the current value of the loop counter, you can change worksheet conditions so that the resulting program operation is systematically varied. For example, a loop can print a series of different reports, as opposed to multiple copies of one report, by systematically calling up a different report during each pass through the loop.

Because the values used by the {FOR} loop counter often take integer values, any function that takes integer arguments has the potential to convert the simple counting of the loop counter into a complex sequence of values or operations. The most notable of such functions are @INDEX and @CHOOSE. @VLOOKUP and @HLOOKUP also fall into this category.

Functions in This Section

Perhaps the common thread running through the functions in this section is that they are all somewhat unusual and therefore likely to be the last mastered (if learned at all). If your experience in learning 1-2-3 was anything like mine, you probably just avoided using these oddball functions if you could find a way to do the same thing with functions you *did* understand. The way these functions work is complicated and hard to grasp. They are the highest-level instructions in 1-2-3 and therefore the most powerful. A previous GUIDELINE recommended that you use functions whenever possible to make your programs shorter and more powerful. I like to think that every time I use one of these functions, I've put a good-sized chunk of my program into high-speed machine language and made the process of program writing that much shorter.

If these functions are new to you, you should take some time to become familiar with how they work. My experience, and one I've heard echoed by many 1-2-3 users, is that after you use and understand these functions, you will wonder how you ever got by without them. If you follow the general axiom that the more immediately obscure the purpose, the more useful the function, you should be able to guide yourself through the process of mastering the best of the bunch.

An Undocumented Improvement

One of the nicest improvements incorporated into Release 2 of 1-2-3 is so subtle that months passed before I even noticed it. Prior to Release 2 (and with Symphony), many functions were fussy about the type of argument used in the parentheses. Many 1-2-3 functions required that address arguments have a specific form: either a range address or a cell address. A *range address* is an address that specifies the corners of a range, such as B2..D4. Conversely, a *cell address* is the address of a single cell, such as B2. Note that the specification of a single cell as a range (B2..B2) is a range address, *not* a cell address. If a function was given a cell address when a range address was expected, the function returned ERR. To confuse matters even further, some functions (@CELL, @S, and @N) that operated on a single cell required the target cell to be specified as a range address.

Prior to Release 2 in 1-2-3 and in Symphony, range names could also cause problems with "fussy" functions. A range name can be assigned to a cell address or range address, but once assigned, no visual indication is provided of which type of assignment has been made. The fussy functions would balk at an improperly assigned range name, which resulted in some difficult debugging problems.

With Release 2, the problem is no more. Functions have been made "friendly." The address arguments must still be in either range address or cell address form, as before, but the conversion now occurs automatically as you type the function. If you inadvertently enter the wrong argument type, 1-2-3 converts the argument for you—a much-needed and, in my copy of 1-2-3, undocumented improvement.

The ! Specification

The functions that required range arguments were first introduced in Symphony. When Lotus released Version 1.1 of Symphony, it included a special function to make entering range addresses easier. Although no longer necessary, this special function is mentioned here for several reasons. First, Release 2 still supports the function. In addition, you might use a command language program originally written for Symphony that uses this feature. Finally, this special function is discussed in the 1-2-3 *Reference Manual.*

To convert a cell address to a range address while entering a formula, you can precede the cell address or range name with an exclamation point (!). 1-2-3 then converts the cell address into a range address. For instance, if you are using the @S function to return the string value of cell A5, you type

   @S(!A5)

As soon as you press the Enter key, 1-2-3 converts the address to a range address and enters the formula as

   @S(A5..A5)

If that cell is named INPUT, you could type

   @S(!INPUT)

1-2-3 would enter this formula as @S(A5..A5), although @S(INPUT) would appear in the control panel.

You can also use the ! specification in POINT mode. Simply enter the ! and then point. When you enter the formula into the cell, 1-2-3 converts all such specifications to ranges. When 1-2-3 is in POINT mode, you can also convert a cell to a range by anchoring that cell while pointing. Unlike the ! specification, anchoring the cell causes it to appear immediately as a range address in the control panel. Mixing the ! and anchoring methods causes no problems; you get a range address using either method or both.

You can also use the ! specification ahead of a range name that's already specified as having a range address. In this case, the ! specification has no effect.

If you use a command language program that was originally written for Symphony, you may find the ! specification used in the program. If you enter the ! ahead of a cell address or range name in a command language instruction, 1-2-3 evaluates the cell in question as a range address. When you enter the ! into a command language instruction, ! appears in that form. The conversion doesn't take place until the program evaluates the formula. For example, suppose that you type

    {IF @N(!A3)=2}{BEEP}

The formula appears exactly as shown in your program, but is evaluated as if you had typed

    {IF @N(A3..A3)=2}{BEEP}

Release 2 of 1-2-3 is tolerant of all types of address specifications in command language programs as well as in the worksheet. You could write the preceding instruction like this, and it would work just fine:

    {IF @N(A3)=2}{BEEP}

Probably the only reason you would ever need the ! specification is for a command language program written in 1-2-3 that was later to be used in Symphony. Note, however, that as of this writing, Symphony is still unfriendly about address types.

The @@ Function

From a programmer's point of view, the @@ function is probably the most powerful 1-2-3 function, and also probably the most difficult to understand. The @@ function is mentioned in the 1-2-3 *Reference Manual*, but that description is brief and incomplete. The @@ function performs what is known as indirect addressing or a *pointer* function. In other languages, pointers form the basis for implementing stacks, queues, linked lists, B-tree structures, sparse matrices, and other fairly advanced data structures.

The primary advantage of pointers is that they enable you to create programs whose execution time is more closely linked to the number of operations performed instead of to the size of the data set. For example, with pointers, adding a name to a sorted customer list would take about the same amount of time whether the customer list contained 5 or 50,000 entries.

Pointers are also used in programming techniques that optimize memory use, such as sparse matrix handling. A *sparse matrix* is an array of numbers (much like a spreadsheet is an array of cells) in which most of the entries are empty. Rather than storing a lot of zeros, you can use pointers to create a simulated array of linked cells. The storage requirement is then reduced to little more than what is required for the nonzero entries.

The @@ function has important uses in the command language. You can use @@ to control the arguments of other functions from within a command language program. Although uses for this capability may not be immediately apparent, when @@ is needed, it is invaluable. The best way to get a feel for how to use @@ is to look at some programs that use it.

Syntax

@@(cell reference)

Figures 8.15 and 8.16 show how @@ works. An additional range is involved in each application. @@'s operation varies according to whether @@ is used separately or as an argument to another function. The operation also varies according to the kind of argument given to @@ and required by the function in which @@ is nested. Because a number of possible configurations are possible, the @@ function will be discussed in some detail.

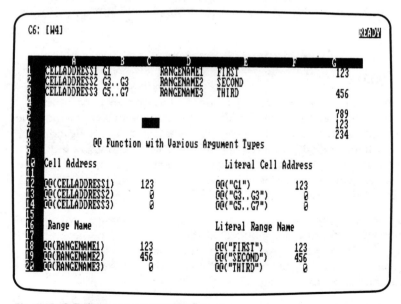

Fig. 8.15. @@ used as a separate function.

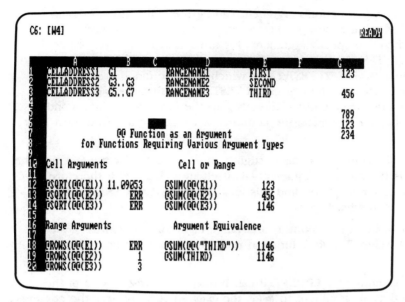

Fig. 8.16. @@ used as a function argument.

Figures 8.15 and 8.16 both contain some reference ranges and range names that the @@ function uses. At the top of the screen, CELLADDRESS and RANGENAME are labels that indicate the range name applied to the cell immediately to their right. This convention is the same one you use in naming macros. The contents of the CELLADDRESS cells are the addresses of the range names on the corresponding lines in the window. The cells containing the address and range names are called the *pointer* cells, and the addresses are the *pointers*, or *target addresses*. The ranges that the pointers point to are at the right of the screen; these cells and ranges are the *targets*.

@@ as a Separate Function

Figure 8.15 shows the @@ function used by itself. You should notice two things about the way in which the @@ function works. The first is that all four methods of specifying the *cell reference* argument have the same effect.

If the @@ function's argument is a range name, the function returns the contents of the cell specified by the address that references the contents of the named range. In other words, the named range contains a pointer to another cell, the contents of which @@ returns. Given a range name, @@ looks in that cell and finds an address. @@ then takes that address and looks up its contents. This pointer may itself be in the form of a cell address or range name.

Alternatively, the @@ function's argument can be the cell address or range name specified as a literal string—that is, enclosed in quotation marks. The same is true when you specify arguments for other functions. If you enter the formula @LEFT("TEST",2), the formula returns the value "TE". You could also enter the formula as @LEFT(TEST,2), in which case the function returns the leftmost two characters in the cell called TEST. In the first case, @LEFT's argument is a literal string entered directly into the formula. In the second case, the argument is a cell reference, the contents of which the function must look up.

Interpreting an @@ function is made slightly more complex by the fact that the string—which is the function argument—is itself an address. You therefore have an address of an address. If you find this idea confusing, try working with the examples and watch what happens.

If the pointer cell's content is not a valid range name or cell address, @@ returns the ERR value. The @@ function returns a zero if the pointer cell is blank.

Note that @CELL and @CELLPOINTER can return an address. If one of these functions is used as an argument to @@, the @@ function returns the contents of the specified cell. This procedure is equivalent to specifying the "contents" argument in @CELL or @CELLPOINTER.

$$@@(@CELLPOINTER("address")) = @CELLPOINTER("contents")$$

Form of Target Address

The second thing to notice about figure 8.15 is that the value that @@ returns depends on the kind of address specified as the pointer. If the target cell specified by the pointer address is a single cell, @@ returns that cell's contents in the manner shown in table 8.2.

A convenient way to think about what @@ returns is that it works as a direct reference to the target cell. That is, @@("G1") returns the same values as +G1.

If the target is a range instead of a cell, @@ returns a zero. If an ERR or NA condition exists in the specified range, however, @@ returns ERR or NA. Note that this kind of reference has no equivalent as has the single cell reference described in the preceding paragraph.

A target address specified as a range address (G1..G3) doesn't have to correspond to any currently assigned range name. The address can refer to any cell or range of cells. Also, although two periods appear in the range specifications, only one is required.

Table 8.2
Values Returned by @@

Contents of Target Cell	@@ Returns
Number	Number
Numeric formula	Formula result
String	String
String formula	Formula result
Repeating label (\ prefix)	Nonrepeating label (left-justified)
Other label (| ' ^ " prefixes)	Left-justified label
Blank	0
ERR, NA	ERR, NA

@@ *as a Function Argument*

You can use @@ as an argument to a second function—an application for which @@ was undoubtedly intended. The function in which @@ is placed then uses the cell or range in the pointer cell as an argument, as if the target range had been entered directly into the function. Therefore, by simply changing the label in the pointer cell, you can apply a different cell or range to the function. Because more than one function can reference the pointer cell, you can alter any number of functions simultaneously by changing one target address.

Figure 8.16 shows how @@ works as the argument to a second function. The @@ function is a model of flexibility when it comes to address type. The @@ function accepts as an argument a one-cell address, a range specified as cell addresses, a one-cell name, or a range name. The parent function's final output depends on the kind of arguments that the functions require.

When the Lotus programmers modified the fussy functions, they missed one. When @@ is used as an indirect address argument, the parent functions display all their old idiosyncrasies. In figure 8.16, the @SQRT function listed under the heading Cell Arguments requires a single cell as an argument. RANGENAME2 and RANGENAME3 contain a single- and multiple-cell pointer range, respectively. Both arguments cause @SQRT to return the ERR value. The @ROWS listing, which requires a range argument, returns the opposite set of ERR conditions.

The first @SUM listing under the heading Cell or Range works with either set of pointers. Any function that takes a "list" as an argument also works with either set of pointers. (See the 1-2-3 *Reference Manual* for details.) The final set of functions in figure 8.16—the two @SUM functions—demonstrates that either using @@ with a literal range name as an argument or using that range name as a cell reference produces equivalent results.

Examples

The @@ function, although complex, can make possible some truly sophisticated programming techniques. The following examples demonstrate some uses in command language programs of this unusual function. The first technique is known in programming as a *circular queue*. This program can operate on a list of data, one item at a time, and then return to the first item after processing the last. The second example uses a small circular queue, only two elements, which alternate as the program executes.

A Circular Queue

The program in figure 8.17 displays data from the first cell in a specific range. The program uses seven ranges; each includes four rows, although only two are used in this macro. The additional rows could contain data that a continuation of the macro would use. For instance, extra rows could contain file names that could be used to retrieve automatically a different file each day.

As listed, the ranges contain only two cells of data each. The first cell contains the name of a day of the week. The second cell contains a pointer, which is the name of the next range in the sequence. Notice that in RANGE7, the pointer is to RANGE1, the beginning of the list. This use of pointers forms a circular queue. Each time you invoke the \d macro, the RANGEREF cell is updated with the pointer contained in the current range. The range specified in RANGEREF then becomes the current range. By repeatedly invoking this macro, you cause the range names to move from RANGE1 to RANGE7 and back to RANGE1 again. Although the operation of this macro is a little complicated, you can easily see how the macro works by running it on your computer. Invoke the macro several times and watch how the various references change.

Cells B14 and B16 contain functions that reference the next range and current range, respectively. The formulas in each of these cells are listed in column D.

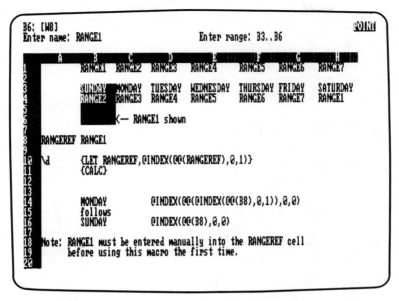

Fig. 8.17. A circular queue macro that uses @@.

Specifying 0 as the last argument of @INDEX returns the data portion of the specified range. Specifying 1 as that argument returns the pointer to the next range. Note that the formula in row 14 can reference the next range in the series by nesting @INDEX references to the pointer. Each additional level of nesting causes the formula to "look ahead" an additional level.

You can rearrange the order of the list by changing the pointers. The name specified as a pointer is always the next range called.

A Toggle Macro

Figure 8.18 shows a simple modification of the macro in figure 8.17. The list of ranges has been reduced to two. This creates a *toggle* condition: first one range is accessed, then the other, then the first again, and so on.

This macro is constructed so that it continues along one of two opposite paths. The first time the macro is invoked, a second window is created, and the cell pointer moves to a specified location in that window. The second time the macro is invoked, it returns the screen to its original, single-window state. The basic macro used to set up the split screen is discussed in detail in Chapter 5, "Macro 4: Macro Window." This strategy, which can be used to alternate any two opposing functions, has the advantage of using only one macro key for execution. Using one key for both functions not only saves an Alt-[letter] key sequence but makes remembering the function easier. You need to memorize only one key instead of two.

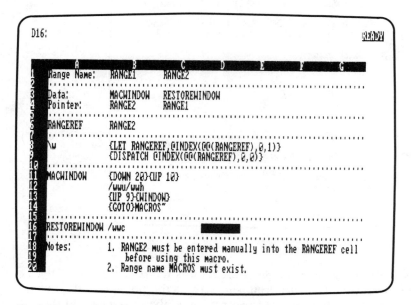

Fig. 8.18. A toggle macro.

Comments

Within command language instructions, the @@ function works only as a source argument. The following operation, for example, is legal:

{LET REFCELL,@@(REMOTE)}

The operation that follows, however, is not legal. An error message appears when you try to execute the function.

{LET @@(REMOTE),REFCELL}

Similarly, you can use @@ in any of the arguments in @INDEX but only as the final (source) argument in {PUT}.

When included in a parent function's argument, the @@ function performs only the pointing function. Notice that in figure 8.19, the unnested version of the formula doesn't work properly. when you use the technique described earlier for assembling complex nested functions, you must include @@ references as a single formula.

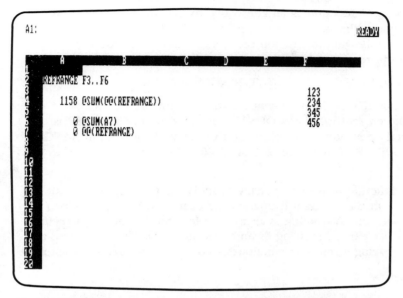

Fig. 8.19. The @@ function placed inside the parent function and used as an indirect argument.

The @@ function can create a test to determine whether a range name specifies a cell or range. The following, for instance, evaluates as TRUE if RANGENAME contains a pointer to a single cell; as FALSE, if RANGENAME contains a pointer to a range.

{IF @ISERR(@ROWS(@@(RANGENAME)))}

You can use the ! specification in the target address. This holds true for target addresses that are cell addresses and target addresses that are range names. You can, for example, use the following in place of G2..G2.

!G2

Or you can use the following to force the parent function to interpret RANGE1 as a range address (as opposed to a cell address).

!RANGE1

You must use the ! specification in the target address and not as the argument to the @@ function. The following constructions are therefore both illegal:

@CELL("type",@@(!RANGEREF))

@CELL("type",!@@(RANGEREF))

Instead of these, use the ! specification on the label contained in RANGEREF.

You can use the @@ function as an alternative to the dynamic command language instructions that are constructed from string formulas (see Chapter 9). For example, the following instruction returns the number of rows in several ranges, placing the result in the cell named REFERENCE:

{LET REFERENCE,@@("range"&@STRING(COUNTER,0))}

The string formula that is the argument for the @@ function is evaluated according to the current value of COUNTER. If the value of COUNTER is one, the string formula evaluates to RANGE1, and the number of rows in RANGE1 is placed in REFERENCE. If the value of COUNTER is two, the number of rows in RANGE2 is placed in REFERENCE.

Using the @@ function instead of a string formula has two advantages: the formula is visible in the program listing instead of hidden behind its string formula result; and the instruction is always recalculated before it is executed (something that isn't true for string formula instructions). The advantages and disadvantages of string formula instructions are discussed further in Chapters 9 and 10.

The @APP Function

Undocumented 1-2-3 Feature

At the time of this writing, Lotus has announced plans to make available for 1-2-3 some add-in application programs. This add-in capability, which is presently available in Symphony, will add to and extend 1-2-3's functions. The application program will become a temporary part of 1-2-3, with its own menu system, commands, and so on.

Details of how the additional applications will be connected to 1-2-3 haven't been announced. If the system is similar to Symphony, however, the @APP function will indicate whether a particular application is loaded.

@APP currently exists in 1-2-3—that is, you can enter it into the worksheet—but it doesn't do anything. Because this function is currently nonfunctional, the description that follows is based on how the function works in Symphony. If you get one of the forthcoming application programs, be sure to test @APP before using it.

In operation, @APP tests for the active presence of an application program. In some sense, @APP parallels @ISERR and @ISNA, except that @APP's syntax is different.

Syntax

@APP(application name,any function)

The @APP function requires two arguments. The first is the application's name; the second, any valid function. If the application is attached, @APP evaluates the second argument. If the application isn't attached, @APP returns ERR. The second argument can be anything that usually can be entered into a cell.

Examples

Figure 8.20 shows several examples of the @APP function. Lines 17 and 18 contain simple examples of the function's use. The macro in line 6 checks to see whether an application (called TOOLS, in this example) is attached, before invoking a command from the attached system. If TOOLS isn't attached, the macro calls a subroutine (named PROMPTDISK) that prompts the user to insert the correct disk; then the macro attaches the application. If the application is already attached, the subroutine is skipped.

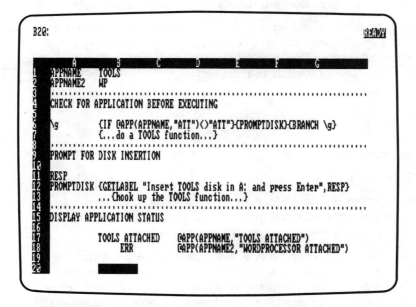

Fig. 8.20. Examples of the @APP function.

Comments

After the attachable applications become available, the @APP function will be important for command language programming. Lacking both an application to test and documentation from Lotus on @APP, I'm unable to offer much insight into the function's use. My guess is that a reason must exist for @APP's double-argument design. The function's primary purpose seems to be to guard against trying to invoke an unattached function or attaching one that is already connected. If the @APP function's only purpose is to guard against this kind of error, I would have preferred, for consistency's sake, a function with the same syntax as @ISERR—for example, an @ISATTACHED function.

The @CELL and @CELLPOINTER Functions

The @CELL and @CELLPOINTER functions provide the kind of information you would ordinarily glean only from visually inspecting the worksheet. These two functions give you, in a sense, a connection to the worksheet's structure. You can use them to create programs that "inspect" the worksheet. @CELLPOINTER in particular enables you to create programs that mimic operations, cursor movements, and all procedures that you usually would perform manually.

Both functions return values based on one of nine arguments. @CELL returns information about a specific cell that is specified as a range address or range name. @CELLPOINTER returns the same information about the cell indicated by the cell pointer at the time of the last calculation.

Syntax

@CELL(string,range)

@CELLPOINTER(string)

For both functions, *string* can be a literal string enclosed in quotation marks, a string formula, or a reference to a cell that contains a string or string formula. The string can be upper- or lowercase, or a mixture of both.

For @CELL, *range* must be a range address, although 1-2-3 will convert the address form for you if you enter a cell address. You can also use the @@ function here. However, the target address, which is a label in the pointer cell, must be in range form. A target address entered as a cell address causes @CELL to return the ERR value.

String Argument Types

You can give @CELL and @CELLPOINTER the following *string* arguments. Note that the values that these functions return pertain to the status of the worksheet at the time of the last recalculation. Any illegal *string* argument causes the functions to return the ERR value.

Address

Address returns the address of the specified cell or position of the cell pointer. The address is returned as a string with dollar signs in the form of an absolute reference—for instance, A100. Range names are not returned.

Col

Col returns the numeric value equivalent to the column number of the specified cell or of the cell pointer. Column A is 1, column B is 2, . . . and column IV is 256. (Also see *Row.*)

Format

Format returns a string code indicating the format setting of the current cell or the cell at the cell pointer location. If no format is specified, *format* returns the /Worksheet Global Format. This last feature creates an interesting effect when the 1-2-3 screen is split into two windows. Because each of the two windows can have its own Global Format, @CELL and @CELLPOINTER can return different results for the same cell. The result returned is tied to the window that contained the cell pointer at the last recalculation, rather than to a specific cell. The *format* codes are the following:

C0..C15	Currency
,0..,15	, (Comma)
F0..F15	Fixed
P0..P15	Percent
G	General
D1..D5	Date
D6..D9	Time
S1..S15	Scientific
+	+/-
T	Text
H	Hidden

These format codes are those that appear in the control panel for a specifically formatted cell. The digits following the letter code therefore indicate decimal places or format type (in the case of **Date** and **Time**). Note that the **Time** formats are a subset of the **Date** formats. What shows as **Time 1** in the **/Range** Format menu appears as code D6 in the cell itself.

Prefix

Prefix returns a one-character string corresponding to the label prefix of the specified cell or of the cell in the cell pointer location. If the cell contains anything other than a label, *prefix* returns a null string. The null string, which appears blank, evaluates as a string and has a length of zero. Here are the possible prefix values:

'	Left-aligned
^	Centered
"	Right-aligned
\	Repeating
|	Printer control

Row

Row returns the numeric value equivalent to the row number of the specified cell or of the cell pointer. Possible values are 1–8192. (Also see *col.*)

Type

Type returns a one-character string for the kind of entry in the specified cell. Here are the possible values:

b	Blank
l	Label
v	Value

Type returns the v string if the cell contains a number, a numeric or string formula, or the ERR or NA values.

Width

Width returns a numeric value equivalent to the width of the specified cell. Possible values are 1–240. Like the **/Worksheet Global Format** setting, when the screen is split, the width of a specific cell is tied to the current window, not to the cell itself. The value that *width* returns depends on which window contained the cell pointer when the worksheet was last recalculated.

Contents

Contents returns the contents of the specified cell as follows:

Cell Contents	Value Returned
String	String
String formula	String
Number	Number
Numeric formula	Number
Blank	0 (zero)
ERR	ERR
NA	NA

The result is also ERR or NA if the current formula evaluates to that value—with one exception. If /Worksheet Global Recalculation is set to Automatic, and you enter @ERR, @NA, or any formula that evaluates to ERR or NA, @CELLPOINTER("contents") returns a zero instead of the expected ERR or NA. Pressing the Calc key (F9) causes @CELLPOINTER("contents") to return the correct values. @CELL works as expected in all cases.

Protect

Protect returns a 0 if the specified cell has been set to Unprotected. If the cell isn't set, the cell is "protected," and the function returns a 1. The /Worksheet Global Protection setting isn't related to the value returned, only to the protection status of the target cell.

Example

This example illustrates how @CELLPOINTER can be used to examine the worksheet and automate an operation that otherwise would require visual inspection of the worksheet. The program presented in this section was developed to eliminate specific kinds of duplicates in a database. The original database contained cost reports for work orders that were updated periodically. As part of an analysis of the accuracy of the work order estimates, the program compared the original estimate to the most recently entered cost. Figure 8.21 shows part of the database.

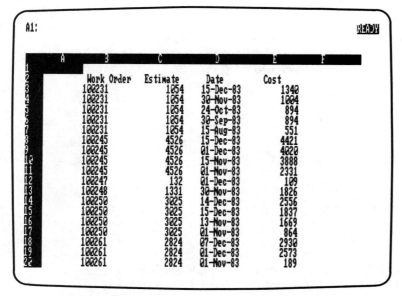

Fig. 8.21. A work order database.

Although the work order numbers and estimates contain duplicates, the unique date and cost information prevented the use of 1-2-3's **/Data Query Delete** or **/Data Query Unique** commands to reduce the database to the required subset of records. In figure 8.21, the database has already been sorted using **Work Order** as the **Primary-Key** (Ascending order) and **Date** as the **Secondary-Key** (Descending order).

When the database is sorted this way, the most recent record (and therefore the one to be kept for analysis) is always at the top of a series of duplicates. Going through the records and eliminating the duplicates is therefore easy. The program in figure 8.22 uses @CELLPOINTER to automate the process.

You start the program with the cell pointer in the **Work Order** field's first record (cell B3 in fig. 8.21).

In line 4, {LET REFCELL, @CELLPOINTER("contents")} copies the cell pointer's current contents to a reference cell called REFCELL.

In line 5, {DOWN} moves the cell pointer down to the next row in the database.

Two tests are then made. Line 6

    {IF @CELLPOINTER("type")="b"}{QUIT}

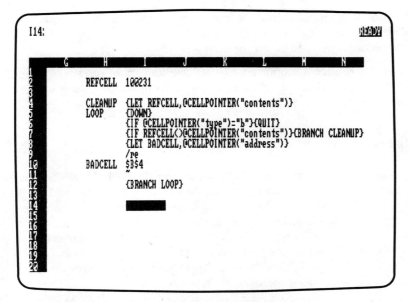

Fig. 8.22. @CELLPOINTER used to eliminate duplicates.

uses the "type" argument to determine whether the cell is blank. If it is, the cell pointer has gone through the entire database, and the program is finished. If the cell isn't blank, the next test is made.

Line 7, {IF REFCELL<>@CELLPOINTER("contents")}{BRANCH CLEANUP}, compares the contents of the cell pointer in its new location with the contents of the cell pointer's previous location (now saved in REFCELL). If the contents aren't the same, the entry isn't a duplicate. The program then starts again, copying the cell pointer's new contents to REFCELL.

Line 8, {LET BADCELL, @CELLPOINTER("address")}, specifies that if the contents are the same, the new row is a duplicate, and the program then copies @CELLPOINTER's "address" argument into the macro at BADCELL.

BADCELL becomes the target address for the /Range Erase command, which begins in line 9 and terminates in line 11. The program thus erases the duplicate cell.

In line 12, the program branches to LOOP, where the macro tests the next entry against the entry stored in REFCELL.

This entire process is repeated until the test in line 6 ends program execution. The result is that the program eliminates all but the first entry for a specific work order number.

When the program is finished, the database can be re-sorted. All the records with erased entries will then appear at the top of the database, leaving the desired subset of records grouped at the bottom.

I used this program to reduce a 3,600-record database with duplicates to 790 records without duplicates. The operation took about 30 minutes, during which time I got to take a break.

Comments

One of the disadvantages of using these functions, especially @CELLPOINTER, is that they have so many characters. Therefore, the functions are tedious to type, and they reach the 240-character formula limit quickly. One way to shorten the typing process, if you are going to use these functions frequently, is to create some brief range names to use as reference cells for the string arguments. If you name a cell *C* and enter the word *contents* into it, you can type *@CELLPOINTER(C)* instead of *@CELLPOINTER("contents")*. This process even saves having to type those bothersome quotation marks.

The @CELLPOINTER function is handy if you are trying to automate a complex process and want to watch what's happening. The disadvantage to using this function is that programs that use it run more slowly than programs that use direct references, @LOOKUP, or @INDEX to access worksheet data.

The @CHOOSE Function

@CHOOSE is one of several functions that takes an integer argument. The integer is used to select from items in a list. Among the @CHOOSE function's more useful aspects are that all its selections are in a single cell and that the list's contents can be anything from simple data to complex expressions.

Syntax

@CHOOSE(key,argument1,argument2,...,argument*n*)

@CHOOSE first evaluates the *key*. Then the function uses that value to select an entry from the list that follows and uses that entry as the cell contents. As with all other functions that use a numbered position, @CHOOSE selects the first item in the list if the value of *key* is zero. If *key* evaluates to 1, @CHOOSE uses the next item, and so forth.

The *key* can be a number, a cell reference, a range name, or a formula. If the *key* isn't an integer, 1-2-3 truncates it and uses only the integer portion.

The *arguments* can be anything that is a valid cell entry. In the same formula, you can use string values, numeric values, string and numeric formulas, and special values (such as @ERR).

@CHOOSE returns the ERR value under any of the following conditions:

1. The *key* evaluates to a negative number.
2. The *key* is a string value.
3. The *key* evaluates to a number larger than the number of items in the contents list.
4. The *key* evaluates to ERR.
5. The selected contents evaluate to ERR.

You can think of @CHOOSE as a specialized form of nested @IF function in which *key* is always evaluated as an integer, and a condition for each value of the argument is required, as in the following example:

@CHOOSE(x,"Yes","No","Maybe")

This formula is equivalent to

@IF(@INT(x)=0,"Yes",@IF(@INT(x)=1,"No",@IF(@INT(x)=2, "Maybe",@ERR)))

Examples

Figure 8.23 shows an example of how you can use @CHOOSE to substitute string values within a macro. The {FOR} loop counter is used as the *key* to the @CHOOSE formula in B7 (notice the formula displayed in the control panel). The {RECALC} instruction ensures that the @CHOOSE formula is updated before it is used.

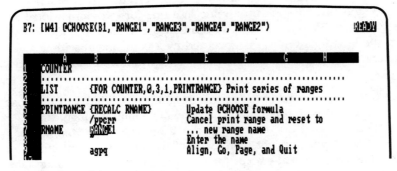

Fig. 8.23. @CHOOSE used to select string values.

Figure 8.24 shows another use for @CHOOSE. The *arguments* are formulas used in a 2-way /Data Table. The {FOR} loop counter is again used as the *key* argument in @CHOOSE. The program runs the /Data Table, then performs a file-extract operation to save the table to a disk file. A second @CHOOSE function provides the extract file names. This process creates a 3-way /Data Table.

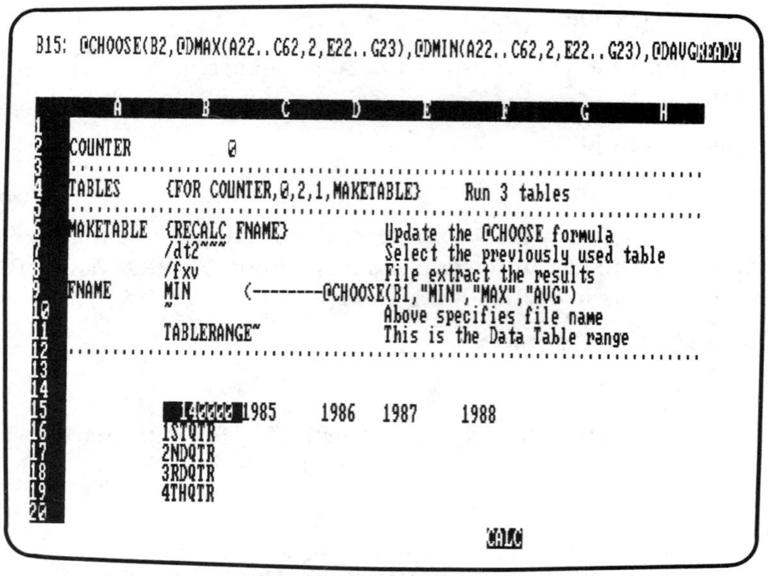

```
B15: @CHOOSE(B2,@DMAX(A22..C62,2,E22..G23),@DMIN(A22..C62,2,E22..G23),@DAVG  READY

        A        B        C      D       E       F        G         H
1
2  COUNTER         0
3  ..............................................................................
4  TABLES     {FOR COUNTER,0,2,1,MAKETABLE}    Run 3 tables
5  ..............................................................................
6  MAKETABLE  {RECALC FNAME}              Update the @CHOOSE formula
7             /dt2~~~                     Select the previously used table
8             /fxv                        File extract the results
9  FNAME      MIN       (--------@CHOOSE(B1,"MIN","MAX","AVG")
10            ~                           Above specifies file name
11            TABLERANGE~                 This is the Data Table range
12 ..............................................................................
13
14
15            14     1985    1986    1987    1988
16            1STQTR
17            2NDQTR
18            3RDQTR
19            4THQTR
20

                                          CALC
```

Fig. 8.24. @CHOOSE used to select formulas.

The @HLOOKUP and @VLOOKUP Functions

@HLOOKUP and @VLOOKUP are probably the most versatile 1-2-3 functions. @HLOOKUP and @VLOOKUP look up a value in a one- or two-dimensional table, according to two different kinds of criteria. In one dimension, the lookup (the value that the functions return) is governed by a comparison with a supplied argument. In the other dimension, the lookup is driven by an integer offset value.

Since Release 1A, these functions have improved significantly; they can now use string values both as returned values and as arguments. Oddly enough, this spectacular improvement isn't documented in the 1-2-3 *Reference Manual* (at least not in my edition), an oversight that I would expect to see corrected. Both these functions are identical except for the orientation of the lookup table they use as a source. Which function you use will probably depend on aesthetics as much as on any practical considerations.

The lookup table is described in figure 8.25. The lookup table itself is specified by the *range* argument (see "Syntax"). Within the *range*, the leftmost column of values (the key range) is used by the lookup function to make comparisons.

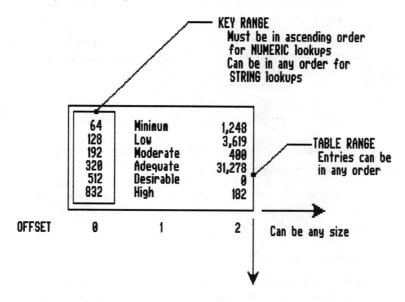

Fig. 8.25. A sample lookup table.

Syntax

@HLOOKUP(test variable,range,row offset number)

@VLOOKUP(test variable,range,column offset number)

The Range Argument

The *range* argument refers to the range of cells in which 1-2-3 performs the comparison and offset lookups. This range, which includes the entire lookup table, must contain at least two cells. Usually, this range consists of a single row or rectangular range. The key to the lookup table is a single row or column in which the comparisons are made. If the comparisons are to be made on a horizontal row of values, you use @HLOOKUP. If the comparisons are to be made on a vertical column of values, you use @VLOOKUP. The comparisons are made on only the leftmost column or the top row, regardless of whether you have specified a multicolumn or multirow range as the *range*.

The *test variables* in the key range of the lookup table can be either string or numeric, but they *all* must be of one type or the other. String and numeric formulas are also valid table range values. For string lookups, the test variable entries can be in any order. For numeric lookups, the entries must both be unique and in ascending order.

If you have used this function with Symphony, you will find that a few changes have been made in Release 2. With Symphony, you don't have to specify the whole lookup table as the *range* argument, and you can use negative offset values. In Release 2, both these characteristics can create recalculation problems by defeating the Natural order Recalculation scheme. For that reason, these capabilities have probably been dropped from the 1-2-3 version of the LOOKUP functions.

The Test Variable Argument

The rules governing the *test variable* differ when a string value, as opposed to a numeric value, is used as a lookup argument.

The Test Variable Argument with a String Value

If the *test variable* argument is a string, 1-2-3 looks for an exact match in the key column or row of the *range*. If no match is found, an ERR value is returned. If 1-2-3 finds a match, the program moves to the right (@VLOOKUP) or down (@HLOOKUP), according to the number of cells indicated in the *offset* argument, to find the value to return.

TRAP: Failure to supply an exact match as a *test variable* argument is the error most frequently made with string lookups.

As with the @EXACT function, the strings must match exactly in order for 1-2-3 to find the *test variable* argument in the table. Capitalization, extra spaces, or foreign-language characters can spoil a match.

TIP: To avoid lookup errors, always use capital letters when you create the key range of your lookup tables and use the @UPPER function on the *test variable* string.

The form of the function would then be

@VLOOKUP(@UPPER(test variable),range,offset)

The Test Variable Argument with a Numeric Value

With numeric test variables, which work somewhat differently from string lookups, approximate matches are possible. If a number doesn't match exactly,

1-2-3 uses the next-higher number in the comparison range as a match. If the *test variable* argument is less than the smallest value in the comparison range, that smallest value becomes the match. ERR is returned if the *test variable* argument is greater than the largest value in the comparison range.

The Offset Argument

The *offset* argument determines how far (in columns or rows) 1-2-3 looks from the matched value in the comparison range to find the table value to return. The column immediately to the right of the comparison range (VLOOKUP) or below the comparison range (HLOOKUP) has an offset of 1. The *offset* argument can be any size, as long as the cell that *offset* specifies is not off the edge of the worksheet.

A zero offset causes the lookup to occur in the comparison range itself. When this offset is specified in a numeric lookup, the value of the matched cell is returned. If zero is specified as the offset for a string lookup, a number is returned that indicates the position of the matched label in the comparison range, with the first position being zero.

@VLOOKUP Recode

If you have used statistical programs, you are probably familiar with the concept of recoding data values. This process enables you to redefine the values in a database or combine several different values into superordinate categories. Using the @LOOKUP functions, you can easily recode data values.

Suppose that you have a database for which you are creating several output reports. The database contains sales data from stores in 12 different states. Your report, however, must show the data for the 4 divisions spread over the 12-state region. The states and their corresponding divisions are listed in figure 8.26.

You can solve this problem in numerous ways. You could add a column to the database and generate a formula that would translate from state to division. Or you could use a criterion range with a row to match each of the state codes. You could also go through your database and physically change all the entries (horrors!). But another still-easier method, which uses a LOOKUP function, is available.

You have already seen, in figure 8.26, the @VLOOKUP table that will generate the translation. To generate a /Data Table showing the total sales for each division, you would use the ranges specified in figure 8.27. The INPUTCELL and DATATABLE ranges are as shown. The Criterion range for the data table is RECODE_CR (B5..B6). Notice the relative reference in the formula

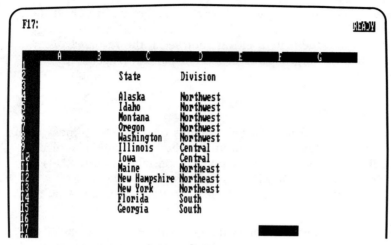

Fig. 8.26. Desired recoding of State to Division.

—STATE—which refers to the state entry in the database. On the other hand, the references to the lookup table (from fig. 8.26) and the INPUTCELL are absolute. If these ranges aren't specified as described, the @DSUM formula won't work properly.

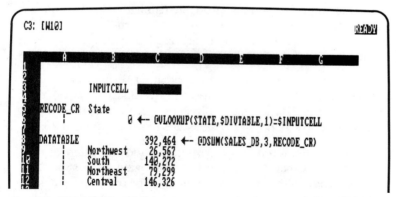

Fig. 8.27. @VLOOKUP recoding.

Case Statement: Data Transformation

If you are accustomed to programming in high-level languages, you probably have encountered something called the *case* statement. The case statement controls program execution when a number of choices are available, similar to the way choices are selected from a menu. Lower-level languages, such as BASIC, don't support the case construct. In those languages, the only way to achieve such selection is with a series of IF statements. For example, the following statements demonstrate computations on an irregular function.

```
100 IF (X > = 0 AND X < 1) THEN Y = 3 * X + 2
110 IF (X > = 1 AND X < 4) THEN Y = X^2
120 IF (X > =4 AND X < 5) THEN Y = X^3
130 IF (X > = 5 AND X < 7) THEN Y = X^4
140 IF X >= 7 THEN Y = X^5
```

The case statement is a specialized form of IF statement that simplifies the handling of such conditions in a much more readable form. Following is an example of how the same function would be written in Pascal.

```
case int(x) of
        0: y := 3 * x + 2;
    1,2,3: y := x^2;
        4: y := x^3;
      5,6: y := x^4;
else
            y := x^5;
end;
```

Note: Standard Pascal does not support the use of the else statement with the case statement. Most implementations of the language, however, provide some sort of extension that allows the else statement to be used this way.

Performing this kind of data transformation in the command language is very simple (see fig. 8.28). The {LET} instruction uses an @VLOOKUP table, which appears in columns D and E.

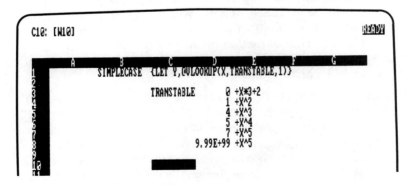

Fig. 8.28. A simple case statement.

Case Statement: Branching

This kind of multiple "if" condition can exist when the result of the test determines the flow of program execution. For example, the following series of instructions might be found at the beginning of a BASIC error-handling subroutine.

```
100 IF ERR = 50 THEN Y = 1: GOTO 1000
110 IF ERR = 51 THEN Y = 2: GOTO 1000
120 IF ERR = 52 THEN GOTO 2000
130 IF ERR = 53 THEN GOTO 3000
140 IF ERR >= 54 THEN Y = 3: GOTO 1000
```

The subroutine returns the variable ERR, which contains an error code. The program branches to different routines that are set up to handle specific kinds of errors. Coding the same program in Pascal would produce something like the following.

```
case ERR of
    50: procedure1(1);
    51: procedure1(2);
    52: procedure2;
    53: procedure3;
else
        procedure1(3);
end;
```

Performing case statement branching in 1-2-3 isn't as elegant as performing case statement data transformations. However, you can use a LOOKUP function to simulate a kind of case statement branching (see fig. 8.29).

Because the procedure is a little complicated, figure 8.29 will be reviewed a section at a time. The main part of the command language program contains the {ONERROR} statement listed in BRANCHCASE, which is the standard command language error-handling instruction. If an error occurs, the error message is entered into ERRMESSAGE. The instruction pointer is then directed to SELECTFIX, which acts as a switching station for the error handling that will be performed in a series of separate routines.

The {DISPATCH} instruction in SELECTFIX uses the @VLOOKUP function to select the subroutine to be executed. {DISPATCH} is described in Chapter 12. {DISPATCH}'s basic function is to transfer the instruction pointer to a location specified by the instruction's argument. In this case, the argument is the @VLOOKUP function, whose *test variable* argument is the error message 1-2-3 placed in ERRMESSAGE. The lookup table for @VLOOKUP is BRANCHTABLE, in B3..D7. The comparison range in the table consists of copies of 1-2-3 error

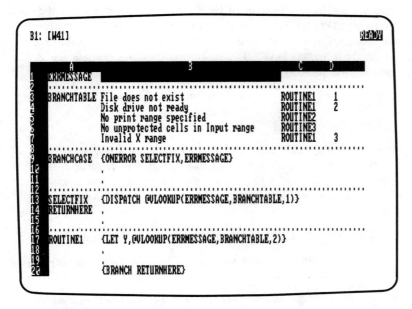

Fig. 8.29. A simulated case statement.

messages. The labels in offset 1 (column C) are the names of the error-handling routines to which the program branches when it finds an error.

Column D in the lookup table demonstrates how to pass parameters to the error routines. A sample error-handling routine appears at the bottom of figure 8.29 (ROUTINE1). The first instruction in ROUTINE1 is another @VLOOKUP to the same table, except with an offset of 2. This procedure sets Y to the appropriate value for use with this specific error.

The last instruction in ROUTINE1 returns the program to the instruction following the {DISPATCH} in SELECTFIX. This is a form of {RETURN} from the routine. The periods in SELECTFIX and ROUTINE1 represent rows where you could add more command language instructions.

Comments

TIP: Use @VLOOKUP on a database range to locate specific items in the database.

You can use @VLOOKUP with a string *test variable* argument to locate a specific record in a database. If the item to be compared is in the first field of the database, you can use the database range name as the *range* argument. If the item isn't in the first field, you must specify a separate range that indicates the column containing the field of interest as that argument. If the item is in the database, @VLOOKUP returns that item's vertical offset within the range. For instance, the following two-line macro positions the cell pointer on the record in the database called DATA_DB, assuming that the comparison string is in the cell named REFERENCE.

```
{GOTO}DATA_DB~                    Go to upper left corner.
{DOWN                             Move down to entry.
@VLOOKUP(REFERENCE, DATA_DB, 0)}
```

To verify the presence of a specific item in the database, you can use a more primitive form of the preceding technique. Because the function returns the ERR value if the comparison string is not found, the following formula is evaluated as TRUE when the comparison is found; otherwise, the formula is evaluated as FALSE.

#NOT#@ISERR(@VLOOKUP(REFERENCE,DATA_DB,0))

TRICK: Use the @HLOOKUP function in a database statistical function to return the proper offset.

The database statistical functions, such as @DSUM and @DCOUNT, are among 1-2-3's most powerful. With these, you can produce totals and counts of selected items in a list without having to go through the bother of Query Extract procedures. Note, however, that these powerful functions can be problematic if you modify (by adding or removing a field, for example) the database to which the functions refer. The problems arise because changing the database can change the offset for the column used by the database statistical function. For instance, suppose that the following line represents the field names in a database named DATA_DB:

```
name    address    income    rating    amount_down
```

For the names listed in the database, the following formula provides the average income of persons who meet a specific criterion (which is contained in the range DATA_CR):

@DAVG(DATA_DB,2,DATA_CR)

No problem arises until you have to modify the database in a way that alters the offset that applies to the income variable. For example, suppose that you insert a column between the address and income columns. If your spreadsheet contains many database statistical functions, this type of change in the database could necessitate much work on those formulas. You can avoid this problem by specifying the offset with an @HLOOKUP function. Another advantage of using this method is that the variable being referenced is named in the formula, which helps in interpretation. Here is the modified formula:

@DAVG(DATA_DB,@HLOOKUP("income",DATA_DB,0),DATA_CR)

With this formula, any modifications to the database are reflected in the value @HLOOKUP returns.

You can use a combination of the techniques just described to perform a "double lookup" and return any item in a database. Suppose that *Smith* is an entry in the database's name field. The following formula returns the income for that person:

@VLOOKUP("Smith",DATA_DB,@HLOOKUP("income",DATA_DB, 0))

By replacing the literal arguments "Smith" and "income" with cell references, you can give a command language program complete access to a database through lookup arguments.

The @ISERR, @ISNA, @ISNUMBER, and @ISSTRING Functions

These functions enable you to test for one of the four special conditions suggested by the function names. In each case, the function returns a 1 if the test evaluates as TRUE; a 0, if the test evaluates as FALSE.

Figure 8.30 shows the results of the functions on various kinds of cell contents. Note that @ISERR and @ISNA return a TRUE result under only those specific conditions. @ISNUMBER, the opposite of @ISSTRING, returns some surprising values. @ISSTRING is TRUE only for strings and formulas with string results. @ISNUMBER is therefore TRUE for everything else, including blank cells, ERR, and NA. Thus, string formulas that return an ERR result are "numbers."

TRAP: @ISNUMBER evaluates as TRUE under some odd conditions.

The good news is that @ISNUMBER stops the "ripple through" effect of ERR and NA. The bad news is that it is not intuitive that ERR (or NA) is a number, so mistakes are likely.

The fact that @ISNUMBER evaluates ERR and NA as numbers also means that this test lacks some discriminating power, which would be useful in programming. The @CELL("type") function helps a little in this regard. This function identifies blank cells and can differentiate between a string formula and a string. You may sometimes want to discriminate between string and numeric formulas that return ERR. To have @ISNUMBER return a FALSE result on ERR would make more sense. In general, the more discriminating power you have in

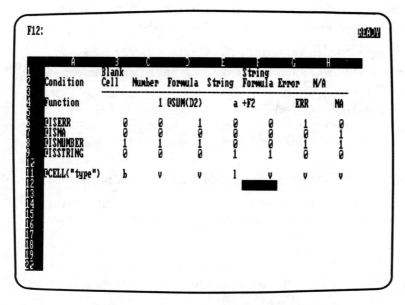

Fig. 8.30. The results returned by the @IS and @CELL("type") functions.

a programming language, the better. Add this change to @ISNUMBER to my "wish list" for the next version of 1-2-3.

Syntax

The general syntax for all the @IS functions is

@ISERR(expression)

@ISNA(expression)

@ISSTRING(expression)

@ISNUMBER(expression)

The *expression* argument can be a number, string, formula, or single-cell range name or cell reference.

Using @IS Functions To Locate Cells with Specific Values

ERR values can frequently be a source of difficulty when you work with 1-2-3. The program in figure 8.31, for example, shows a database called DATA_DB that contains ERR values. These errors arose in the process of putting together the database. Now the errors are just a left-over nuisance that make using database statistical formulas impossible.

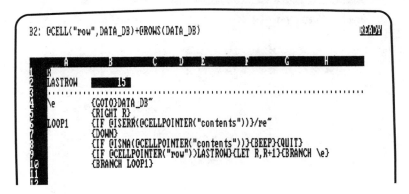

Fig. 8.31. A program using @ISERR and @ISNA.

This example illustrates a general problem that arises when identifying and operating on specific values that occur within a specific range of data. In this example, the intent is to eliminate the ERR values, but the program's main function is to locate them. By modifying the instructions following the {IF} statement in line 6, you could make the program perform any operation. Likewise, you could make the program search any range, including one defined to encompass the entire worksheet.

The program uses the @IS functions in two ways. @ISERR tests for ERR-valued cells. @ISNA takes advantage of the fact that the NA value rarely appears in the worksheet. In this program, the test for NA terminates program execution. To use @ISNA in this fashion requires that you put an NA value in the path of the cell pointer as it is guided by the program. Figure 8.32 shows DATA_DB and the placement of the NA value.

In figure 8.31, cell B1, named *R*, contains an argument for the {RIGHT} instruction in cell B5. On each pass through the program, R is incremented by one and causes the cell pointer to move another column to the right from the starting point in the upper left corner of DATA_DB.

The formula in cell B2 uses the @CELL("row") function and the @ROWS function to compute the last row in DATA_DB. The formula is used later as a test value in the {IF} instruction in cell B9.

Cell B4 starts the program by placing the cell pointer in the upper left corner of DATA_DB.

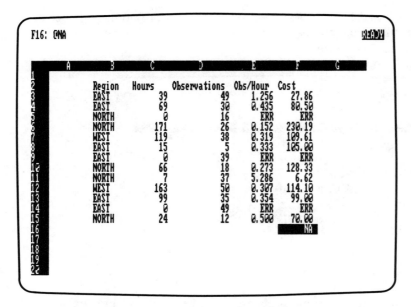

Fig. 8.32. The database range used in the program in figure 8.31.

Cell B5 moves the cell pointer right the number of columns specified by R (cell B1). If R is zero, no movement occurs.

Cell B6 tests the current cell pointer contents for ERR. If the ERR test is TRUE, control passes to the other instructions on this line; those instructions erase the cell contents. If the ERR test is FALSE, the other instructions are skipped. This line is also the reentry point for the {BRANCH} instruction in cell B10.

Cell B7 moves the cell pointer down to test the next cell.

The {IF} instruction in cell B8 tests for the NA value. If the current cell pointer contents are NA, which will be the case after the program traverses the entire range, the computer beeps once and stops. Note that this test must come before the test in B9.

The {IF} test in cell B9 will be TRUE after the cell pointer moves past the last row of the range. R is then incremented by one, and program control passes to the initial instruction in cell B4.

The instruction in cell B10 branches to LOOP1 and causes the program to test sequentially all the cells in a specific column.

Many methods are available for implementing a program that tests all the cells in a range. The primary advantage to this method is that all the operations are tied to the cell pointer; you can therefore monitor the program's progress. This kind of program would also be useful if you wanted to perform manual operations on a cell after the test value was located.

Comments

ERR and NA can cause some problems in tests involving compound comparisons—that is, multiple TRUE-FALSE tests linked with the Boolean operators AND and OR. Figure 8.33 demonstrates the effect of combining ERR and NA with TRUE and FALSE results. In all cases, the ERR or NA result overrides the TRUE or FALSE result and causes the test to return the ERR or NA value.

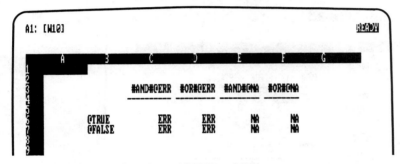

Fig. 8.33. Boolean combinations with ERR and NA.

What is important here is that 1-2-3 interprets an ERR or NA result in a test as FALSE. Compound comparisons can therefore return unintended results. Look, for example, at the following test, which is contained in a command language {IF} instruction.

```
{IF RESPONSE="yes"#OR#INCOME<0}
```

In this example, an action (whatever follows the {IF} statement) will be performed if the user enters a "yes" response or if the value in the cell named INCOME is less than zero. The user could answer "no" or give any other response, but the action would still be executed under negative income conditions. However, if the user types a nonstring response, such as a number, the left part of the comparison returns ERR as a result. Under these conditions, the {IF} test is always evaluated as FALSE, regardless of the result of the INCOME<0 part of the test, because the ERR result forces the entire compound comparison to return ERR and therefore is evaluated as FALSE.

This example is used because string comparisons that return an ERR result are common. However, any test that returns an ERR or NA result causes the same problem. The solution is to enclose in an @IF statement any test that is subject to returning an ERR result. For instance, you can use this equation:

@IF(@ISERR(YOURTEST),0,YOURTEST)

Figure 8.34 shows the possible combinations of TRUE, FALSE, and ERR under AND and OR conditions. The equation causes an ERR result to act as if it were a FALSE result. This strategy also enables you to define arbitrarily an ERR result as TRUE. You do this by replacing the 0 in the equation with a 1, as in the following example:

@IF(@ISERR(YOURTEST),1,YOURTEST)

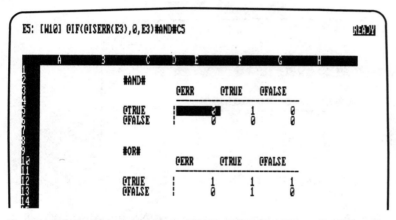

Fig. 8.34. All possible combinations of TRUE, FALSE, and ERR under AND and OR conditions.

The @INDEX Function

@INDEX is one of those functions that looks interesting but can also leave you with a "so what?" feeling, especially if you are used to thinking of functions in terms of how you can use them in a worksheet. In fact, I don't think I have ever used @INDEX as a simple worksheet function. From a programming perspective, however, @INDEX is probably the most useful of 1-2-3's functions. It enables you to treat the cells in a specific range as entries in a two-dimensional array. With @INDEX, you can use in the command language any of the standard programming techniques that apply to arrays.

@INDEX is similar to the @LOOKUP functions in that it returns the contents of a cell in a two-dimensional array. The difference is that the @LOOKUP functions take a *test variable* argument and an *offset* argument, whereas

@INDEX takes two *offset* arguments. Thus, both the column and row locations in the specified range are given as numbers.

Syntax

@INDEX(range,column offset,row offset)

As with all offsets in 1-2-3, the offsets for the @INDEX function begin numbering with zero. Therefore, to access the upper left corner of a range, you would use

@INDEX(range,0,0)

The last row or column in the range has an offset number that is one less than the corresponding number of rows or columns. Therefore, to access the lower right corner of the range, you would use

@INDEX(range,@COLS(range)-1,@ROWS(range)-1)

@INDEX, like all other functions, can't be used to enter values into a range. @INDEX can return only the values that are in a range. Therefore, the following is legal:

{LET RNAME,@INDEX(range,col,row)}

But this is not:

{LET @INDEX(range,col,row),RNAME}

@INDEX has a "companion" command language instruction that enters data into a range. See {PUT} in the following example and in Chapter 12.

Example

Figure 8.35 is a modified version of the program described in the section about the @ISERR function. In that program, the @CELLPOINTER function was used to traverse physically the range being modified; when an ERR value was encountered, the cell was erased. In this example, the @INDEX function and its companion command language instruction, {PUT}, test and modify the range.

Four major differences exist between this program and the previous program that performed the same function:

1. This program substitutes zeros for the ERR values rather than erasing them. Executing an erase function with this kind of program is possible, but involves constructing a command language instruction

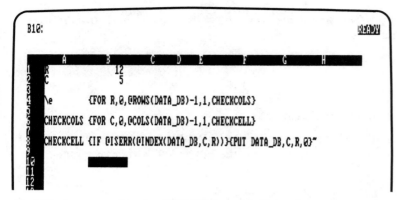

Fig. 8.35. A program that uses @INDEX to remove ERR values.

from a string formula, which is a more advanced topic than is appropriate for this example. If you are going to use such a program, you must decide whether the substituted values should be zeros or blanks, because the results of such formulas as @AVG and @COUNT will be affected.

2. This program doesn't require any limiting values such as the NA value that was used in the other program. This program uses the @INDEX function and two {FOR} loops driven by the dimensions of the range. Therefore, the program operates on that range and nothing more, and is self-limiting.

3. Nothing happens on the screen as this program runs; all operations occur internally. If you want to monitor the program's progress, this lack of on-screen action can be a drawback. However, see the next two items for the tradeoffs.

4. This program is three lines shorter.

5. This program runs four times faster. The fact that it doesn't erase the cells doesn't affect its execution speed.

Comments

The greatest advantage of @INDEX is that it frees you from the confines of cell addresses. You can write a program that can access any location in a range, regardless of where the range is in the worksheet. Furthermore, no restrictions apply to the contents of that range. Restrictions do apply when you use @LOOKUP functions. Therefore, you can treat the range and its contents as if they were a two-dimensional array in a standard programming language.

Another big advantage to using @INDEX is that it gives you the most mobility within the worksheet. Compared to the alternatives, programming with @INDEX is *fast*. The speed increase in the example in figure 8.35 is typical. Much of 1-2-3's sluggishness can be attributed to the overhead involved with updating the screen. Watching the cell pointer move around and perform its various tasks is fun but does carry a significant time penalty.

TRICK: Use @INDEX as a search-and-replace function for the entire worksheet.

The preceding example is a small-scale version of a search-andreplace operation, much like you might use with a word processor. By assigning a range name to the whole worksheet, you can alter it systematically instead of being limited to one column of labels. Also, if the program contains the appropriate tests, you can find and alter numbers and formulas as well as labels.

String Functions

With Release 2, 1-2-3 users now have access to the same powerful string functions that most Symphony users have long found indispensable. Using string functions, you can perform calculations on words and characters (or anything else contained in a label), much the same as you would do with numbers. This capability is important in almost all spreadsheet work, because words are the link between numeric calculations and the people who must interpret the numbers. Using string functions, you can make the labels and descriptions that accompany the numbers in a spreadsheet as dynamic as the numbers themselves. When the calculations change, the labels can change to reflect the new numeric results.

More important, however, is the fact that numbers are only one form of data you can use. In addition to the numeric value of a calculation, you can work with attributes of numbers, such as categorical (nominal) membership. For example, to track sales performance, you could group and compare sales data according to the categories of region, salesperson, and product. String functions enable you to deal with these various forms of categorization directly rather than through some intermediary code. You will find this capability especially valuable when you work with databases, which by their very nature are almost always a mixture of nominal and numeric data.

In some cases, numbers are used as labels rather than as numbers for calculations. A common street address is one example of numbers used as labels. Another would be a product code, as described in the "Nesting Functions" section at the beginning of this chapter. Such a code might contain several hyphenated numeric sequences or even a mixture of number and letter codes. String functions give you an easy way to deal with this complex form of information coding, enabling you to extract portions of the code or even convert the code to a numeric form so that mathematical operations can be applied.

String functions play a special role in macros and command language programming. Because the instructions for macros and programs are nothing more than strings themselves, constructing an instruction from a string formula is a simple matter. This capability gives your programs virtually unlimited flexibility. Not only can you construct instructions that change dynamically with the contents of the worksheet (possible only with complicated /Copy operations in Release 1A), but you can create string formulas that allow command language instructions to perform beyond their design limitations. Chapter 9 goes into more detail on this subject; this chapter examines some of the basic tools for manipulating strings.

An Overview of String Functions

Release 2 of 1-2-3 has 18 functions that deal directly with strings. Along with these are 2 date functions, 3 logical functions, and 7 special functions that can deal indirectly with strings. String functions can be divided into 4 categories, according to how the functions operate on the arguments the functions are given: formatting functions, character-manipulation functions, character/numeric-conversion functions, and special functions.

The first group of string functions manipulates the appearance of a string without making any substantial changes to the string's contents. These functions are the following:

@CLEAN	Removes control characters from a string
@TRIM	Removes extra spaces from a string
@LOWER	Converts to all lowercase characters
@UPPER	Converts to all uppercase characters
@PROPER	Capitalizes the first letter in each word

The second group of functions alters the contents of a string by adding, deleting, or extracting characters. These functions are the following:

@LEFT	Extracts characters from the left edge of a string
@RIGHT	Extracts characters from the right edge of a string

@MID	Extracts characters from the middle of a string
@REPEAT	Creates a string by repeating characters a specified number of times
@REPLACE	Removes characters from a string and replaces them with other characters

Also included in this category is the concatenation operator—the ampersand (&)—which is described in the "Basic String Mathematics" section.

The third group of functions performs conversions between characters and numeric values. These functions are the following:

@CHAR	Converts ASCII/LICS number to equivalent character
@CODE	Converts character to ASCII/LICS number
@FIND	Locates the position of a character or string within another string
@LENGTH	Returns the number of characters in a string
@STRING	Converts a number into a string that looks like a number
@VALUE	Converts a string that looks like a number into a number
@DATEVALUE	Converts a string that looks like a date into its Julian-date numeric equavalent
@TIMEVALUE	Converts a string that looks like a time into its time-value equavalent

Logical functions could also be included in this group because they convert string arguments into FALSE and TRUE, which are equivalent to zero and nonzero, respectively. The logical functions are the following:

@IF	Tests a Boolean condition
@ISSTRING	Tests to see whether an entry is a string
@EXACT	Tests to see whether two strings are exactly equivalent, including case structure and foreign-alphabet characters

1-2-3's special functions perform a variety of operations using or returning strings as arguments. Four of these functions (all described later in this chapter) perform table lookups that can return strings as well as numeric values. These functions are the following:

@VLOOKUP
@HLOOKUP
@INDEX
@CHOOSE

Two of the special functions are designed specifically to deal with the fact that strings are a special type of data and can't be combined with numbers. If you supply a numeric value to a function that requires a string argument, or vice versa, an ERR condition results. Because the data type can sometimes be unpredictable, the following "housekeeping" functions are available to ensure that the data is interpreted consistently as either string or numeric.

@S
@N

Two more of the special functions that were described earlier in this chapter can return the string contents of cells or, more frequently, strings that describe the attributes of cells.

@CELL
@CELLPOINTER

Finally, the @@ function, also described earlier, qualifies as a string function because it requires a string (in the form of a cell address) as an argument.

@@

Basic String Mathematics

You can start working with strings without using functions. Much like numbers, strings can be manipulated directly in an equation. For instance, you can add two or more strings together. The result is a little different than what you would get if you were adding numbers, because the result of adding A to B is AB, not C. This process of joining two strings is called *concatenation*. Rather than using a plus sign (+), this form of string addition uses the ampersand (&).

You can refer to the strings in your equation in three ways. You are probably already familiar with the first two methods: cell addresses and range names. The third method, called a *literal string*, uses the string's actual characters, enclosed in quotation marks. Without the quotation marks, 1-2-3 tries to interpret the string as a range name. The following are all valid string equations (concatenations):

+A1&A2   Both A1 and A2 contain strings.

+FIRST&LAST   FIRST and LAST are range names.

+"Hello "&"there!"

Any mixture of range name, cell specification, or literal string is also valid.

Here are several points to keep in mind when you use string equations:

1. Blank cells are considered numeric. Therefore, the first two of the preceding examples return an ERR result if any of the cells or ranges referenced are blank (or contain numbers or numeric formulas).

2. String equations, like numeric equations, must begin with a plus sign (+). If you use an ampersand (&), 1-2-3 interprets the equation as a label. The plus sign, however, is not valid as an operator for joining strings. You must use the ampersand (&) for that purpose.

3. A string that contains no characters is valid; this is called a *null string*, and it has a length of zero. Any cell containing only a label prefix character is a null string. A null string can also be represented by two quotation marks in succession (+"").

4. By using two quotation marks in succession, you can create a string equation that displays quotation marks. Be careful not to confuse this with a null string; the two look identical but appear in different contexts. For instance, assume that cell A1 contains the string *Bob* and compare the following:

Formula	*Result*
+A1&" says "&""&"John"	Bob says John
+A1&" says ""Hello"" John"	Bob says "Hello" John

5. A cell formula displayed with the Text format setting is not a string, even though it looks like one.

Formatting Functions

Five of the string functions included in Release 2 can be considered formatting functions. These functions alter the appearance of the string supplied as an argument without significantly altering the string's content.

The @CLEAN Function

@CLEAN strips all control characters from a string. Control characters are those with ASCII codes of less than 32. Typically, control characters include such things as tab characters, carriage returns, backspace characters, line feeds, and other nontext characters. 1-2-3 has two carriage return characters: the standard soft return (ASCII 13) and a hard return (LICS 20). The hard return is currently used in Symphony's DOC environment and has no immediate application in 1-2-3, although if you load Symphony files into 1-2-3, these characters may be present. @CLEAN removes both types of carriage return characters from a string.

@CLEAN is used primarily to process data that has been brought into the worksheet from an external source (such as an imported text file) or file data read with {READ} or {READLN}.

   @CLEAN(string)

The *string* argument can be a literal string, string expression, range name, or cell reference to cells containing a label or string expression. The string @CLEAN produces is exactly like the string supplied to the function as an argument, except that @CLEAN removes the control characters. @CLEAN deletes the spaces the control characters occupy; therefore, the resulting string is shorter than the original. Figure 8.36 shows the "before" and "after" versions of such a string. Notice that the hard carriage return character (LICS 20; notice its appearance as a triangle in the command line) is perceived as one of the eight control characters in this example and is stripped by @CLEAN.

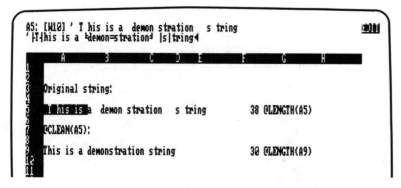

Fig. 8.36. The results of an @CLEAN function.

TIP: To make control characters visible, use EDIT mode.

Control characters are usually not visible in the worksheet, but they do appear in the second line of the control panel when 1-2-3 is in EDIT mode. Control characters only appear, however, when they are part of a label string. When they are part of string formula, or when they are generated by the @CHAR function, they appear as spaces. When 1-2-3 is in EDIT mode and when characters are enclosed in quotation marks, the characters appear as a substring that is part of the string formula.

TIP/TRAP: Control characters do not execute in a macro.

I'm not sure whether to call this statement a TIP or a TRAP, because, depending on the situation, you may or may not want to execute control characters. In either case, if your macro or command language program contains control characters, they don't execute. If you try to execute the demonstration string in figure 8.36 as a macro (which would type the string), the result would be exactly the same as the result of the @CLEAN function: the control characters are ignored. If a cell in a macro contains only control characters, that cell doesn't halt macro execution, but neither does anything occur as a result of the control characters' execution.

The @TRIM Function

Similar to @CLEAN, @TRIM returns its string minus some specific characters. The specific characters in figure 8.37 are multiple spaces; @TRIM removes any leading or trailing spaces in a string and compresses all internal multiple spaces to a single space each. @TRIM operates on only standard "soft" spaces—those 1-2-3 inserts when you press the space bar. The "hard" space generated as a compose character is not affected.

@TRIM(string)

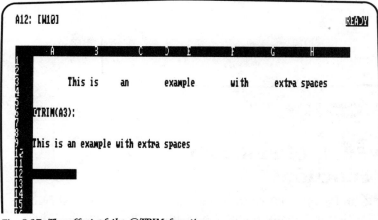

Fig. 8.37. The effect of the @TRIM function.

The *string* argument can be a literal string, string expression, range name, or cell reference to cells containing a label or string expression.

TRAP: @TRIM can appear to leave a trailing space.

Figure 8.38 shows another use of the @TRIM function. In this example, a trailing space appears not to have been removed. The argument string for @TRIM ends in a hard carriage return. Because trailing spaces are defined as those that come after the last nonspace character in the string, the spaces preceding the hard carriage return are perceived as internal spaces. @TRIM therefore treats them as any other set of internal spaces, compressing them to one space. Two spaces appear to be at the end of the "trimmed" string. The second space is actually a hard carriage return character. The last line of this figure shows how to get all the "junk" out of the source string: use a combination of @CLEAN and @TRIM.

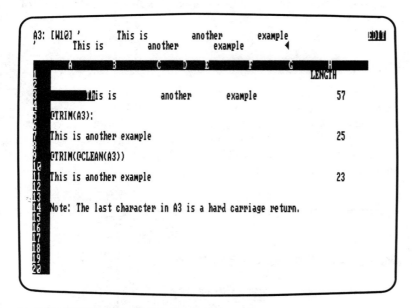

Fig. 8.38. @TRIM used with hard carriage returns.

The @LOWER, @UPPER, and @PROPER Functions

@LOWER, @UPPER, and @PROPER control the case structure of the characters in a string—that is, which letters are uppercase or lowercase. These functions are useful for controlling string-matching comparisons. As shown in figure 8.39, the functions' names describe the functions' purpose. Note that the functions operate on all the words in a string.

@LOWER(string)

@UPPER(string)

@PROPER(string)

The *string* argument can be a literal string, string expression, range name, or cell reference to cells containing a label or string expression.

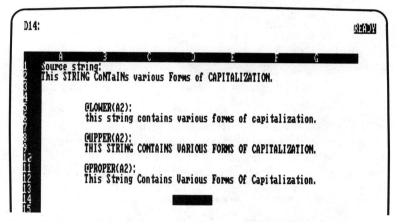

Fig. 8.39. The effects of the @LOWER, @UPPER, and @PROPER functions.

Character-Manipulation Functions

Character-manipulation functions provide access to the individual characters in a string. With these functions, you can make long strings out of short strings, make short strings out of long ones, and separate a string into pieces. These capabilities are what allow you to use strings as data.

The @LEFT and @RIGHT Functions

@LEFT and @RIGHT are the first of the character-manipulation functions. Both return a subset of characters from their string arguments. Those characters are the left- or rightmost characters of the specified length.

@LEFT(string,length)

@RIGHT(string,length)

The *string* can be a literal string, string expression, range name, or cell reference to a cell containing label or string expression.

Length, the second argument in the function, specifies the number of characters to return. The *length* can be a number, numeric expression, range name, or cell reference to a cell containing a number or numeric expression. The *length* must be a positive number or zero. Using numbers larger than 240 is equivalent to specifying 240. If *length* is not an integer, 1-2-3 truncates the fractional part of the number. Negative numbers return ERR.

Figure 8.40 shows several examples of each function. Notice the appearance of the source string in the control panel. Several things are worth noting in these examples:

1. When the *length* is zero, the result is a null string with a length of zero, which is not the same as a blank.

2. When the *length* is greater than the string length, the function returns the whole string. No extra characters are added to the result, and the oversized *length* argument is ignored.

3. When the rightmost character is a hard carriage return, @RIGHT counts that character and returns it, even though hard carriage returns may not otherwise be visible. The same is true for other control characters; they appear as spaces in the string that is returned.

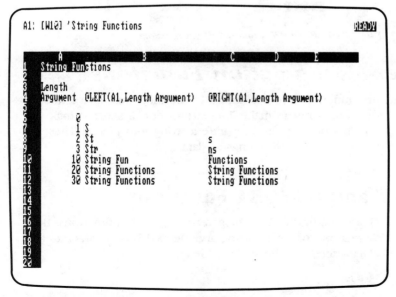

Fig. 8.40. The effects of the @LEFT and @RIGHT functions.

The @MID Function

@MID, a more general form of the preceding functions, returns a substring result from anywhere in the string. @MID's syntax is slightly more complicated than that of @LEFT and @RIGHT.

@MID(source string,start position,length)

The *source string* can be a literal string, string expression, range name, or cell reference to a cell containing a label or string expression.

The *start position* and *length* can be numbers, numeric expressions, range names, or cell references to cells containing numbers or numeric expressions. Both these arguments must be positive numbers or zero. Using numbers larger than 240 is equivalent to specifying 240. If neither argument is an integer, 1-2-3 truncates the fractional portion of the number. Negative numbers return ERR.

Figure 8.41 shows several variations of @MID. In particular, you should notice the following:

1. Character numbering, as with all other offset-type arguments, begins with zero. Therefore, @MID(source string,0,1) returns the first character in *source string*.

2. If the *start position* value is larger than the string *length*, the result is a null string.

3. If the *length* is zero, the result is a null string.

4. When the *length* plus the *start position* equals a value larger than the length of the string, @MID returns the characters from the start position to the end of the string.

5. When the *start position* is specified as zero, the @MID function is equivalent to the @LEFT function.

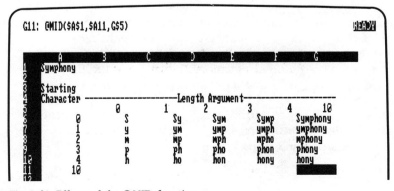

Fig. 8.41. Effects of the @MID function.

The @REPEAT Function

@REPEAT differs from the previous three functions in that it generates rather than reduces strings. That is, @REPEAT makes long strings out of short strings rather than short strings out of long ones. @REPEAT is similar to the repeating label prefix (backslash) but isn't limited by the cell boundary (as is the repeating label).

Syntax

@REPEAT(string,repeat number)

The *string* argument can be a literal string, string expression, range name, or cell reference to cells containing a label or string expression.

The *repeat number* can be a number, numeric expression, range name, or cell reference to a cell containing a number or numeric expression. The *repeat number* must be a positive number or zero. Using numbers larger than 240 is equivalent to specifying 240. If the *repeat number* isn't an integer, 1-2-3 truncates the fractional part of the number. Negative numbers return ERR.

Examples

@REPEAT can be valuable in formatting output. Most standard programming languages, in which the output is generated a line at a time, have an equivalent function that places the output under the control of a variable. For example, BASIC uses the SPACE$(n) function to create a string of spaces. Figure 8.42 demonstrates one use for this kind of control. In this example, a formula using the @SIN function generates the *number* argument. The result of a whole series of such equations is the plot of the sine function.

With @REPEAT, you can position various kinds of indicators on the screen dynamically. Figures 8.43 and 8.44 show @REPEAT used to emphasize specific words in a sentence. In both examples, the first letter of the word is entered into the Start character cell. The other equations shown cause the first occurrence of a word beginning with that letter to appear underlined.

@REPEAT can generate strings up to 240 characters long. If you try to generate a longer string—by repeating *xyz* 100 times, for instance—the function generates a 240-character string and stops.

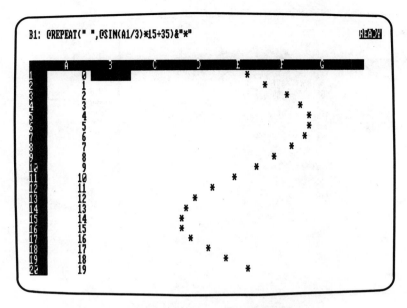

Fig. 8.42. The @REPEAT function used to generate graph plots.

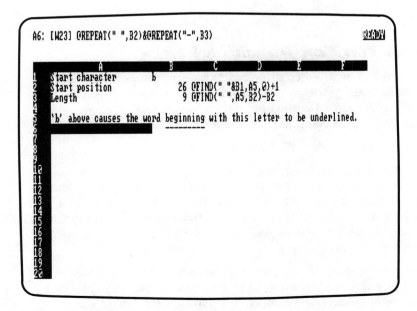

Fig. 8.43. @REPEAT used to emphasize text areas.

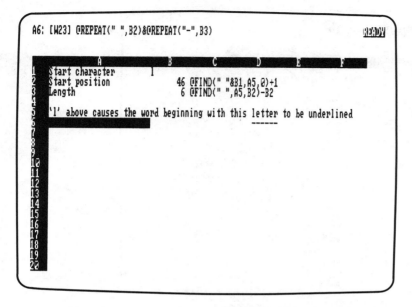

Fig. 8.44. A changed start character that causes a different word to be underlined.

Other Tricks You Can Do with @REPEAT

By combining @REPEAT with other string functions, you can perform some simple, but useful formatting tricks. For example, you can use @REPEAT with @CELL("width") to generate a dashed line that is always one character shorter than the column width. You could use a formula similar to the following:

    @REPEAT("-",@CELL("width",B2..B2)-1)

This "short line" formula helps make multicolumn worksheet displays more readable (see fig. 8.45). I've seen more than one 1-2-3 user create such lines by carefully typing the requisite number of dashes, only to redo many of them later when changing column widths became necessary. This combination of functions makes the line self-adjusting and saves you a lot of reformatting work if you use short lines in your worksheets.

When using the @REPEAT function, you should keep a number of things in mind. First, the cell referenced by the @CELL function (in this example, B2) should be in the same column as the function itself. However, don't use the formula cell itself because that creates a circular reference. A good rule of thumb is to use the cell immediately above or below the formula cell.

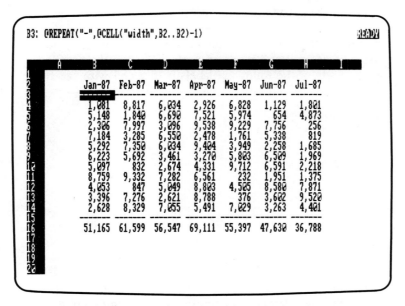

Fig. 8.45. The "short line" function used to make column formats more readable.

Second, the formula does not recalculate when you change the column widths. However, it will be updated the first time the worksheet is recalculated, either manually or automatically.

Third, a hidden column has a width of zero, which, when applied to this formula, generates a *repeat number* argument of –1. This negative value for *repeat number* generates an ERR condition instead of a "short line." This effect is visible only when columns are "unhidden" with the /Worksheet Column Display command or when hidden columns are temporarily made visible during certain operations such as /Copy. The ERR condition corrects itself as soon as the worksheet is recalculated.

Finally, because column widths are independent in 1-2-3's two windows, you can get two different results from this formula, depending on which window contains the cell pointer. The formula will display a line that is one character less than the width of the column that contained the cell pointer when the worksheet was last recalculated. The formula will appear the same in both windows.

Another trick you can perform with a variant of the "short line" formula is to create an "underscore" to emphasize a worksheet heading. By using an @LENGTH function as the *repeat number* argument, you make the formula return a line of dashes the same length as the cell that provides the argument to @LENGTH. Placing the @REPEAT function directly below the label cell creates the appearance of an underscore. The advantage of entering underscores with a formula is that they always adjusts to the current label. The same formula can be copied to many places and still work properly, adjusting to changes in the label. For example, if any of the following labels is in a cell with the range name LABELCELL, the formula would be

@REPEAT("−",@LENGTH(LABELCELL))

Examples:

This is an example label

So is this

The @REPEAT formula is directly below each of these labels.

The @REPLACE Function

@REPLACE is the most complex string function because of the number of arguments required and the complexity of operation. This string function duplicates the search-and-replace command typically found in word-processing programs, deleting one portion of a string and inserting another string in its place.

@REPLACE(source string,start position,length,insert string)

The *source string* and the *insert string* can be literal strings, string expressions, range names, or cell references to cells containing labels or string expressions.

The *start position* and *length* can be numbers, numeric expressions, range names, or cell references to cells containing numbers or numeric expressions. Both arguments must be positive numbers or zero. Using numbers larger than 240 is equivalent to specifying 240. If either argument is not an integer, 1-2-3 truncates the fractional portion of the number. Negative numbers return ERR.

Remembering the syntax of the @REPLACE function is a little easier if you keep in mind that the first three arguments are the same as those of @MID. If the *insert string* is a null string, @REPLACE becomes the opposite of @MID (see fig. 8.46).

You also can think of @REPLACE as performing two separate operations: deleting a specific number of characters and inserting another set of characters. The two operations are independent, except that they occur at the same location in the *source string*. Creating a separate operation to delete characters prior to performing an insertion is therefore unnecessary.

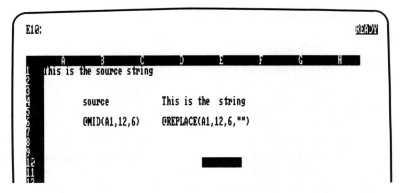

Fig. 8.46. The effects of the opposite functions @REPLACE and @MID.

The *length* argument determines the number of characters to delete. If the *length* is equal to zero, nothing is deleted. The number of characters inserted is specified in the *insert string*.

Figure 8.47 shows several examples of @REPLACE. @REPLACE can act as a true search-and-replace function when used with @FIND and @LENGTH, as shown in lines 14 and 15. These functions provide the arguments necessary to locate and delete a specific string.

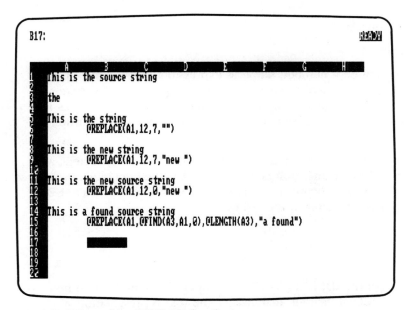

Fig. 8.47. Effects of the @REPLACE function.

Character/Numeric-Conversion Functions

Character/numeric-conversion functions do exactly what their name implies: they convert characters to numbers or numbers to characters. These conversions are important for two reasons. First, by converting strings that look like numbers into actual numeric values, you can perform mathematical operations on strings. Second, some of the numeric information generated by a conversion can be used as argument values by other string functions. The following descriptions provide an introduction to the concepts involved. As you will see throughout the rest of the book, these character/numeric conversions form the foundation for many powerful applications of the command language.

The @CHAR and @CODE Functions

The @CHAR and @CODE functions, compliments of one another, translate the machine-code representation of a character into its character representation, or vice versa. @CODE returns the ASCII/LICS numeric equivalent of a character, whereas @CHAR turns that number back into a character.

Syntax

@CHAR(code number)

@CODE(character)

The *code number* can be a number, numeric expression, range name, or cell reference to a cell containing a number or numeric expression. The *code number* must be in the range 1–255. Any value outside this range returns ERR. If the *code number* is not an integer, 1-2-3 truncates the fractional portion of the number.

The *character* argument can be a literal string of one or more characters, a string expression, a range name, or a cell reference to a cell containing a label or string expression. If the *character* contains more than one character, 1-2-3 uses only the leftmost character in the string.

Comments

When you use 1-2-3's {READ} and {WRITE} disk operation functions on nontext files, you will find @CODE helpful. It translates the text representation of the character into its numeric equivalent. When a program stores numbers in binary form, the numbers can't be read from their text representation. For example, the binary form of the number 100 looks like the lowercase letter *d*. However, because @CODE("d")=100, the text can be translated back into its numeric equivalent.

With @CHAR, you can create characters in situations in which doing so would otherwise be difficult. For example, @CHAR can serve as an alternative to the method of inserting quotation marks into a string formula (described in the "Basic String Mathematics" section). If you need a string whose result contains some quotation mark characters, you can use @CHAR to insert them, as shown in figure 8.48.

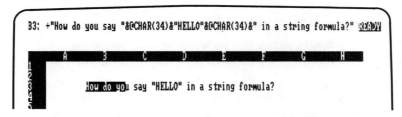

Fig. 8.48. *The @CHAR function used to insert quotation marks in a string formula.*

You can also use @CHAR with the @CELL function to return the current column letter. For instance, look at the following:

@CHAR(@CELL("col",B2..B2)+64)

This returns the letter B. If you need a formula that works beyond columns A through Z, use the following:

@MID(@CELL("address",AB1..AB1),1,@FIND("$",@CELL("address", AB1..AB1),1)-1)

You can also use @CODE and @CHAR together in order to return the next letter in the ASCII/LICS alphabet. Look at the following:

@CHAR(@CODE(B1)+1)

This returns the letter B if cell B1 contains the letter A. This kind of manipulation is the most common use for these functions. You can perform mathematical transformations on characters by turning them into numbers and then back into strings again.

TRICK: Use @CHAR to create strings that contain control characters.

@CHAR can create 255 characters, including the control characters represented by ASCII/LICS codes 1–31. You can use these characters to create binary-type data for use with programs that require data in this form. This use, however, is limited by the @CHAR function's incapability to create a character for ASCII/ LICS' zero.

The @FIND Function

@FIND returns a number that refers to the location of a specific character (or set of characters) in a string.

Syntax

@FIND(match string,source string,starting character)

The *match string* and the *source string* can be literal strings, string expressions, range names, or cell references to cells containing labels or string expressions.

The *starting character* can be a number, numeric expression, range name, or cell address referring to a cell containing a number or numeric expression. The *starting character* must be a positive number or zero. Using numbers larger than 240 is equivalent to specifying 240. If the *starting character* is not an integer, 1-2-3 truncates the fractional portion of the number. Negative numbers return ERR.

The *starting character* specifies the location in which @FIND begins looking for a match. Thus, you can skip parts of the string during the search. As always, the numbering scheme for the characters starts with zero. If @FIND finds a match, the function returns the number referring to the location in the *source string* of the first matching character specified in the *match string*. If no match is found, @FIND returns the ERR value. The match must be exact; for instance, *A* and *a* are not equivalent. Figure 8.49 shows the results of @FIND with various arguments.

Comments

@FIND is the link between the kinds of things you usually will want to do with a string, which are character oriented, and most of the string functions, which require numeric arguments. @FIND provides the search function for search-and-replace operations using @REPLACE as shown in figure 8.47. @FIND can also be used to isolate substring segments, as was described in the text accompanying figure 8.7. You can also use @FIND to supply arguments to another @FIND (see fig. 8.8). Altogether, @FIND is a versatile and an important function.

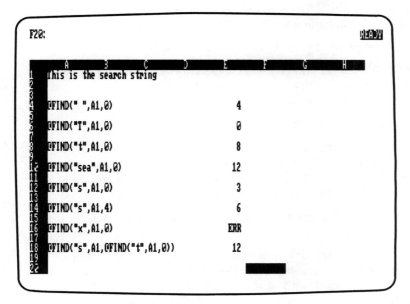

Fig. 8.49. Effects of the @FIND function.

TRAP: In the 1-2-3 manuals, the explanation of how @FIND functions in a Boolean expression can be misleading.

The 1-2-3 *Reference Manual* states:

> If the search fails, the result is ERR. In a selection criterion formula, this result is the logical condition FALSE.

What this statement means is that the ERR result is interpreted as a FALSE result. The restrictions regarding ERR results in Boolean expressions combined with AND and OR (as described in this chapter's @ISERR section) still apply. The ERR response from @FIND forces the entire test to be FALSE, regardless of the results of other parts of the test.

The @LENGTH Function

@LENGTH returns the number of characters in a string. The length of a string can vary from 0 to 240.

@LENGTH(string)

The *string* argument can be a literal string, string expression, range name, or cell reference to a cell containing a label or string expression.

Figure 8.50 illustrates some general facts about the function:

1. Notice that in cells A1 and A2, what appear to be identical entries have different lengths. This difference occurs because the second entry has a space following the word.

2. The blank cell in A3 causes an ERR result.

3. The cell in A4 is a null string, a string with no characters. As shown in the control panel, a null string in 1-2-3 appears as a label prefix character only. Because the label prefix character is not counted as part of the string, it has a length of zero.

4. The null string can be repeated (or concatenated) an indefinite number of times and still have a length of zero, as shown in line 5.

5. Lines 8, 9, and 10 show that @LENGTH can be applied to string formulas as well as to strings *per se*. However, the 240-character limit still applies, and if the length of the string formula exceeds that limit, an ERR results.

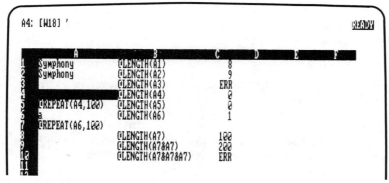

Fig. 8.50. Limits of the @LENGTH function.

The @STRING and @VALUE Functions

@STRING and @VALUE are another set of complementary functions. Their purposes, respectively, are to change the data type from numeric to string or from string to numeric.

@STRING(number to convert,decimal places)

@VALUE(string)

For @STRING, *decimal places* specifies the number of digits to the right of the decimal to be displayed. The *decimal places* argument can be a number, range name, or numeric expression in the range zero to 15. If the number is zero, the result appears as an integer (without a decimal point). Negative values or values greater than 15 cause @STRING to return ERR.

The *number to convert* argument can be a number, formula, or cell reference.

For @VALUE, *string* must be a string that looks like a number. You can't use nonnumeric characters. 1-2-3 ignores leading and trailing spaces.

@STRING is especially useful in command language programming. With this function, you can convert calculated numbers into a string, which you can incorporate into a program (see fig. 8.51).

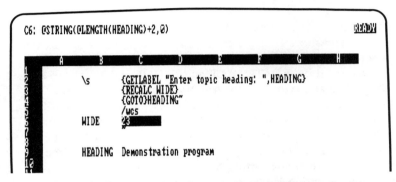

Fig. 8.51. The @STRING function used to convert a calculated number into a string and incorporate the result into a program.

You can use @STRING and @VALUE together to perform mathematical operations on strings. For example, the following formula adds 1 to a numeric string (a label) in cell A1 and returns a string value.

@STRING(@VALUE(A1)+1,0)

The following formula returns the number of digits to the left of the decimal in a number in cell B3.

@VALUE(@LENGTH(@STRING(B3,0)))

The @DATEVALUE
and @TIMEVALUE Functions

The @DATEVALUE and @TIMEVALUE functions convert string arguments that look like dates or times into their Julian number equivalents.

Syntax

@DATEVALUE(date string)

@TIMEVALUE(time string)

The *string* argument can be a literal string, string expression, range name, or cell reference to a cell containing a label or string expression.

The form of the *string* argument for @DATEVALUE and @TIMEVALUE must be a valid date or time format, respectively. Valid date or time formats are any of the formats 1-2-3 displays.

Comments

Choosing a format is somewhat complicated by the fact that the International formats, as set in the /Worksheet Global Default International settings, can vary from their default settings. When you change an International Date or Time setting, the formats accepted by @DATEVALUE and @TIMEVALUE change as well. 1-2-3 uses three date and two time formats that don't change as the International settings change. These are: D1, D2, and D3 for date; D6 and D7 for time. These formats are always valid for @DATEVALUE and @TIMEVALUE. If, however, you use an International Date or Time setting that is not the one currently in use, the functions return ERR. Formulas that are already in the worksheet and that use International setting formats for date and time convert to ERR if the International setting is changed after the fact. Table 8.3 shows the available formats for date and time.

Table 8.3
Formats Accepted by @DATEVALUE and @TIMEVALUE

	Format	Example
Date Formats		
Standard		
(D1)	DD–MMM–YY	04–Jul–86
(D2)	DD–MMM	04–Jul
(D3)	MMM–YY	Jul–86

International

(D4)	MM/DD/YY	07/04/86
	DD/MM/YY	04/07/86
	DD.MM.YY	04.07.86
	YY–MM–DD	86–07–04
(D5)	MM/DD	07/04
	DD/MM	04/07
	DD.MM	04.07
	MM–DD	07–04

Time Formats

Standard

(D6)	HH:MM:SS AM/PM	03:15:30 PM
(D7)	HH:MM AM/PM	03:15 PM

International

(D8)	HH:MM:SS	15:15:30
	HH.MM.SS	15.15.30
	HH,MM,SS	15,15,30
	HHhMMmSSs	15h15m30s
(D9)	HH:MM	15:15
	HH.MM	15.15
	HH,MM	15,15
	HHhMMm	15h15m

@DATEVALUE and @TIMEVALUE are lenient with respect to the exact format required. Both functions accept strings formatted without leading zeros. Therefore, you can, for instance, type 7/4/86 instead of 07/04/86; 3:5 PM, instead of 03:05 PM. In addition, both functions accept partially formatted entries, although the result of a partial argument depends on its exact format. Table 8.4 describes the partial argument types and results.

Table 8.4
Partial Formats Accepted by @DATEVALUE and @TIMEVALUE

Format	Example	(D1) Result
Date Formats		
Standard		
DD–MMM	04–Jul	04–Jul–86 *
MMM–YY	Jul–81	01–Jul–81
MMM–	Jul–	01–Jul–00
International		
MM/DD	7/4	04–Jul–86 *
MM/	7/	01–Jul–86 *
MM//	7//	01–Jul–00
MM//YY	7//81	01–Jul–81

*Note: When the year is unspecified, the year value is supplied from the current setting of the computer's system clock.

Time Formats		
HH:	3:	03:00:00 AM
	15:	03:00:00 PM
HH: AM/PM	3: PM	03:00:00 PM
HH::SS	3::30	03:00:30 AM
	15::30	03:00:30 PM
HH::SS AM/PM	3::30 PM	03:00:30 PM
:MM	:15	12:15:00 AM
:MM AM/PM	:15 PM	12:15:00 PM
::SS	::30	12:00:30 AM
::SS AM/PM	::30 PM	12:00:30 PM

The partial formats operate as follows:

1. If the year is omitted from the date, the date from the computer's system clock is used as a default.

2. If the day is omitted, the first of the month is used as a default.

3. If the year is omitted, but the separator character for the year is included, the year is set to zero (1900).

4. If AM and PM are omitted from the time, AM is assumed.

5. If minutes or seconds are omitted from the time, zero is used as a default.

6. If hours are omitted from the time, 12 AM is used as a default unless PM has been specified.

Logical Functions: @IF and @EXACT

1-2-3's logical functions provide a way to perform tests on strings. The @IF function was available in 1-2-3 Release 1A but has been expanded in Release 2 to allow tests on string values. The @EXACT function is a special function that is case and special-character sensitive.

Both @IF and @EXACT can perform tests on string data. The @IF function, the workhorse of most spreadsheet formula testing, is the general form of 1-2-3's conditional testing function. @IF takes three arguments, the first of which is usually a Boolean expression, either string or numeric. @EXACT, on the other hand, is a specialized Boolean function designed to test the exact equivalence of two strings.

@IF(a,vtrue,vfalse)

@EXACT(string1,string2)

The *a* argument can be a number, cell reference, range name, or any sort of numeric expression, Boolean or otherwise. If *a* evaluates to zero (FALSE), the *vfalse* result is returned. If *a* evaluates to anything but zero, the result is TRUE, and the *vtrue* result is returned. The *v* arguments can be numbers, strings, numeric or string expressions, range names, or cell references. @IF evaluates to ERR if *a* is a string or a cell reference to a label or string formula. Boolean expressions using strings, however, are permitted.

The *string1* and *string2* arguments can be literal strings, cell addresses, or range names that refer to labels or string formulas. If either *string* argument is not a string, @EXACT evaluates to ERR.

1-2-3 uses an approximate matching scheme for strings and characters used in Boolean expressions. Case structure and the modifications of certain characters for use in foreign alphabets are ignored. When @EXACT is used to test the equivalence of the two strings, case structure and foreign characters must match exactly in order for the result to be TRUE. Here is a comparison of the two methods of testing string equivalence:

Boolean Expression	Result
"A"="A"	TRUE
"A"="a"	TRUE
"â"="a"	TRUE
@EXACT("A","A")	TRUE
@EXACT("A","a")	FALSE
@EXACT("â","a")	FALSE

Special Functions: @S and @N

1-2-3 provides two special functions with which you can create formulas that mix strings and numbers. These functions are the @S and the @N functions.

The @S and @N functions "guard" against errors that can arise from giving a function an argument of the wrong data type. A few functions take either numeric *or* string arguments. Most functions, however, require one or the other and produce an ERR result if given the wrong one.

The syntax for @S and @N is peculiar, to say the least. Like the @CELL function, both require a *range* argument, but process only one cell. When entering the formula, however, you need only specify a cell address argument. When the formula is entered into the worksheet, 1-2-3 converts the argument to a range address. Again, like the @CELL function, @S and @N process only the upper left corner cell of the specified range if the range consists of more than one cell. @S and @N return ERR if anything besides a cell address is supplied as an argument. You can't, therefore, nest other functions inside either @S or @N.

@S(range)

@N(range)

@S and @N "force" an argument to be interpreted as either a string or number, respectively. Figure 8.52 demonstrates the effect of the two functions on numbers (lines 4–5), blank cells (line 6), labels (lines 7–8), and ERR and NA values (lines 9–10). @S returns a blank (null string) for every numeric argument. @N returns a zero for all string arguments. Both @S and @N pass the ERR and NA values.

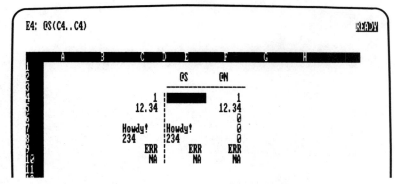

Fig. 8.52. The effects of @S and @N on various data types.

Figure 8.53 demonstrates the use of @S and @N as argument modifiers for other functions and formulas. In lines 4–10, @LENGTH returns an ERR value for numeric and blank cells. With @S modifying the argument, however, @LENGTH interprets all the cells as strings. If the cell has a numeric value, @S returns a null string. In the lower part of the screen, two cells with opposing data types are combined, first numerically with +, then as string concatenations with &. Including the @S or @N function causes the formula to work correctly for its respective data type.

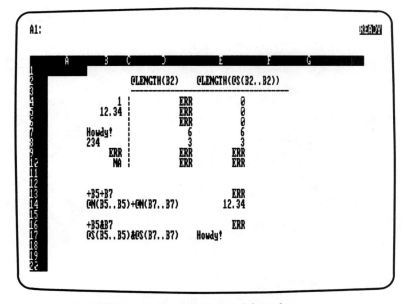

Fig. 8.53. @S and @N used with functions and formulas.

9

The Command Language

This chapter begins to introduce you to the really powerful aspects of programming in the command language. While the macros covered in the previous chapters represent a form of programming, macro programming is limited both in complexity and in power. Although using macros to automate sequences of commands can be a tremendous productivity enhancer, the capability of the command language to add selection and repetition to your programming arsenal opens up whole new realms of possibility.

With the command language, you have a much greater degree of control over 1-2-3. You can use the command language to turn 1-2-3 into a complete computing system and build applications as complex as a complete accounting system. Or, you can program a much greater degree of automation into your daily work, extending the concept of macros far beyond simple command automation.

This chapter begins with a discussion of how many of the string functions discussed in Chapter 8 can be used to overcome some of the limitations of the command language. Using the techniques described, you can create string formulas that act as command language instructions, but which perform programming tasks that could not be accomplished otherwise.

When you start programming in the command language, you are also leaving behind the safe and easy world of spreadsheet building and entering the more complex and disciplined world of programming. The type of programming you do with the command language is not as forgiving as the process of model building with a spreadsheet. Your programs will have to contend with user input, generation of output in the proper sequence, and the processing of errors and unexpected problems. Fortunately, the problems associated with writing programs have been addressed by programmers working in more conventional languages, such as FORTRAN and Pascal.

This more mature discipline of conventional programming uses some terminology that, although useful, may be unfamiliar to those of you without formal computer backgrounds. For a review of command language programming terms, see the glossary at the end of this book. The terms explained in the glossary will appear with some frequency in the chapters that follow. Familiarize yourself with this terminology. Although it is, in a sense, jargon, many of the terms used provide a convenient way to think and talk about programming. Speaking the common tongue will make using the multitude of material written for conventional programming easier for you.

Those of you already familiar with Release 1A of 1-2-3 are probably familiar with the primitive programming features available as part of Release 1A's macro language. Veteran Release 1A users will find two major changes in those macro features, which are discussed in the last part of this chapter. First, most macro keywords now accept a form of argument that allows them to repeat automatically. Second, the old /x commands, although still a part of Release 2, have been supplanted by newer command language equivalents.

Command Language Syntax

Command language instructions, which are extensions of macro instructions, are a special set of keywords. The command language instructions, like macro keywords, are enclosed in braces ({}). Some command language instructions can accept arguments in the same way that 1-2-3 functions do. Note that virtually all macro keywords also can accept arguments. (This wasn't explained previously because using arguments with keywords relates more to programming, as I defined it earlier, than to macros.)

The syntax for command language instruction arguments, which is similar to that of function arguments, has three requirements. First, the arguments follow the keyword. Second, the arguments are separated from the keyword by a single space (which is required). If an instruction contains multiple arguments, those arguments must be separated by a comma or semicolon. Third, the arguments are included with the keyword inside the braces. Following is an example:

{KEYWORD argument1,argument2,...argumentn}

└─Required space

Like an @ function, a command language instruction can have one, several, or no arguments. 1-2-3 "acts" oddly if the number of arguments included in an instruction isn't correct. If you include more arguments in an instruction than are required, 1-2-3 almost always ignores the extra argument. An omitted argument, however, causes a run-time error when you try to run the program. A run-time error also occurs if you omit the closing brace.

Using String Formulas To Create Command Language Instructions

The fact that 1-2-3 executes string formulas makes the command language almost completely flexible. You can create instructions that are automatically modified by data in the worksheet, instructions that are modified by other parts of the command language program, and even instructions that modify themselves. For an instruction to be executable, all that is required is that what appears in the cell must have correct syntax. (Note that when the cell is formatted to Text, the formula itself will appear.)

Instructions That Update Automatically

You have already seen several examples of instructions that contain string formulas. In Chapter 6, the Slide Show macro demonstrated the use of string formulas in a macro. Chapter 8 described how to use @CHOOSE and @STRING to combine information into a program. Figure 9.1 shows another example. This short program inserts data into a database, according to a simple formula in cell B5. The instruction in B5 is tied to the counter variable (CTR) used by the {FOR} instruction in line 3. The formula that creates the instruction in B5, which appears in the control panel, calculates a new value from the counter variable during each pass. The @STRING function then converts the calculated result to a form that allows the result to be entered directly into the input form of a database.

"Impossible" Instructions

Some command language instructions take string arguments. According to the 1-2-3 *Reference Manual*, three such instructions exist for which the string must be typed directly into the instruction rather than specified as a cell reference. These instructions are {GETLABEL}, {GETNUMBER}, and {INDICATE}.

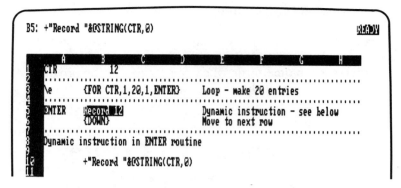

Fig. 9.1. Dynamic instructions.

With {INDICATE}, you can control the appearance of the mode indicator that appears in the upper right corner of the screen. The usual syntax for this instruction is

{INDICATE message}

When 1-2-3 executes this instruction, a *message*, which can be up to five characters long, appears in place of 1-2-3's usual mode indicator. Notice that no quotation marks are required around the *message* argument. Usually, when you use a string without quotation marks as an argument to either an @ function or a command language instruction, that string is interpreted as a range name. The syntax for {INDICATE}, therefore, is somewhat unique. If you try to apply the more standard syntax to {INDICATE} by using a cell address or a range name as an argument, the results may not be what you expect.

In figure 9.2, C3, which appears as an argument to the {INDICATE} instruction, looks like a cell reference. If C3 was a cell reference, however, you would expect the word hello to appear in the mode indicator. Instead, what appears is C3—a literal copy of the argument supplied to {INDICATE}, not the contents of cell C3.

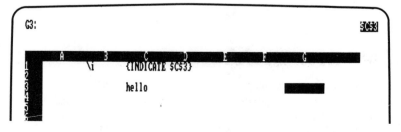

Fig. 9.2. The cell reference used with {INDICATE} is not recognized as such.

You *can* make an {INDICATE} instruction display the contents of another cell. You simply construct a string formula whose result is the desired instruction (see fig. 9.3).

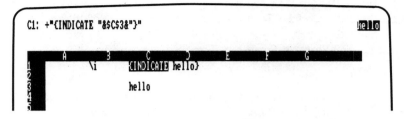

Fig. 9.3. A string formula used to make {INDICATE} accept referenced arguments.

By adding a few characters, you can convert the instruction into a string formula, the result of which is

{INDICATE hello}

As you can see, the resulting string formula produces an {INDICATE} instruction that uses a cell reference to supply the string argument.

The Problem of Quotation Marks

Any command language instruction can be constructed with a simple string formula like the one in figure 9.3, unless the instruction's usual syntax requires that quotation marks surround the argument. Quotation marks are required when the argument contains standard delimiter characters such as commas or semicolons, or when the argument contains certain special characters such as a left brace ({). The quotation marks keep 1-2-3 from interpreting commas or semicolons as argument separators and the left brace as the beginning of a new command language instruction. When quotation marks are used to delimit strings in a string formula, you must take special steps to include quotation marks as part of a delimited string.

You can use three methods to include quotation marks as part of a delimited string. With the first method, you use two quotation marks in a row, which 1-2-3 interprets as a single quotation mark within a string. For instance, suppose that you want to create the following string:

Bob says "Hi!"

You use the string formula

+"Bob says ""Hi!"""

Notice that the formula ends with three quotation marks in a row. 1-2-3 interprets the first two as a single quotation mark following the exclamation point. The last quotation mark is the final delimiter for the string formula.

The second method uses the @CHAR function. @CHAR(34) represents the quotation mark character. Therefore, including @CHAR(34) in a string formula causes a quotation mark to appear. If you apply this method to the preceding example, the result is the following formula:

+"Bob says "&@CHAR(34)&"Hi!"&@CHAR(34)

Figure 9.4 shows how you can apply this method to the {INDICATE} instruction in order to cause 1-2-3 to display a colon centered in a five-character field.

Fig. 9.4. @CHAR(34) used to include quotation marks in string formulas.

The third method involves splitting the command language instruction into three cells and combining them all with a simple concatenation formula (see fig. 9.5). This method uses the simplest formulas, but takes up the greatest number of cells.

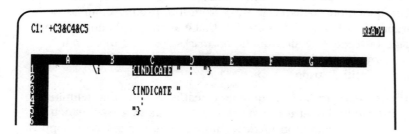

Fig. 9.5. Multiple references used to include quotation marks in string formulas.

The Calculation Problem

Dynamic instructions, of which the preceding is only one example, are powerful additions to the command language instruction set. However, one important restriction applies to the use of these instructions created from string formulas: they are formulas and, like all formulas, they display current results only when recalculated.

TRAP: 1-2-3 doesn't recalculate all cells during macro or program execution.

Some command language instructions, such as {IF}, force 1-2-3 to recalculate the instructions' contents before proceeding. However, even when Recalculation is set to Automatic, 1-2-3 doesn't recalculate most cells in the worksheet after executing an instruction. Evidently 1-2-3 doesn't consider the execution of a program instruction sufficient reason to recalculate the worksheet. Considering how slow the command language is, you probably wouldn't want 1-2-3 to perform such recalculations. If your program alters the worksheet, however, many formulas in the worksheet won't reflect these alterations until something else forces recalculation. This failure to recalculate happens when you use dynamic instructions, which are formulas. When you use dynamic instructions, you must be sure that prior to executing the instruction, 1-2-3 recalculates the cell containing the instruction's formula.

GUIDELINE: Always include a {RECALC} instruction in a dynamic instruction formula.

To make sure that 1-2-3 updates your dynamic instruction, you must do two things. First, you must assign a range name to the cell containing the formula. Second, you must use a {RECALC} instruction in the formula.

In the example in figure 9.6, the dynamic instruction cell is also the entry point for a subroutine and already has a name. This arrangement causes 1-2-3 to alter the very instruction the program is executing. Even so, I've never had any difficulty with this method. You must be sure, however, that the {RECALC} instruction is the first item in the formula.

GUIDELINE: Always leave dynamic instruction formulas showing the formula result, but include a copy of the formula in your listing.

Dynamic instructions pose a problem for program documentation because the instruction that appears on the screen or in a listing isn't the only form the instruction can take. Any given listing will not describe how the program operates when the dynamic instruction changes appearance. Therefore, dynamic instructions require special documentation.

One way to document dynamic instructions might be to set their cell formats to Text so that the formulas themselves are visible. This idea, however, is actually

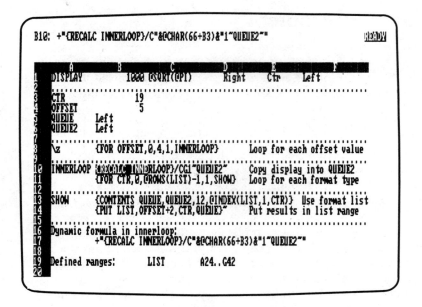

Fig. 9.6. The {RECALC} instruction in a dynamic instruction formula.

very bad. When you read a program listing that contains text listings of dynamic instructions, deciphering the final form of the instruction by simple examination is virtually impossible. You have to re-create the formula and its final result in your head. Even if you are a whiz at interpreting formulas, the translation process interrupts the flow of understanding the program.

A better way to document a dynamic instruction is to leave it in its final form, but flag it as dynamic and include a listing of the formula, as a string, close to the instruction itself. If you include a {RECALC} instruction with each dynamic formula, you will necessarily have a range name assigned to each dynamic instruction. You can use that range name to identify the instruction as dynamic.

The Display Problem

Many command language instructions cause changes in the worksheet that don't immediately appear on the screen. To reduce the time needed for 1-2-3 to execute a command language program, Lotus software engineers decided not to update the screen with every operation. The result is that some command language instructions operate "behind the scenes." The worksheet is modified, but the modifications are invisible.

To view the results of the program, you may have to press Enter or some other key on the keyboard (either manually or with the program). This procedure isn't always necessary; some instructions, such as {WINDOWSON}, force updating of the screen. If your program doesn't appear to be working properly, check to be sure that the screen is up-to-date.

What you gain for not being able to see the screen activity is speed. Because the command language is slow, any gain in speed is usually valuable. If you want to watch everything on your screen as it happens (a good idea when debugging a program), you can force frequent screen updating, but only at a significant increase in execution time.

Conventions Used in This Chapter

In this chapter, command language instructions often are referred to without their arguments, as if the instructions were macro keywords. For example, {INDICATE} appears in this sentence as if the instruction had no arguments, which is only sometimes the case. When I use a command language instruction without arguments in the text, I'm usually referring to the keyword and not necessarily using acceptable syntax.

Arguments

Many command language instructions require another value, address, or keyword within the braces. These values, called *parameters*, are also known as *arguments*. Some instructions have optional arguments, in which case the arguments appear in brackets.

For most of these optional arguments, an additional argument delimiter is required, which also appears inside the brackets. Following is the syntax listing for an instruction with one required argument and one optional argument.

    {KEYWORD required_argument[,optional_argument]}

Addresses

A *cell address* in the syntax descriptions refers to a column and row location, and can take any of the relative or absolute forms:

    A12
    A12
    $A12
    A$12

A *range address* refers to cell address specifications that indicate range corners, such as

A12..G15

A range address can specify a single cell or group of cells. Either of the cell addresses can be in any of the relative or absolute forms.

If the syntax specifies *address* rather than *cell address* or *range address*, either of these forms is acceptable. Unless otherwise stated, *address* can be a range name.

Range Names

One of the most important points I have tried to make throughout this book is the importance of creating and documenting programs in a form that makes them easy to maintain. Program code is inherently difficult to read and understand, and as the length of your programs grows to beyond a few lines, small differences in readability become magnified. As one of a family of Que Corporation books about 1-2-3, the program listings in this book are bound by the conventions established for coding macros. According to those conventions, both keywords and range names are presented in uppercase letters.

You can make your own program listings more readable, however, if you use a combination of upper- and lowercase letters for writing programs. Human factors researchers discovered some time ago that programmers make fewer errors if the standard language elements are listed in uppercase and the remainder of the program is in lowercase or mixed case. To incorporate this idea into your command language program writing, you should use uppercase for listing keywords and functions, such as {BRANCH}, {IF}, or @STRING, and lowercase for all range names, including those used in functions.

Using this mixture of cases has two distinct advantages over other methods. First, when you create a subroutine, the call to that subroutine will appear as the range name assigned to the subroutine enclosed in braces. For example, if you want to call a subroutine called LOAD, the listing would appear as

{load}

When this type of listing is included in a program, you can easily distinguish the subroutine calls you have created from the standard language elements. When you are debugging a program, using this convention makes it much easier to trace backward from a subroutine to the place or places the routine was called in the main program.

Second, many programs you write will have code that contains several command language instructions on the same line. When this occurs, using lowercase for range names breaks up the long strings of characters and allows you to distinguish the individual instructions. For example, compare the following lines.

All uppercase:

{IF @INDEX(DRANGE,COL,ROW)=OLDCELL}{BEEP}{REDO}{LET OLDCELL,NEWCELL}

Mixed cases:

{IF @INDEX(drange,col,row)=OldCell}{BEEP}{redo}{LET OldCell,NewCell}

You may have noticed in the preceding example and elsewhere in this book my rather peculiar habit of running several words together in a range name. Using such compound range names allows you to use more descriptive names in your programs. This practice can help readability considerably.

In the days when computers did not have lowercase characters, programmers compounded names by separating the sections of the name with a special character, usually the underscore. Using the underscore, you would create names such as RANGE_NAME. The name is readily distinguishable as a single name, and is fairly readable. Because you have lowercase letters on your computer, you can use a mixture of uppercase and lowercase letters to accomplish the same effect, as in RangeName. This convention, which is borrowed from Pascal, is one I use in all my program writing. Mixed-case range names are easier to type than underscore-separated range names. In addition, because 1-2-3 limits range names to 15 characters, leaving out the underscore allows more room for words. You can use mixed case to create very long range names. For example,

OutOfTheWayCell

is more readable than

OUTOFTHEWAYCELL

and is easier to type (and more grammatical) than

OUT_OF_WAY_CELL

These differences may seem minor at first, but the effects add up in a long program listing. Remember that program code is intrinsically difficult to read. Anything you can do to enhance readability is virtually mandatory for serious command language programmers. To formalize my recommendations regarding program coding conventions, I offer the following guidelines.

GUIDELINE: Use these conventions for coding programs:

1. Use uppercase letters for all keywords and command language instructions.

2. Use lowercase letters for range names, and mixed case for range names compounded from more than one word.

3. Make your range names as descriptive as possible.

In Chapter 3, I recommended that you adopt a convention to distinguish range names from keywords and macro commands, using uppercase for one and lowercase for the other. In that discussion I suggested that which you capitalized and which you left in lowercase did not matter. When establishing a convention for use with the command language, however, another consideration is involved. The {GET} instruction, which is used in the Automatic Macro program, and its companion instruction {LOOK}, both capture keystrokes in uppercase. If you use uppercase for keywords, your instruction coding will be compatible with the output from these two command language instructions.

The selection of range names for use in command language programs poses the same dilemma for 1-2-3 programmers as for programmers of other computer languages. Short, abbreviated names are easy to write, but hard to read. Because a certain amount of tedium is associated with writing a program, most programmers are tempted to use the shortest possible names. The result is code that is difficult to interpret. For example, compare the readability of the two listings that follow. The module shown performs the iterative calculations for a goal-seeking program (listed in full in Chapter 11). Notice how much easier the second listing is to follow.

Listing 1: Heavily abbreviated

```
it        {RECALC it}{LET $D$166,inc+ll}
          {CALC}
          {IF @ROUND(@@(ca),tol)=@ROUND(gl,tol)}{FORBREAK}
          {IF @@(ca)<gl}{LET ll,ll+inc}{RETURN}
          {IF @@(ca)>gl}{LET inc,inc/2}{RETURN}
```

Listing 2: Expanded range names

```
Iterate   {RECALC Iterate}{LET $D$166,Increment+LowerLimit}
          {CALC}
          {IF @ROUND(@@(CheckAddress),Tolerance)=
             @ROUND(Goal,Tolerance)}{FORBREAK}
          {IF @@(CheckAddress)<Goal}{LET LowerLimit,LowerLimit+Increment}{RETURN}
          {IF @@(CheckAddress)>Goal}{LET Increment,Increment/2}{RETURN}
```

Longer, more descriptive range names can enhance program readability considerably, but they also slow down the process of writing the program. As a compromise, here are some guidelines for using range names in a command language program.

GUIDELINE: Use the following guidelines for range names in a command language program:

1. If the module you are writing is complicated or uses some tricky programming to accomplish its goals, use long range names. The more complex the module, the more descriptive your names should be.

2. If the module is part of a long program, use long names. When you use many abbreviations in a long program, you are likely to repeat, causing a horrible debugging problem. Also, when you have many names to keep track of, as in a long program, more descriptive names make the program easier to follow. Use the "rule of 3s" definition of a long program: a program that has more than 30 lines, more than 3 modules, or more than 3 levels of subroutine nesting.

3. Use descriptive names for constants and variables, that is, the cells that contain values or strings used by the program in computation.

4. Always use the most descriptive names possible to name subroutines. Describe a subroutine's function in its name, and your program will become almost self-documenting.

5. Use short range names for loop reentry points or recalculation cells that appear in subroutines. One trick I use frequently when a subroutine contains a number of reference points is to create names using the first three characters of the subroutine name and a sequential number. Thus, if a subroutine is named *message*, the reference points would be named *mes1*, *mes2*, *mes3*, and so on. This naming technique also creates a "family" of names that helps identify the origin of a variable or subroutine. You should use at least three characters from the subroutine name in order to avoid creating a name that is also a cell address.

6. Use short names for the variables within complicated formulas. At some point, the length of a long formula begins to make it difficult to read, and a compromise is in order. Shorter names allow you to display more of the logic of a formula on the screen at one time. Use this technique sparingly.

More than Macros: Programming 1-2-3

This section is for everyone, but especially for veteran 1-2-3 Release 1A programmers. Release 2 contains some significant improvements over the macro facility of Release 1A. Keywords may be automatically repeated, and the /x commands have been improved.

Repetition Arguments for Macro Keywords

With Release 2 of 1-2-3, you can specify repetition arguments for macro keywords. Veteran 1-2-3 macro users will immediately appreciate the value of this feature. For example, if you want to move down 19 rows in Release 1A, you have to type 19 {DOWN} keywords into the macro—a tedious process that generates a cluttered-looking macro.

    {DOWN}{DOWN}{DOWN}{DOWN}{DOWN}{DOWN}{DOWN}
    {DOWN}{DOWN}{DOWN}{DOWN}{DOWN}{DOWN}{DOWN}
    {DOWN}{DOWN}{DOWN}{DOWN}{DOWN}

With 1-2-3, you type

    {DOWN 19}

or

    {D 19}

One advantage of this procedure is immediately apparent: it's quick and easy to implement. Another more powerful advantage is that instead of a number, you can use a formula or cell reference as a repetition argument (see fig. 9.7).

If the repetition argument is not an integer, 1-2-3 truncates the fractional part of the argument. For example, {DOWN 19/10} moves down only 1 row because 1-2-3 truncates 1.9 to 1. 1-2-3 ignores the sign of the repetition number. {DOWN –3}, for instance, is equivalent to {DOWN 3}.

You can also specify an argument of zero, in which case 1-2-3 doesn't execute the instruction. Also, if the repetition argument is ERR or NA, 1-2-3 doesn't execute the instruction.

You can use the @@ function to reference the repetition count indirectly as long as the address used in the pointer cell is a cell address. If a range address is used in the pointer cell, 1-2-3 treats the repetition count as zero.

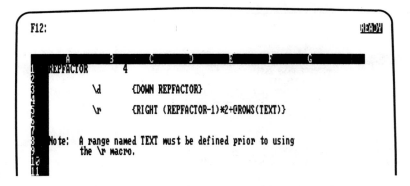

Fig. 9.7. Repetition factors specified with macro keywords.

TRAP: The maximum value for a repetition argument is 32767.

A limit exists to the number of repetitions you can specify for a keyword: 32767. This number is extremely large and one you are unlikely to encounter during normal programming. If you exceed this limit, the instruction treats the repetition argument as if it were zero, and the instruction doesn't execute. The most likely scenario for encountering this limitation is when you use a formula to calculate the repetition number, and something goes awry with that formula, returning a number that is much higher than expected.

By controlling the number of times 1-2-3 executes an instruction, you can create some interesting applications. For example, the program in figure 9.8 enables you to edit any cell in a database, given the record number and field name as inputs. If you know the exact record number, you can use this method as an alternative to /Data Query Find.

The program operates on a database such as the one shown in figure 9.9. The operator simply enters the record number and field name in response to the {GETNUMBER} and {GETLABEL} prompts (see fig. 9.8), and the cell pointer is moved to the appropriate location.

The argument in the {DOWN} instruction uses as a repetition argument the value the user enters in response to the {GETNUMBER} instruction's prompt. Because the top row of a database is not a data record, the {GOTO} instruction places the cell pointer on what is, in effect, record zero of the database. If the user types the number 1 in response to the {GETNUMBER} instruction's prompt, the repetition argument will be 1, the {DOWN} keyword will repeat once, and the cell pointer will come to rest on the first record.

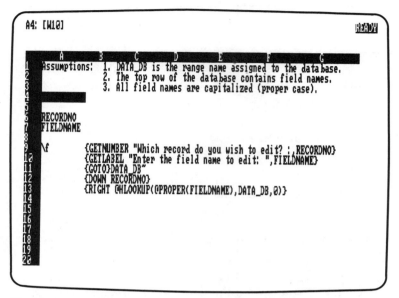

```
A4: [W10]                                                        READY

          A      B       C        D        E        F        G
 1  Assumptions:  1. DATA_DB is the range name assigned to the database.
 2                2. The top row of the database contains field names.
 3                3. All field names are capitalized (proper case).
 4
 5
 6  RECORDNO
 7  FIELDNAME
 8
 9  \f        {GETNUMBER "Which record do you wish to edit? :,RECORDNO}
10            {GETLABEL "Enter the field name to edit: ",FIELDNAME}
11            {GOTO}DATA_DB~
12            {DOWN RECORDNO}
13            {RIGHT @HLOOKUP(@PROPER(FIELDNAME),DATA_DB,0)}
14
15
16
17
18
19
20
```

Fig. 9.8. A program that edits any cell in a database.

```
A1: [W10]                                                        READY

          A       B        C        D        E        F         G
 1
 2  Customer  Outlet   Order#  Invoice#  Quantity  Product    Salesperson
 3      272   East     35466     1898        10    Cologne        126
 4      272   West     27356     1916         3    Shirt          129
 5      272   Downtown 43699     1749         7    Disk           145
 6      293   East     33811     1042         8    Dishpan        575
 7      293   Downtown 36991     1825         8    Lantern        576
 8      371   East     49874     1497         8    Coffee         327
 9      371   West     49003     1397         4    Backpack       551
10      451   Downtown 88202     1829         5    Wrench         463
11      451   West     28127     1728         8    Computer       203
12      451   East     35077     1346        11    Pant           117
13      466   East     43188     1179        11    Mixer          129
14      466   West     50757     1171         4    Skirt          309
15      526   West     47302     1381         9    Notebook       384
16      526   Downtown 27488     1037         3    Blouse         115
17      998   West     17775     1292         9    Light bulb     498
18      998   Downtown 64110     1206         7    Silverware     141
19
20
```

Fig. 9.9. A database on which the program in figure 9.8 could operate.

The @HLOOKUP function calculates the argument for the {RIGHT} keyword, based on the field name the user enters in response to the {GETLABEL} instruction's prompt. The @HLOOKUP function returns the offset of the specified field name in the database, and the cell pointer comes to rest in the desired column. Notice that if the user selects the first field in the database, @HLOOKUP returns an offset of zero, and the {RIGHT} instruction doesn't execute.

Keyword Listing

You can use a repetition argument with the following macro keywords:

{ABS}
{BACKSPACE} or {BS}
{BIGLEFT}
{BIGRIGHT}
{CALC}
{DELETE} or {DEL}
{DOWN} or {D}
{EDIT}
{END}
{ESCAPE} or {ESC}
{GOTO}
{GRAPH}
{HOME}
{INSERT} or {INS}
{LEFT} or {L}
{NAME}
{PGDN} or {BIGDOWN}
{PGUP} or {BIGUP}
{QUERY}
{RIGHT} or {R}
{TABLE}
{UP} or {U}
{WINDOW}

With some of these keywords, the repetition argument is not very useful. I know of no instance, for example, in which repeatedly pressing the Home key or the GoTo key (F5) accomplishes anything more than pressing the key once accomplishes.

You should also be aware that macro program control is suspended when the {GRAPH} keyword is used. The program resumes when the user presses a key on the keyboard. If you specify a repetition argument for {GRAPH}, 1-2-3 will display the graph, if one is defined, the number of times specified by the argument. Each time the graph is displayed, the user will have to press a key to resume program execution. Suppose, for instance, that you specify {GRAPH 3}. The graph will be displayed, 1-2-3 will stop program execution, and you will have to press a key—in that sequence, three times.

The /x Commands

In addition to the 26 keywords and 40 or so command language instructions, 1-2-3 has 8 special macro functions usually referred to as the /x commands. I think of these commands as the tailbone of 1-2-3, something left over from more primitive times. The /x commands were meant to be similar in operation to the other 1-2-3 commands, beginning with a slash (/) and ending with a tilde (~). The enthusiasm that users exhibited for this rudimentary programming capability led Lotus to develop the full-blown programming language that is the subject of this book.

To maintain compatibility with spreadsheets and macros created in Release 1A, Release 2 still has the /x commands. All, however, have equivalents in the command language. Table 9.1 shows the /x commands and their corresponding command language instructions.

Table 9.1
/x Commands and Their Command Language
Instruction Equivalents

/xg	{BRANCH}
/xm	{MENUBRANCH}
/xc	{name}
/xr	{RETURN}
/xq	{QUIT}
/xi	{IF}
/xl	{GETLABEL}
/xn	{GETNUMBER}

The functions of the corresponding /x commands and command language instructions are almost exactly the same. The few differences that do exist are subtle.

1. The /x commands don't need to be written on a single line, as do the command language instructions. With the exception of /xi, the /x instructions can even be written one character to a line. The second part of the /xi instruction executes only if the test contained in the first part evaluates as TRUE. This second, conditional portion of the command must be on a single line following the tilde that separates the two parts of the instruction.

2. The /xl and /xn commands can place the user response in the current cell. This is something that the companion {GETLABEL} and {GETNUMBER} instructions can do only with some tricky programming.

3. The /xn command won't allow the user to enter characters (except range names or cell addresses) or to give no response (Enter). The command displays an error message and lets the user retry the entry. If characters or Enter are entered with {GETNUMBER}, the response is accepted, but ERR is placed in the destination cell.

4. The /x commands process their instructions with the same mechanisms 1-2-3 uses to process manual commands. The contents of the commands are actually typed into the command line as the commands execute. If you operate the commands in STEP mode, you can monitor this activity, which includes an appearance by the command menu when a command is first invoked.

    The corresponding command language instructions, on the other hand, operate internally. When the command language instructions execute, no external evidence exists of their operation. Because of this difference in operation, the command language instructions are lightning fast compared to their /x counterparts. The speed advantage is somewhere on the order of 50 to 100 times faster, depending on the application.

Two other important differences exist between the /x commands and command language instructions. First, compared to their command language equivalents, /x commands create cryptic, difficult-to-read programs. Second, /x commands are prone to syntax errors because of omitted tildes. With Release 1A of 1-2-3, a true macro expert was someone who could actually read existing macros and understand their functions.

In summary, the /x commands are truly holdovers from the old release of 1-2-3. With the minor exceptions described earlier, everything that can be accomplished with /x instructions can be accomplished with the command language equivalents. In addition, using the command language instead of the /x commands results in programs that are easier to read and less prone to syntax errors. Moreover, command language programs can run up to 100 times faster.

GUIDELINE: Always use the command language instructions instead of the /x commands.

Experienced 1-2-3 macro programmers will be tempted to continue using the /x commands because they are familiar and easier to write. Even though short range names are easier to use, they have certain disadvantages (see the "Range Names" section in this chapter). If you are an old hand at using /x commands, the time has come for you to graduate to a real programming language.

You may encounter some rare application in which the /x commands are easier to use than the command language—for example, using /xl or /xn to enter data into the current cell pointer location. However, you can accomplish almost any other function by using a command language instruction. For documenting your programs, the /x commands are just awful. Although the command language instructions have more characters, the payoff in readability, debugging time, and ease of program modification will more than repay the effort needed to make the switch.

10

Programming

Including in this book a chapter simply titled "Programming" is perhaps a little presumptuous. The subject of writing programs is one whose scope encompasses an entire book or perhaps several books and a few college-level courses. If you have read the previous chapters and worked your way through the programming examples, you are probably getting a feel for how to construct programs. At this point, however, you could say that what has been covered is enough knowledge to be dangerous. The examples merely demonstrate the use of the command language's instruction set and haven't addressed some of the larger issues that pertain to writing programs.

These important issues will be addressed in some form in this chapter. You won't learn everything you need to know about programming, but you should come away with some guidelines that will help get you started as a programmer. If you get really ambitious, and you don't have any programming experience or training, you should look into additional sources of programming information.

You can do a tremendous amount with the command language without running into most of the issues described in this chapter. If all you intend to do with the command language is write programs that are similar in size and scope to the examples in the previous chapters, you probably can skip this section. You should, however, consider the Law of the Hammer (which is crudely paraphrased here): "If you give someone a hammer, sooner or later he or she is gonna pound something." That is, as you become familiar with the command language, the possibilities for larger and larger applications will become irresistible. You may start out innocently enough writing simple File Save macros. But after a while, you can easily find yourself thinking about such things as relational databases, general ledger systems, or simulation of human thought. If you expect your command language applications to become increasingly complicated, read on.

The Problem of Structure

As much as I'm excited about 1-2-3's potential as a new form of computer language, the program holds a number of pitfalls for the unwary. One criticism I've heard about spreadsheets in general is that they are too unstructured; that is, you can construct anything you want any way you want without worrying about the consequences of your work. Of course, others have said that this very lack of structure is the reason for the spreadsheet's popularity. You simply throw into the spreadsheet whatever information you have at hand, and you gradually shape the final result by adding, deleting, and modifying the initial setup.

This cut-and-try method is probably a lot closer to the way our brains work than most computer programming. Depending on how well you use this method, it could be said to resemble either sculpting with clay or cooking by throwing a lot of leftovers into a pot. The difference is that sculptors not only see their work clearly, but probably have a specific image of what end point they are trying to reach. Cooks, on the other hand, working without a recipe or plan, could easily ruin the food by adding one spice too many. Many an unsavory stew can trace its beginnings to just such efforts.

When building a spreadsheet, you can be either a sculptor or a haphazard cook. You can set up numbers and formulas logically or randomly. You can document thoroughly or not at all. You can write formulas with meaningful range names, obscure range names, or uninterpretable cell addresses. In other words, a spreadsheet allows, but does not force, an organized approach to the work. In other words, along with flexibility comes the potential for creating incredible messes.

The lack of forced structure is most serious when applied to programming. Consider what you could do with a command language program if you deliberately tried to make it difficult to follow. You could use cell addresses instead of range names, hide parts of the code, or document nothing. You could easily write programs so that the long labels containing the instructions overlapped each other and could be read only a cell at a time in EDIT mode.

Unfortunately, such things sometimes happen unintentionally in command language programming. I've been guilty of each of the preceding offenses; they creep up on you when you aren't looking. The heart of the problem is the process of translating abstract thoughts about a problem into the literal, simplistic, sequential language of the computer. The conceptual distance between human thought and computer language is vast. If you don't bridge the gap by using a clearly organized approach and writing documentation, the whole process can fall apart.

How Computer Programmers Get into Trouble

Few people can write computer code in one sitting. You may plan carefully, but every system has enough vagaries to make testing and refinement necessary before the system works. For most people, the process of developing a program is iterative: they achieve the final result by using a series of successive approximations. 1-2-3's highly visual mode of programming encourages this kind of development.

The problems begin to arise as you make refinements to the pieces of program that comprise the solution. When you lay out your first rough program, it will probably be fairly coherent. It will have an identifiable beginning, middle, and end. And the program's purpose and direction probably will be immediately obvious (at least to you). With each change you make, however, you lose some coherence. Some changes will be the result of incomplete planning; others, the result of refinements you think of as you begin working with the program and see it in action. Some changes will be forced upon you by an idiot mechanical intelligence that does exactly what you tell it to do and not what you want it to do. Still other changes will be the result of bugs in the way the system operates.

As you refine a program, nothing forces you to maintain the original logic and flow of the initial, conceptual-level approach. In fact, if the program structure reflects the order in which you make the refinements, the program tends to become tangled and obscure to the point that following what the program does becomes harder and harder. The program may eventually become so difficult to follow that a change that corrects one problem creates another somewhere else. Three major factors lead to such problems:

1. A tendency to see time spent in planning and documenting as unproductive because you see no tangible progress toward the goal. Planning and documenting are usually the first to be omitted when time pressures are involved.

2. The general hassle associated with planning and documentation. Some people derive great satisfaction from being methodical and thorough. If you aren't one of these people—and few programmers appear to be—you are likely to find tedious many tasks associated with structured programming.

3. Adherence to an original design that was flawed. This problem is more likely to arise after you spend a great deal of time getting your program to work. The less structured you are about building programs, the more this problem becomes a factor. Think of an unstructured program as a large ball of string: by trying to untangle a tangled mess,

you may pull all the knots tighter. At some point, throwing the program away and starting again is the only sensible solution. In other words, a large number of small changes may destroy the original logical flow of your programming approach.

The Consequences of Unstructured Programming

In the real world of commercial computer programs (the kind found on mainframes and minicomputers), programmers spend more than 75 percent of their time maintaining programs. This percentage is staggering, considering that the time is largely unproductive. This situation has arisen for two reasons. First, every program requires at least some maintenance. As more and more programs accumulate, the little chunks of maintenance time grow until they occupy all of a programmer's time. This condition is probably unavoidable. The second reason has to do with programming practices that make programs difficult to maintain. This condition *is* avoidable.

Unless software is just thrown away after being used once, *all* software eventually must be maintained. Although all programs are tested as thoroughly as possible, they are rarely tested for all potential conditions. For example, 15 passes through a program that contains 7 branches of 3 choices each can generate more than 200 trillion unique paths through the program. Testing each path in such a program, even at 1-2-3's blinding speed of about 10 tests per second (most 1-2-3 functions are slower), is roughly equal to the time needed for the San Andreas fault in California to move 25 miles: about 600,000 years.

If you bear in mind such statistics, the more cost-effective option is probably to do the best job of testing that is practical, and then fix mistakes when they surface. Even if you could test a program completely, maintenance would still be required to make changes arising from user requests, changes in the form of the input data, plain old mistakes, and so forth.

Because some program maintenance is inevitable, any time spent preparing for that process is well spent. And the larger the program, the more this maxim applies.

A Structured Approach to Programming

Programmers are divided into two major groups: bottom-up and top-down. Bottom-up programming, also known as data structured design, has many adherents and has been applied successfully to many complex programming tasks. Its basic tenet states that the way to construct a program is to start with the data, both inputs and outputs, on which the program will operate. By applying a series of rules to the transformations of the data, the programmer eventually constructs a program from the bottom up.

Bottom-up programming may be the programming method of choice for extremely complicated data sets, such as those involving multiple databases, varied inputs, and numerous interrelated reports. I will say no more on the topic of bottom-up programming because my experience has been that beginners have a difficult time getting started with this approach. If you are interested in pursuing this subject further, an excellent book on the subject is *Data Structured Program Design* by Kirk Hansen (Topeka, Kans.: Orr, Ken & Associates, Inc., 1983).

Top-down programming probably seems more natural to most people because it more closely resembles the way people think about a problem. You start with the most global description of the problem and break the solution down into substeps. Then you break down each substep into another level of substeps, and so on, until you can't make further logical refinements. Each of the lowest-order substeps, which can be considered a program *module*, translates easily into program code. Another name for this process is *functional decomposition* because the program is decomposed into smaller parts, according to the functions each part performs.

Each time you break a task into subtasks, you create a hierarchy of task description. That is, the subtasks are the parts that make up the task, just as the tasks are the parts that make up the program. Most programming languages use a program-listing convention that helps keep the hierarchical relationship of the program parts clear: for each level of program hierarchy, the left margin of each portion of the listing is indented a little further. The program name isn't indented, but the first level of decomposition is indented 5 spaces, and the subtasks for each first-level task are indented 10 spaces. For each level of indentation, the left margin moves right another 5 spaces (although the exact number of spaces for each level of indentation is arbitrary). The program descriptions that follow use this indentation convention.

Whenever people approach a project of any magnitude, they use functional decomposition. Suppose, for example, that you want to perform the following task:

Make a meal.

You can divide this task into subtasks:

Decide what to fix.
Make a salad.

Make the main dish.
Make a dessert.
Serve the meal.
Eat.
Clean up.

You can divide each subtask into "sub-subtasks," creating multiple levels of hierarchy. For instance, you could divide *Decide what to fix* into

Check available ingredients.
Compare ingredients to recipes.
Select a recipe.

The sub-subtasks for *Make a salad* might be

Get a bowl.
Get the lettuce.
Get the garbanzo beans.

Of most importance here is that each listing completely describes the superordinate task—the label that heads the category containing the listing. Notice also that by reading all the entries at any level of indentation, you can follow the entire process. At the deeper levels of decomposition, however, the individual steps are easy to follow, but ascertaining what the overall task was originally becomes more and more difficult.

The advantage to decomposing a task into a series of steps is that you describe the task at several levels simultaneously. At the deeper levels, the tasks are described in great detail. At the higher levels, following the purpose and flow of the overall task is easy.

The Design Process

GUIDELINE: Gather your apples before you cook your pie.

In program construction, you can use two approaches. One is right, and the other is wrong. The preceding metaphorical guideline should give you a clue as to the major difference between the two. The wrong way, which seems easier in the short run, is the "Let's see, what do I do next?" programming method. It works for *very* short programs, but can also generate programs like balls of string (and is almost certain to do so for long programs). The alternative, of course, is to sit down and plan the program before you write any code.

Major Issues in Program Design

The issues presented here address a worst-case situation in which someone asks you to write a program to perform a task. Even when you write programs for yourself, keeping in mind what is presented here will help clarify your own thinking.

More important than anything else is that a programmer must know what the program is supposed to do. This issue may seem trivial, but it isn't. People don't think like computers and generally have little conception of how stupid these machines really are. After you have been programming a while, you begin to appreciate the difficulty of translating human thought into program instructions. People tend to think and speak using "fuzzy" terminology that works moderately well when another human is at the receiving end. Computers, however, can't handle the least bit of "fuzziness."

People who request a computer program are rarely sure what they want. Suppose that you have to write a program to manage a company checking account. What exactly does that mean? What form will the input take? Who will use the system? What kinds of outputs are desired? How much flexibility is necessary? Get as much of this kind of information as possible. Otherwise you may find that you have written a program that solves the wrong problem.

Knowing what the program is supposed to do is the most difficult and most important part of developing a program. Unfortunately, people with enough authority to order a program rarely have the time or inclination to specify the kind of detail a programmer needs in order to generate the correct program. The programmer must make several tries at writing the program before everyone is happy. Note that even when you are writing a program for yourself, you aren't immune to these issues. You will encounter these kinds of problems if you start writing before mentally clarifying what you want.

When you design a program (for yourself or for someone else), you must consider three major issues: input, output, and errors. The more of these three areas you can successfully address before you start writing code, the more smoothly the process is likely to go.

Input

Here are some issues to consider when you are designing the input for a program:

1. What form will the input take? Will the data fed into the computer be entered by hand or from some automated source?

2. If data is entered by hand, will the data be entered using standard forms?

3. Must the data be entered in a particular order?

4. What data volume can be expected? A program that handles a dozen inputs will be very different from one designed to handle thousands. With 1-2-3, another data volume issue is whether all the data will fit into one worksheet or whether the program will have to handle multiple worksheets or data files.

5. What are the value limits for the data? What are the highest and lowest values that can be expected for numeric data? Does categorical data have a defined set? Will the data be entered as labels, numbers, time, date, and so on? Can some data values be computed instead of entered?

GUIDELINE: Create a design file for all your programs.

Be organized in your approach to programming. Keep any notes you make on a notepad inside your design folder. Keep everything you generate during the design process; you never know what will be valuable. When the program is fully operational, you can clean out the folder.

GUIDELINE: Compile a list of all input variables, along with data volume and value limits for each.

A list of all input variables is sometimes known as a *data dictionary*. Note that a complete data dictionary lists all variables used by the program, along with a brief definition of each variable.

GUIDELINE: Get examples of any data forms that will be used in the input process.

Keep in your design folder a copy of your data dictionary and sample input forms.

One bit of computer jargon that has enjoyed general usage is "Garbage In—Garbage Out," sometimes abbreviated as GIGO. The idea behind this phrase is that a computer program can't produce valid output if given invalid input. If human operators will input data into a computer system you are designing, you are about to come face to face with the GIGO effect. You can, however, do a number of things to minimize the likelihood of input errors.

The first thing you must keep in mind is that humans aren't very good at performing routine tasks, such as data entry, with great accuracy. To optimize operator performance on data input, I offer the following guideline.

GUIDELINE: Make all data input procedures as mechanical as possible.

If you eliminate as much thinking as possible from the data entry process, operators will enter the data with fewer errors. I used to worry that mechanizing the input process too much would frustrate operators, but my experience has proved the opposite. Long and tedious tasks that also require a lot of brainwork can be extremely tiring. If the task must be long and tedious, make it fairly mindless as well to make time go by faster. Be sure to give your data entry people other, more stimulating tasks to keep them happy.

Conversely, if the task does require some care, don't make the task mindless. Otherwise, when the time comes to engage the brain, it will be occupied doing other things. For data entry that involves a great deal of thought, you will have to contend with slower entry and more potential for errors.

GUIDELINE: If data is being input to the computer from a form, use in your program the /Range Input command to display on the screen as exact a copy of that form as possible.

What you want to do, whenever possible, is to create a visual analogue of the data. That is, you want to make the screen look like the form on which the data appears. For instance, match upper- and lowercase letters; and use the same key words (whenever possible).

If the data is being input from a checklist, such as the one in table 10.1, consider using a {GET} instruction and assigning two special keys to serve as positional analogues for the data items in the checklist. {GET} enables the operator to enter data by pressing a single key, without having to press the Enter key for each data point.

In this example, {GET} captures the number 1 and converts it into a TRUE response, and converts the number 2 into a FALSE response. The operator presses the key on the left to enter TRUE and the one on the right to enter FALSE. This is the same arrangement as the boxes in the checklist. With this method, the keys the operator must press to enter data have the same left/right relationship as the data listing. The operator doesn't have to think about TRUE and FALSE, only left and right, and therefore can enter several items per second.

The module in figure 10.1 enters a column of TRUE or FALSE responses. The operator stops the program by pressing 0. If you have never spent any time entering data, try setting up this example and see how fast you can enter data. Then, to really see the effect of the visual analogue, set up the input keys in reverse order from the data form. The difference should be dramatic.

GUIDELINE: Don't make the operator perform calculations, look up values, or perform data transformations while entering data.

Table 10.1
A TRUE/FALSE Checklist Used as a Data Source

	TRUE	FALSE
Item 1	[X]	
Item 2	[ ]	[X]
Item 3	[ ]	[X]
Item 4	[ ]	[X]
Item 5	[X]	[ ]
Item 6	[X]	[ ]
Item 7	[ ]	[X]
Item 8	[ ]	[X]
Item 9	[X]	[ ]
Item 10	[X]	[ ]
Item 11	[ ]	[X]
Item 12	[X]	[ ]
Item 13	[X]	[ ]
Item 14	[X]	[ ]
Item 15	[X]	[ ]

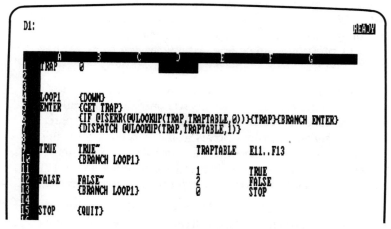

Fig. 10.1. A data entry module that enters TRUE or FALSE by pressing 1 or 2.

Computers are better at calculations than people. If you want the calculations to be correct every time, let the computer do them. The extra effort required to program the computer to perform the calculations will more than pay off in fewer errors. For example, if you are entering monthly income data, and the raw data you are working with is annual income, let the computer divide by 12. Even simple calculations, such as adding 1 or dividing by 10, are prone to data entry errors.

GUIDELINE: When entering names or other categorical data, use abbreviations whenever possible.

If you are entering data into a database, use 1-2-3's LOOKUP capabilities to transform the data from abbreviations into final form. People unfamiliar with computers have an especially difficult time understanding that adding a space after a word makes that entry different from the same word without the space, or that the word *Street* doesn't match the abbreviation *St*. Computers, however, readily detect such differences, which can cause serious problems in a program's operation. You will find that correcting a program for such data entry anomalies after the data has been entered is much more difficult than making sure that the data is correct when it is first entered.

Output

1. What form of output will be generated? The four common forms of output are the following:

   - Disk files

   - Information printed to only the screen

   - Printed reports and graphs

   - Information transmitted to another computer

2. If disk files will be used, will automatic backup copies be required?

3. For printed reports, what will be the output device? Will dot matrix suffice? Is letter quality required? What size paper is necessary? How many copies will be needed?

4. For graphs, what quality, size, and labeling information is required?

GUIDELINE: Get an example of what the final outputs will look like. If such examples aren't available, make mock-ups.

Errors

When you design a program, anticipate errors by considering the following:

1. What kinds of errors can be expected? Will the data contain illegal values that must be trapped on input?

2. How "bulletproof" must the system be? Will the person operating the system be knowledgeable about 1-2-3? Can you assume some user sophistication, or will you have to trap every conceivable error?

3. Can you make trade-offs between user training and programming? The error-trapping parts of a program are more often than not as large as the productive part of the program, and no matter how sophisticated your error-trapping routines are, humans can always find new and creative ways to make a computer "unhappy." At some point, anticipating every possible error becomes more expensive than teaching people not to make the errors.

4. What are the recovery procedures for each error? You should be especially alert for errors that can destroy data.

The answer to these questions will depend in part on whether someone will be able to troubleshoot new problems that arise as a result of user errors. If you are that person, how much time can you devote to troubleshooting?

Designing the Program

You are now ready to start laying out the design of the program. Remember that your first pass probably won't be your last; expect an iterative process. Good program design is always something like taking two steps forward and one step backward.

GUIDELINE: Before starting to design the program, go over the input, output, and error conditions and processing requirements at least twice.

If you create a rough model of your entire program, the model is likely to illuminate the weak spots and gaps in the design. Make sure that you have prepared everything fairly well before you even turn on the computer.

GUIDELINE: Don't be afraid to make changes if you see a better way of doing something.

If you design your program in modular form (explained later in this chapter), making changes will be easier. Especially important is keeping an open mind about radically different approaches to a problem. Don't get emotionally attached to the first solution you create. Chances are that after you work on a program for a while, you will find a new way to solve the problem. If the new approach is much better than the old, throw away the old.

GUIDELINE: Get your design approved before you start programming.

If you are writing a program for other people, have them review the overall design, including input and output forms, before you start to construct the program. You will probably be surprised at how many changes are made at this point. The reason for these changes is not necessarily that you didn't design the program as ordered; chances are that the program wasn't ordered correctly. When some mock-ups or samples of output are first made available, the person requesting the program will be better able to determine exactly what is wanted.

If you are writing programs for your own use, take this opportunity to ask yourself the same question: Is this really what you want? Often, stepping back from the design process to get a broader perspective on the system can be an illuminating experience. The more complicated your program, the more important this procedure becomes. Making changes at this stage is easy. After you start generating program code, however, altering the direction of your efforts will be much more difficult.

Describing the Program

As you begin building a program, focus initially on *what* you want the program to do. For example, suppose that you want to build a program to manage a database of names and addresses. To make the data management process as easy as possible, you will want to create a form-type database in which the records appear as fill-in-the-blank entries rather than as a grid of information in the spreadsheet.

You can pattern the initial operational design after any number of database programs available for the PC. Borrowing from the features usually found in such programs, you will want your program to enable you to enter data through the form image; page backward and forward through the data and have the records appear in the form; move immediately to the first, last, or a numbered record; edit or delete the current record; and select a subset of records for viewing or editing.

The starting point for the program is the high-level description of the program's purpose:

> Manage a database.

The next task is to examine the program's input, output, and error requirements. You will have as inputs the following:

> The information to be tracked by the database.
> A name for the database and associated Criterion range.
> Commands for paging through the database.
> Commands for editing the database.
> Criteria entered for selective viewing and editing.

The next step is to describe the inputs to the program in as much detail as you can (see table 10.2). As you develop this list, you will have to give some thought to exactly what you want the program to do. The input listing task is intended to assist you in "fleshing out" the program's detailed structure. As you will see in the remainder of the example, each step in the development process provides similar assistance in moving from a loosely defined concept to the details of the program code itself.

Table 10.2
Input Variables To Be Used in the Program

Variable Description	Variable Type
Database	
Last Name	Label, 35 characters
First Name	Label, 35 characters
Company/Affiliation	Label, 35 characters
Street Address 1	Label, 45 characters
Street Address 2	Label, 45 characters
City	Label, 35 characters
State	Label, 2 characters
ZIP	Label, 10 characters
Salutation	Label, 25 characters
Group Code	Label, 10 characters
Reference	Label, 60 characters
Database names	
DATABASE	Range name, 14 characters, max
DATABASE_CR	Range name, 14 characters, max
Commands for paging through the database	
View First Record	Menu selection
View Last Record	Menu selection
View Next Record	Menu selection
View Previous Record	Menu selection
View Selected Record	Menu selection, then number
Commands for editing the database	
Reset Entries in Current Record	Menu selection
Edit Current Record	Menu selection
Delete Current Record	Menu selection

Selective viewing and editing

Enter Matching Criteria	Menu selection
Matching Criteria	Matching labels

Commands for sorting

Select Primary-Key	Menu selection
Primary-Key	Cell address
Sort Direction	A or D
Select Secondary-Key	Menu selection
Secondary-Key	Cell address
Sort Direction	A or D
Clear Sort keys	Menu selection
Perform Sort	Menu selection

Form-letter printing

Form letter	Text
Form-letter formulas	Formulas
Form-letter specification	Range name

Outputs from this program will primarily be screen displays. Besides displaying the data from the database itself, the screen will indicate which record is currently displayed and how many total records are in the database. When selection criteria are applied to the viewing process, the screen should also indicate how many matching records exist. In addition, with a little bit of formula construction, the program will be able to generate form letters (described later in this chapter).

The program must cover several error conditions. When a user is viewing records, the program must guard against the user trying to back up to before the first record in the database or trying to move past the last record in the database. Other errors that users may commit include trying to view selected records when no existing records match the specified criteria, trying to sort the database when no sort keys have been specified, and deleting data accidentally.

Decomposing the Program

After you have generally defined the inputs, outputs, and error conditions, you can start breaking down the task into manageable proportions. To decompose the problem functionally, you can mentally review the sequence of steps you will go through whenever you use the final system.

The Initial Decomposition

The first step in creating a database is to put the information into the computer. After entering the information, you will have to be able to examine the records. You will also need to be able to change the contents of the database as well as to delete unwanted records. If you want to be able to examine a subset of the records in the database or to print a form letter based on a subset of the database, you will have to be able to enter selection criteria.

You have now completed the first step in your functional decomposition of the program: you have divided the program into several subtasks that can be performed separately. The results of the first stage of the functional decomposition process can be summarized as follows:

Overall program task:

  Manage a mailing list database.

Subtasks:

    Enter data into the database.
    Edit existing data.
    Select a subset of records.
    Sort the database.

You can now apply the same basic mental process to each subtask and divide it into sub-subtasks. Notice in the preceding listing that the subtask names are indented from the overall program task description. As described previously, the indentation is deliberate and emphasizes the hierarchical nature of the decomposition process. As you break down each subtask into sub-subtasks, you add another level of indentation and hierarchy. You won't add the list of sub-subtasks into the preceding listing; instead, you will create subroutines for each sub-subtask.

The process described in the preceding paragraph is the key to top-down programming. When you create the actual program, you will have a series of subroutine calls or menu options virtually identical to those in the preceding listing, and this series will be your main program. The subroutines will contain additional subroutines, as required.

This arrangement has nothing to do with how the program works; any number of command language instruction groupings could perform the task. What you gain by imposing this structure on the program-generation process is an effective way to approach the problem. This method also helps bridge the gap between the goal you want to achieve and the program instructions. Probably the most important aspects of the top-down structure are that it enables you to follow logically what you create as you write the program, and enables you and others to follow the program's operation after you complete the program.

Decomposing the Tasks Further

GUIDELINE: Limit your program modules to 10 lines or less.

As you proceed with the functional decomposition, the question that arises is "How far do I carry this process?" Decomposition has two limits. You reach the first limit when a single command language instruction can execute each decomposed step.

The second limit has to do with readability. As a rough guideline, I try to keep all my modules (subroutines) to no more than about 10 lines—that is, 10 to 20 command language instructions. For purposes of readability, if a module doesn't fit on the screen, decompose the module further.

Guidelines for Good Decomposition

Breaking up a program into subroutine modules involves more work than arbitrarily dividing the instructions into groups. The following explanation begins to delve into some of the more sophisticated aspects of program design and should help you get an idea of how to proceed on your own with this task. The ideas in this section were adapted from David King's *Current Practices in Software Development* (New York: Yourdon Press, 1984). That book contains much additional useful information for anyone wanting to pursue program construction beyond what is described in this book.

The two basic guidelines for module construction are that the module should have high cohesion and low coupling.

Cohesion

Cohesion, which is sometimes referred to as the strength of a module, is the degree to which a module performs one definable task. Another way to think of cohesion is as internal consistency. A highly cohesive module performs one task that is clearly defined. Furthermore, the module performs that task, and only that task, completely. A cohesive module typically has a single input, which the module transforms into a single output.

Other than a module's function, the following factors can also determine the module's internal consistency:

1. Modules can either perform several activities that must be done in sequence or perform successive transformations on the same data. This form of cohesion isn't as good as functional cohesion but isn't bad either.

2. Modules can perform unrelated activities that are either performed at the same time or grouped at random. Try to avoid using this kind of grouping; it can make the program difficult to follow and maintain.

3. You can also design modules so that one module performs one of several similar tasks, depending on the values of some other variables. Such a module is not the same as a subroutine that performs the same task on different data. Modules that modify their function to perform more than one task are usually constructed to save space and are actually a combination of two separate routines with overlapping functions. Definitely avoid this kind of construction; it's almost impossible to maintain.

Coupling

Coupling is the degree to which any module interacts with other modules in a program. Modules coupled by data only are those that take specific information and perform an operation on that information. Modules coupled by data only are the most desirable. The result of the coupling will be either new data or a transformation of the original data.

You can think of 1-2-3's functions and commands as models of good module construction because they are all functionally cohesive and data coupled. The @SUM function, for instance, takes a specified list of values as inputs and returns a new value based on those inputs. An example of a module that transforms data is the /Range Value command. This command takes a range specification as an input and transforms the data into a new form: the range's displayed values.

Modules coupled via anything besides a simple data transformation usually invite trouble. Undesirable coupling occurs when one module sets a flag that determines the operation of another module, or when one module changes the contents of another or branches to a point inside the second module. In such cases, if you make a change in one module, you may have to alter the modules it is coupled to so that the program continues to work. Unfortunately, the fact that modules are coupled isn't always obvious. You usually realize that modules are coupled when you make a small, innocuous change in a module, and the whole program suddenly crashes.

The guidelines for cohesion and coupling are, of course, idealized, and adhering to them is sometimes difficult. The command language has some limitations that can stifle your good programming habits. For example, in most high-level structured languages, subroutines have "local" variables. Local variables are created when the subroutine is called, and they disappear when it is finished. In 1-2-3, this arrangement would be like having each subroutine in its own separate worksheet. Nothing you could do in this "local" spreadsheet would affect the main spreadsheet.

With this kind of construction, subroutines must also be able to pass the results of the subroutines' operations back to the calling program. 1-2-3 allows variables to be passed into but not out of a subroutine. Therefore, subroutines in 1-2-3 must always place their results in "global" variables, which, in a spreadsheet, are worksheet cells and (by definition) are available to any routine. Global variables make creating what David King refers to as "pathological coupling" easy. They even make creating accidental coupling possible—for example, if you use in a subroutine a range name that had already been used in another subroutine. Pathological and accidental coupling create program structures that are inherently difficult to maintain and that easily lead to inoperative programs. Those types of coupling should be studiously avoided.

When you are constructing programs, keep these guidelines in mind, even if you can't adhere to them exactly. In general, the longer the program, the more important the guidelines become. If you are working on a program more than 100 lines long, the extra effort—even to the point of redesigning and rewriting some modules—is worthwhile.

The Example Continued

To continue further the decomposition task, you will have to define some of the structure of the worksheet. Entering data into the worksheet is actually a form of programming, as mentioned in the introduction to this book. Entering data, however, is very different from command language programming and has its own set of issues. For the purposes of this example, only the problems of constructing the command language program are considered. You will, however, have to construct some ranges and formulas to serve as the foundation for the database program.

Initially, if the data is to be entered and viewed as a fill-in-the-blanks form, you will have to construct a form image. Figure 10.2 shows the layout of a form designed around the data fields defined previously in table 10.2. Also shown in this figure is a message line (line 15) that describes which record is currently being viewed. The form is constructed using the following column widths:

Default	9
Column A	11
Column C	11
Column D	6
Column E	11
Column F	5

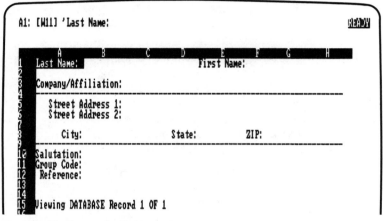

Fig. 10.2. The layout for the input form.

The easiest way to put data into such a form is to use 1-2-3's /Range Input command. Using this command requires that the input cells be unprotected, using the /Range Unprotect command. The cells to unprotect are the following:

B1
F1
C3
C5
C6
B8
E8
G8
B10
B11
B12

To facilitate using this range in the command language program, assign A1..H12 the range name INPUTRANGE.

Two other ranges need to be constructed. The first is the Database range itself. Because the database contains no data yet, the range will consist only of a set of field names, all in a single row. This example uses the field names that appear in the input form (minus the colons), arranged in the same order as they appear in the form, reading left to right, top to bottom. This line of field names is given the range name DATABASE. At the start, the Database range will contain only one row—the field names themselves. For this example, the Database range is I1..S1.

The database manager also requires a Criterion range. At the beginning, the Criterion range is identical to the Database range, containing only field names. In this example, the Criterion range, AA1..AK1, is named DATABASE_CR.

Returning to command language programming, you have broken down the overall program description so that the first level of decomposition looks like the following.

Overall program task:

> Manage a mailing list database.

Subtasks:

> Enter data into the database.
> Edit existing data.
> Select a subset of records.
> Sort the database.

You can decompose each subtask further. Start with the first subtask:

> Enter data into the database.

This first subtask is concerned with the entry of new information into the database, which is similar to editing but not identical. To enter new data, your program will have to do the following:

> Erase any entries currently in the form.
> Determine the record number for the new entry.
> Display an indicator showing which record is being entered.
> Adjust the size of the Database range name.
> Transfer the data to the Database range from the form.

For some entries, further decomposition is required.

> Transfer the data to the Database range from the form.

>> Erase all destination cells in the database.
>> Move nonblank entries into the database.

Next, you can decompose the second subtask:

>   Edit existing data.

Editing existing data combines viewing records (browsing) and altering records (editing). These procedures can be broken down into the following:

>   Display the first record in the database.
>   Display the last record in the database.
>   Display the record subsequent to the one currently being viewed.
>   Display the record previous to the one being viewed.
>   Change the current record.
>   Delete the current record.

These procedures can be further decomposed:

>   Change the current record.

>>   Allow manual changes to each entry.
>>   Transfer the changes to the database.

>   Delete the current record.

>>   Get user confirmation to delete.
>>   Remove the data from the database.
>>   Adjust the Database range size.
>>   Adjust the on-screen indicator.

Now go on to decompose the third subtask:

>   Select a subset of records.

Selecting records is a two-step process. First, records must be selected according to some criteria. 1-2-3 provides the engine to "drive" this process, in the form of the /Data Query Find command. Using this command requires that you enter into the system a range specification for the database and a range specification for the Criterion range. Before you can actually select (Find) records, you must also enter into the Criterion range some criterion-matching labels or formulas. For the sake of simplicity in an already complicated example, the only selection criteria that this example will address is label matching.

To keep within the definition of the task, you must adapt the actions of the /Data Query Find command to the form-oriented presentation of this system. Because the Database and Criterion ranges are both horizontal ranges that can contain multiple records, you can readily convert the routines used to put data into the database and use them to put matching labels into the Criterion range as well. Using the existing routines also makes creating multiple-record criterion matches easy (see the 1-2-3 *Reference Manual* for more detail on criterion matching).

The outline listing of these tasks then becomes the following:

Enter the criteria via the form.

Switch operation of the routines to run on the Criterion range.
Enter new entries into the Criterion range.

Erase any entries currently in the form.
Determine the record number for the new entry.
Display an indicator showing which record is being entered.
Adjust the size of the Criterion range name.
Transfer the data to the Criterion range from the form.

Erase all destination cells in the Criterion range.
Move nonblank entries into the Criterion range.

Edit existing criterion data.

Display the first record in the Criterion range.
Display the last record in the Criterion range.
Display the record subsequent to the one currently being viewed.
Display the record previous to the one being viewed.
Change the current record.

Allow manual changes to each entry.
Transfer the changes to the Criterion range.

Delete the current record.

Get user confirmation to delete.
Remove the data from the Criterion range.
Adjust the Criterion range's size.
Adjust the on-screen indicator.

The second step in the process is to select the matching records. Selecting them requires that the program transform the outputs of the /Data Query Find command so that the records can be displayed in the form. A little creative programming is required to accomplish this task. By combining the @CELLPOINTER function with /Data Query Find, you cause the program to make a list of matching record numbers (by converting the worksheet row number). This numeric list can then be tapped to run the form display.

Display matching records.

Create a list of matching record numbers.

Erase any entries in current record list.
Call /Data Query Find command.

> If a match occurs, then save the record number.
> > Repeat until no matches are found.
> If no matches, display that fact on the screen.

> Display the total matches and which of that total is currently being displayed.
> Display the first record in the database.
> Display the last record in the database.
> Display the record subsequent to the one currently being viewed.
> Display the record previous to the one being viewed.

One last task must be described: the printing of the form letter, using matching criteria. This operation could be placed as a main task or subtask of record finding. Because this example treats the print operation as another way of displaying the selected records, you should include the operation at that level.

Printing a form letter requires that one more area be set up in the worksheet. For the example, a range called FORMLETTER will be entered from CA1..CG19. Using the routines that display selected records, the program will use string formulas to tie the display form to the letter form. To print the form letter, the program will call each of the matching records to the screen within the data form and print one copy of the form letter for each of the displays. To "cycle" through the selected list automatically, the program can use the same routines used to view the selected list manually.

> Print the form letter.

> > Get range name for form letter.
> > If matching records exist, display and print each match.
> > If no records match, display an on-screen message.

Finally, you can decompose the fourth subtask:

> Sort the database.

The final task for the database manager is to allow the sorting of the database. Again, the program will adapt the existing 1-2-3 /Data Sort command to the new format. Because only one database must be sorted, the program can be written to specify automatically the database as the Data-Range required by the /Sort command. The command language program can also incorporate the setting and resetting of sort keys into the program's command structure. This part of the program should include error checks to prevent the /Sort command from being activated when no Data-Range is specified.

> Clear any existing sort keys.
> Set a primary sort key.

Display a prompt for sort-key setting.
Get the sort-key column specification.
Indicate that a sort key has been selected.
Get the sort direction (Ascending/Descending).

Set a secondary sort key.

Display a prompt for sort-key setting.
Get the sort-key column specification.
Indicate that a sort key has been selected.
Get the sort direction (Ascending/Descending).

Perform the sort.

If a sort key has been set, enter the information for the /Sort command.

Specify the Database range as the Data-Range.
Adjust the entered range to exclude the top row of field names.
Sort.

If a sort key hasn't been set, display an indication of that fact.

Converting the Program Description into Instructions

The process of decomposition described in this chapter requires some time and thought. This time, however, is little compared to the time you save writing the actual program code and the time that would otherwise be spent debugging. The decomposition process divides your task into small, manageable steps. During the process, you are actually beginning to write the program. As you will see, not only is the generated outline a conceptual map of the program, but also is a fairly explicit guideline for the actual program steps. You will be able to convert some of this description into program code on a line-for-line basis.

As you write your program, keep in mind that your ultimate goal is readability. This program is now complex enough that you must be fairly fastidious about documentation procedures. As you review the guidelines that follow, refer to the sample letter in figure 10.3 and to the final program listing in figure 10.4.

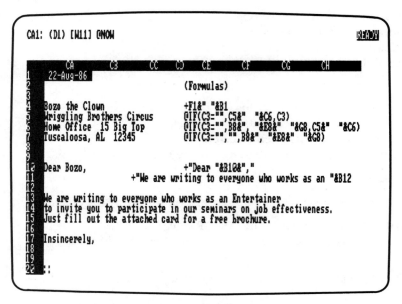

Fig. 10.3. A sample form letter showing formulas tied to input form.

```
21                      Range      Starting  Ending   Screen
22                      Names      Column    Column   Label
23              ----------  --------  -------- --------
24 REFTABLE      DATABASE   J         T        DATABASE
25      !        DATABASE_CR AB       AL       CRITERION
26 ----------------------------------------------------------------------------
27 REFERENCE VARIABLES
28
29 RANGE         DATABASE                               Reference for @@ in formulas
30 RESPONSE                 1                           OK to delete response
31 RECORDNO                 1                           Currently displayed record
32 I                        1                           Loop counter
33 ADDRESSREF    $I$10                                  Reference for use with find
34 LETTERRANGE   FORMLETTER                             Form letter range name
35 KEY           $J$1                                   Sort key address - to confirm one is set
36 MESSAGE1      Point to the sort key and press Enter  Message displayed for setting sort keys
37 ----------------------------------------------------------------------------
38 LIST OF CELLS IN INPUT RANGE
39
40 CELLLIST      B1
41      !        F1
42      !        C3
43      !        C5
44      !        C6
45      !        B8
46      !        E8
47      !        G8
48      !        B10
49      !        B11
50      !        B12
```

```
51  ---------------------------------------------------------------------------------
52  BROWSEFORM RANGE:
53  =================================================================================
54  Last Name:     Clown                      First Name:Bozo the
55
56  Company/Affiliation:    Wriggling Brothers Circus
57  ---------------------------------------------------------------------------------
58     Street Address 1:     Home Office
59     Street Address 2:     15 Big Top
60
61        City:  Tuscaloosa          State:  AL       ZIP:    12345
62  ---------------------------------------------------------------------------------
63  Salutation:    Bozo
64  Group Code:    5
65   Reference:    Entertainer
66  =================================================================================
67  Formula reference (Offsets in aINDEX vary with each entry):
68
69  aIF(aISSTRING(aINDEX(aa($RANGE),0,$RECORDNO)),aINDEX(aa($RANGE),0,$RECORDNO),"")
70  ---------------------------------------------------------------------------------
71  MASTER CALL MACRO
72
73  \d          {HOME}                                     Position cell pointer
74              {MENUBRANCH MAINMENU}                      Call menu
75  ---------------------------------------------------------------------------------
76  MENU SECTION
77
78  MAINMENU     Enter     Reset    Browse   Sort      CriterionFind     Quit
79              Enter new DaErase theLook throSort the daEnter selFind recoExit Data
80              {NEWRECORD} {ERASE}   {BROWSE} {MENUCALL S{SPECIFY}{FIND}          {RETURNTODB}
81              {MENUBRANCH {MENUBRAN{MENUBRAN{MENUBRANCH{MENUBRAN{MENUBRANCH MAINME{MENUBRANCH MAINMENU}
82
83  Dynamic Formulas For Option "Database" (Follows Quit)
84  aIF(aINDEX(REFTABLE,0,1)=RANGE,"Database","")
85  aIF(aINDEX(REFTABLE,0,1)=RANGE,"Return to Database","")
86  ---------------------------------------------------------------------------------
87  ENTER A NEW RECORD INTO THE DATABASE OR CRITERION RANGE
88
89  NEWRECORD     {ERASE}                                  Erase current display
90              {LET RECORDNO,aROWS(aa(RANGE))}            Set record counter to 1+maximum currently in range
91              {ENTER}                                    Get and transfer data
92  ---------------------------------------------------------------------------------
93  BLANK ALL ENTRIES IN INPUT FORM
94
95  ERASE        {FOR I,0,aROWS(CELLLIST)-1,1,WIPECELL}~
96  ---------------------------------------------------------------------------------
97  BLANK AN INPUT FORM CELL
98
99  WIPECELL      {RECALC WIPECELL2}                       Recalculate {BLANK} instruction
100 WIPECELL2    {BLANK F1}                                Erase one cell
101
102 Formula in WIPECELL2:
103 +"{BLANK "&aINDEX(CELLLIST,0,B42)&"}"
104 ---------------------------------------------------------------------------------
105 ALLOW DATA ENTRY INTO FORM AND TRANSFER
106
107 ENTER        {LET POINTER,+"Entering "&aVLOOKUP(RANGE,REFTABLE,3)&" Record: "&aSTRING(RECORDNO,0):VALUE}
108             /riINPUTRANGE~                             Above: show current record.  This line: get input.
109             {TRANSFERDATA}                             Move data from the form into the appropriate range
110 ---------------------------------------------------------------------------------
111 MOVE DATA FROM INPUT FORM TO DATA BASE OR CRITERION RANGE
112
113 TRANSFERDATA  {RECALC COPYCELL2}                       Recalc to display destination range
114             {IF RECORDNO>aROWS(aa(RANGE))-1}{SIZECHANGE "{DOWN}"}     If current record is new, expand the rang
115             {RECALC TRANSFERDATA2}
116 TRANSFERDATA2 {BLANK J2..T2}                           Blank the target cells in destination range
117             {FOR I,0,aCOLS(aa(RANGE))-1,1,COPYCELL}    Send each cell to destination
118
```

```
119 Formula in TRANSFERDATA2:
120 +"{RECALC TRANSFERDATA2}{BLANK "&@VLOOKUP(RANGE,REFTABLE,1)&@STRING(RECORDNO+1,0)&".."
121    &@VLOOKUP(RANGE,REFTABLE,2)&@STRING(RECORDNO+1,0)&"}"
122 --------------------------------------------------------------------------------------------------
123 MOVE ONE CELL OF DATA
124
125 COPYCELL    {IF @CELL("TYPE",@@("!"&@INDEX(CELLLIST,0,I)))="b"}{RETURN}        Do not transfer if source cell i
126             {IF @CELL("CONTENTS",@@("!"&@INDEX(CELLLIST,0,I)))=""}{RETURN}     ... or if it is a null string
127 COPYCELL2   {PUT DATABASE,I,RECORDNO,@CELL("CONTENTS",@@("!"&@INDEX(CELLLIST,0,I)))}
128
129 Formula in COPYCELL2:
130 +"{PUT "&RANGE&",I,RECORDNO,@CELL(""CONTENTS"",@@(""!""&@INDEX(CELLLIST,0,I))))}"
131 --------------------------------------------------------------------------------------------------
132 EXPAND OR CONTRACT SIZE OF DATA BASE OR CRITERION RANGES
133
134 SIZECHANGE  {DEFINE MOVEMENT}
135             {RECALC SIZECHANGE2}
136             {WINDOWSOFF}                                Hide the action
137             /rnc                                        Call the Range Name Create command
138 SIZECHANGE2 DATABASE
139             ~
140 MOVEMENT    {DOWN}                                      Expand or contract (passed parameter)
141             ~
142             {WINDOWSON}                                 Restore screen action
143
144 Formula in SIZECHANGE2:
145 +RANGE
146 ==================================================================================================
147 ALLOW BROWSING THROUGH DATA BASE OR CRITERION RANGE
148
149 BROWSE      /cBROWSEFORM~INPUTRANGE~                     Copy range of @INDEX formulas to input form
150             {LET RECORDNO,@MIN(RECORDNO,@ROWS(@@(RANGE))-1)}  Make sure record number isn't larger than the cu
151             {DISPLAYPLACE}                              Show which record is displayed
152             {MENUCALL EDITDB}                           Call the browsing menu
153 --------------------------------------------------------------------------------------------------
154 DISPLAY CURRENT RECORD INFORMATION IN INPUT FORM
155
156 DISPLAYPLACE {LET POINTER,+"Viewing "&@VLOOKUP(RANGE,REFTABLE,3)&" Record "&@STRING(RECORDNO,0)
                 &" of "&@STRING(@ROWS(@@(RANGE))-1,0):Value}~
157 --------------------------------------------------------------------------------------------------
158 MENU FOR CONTROL OF BROWSING OPERATIONS
159
160 EDITDB      Next       Previous First    Last      RecordNumEdit    Delete   Quit
161             Display the Display tMove to tMove to theView a spEdit the Delete thReturn to main menu
162             {NEXT}     {PREVIOUS{FIRST}  {LAST}    {VIEWNUMB{EDITRECO{DELETERECORD}
163             {MENUBRANCH {MENUBRAN{MENUBRAN{MENUBRANCH{MENUBRAN{MENUBRAN{MENUBRANCH EDITDB}
164 --------------------------------------------------------------------------------------------------
165 RECORD MOVEMENT ROUTINES
166
167 NEXT        {CHANGERECORD @MIN(@ROWS(@@(RANGE))-1,RECORDNO+1)}     Next record but not beyond the last recor
168
169 PREVIOUS    {CHANGERECORD @MAX(1,RECORDNO-1)}           Previous record but not beyond the first
170
171 FIRST       {CHANGERECORD 1}                            Go to record 1
172
173 LAST        {CHANGERECORD @ROWS(@@(RANGE))-1}           Go to the last record
174 --------------------------------------------------------------------------------------------------
175 MOVE TO A SPECIFIC RECORD
176
177 VIEWNUMBER  {GETNUMBER "View which record number? : ",RECORDNO}    Get record number from user
178             {LET RECORDNO,@MAX(@MIN(RECORDNO,@ROWS(@@(RANGE))-1),1)}  Restrict to existing records
179             {CHANGERECORD RECORDNO}                     Display the selected record
180 --------------------------------------------------------------------------------------------------
181 MOVE TO A DIFFERENT RECORD
182
183 CHANGERECORD {DEFINE RECORDNO:VALUE}                    Put new record number directly into record pointer
184             {RECALC INPUTRANGE}                         Update the formulas
185             {DISPLAYPLACE}                              Update the reference display
```

```
186 ------------------------------------------------------------------------------------------------
187 ALLOW EDITING OF CURRENTLY DISPLAYED ENTRY
188
189 EDITRECORD    /rvINPUTRANGE~INPUTRANGE~                          Convert formulas to values
190               {ENTER}                                            Allow changes and transfer
191               /cBROWSEFORM~INPUTRANGE~                           Restore browsing formulas
192 ------------------------------------------------------------------------------------------------
193 DELETE THE CURRENTLY DISPLAYED RECORD
194
195 DELETERECORD  {LET RESPONSE,0}                                   Set response to false
196               {MENUCALL AREYOUSURE}                              Get confirmation
197               {IF RESPONSE}{OKTODELETE}                          If response has changed, call delete routine
198 ------------------------------------------------------------------------------------------------
199 CONFIRM DELETE OPERATION BEFORE DOING
200
201 AREYOUSURE    No           Yes
202               Delete the cDelete the current record and contract database ???
203               {LET RESPONS{LET RESPONSE,1}
204 ------------------------------------------------------------------------------------------------
205 COMPACT RANGE TO DELETE ENTRY
206
207 OKTODELETE    {RECALC OKTODELETE2}
208               {SIZECHANGE "{DOWN}"}                              Expand current range name
209 OKTODELETE2   /mJ3..T16~J2~                                      Move subsequent rows on top of deleted row
210               {SIZECHANGE "{UP}"}                                Contract range name
211               {IF RECORDNO<@ROWS(@@(RANGE))}{RETURN}             If not the last record, done
212               {CHANGERECORD @MAX(1,RECORDNO-1}                   Otherwise adjust record number
213               {DISPLAYPLACE}                                     Update display
214
215 Formula in OKTODELETE2
216 +"/m"&@VLOOKUP(RANGE,REFTABLE,1)&@STRING(RECORDNO+2,0)&".."&@VLOOKUP(RANGE,REFTABLE,2)&@STRING(@ROWS(@@(RANGE))+2,0)
217   &"~"&@VLOOKUP(RANGE,REFTABLE,1)&@STRING(RECORDNO+1,0)&"~"
218 ================================================================================================
219 MASTER SORTING MENU
220
221 SORT          Go           PrimaryKeSecondaryReset      Quit
222               Sort the datEnter theEnter theClear the sExit back to the previous menu
223               {DOTHESORT} {KEYSET P{KEYSET S{CLEARKEYS}
224                           {MENUBRAN{MENUBRANCH SORT}
225 ------------------------------------------------------------------------------------------------
226 PERFORM THE SORT OPERATION
227
228 DOTHESORT     {IF @CELL("TYPE",!KEY)="b"}{MENUCALL NOKEYS}{RETURN}  Don't sort if no keys set
229               {LET DOTHESORT2,@INDEX(REFTABLE,0,0):VALUE}          Enter current database range name into the Sort command
230               {ESC}/dsd                                            Call the Sort command
231 DOTHESORT2    DATABASE                                             Database range name
232               ~                                                    Enter the name
233               d..{DOWN}~                                           Recall the name and adjust to eliminate field name row
234               g                                                    Do the sort
235 ------------------------------------------------------------------------------------------------
236 SET PRIMARY OR SECONDARY SORT KEY
237
238 KEYSET        {DEFINE WHICHKEY}                                  Select Primary or Secondary
239               {WINDOWSOFF}{GOTO}MESSAGE1~{PANELOFF}              Freeze windows, get prompt in control panel, and freeze panel
240               {LET KEYSET2,@INDEX(REFTABLE,0,0):VALUE}           Put in current range name
241               {GOTO}                                             Go there
242 KEYSET2       DATABASE
243               ~
244               {WINDOWSON}{?}                                     Restore window action and get response
245               {IF WHICHKEY="p"}{LET KEY,@CELLPOINTER("ADDRESS")}     Save if primary key
246               {LET KEYSET3,@CELLLPOINTER("ADDRESS")}            Save the current address
247               {HOME}                                            Go back to input form
248               {PANELON}                                         Restore panel action
249               /ds                                               Call Sort command
250 WHICHKEY      p                                                 Enter the key (passed parameter)
251 KEYSET3       $J$1
252               ~
253               {?}~q                                             Let user select Ascending or Descending and quit
```

```
254 ---------------------------------------------------------------------------------
255 RESET CURRENTLY DEFINED SORT KEYS
256
257 CLEARKEYS      /dsrq                                      Delete all current Sort settings
258               {BLANK KEY}                                Erase reference key
259 =================================================================================
260 CHANGE TARGET RANGE TO CRITERION FOR EDITING OPERATIONS
261
262 SPECIFY        {LET RANGE,@INDEX(REFTABLE,0,1):VALUE}     Switch reference range from database to criterion
263               {LET RECORDNO,1}                           Set record number to first
264               /cBROWSEFORM~INPUTRANGE~                    Load the browsing form
265               {DISPLAYPLACE}                             Display the current position
266               {BROWSE}                                   and Browse
267 =================================================================================
268 GET A LIST OF MATCHING RECORD NUMBERS
269
270 FIND           {WINDOWSOFF}                               Hide window action
271               {HOME}                                     Position cellpointer at beginning
272               {BLANK RECORDLIST}                         Erase currently stored record number list
273               /rncRECORDLIST~{ESC}.{END}{DOWN}~          Expand range name to bottom of sheet (allows use of {PUT})
274 FIND2          {RECALC FIND2}/dqiDATABASE~cDATABASE_CR~   Set Input and Criterion ranges in Data Query
275               f                                          Activate Find command
276               {LET ADDRESSREF,"$A$1"}                     If cellpointer still at home, then find failed
277               {GETLIST}                                  If not at home, get a list of matches
278               ~q                                         All done here
279               {RESETNAME}                                Reset the range name to reasonable size
280               {IF @COUNT(RECORDLIST)=0}{MENUCALL NONEFOUND}{RETURN}   If no matches found, let the user know
281               {LET RECORDNO,@VALUE(@INDEX(RECORDLIST,0,0))}   Enter the first matching record number
282               /cBROWSEFORM~INPUTRANGE~                    Load the browse form
283               {DISPLAYMATCH}                             and display X of Y matches
284               {WINDOWSON}                                Restore window action
285               {MENUCALL EDITMATCH}                       Browse the matching records
286
287 Formula in FIND2:
288 +"{RECALC FIND2}/dqi"&@INDEX(REFTABLE,0,0)&"~c"&@INDEX(REFTABLE,0,1)&"~"
289 ---------------------------------------------------------------------------------
290 GET AND SAVE MATCHING RECORD NUMBERS (DO-UNTIL LOOP)
291
292 GETLIST        {IF @CELLPOINTER("ADDRESS")=ADDRESSREF}{RETURN}   If cell pointer has not moved, then this is the last match
293               {LET ADDRESSREF,@CELLPOINTER("ADDRESS")}    Save the current location for the above test
294               {PUT RECORDLIST,0,@COUNT(RECORDLIST),@STRING(@CELLPOINTER("ROW")-1,0)}   Add this record number to the
295               {DOWN}                                     Try to find another
296               {BRANCH GETLIST}                           Loop until done
297 ---------------------------------------------------------------------------------
298 SET RECORDLIST RANGE NAME TO SIZE OF CURRENT ENTRIES
299
300 RESETNAME      /rncRECORDLIST~{ESC}.                       Reset size of record list range
301               {DOWN @MAX(@COUNT(RECORDLIST),1)}~          But leave at least 2 rows so it is a range
302 ---------------------------------------------------------------------------------
303 BROWSING MENU FOR MATCHES
304
305 EDITMATCH      Next       Previous First    Last      Edit     Output   Quit
306               Display the Display tMove to tMove to theEdit the Print a fReturn to main menu
307               {NEXTMATCH} {PREVIOUS{FIRSTMAT{LASTMATCH{EDITRECO{OUTPUT} {EXITFIND}
308               {MENUBRANCH {MENUBRAN{MENUBRAN{MENUBRANCH{MENUBRAN{MENUBRANCH EDITMATCH}
309 ---------------------------------------------------------------------------------
310 RECORD MOVEMENT ROUTINES FOR MATCHES       These routines enter the record number sequence from the record list range
311
312 NEXTMATCH      {CHANGERECORD @VALUE(@INDEX(RECORDLIST,0,@MIN(@VLOOKUP(@STRING(RECORDNO,0),RECORDLIST,0)+1,@COUNT(RECORDLIST)-1)))}
313               {DISPLAYMATCH}
314
315 PREVIOUSMATCH  {CHANGERECORD @VALUE(@INDEX(RECORDLIST,0,@MAX(@VLOOKUP(@STRING(RECORDNO,0),RECORDLIST,0)-1,0)))}
316               {DISPLAYMATCH}
317
318 FIRSTMATCH     {CHANGERECORD @VALUE(@INDEX(RECORDLIST,0,1))}
319               {DISPLAYMATCH}
320
321 LASTMATCH      {CHANGERECORD @VALUE(@INDEX(RECORDLIST,0,@COUNT(RECORDLIST)-1))}
322               {DISPLAYMATCH}
```

```
323 --------------------------------------------------------------------------------------------------
324 DISPLAY INDICATION OF WHICH MATCH IS DISPLAYED
325
326 DISPLAYMATCH   {LET POINTER2,+"Match "&@STRING(@VLOOKUP(@STRING(RECORDNO,0),RECORDLIST,0)+1,0)
                   &" of "&@STRING(@COUNT(RECORDLIST),0):VALUE}~
327 --------------------------------------------------------------------------------------------------
328 PRINT A FORM LETTER FOR CURRENT MATCHED RECORDS
329
330 OUTPUT         {IF @COUNT(RECORDLIST)=0}{NONEFOUND}{RETURN}      Abort of no matches current
331                {GETLABEL "What is the range name for the form letter: ",LETTERRANGE}
332                {LET OUTPUT2,LETTERRANGE}
333                {RECALC PRINT3}                                  Reset the command which will update the form letter
334                /ppcrr                                           Clear the current range setting and reset
335 OUTPUT2        FORMLETTER                                       to the new range
336                ~q                                               and quit for now
337                {FOR I,0,@COUNT(RECORDLIST),1,PRINT}             Call the print routine for each match
338 --------------------------------------------------------------------------------------------------
339 PRINT ONE FORM LETTER
340
341 PRINT          {LET RECORDNO,@VALUE(@INDEX(RECORDLIST,0,I))}    Get the record number of the selected item
342                {RECALC INPUTRANGE}                              Update the input form display
343 PRINT3         {RECALC FORMLETTER}                              Update the form letter
344                /ppagq                                           Print
345 --------------------------------------------------------------------------------------------------
346 CLEAR THE INDICATOR SHOWING MATCHED RECORDS
347
348 EXITFIND       {BLANK POINTER2}~                                Delete the X of Y match display
349 ==================================================================================================
350 RESET OPERATIONS TO DATABASE RANGE FROM CRITERION
351
352 RETURNTODB     {LET RANGE,@INDEX(REFTABLE,0,0):VALUE}           Reset reference range from criterion to database
353                {DISPLAYPLACE}                                   Update the record display
354                {CALC}                                           Update everything
355 ==================================================================================================
356 MESSAGE MENU : No sort keys set
357
358 NOKEYS          ******* Unable to Sort ********
359                No Sort Keys set.  Select Sort Keys and try again.  - Press Enter
360 --------------------------------------------------------------------------------------------------
361 MESSAGE MENU : No matching records found
362
363 NONEFOUND       *********** No records matching criteria found *************
364                         Press Enter to continue
365 ==================================================================================================
366 MENU DOCUMENTATION
367
368 MAINMENU                                                                       {MENUBRANCH MAINMENU}
369 Enter          Enter new Data into the database                 {NEWRECORD}    {MENUBRANCH MAINMENU}
370 Reset          Erase the current database entry                 {ERASE}        {MENUBRANCH MAINMENU}
371 Browse         Look through the database                        {BROWSE}       {MENUBRANCH MAINMENU}
372 Specify        Enter selection criteria for printing or locating records  {SPECIFY}  {MENUBRANCH MAINMENU}
373 Find           Find records that matches the specification criteria  {FIND}   {MENUBRANCH MAINMENU}
374 Quit           Exit Data Management System
375 Database       Return to Data base                              {RETURNTODB}   {MENUBRANCH MAINMENU}
376 --------------------------------------------------------------------------------------------------
377 EDITMATCH
378 Next           Display the next record in the database          {NEXTMATCH}    {MENUBRANCH EDITMATCH}
379 Previous       Display the previous record in the database      {PREVIOUSMATCH} {MENUBRANCH EDITMATCH}
380 First          Move to the beginning of the database            {FIRSTMATCH}   {MENUBRANCH EDITMATCH}
381 Last           Move to the end of the database                  {LASTMATCH}    {MENUBRANCH EDITMATCH}
382 Edit           Edit the currently displayed entry               {EDITRECORD}   {MENUBRANCH EDITMATCH}
383 Quit           Return to main menu                              {EXITFIND}
384 --------------------------------------------------------------------------------------------------
385 AREYOUSURE
386 No             Delete the current record and contract database ???   {LET RESPONSE,0}
387 Yes            Delete the current record and contract database ???   {LET RESPONSE,1}
```

```
388 ---------------------------------------------------------------------------------------------------------------
389 EDITDB
390 Next          Display the next record in the database             {NEXT}              {MENUBRANCH EDITDB}
391 Previous      Display the previous record in the database         {PREVIOUS}          {MENUBRANCH EDITDB}
392 First         Move to the beginning of the database               {FIRST}            {MENUBRANCH EDITDB}
393 Last          Move to the end of the database                     {LAST}             {MENUBRANCH EDITDB}
394 RecordNumber  View a specified record                             {VIEWNUMBER}        {MENUBRANCH EDITDB}
395 Edit          Edit the currently displayed entry                  {EDITRECORD}        {MENUBRANCH EDITDB}
396 Delete        Delete the currently displayed entry                {DELETERECORD}      {MENUBRANCH EDITDB}
397 Quit          Return to main menu
398 ---------------------------------------------------------------------------------------------------------------
399 SORT
400 Go            Sort the database using the specified sort keys      {DOTHESORT}
401 PrimaryKey    Enter the primary sort key                          {KEYSET p}         {MENUBRANCH SORT}
402 SecondaryKey  Enter the Secondary sort key                        {KEYSET s}         {MENUBRANCH SORT}
403 Reset         Clear the sort keys                                 {CLEARKEYS}
404 Quit          Exit back to the previous menu
405 ===============================================================================================================
406 RANGE NAME TABLE:
407
408 ADDRESSREF     C33
409 AREYOUSURE     C204
410 BROWSE         C150
411 BROWSEFORM     B54..H65
412 CELLLIST       C40..C50
413 CHANGERECORD   C185
414 CLEARKEYS      C260
415 COPYCELL       C126
416 COPYCELL2      C128
417 DATABASE       J1..T14
418 DATABASE_CR    AB1..AL2
419 DELETERECORD   C198
420 DISPLAYMATCH   C331
421 DISPLAYPLACE   C158
422 DOTHESORT      C231
423 DOTHESORT2     C234
424 EDITDB         C162
425 EDITMATCH      C309
426 EDITRECORD     C192
427 ENTER          C108
428 ERASE          C95
429 EXITFIND       C354
430 FIND           C274
431 FIND2          C278
432 FIRST          C173
433 FIRSTMATCH     C322
434 FORMLETTER     CB1..CH19
435 GETLIST        C296
436 I              C32
437 INPUTRANGE     B1..H12
438 KEY            C35
439 KEYSET         C241
440 KEYSET2        C245
441 KEYSET3        C254
442 LAST           C175
443 LASTMATCH      C325
444 LETTERRANGE    C34
445 MAINMENU       C78
446 MESSAGE1       C36
447 MOVEMENT       C141
448 NEWRECORD      C89
449 NEXT           C169
450 NEXTMATCH      C316
451 NOKEYS         C364
452 OKTODELETE     C210
453 OKTODELETE2    C212
454 OUTPUT         C335
455 OUTPUT2        C340
```

```
456 POINTER       B15
457 POINTER2      B16
458 PREVIOUS      C171
459 PREVIOUSMATCH C319
460 PRINT         C346
461 PRINT3        C348
462 RANGE         C29
463 RECORDLIST    C500..C506
464 RECORDNO      C31
465 REFTABLE      C24..F25
466 RESET2        C305
467 RESETNAME     C304
468 RESPONSE      C30
469 RETURNTODB    C358
470 SIZECHANGE    C135
471 SIZECHANGE2   C139
472 SORT          C224
473 SPECIFY       C265
474 TRANSFERDATA  C114
475 TRANSFERDATA2 C117
476 VIEWNUMBER    C179
477 WHICHKEY      C253
478 WIPECELL      C99
479 WIPECELL2     C100
480 \D            C73
481
482 ==================================================================================================
483 RECORDLIST    1           Note: Can grow to any length.
484     ¦         2                 Do not put anything below this range.
485     ¦         3
486     v         6
487               9
```

Fig. 10.4. The final version of the database program.

From the start, you should adopt the same kind of documentation structure you used for macros:

1. Use the **/Range Name Labels Right** command to generate names for your routines. Leave the range names visible in the left column of the window.

2. For the program instructions, use several columns in the center of the window.

3. Use columns along the right side of the window for comments that describe and explain the function of the instructions on each line.

To these guidelines you will add several others:

1. The input form should be in the upper left corner of the worksheet.

2. The Database range should be to the right of the input form, with the field names in the first row of the worksheet.

3. The database name should be assigned to this one-row list of field names. You can set the column widths to accommodate the widths of the field names or the data, because nothing will be below this range.

4. Initially, the Criterion range should be identical to the Database range: one row of field names in worksheet row one, with the Criterion range name assigned to that single row of labels.

5. The DATABASE range name should be entered in uppercase in the upper left corner of the REFTABLE range (cell B24 in this example). The Criterion range name should be entered, in all caps, just below the DATABASE range name.

6. A list of cell addresses that are the input cells from the input form should be created. The list should be assigned the range name CELLLIST.

7. Each input cell in the input form should be unprotected. The range name INPUTRANGE should be assigned to the input form area.

8. A copy of the input form should be constructed and assigned the range name BROWSEFORM. Each of the input cells should be replaced with a variation of the following formula:

   @IF(@ISSTRING(@INDEX(@@($RANGE),<offset>,$RECORDNO)),
   @INDEX(@@($RANGE),<offset>,$RECORDNO),"")

   The <offset> in the formula should be replaced with a number representing the column location of the variable represented by each input cell in the BROWSEFORM range. That is, the offset for the first entry in BROWSEFORM should be 0; for the second entry, 1; and so on.

   Note that the range names RANGE and RECORDNO must be created before the formula can be entered. The position of these ranges is shown in figure 10.4.

9. A form-letter range should be created if you want to print form letters. This range should be assigned a range name. You may have more than one such range. The display of the form letter should be tied to the input cells in INPUTRANGE with string formulas so that the form letter displays whatever information is in the input form as part of its text.

GUIDELINE: At the beginning of the program listing, include a list of important assumptions.

The list is for your reference and for others who might want to know about the design of your program. In the sample program, you have already made numerous assumptions that affect how the program works.

GUIDELINE: The second area in your listing should be a place for all your reference variables.

Reference variables are the counters used by {FOR} loops, the cells that store the results from {GETLABEL} instructions, and the like. Any values that are not a part of the program listing but are used by the program should appear here. This convention, adapted from Pascal, requires that all variables in a program be declared at the beginning of the program. In this way, you always know where to look for the reference values.

GUIDELINE: Clearly separate all your subroutines from each other.

In the program listing for the example, a dashed line separates each subroutine. This arrangement makes following the program and identifying the various routines easy, but has to be done a certain way. The line in the listing is actually a long label in the left column. The cells separating the modules themselves *must be blank*; the blank cells stop the modules. Don't use a repeating label prefix copied across the width of the screen. The program will interpret these label cells as part of the program, connect all your modules together, and, in short, won't run.

The sample program consists of several separate operations called from a master menu. The program listing shows each of these operational areas separated by a double dashed line (equal signs). Although the effect does not appear in the printed listing (shown in fig. 10.4), you can enhance the readability of the program in the worksheet by using the /Range Unprotect command to unprotect the dividing lines between the subroutines. Unprotecting these cells makes the dividing lines appear highlighted or in color (depending on your monitor) and makes the divisions between routines prominent.

GUIDELINE: Include a global description of each subroutine above the routine itself.

The global description will help remind you of the overall function of each routine without requiring that you interpret each routine's code. Use the /Range Unprotect command to highlight this description along with the dividing lines between modules.

GUIDELINE: List all the modules in the order in which the program executes them.

This guideline, which makes the program easy to follow, is also borrowed from Pascal. In fact, if you don't follow this convention in Pascal, the program refuses to run. When you review a program listing, you will be able to find a specific module quickly by keeping in mind that subroutines are always listed immediately after the routine that contains the subroutine call.

Usually, following this guideline exactly isn't possible because some modules are called from several places in the program. The more order you can impose on the listing, however, the better. In a program as long as the one in this example, you could waste a lot of time simply searching for randomly placed routines. After writing my programs, I usually take the time to rearrange them to optimize their readability. This practice helps reduce the clutter that is inevitable during program construction.

Note: Pascal users will notice that this convention is the opposite of the Pascal convention that requires that routines be listed before they are called. Because the command language isn't a compiled language, that requirement doesn't pertain. The goal here is to create a readable program. For most people, having what comes first on the top is the natural way to list a program, especially considering that the individual instructions are executed from top to bottom.

GUIDELINE: Avoid dynamic instructions whenever possible.

Dynamic instructions, which are instructions created from string formulas, are powerful, but difficult to document and follow. These instructions are a form of self-modifying code that is generally frowned on in structured programming circles because you can't necessarily tell what the instruction is by reading the listing. According to one story, a major software house circulated a memo to the effect that any programmers found writing self-modifying code would be summarily shot. I assume that the company didn't intend to carry out the threat, but I bet the programmers got the point.

With the command language, dynamic instructions create problems beyond readability. Because dynamic instructions are worksheet formulas, you must take special care to see that they are recalculated prior to their use. This process requires extra program steps and is a prime source of hard-to-find errors. Furthermore, although you should include a {RECALC} in the dynamic instruction itself to be sure that the formula is updated, this method won't work if the formula references a cell that results in ERR. When a cell displays ERR, it can't recalculate itself. The ERR problem can easily occur with instructions that reference the counter to a {FOR} loop.

The preceding paragraphs probably read like heresy coming from someone who, in Chapters 8 and 9, made a big deal about how great dynamic instructions are. I'm not saying that you shouldn't use dynamic instructions. In fact, the program you have been working with has six of them. What I *am* saying is not to use them if you don't have to. One of the most difficult things for a programmer to do is to resist the temptation to be clever, and I succumb to the temptation frequently. However, your programs will run better and faster and have fewer bugs if you keep dynamic instructions to a minimum. Note the use of @@ in the sample program, which in almost all cases accomplishes an action that would otherwise require a dynamic instruction.

GUIDELINE: If you must use dynamic instructions, include a copy of the formula in the module listing.

In your program listing, leave the dynamic instruction in its final form—that is, as the instruction is read by the program when the instruction executes. Don't convert it to a formula or use a literal format in your listing. Program code is hard enough to read when all the instructions appear in normal form (when the result of the formula is visible). Do include a listing of the formula in a separate line, along with your module listing. Make sure that your formula listing uses the range names of the variables involved rather than cell addresses. And be sure to identify which instructions in your module listing are dynamic.

GUIDELINE: In a command language instruction, never use a cell address when you can use a range name.

You have seen this guideline before, but it bears repeating. The sample program uses cell address manipulation to calculate the record numbers. This process requires that the Database and Criterion ranges be in worksheet row one. This requirement is carefully documented in the program assumptions.

Although you could write your program so that it would work even when the Database and Criterion ranges are placed in locations other than worksheet row 1, a compromise was made in this case for the sake of simplifying the example. For instance, the column locations of the Database and Criterion ranges can be anywhere in the worksheet, even though these column locations are used as part of the cell address operations. To make the program flexible with regard to column location, the beginning and ending columns are included in REFTABLE and are calculated by formulas. The formula for calculating the starting column (in C24) is

```
@IF(@CELL("col",@@(B24))<27,@CHAR(@CELL("col",@@(B24))+64),
@CHAR(@INT((@CELL("col",@@(B24))-1)/26+64))&
@CHAR(@MOD(@CELL("col",@@(B24))-1,26)+65))
```

The formula for the ending column (in D24) is

```
@IF(@CELL("col",@@(B24))+@COLS(@@(B24))-1<27,
@CHAR(@CELL("col",@@(B24))+@COLS(@@(B24))+63),
@CHAR(@INT((@CELL("col",@@(B24))+@COLS(@@(B24))-2)/26+64))
&@CHAR(@MOD(@CELL("col",@@(B24))+@COLS(@@(B24))-2,26)+65)))
```

GUIDELINE: Whenever possible, avoid the use of {BRANCH}.

The sample program, which is quite complex, is written almost entirely without the use of {BRANCH}. In fact, the only branching of any sort in the program is accomplished with {MENUBRANCH}, which returns operation to the menus, and two routines that use {BRANCH} to simulate a DO-UNTIL loop, a construct not otherwise supported by the command language. All the transfers between routines are accomplished by setting up a series of subroutines.

If you find yourself writing code with {BRANCH} instructions at the end of each routine, watch out. Such programs can become a nightmare to debug. Virtually any program can be written without {BRANCH} if you control the order of the program by sequencing a series of subroutines. Again, programming without {BRANCH} instructions takes more thought beforehand, but pays for itself later. You will find that rewriting a program in order to get rid of {BRANCH} instructions is worthwhile.

Coding the Example

Now that the program is fairly well decomposed, you can begin turning the program description into command language instructions. For comparisons between description and code, refer to the program description in a previous section.

The major functions of the program, as initially decomposed, are independent. This program actually will be a collection of several small programs, which you will link by calling the main routines from a series of menus.

To call the main menu, you will need an Alt-[letter] macro. To be sure that the input form is correctly displayed when the main menu is called, you can include a {HOME} instruction.

```
\d          {HOME}
            {MENUBRANCH MAINMENU}
```

The main menu can simply be a listing of the main tasks described in the first level of program decompositions. To keep the first characters of the menu choices unique, you can use the selections that follow. Because specifying matching criteria and finding matching records are also independent operations, they should each have a separate main menu entry.

MENU:

Enter   Browse   Sort   Criterion   Find   Quit

Notice that this order parallels the order in which the user would execute each of the tasks performed by the system. The user should be returned to the main menu after each task is completed. Therefore, the general format for construction of the menu is the following:

```
Short Prompt
Long Prompt
{SUBROUTINE}
{MENUBRANCH MAINMENU}
```

Note also how readily the menu construction "falls" from the program decomposition. After specifying the menu, you can follow the decomposition outline and create the supporting subroutines.

The first operation is the entry of new records into the database. You can begin by choosing a descriptive subroutine name such as {NEWRECORD}. This subroutine must first erase the existing entries—a process that can be put into a separate subroutine. The {NEWRECORD} subroutine must then determine which entry is being entered. The calculation for this task can be performed with the @ROWS function. Because record numbers begin with zero, the number of rows in the range will be the next available record number. The resulting number can be stored in a cell named RECORDNO. This cell can then be used as a master pointer for subsequent record operations.

At this point, a little thinking ahead is in order. Recall that in the decomposition process, you used the same entry routines for entering data into the database and for entering data into the Criterion range. By using the @@ function as an argument, you can make functions reference more than one source. Therefore,

@ROWS(@@(RANGE))

will return the number of rows contained in the range specified by the range name contained in the RANGE cell. In other words, if RANGE contains DATABASE, then @ROWS(@@(RANGE)) is the same as @ROWS(DATABASE). When RANGE contains DATABASE_CR, then @ROWS(@@(RANGE)) is the same as @ROWS(DATABASE_CR).

The last function of this subroutine—the actual entry and transfer of the data from the input form into the appropriate range—can also be a separate subroutine. Thus the final form for the current routine is the following:

```
NEWRECORD    {ERASE}
             {LET RECORDNO,@ROWS(@@(RANGE))}
             {ENTER}
```

The {ERASE} routine can use the list of cells (CELLLIST) that was specified earlier. This routine can simply call another subroutine that erases one cell, once for each cell in the list. Using the range name assigned to the list of cells also makes the program adapt to changes or different forms. Notice that the loop variable begins with zero and ends one short of the number of rows in the range.

```
ERASE        {FOR i,0,@ROWS(CELLLIST)-1,1,WIPECELL}
```

The {WIPECELL} routine must erase one cell, using information in the list. The fastest way to accomplish this task is to create a dynamic instruction. By using @INDEX in a string formula, you can construct a {BLANK} instruction.

```
+"{BLANK "&@INDEX(CELLLIST,0,i)&"}"
```

This instruction must be recalculated prior to execution. Otherwise, the reference to the cell to erase won't change. Because @INDEX uses the loop variable from the {FOR} instruction to cycle through the entries in CELLLIST, and because the {FOR} instruction always includes one extra increment beyond the stop value specified, the loop will terminate with an invalid offset for the @INDEX function. The instruction will, in that case, display ERR. Because of the ERR condition, the recalculation for the updating of this dynamic instruction must be performed separately. The final form for this routine then becomes the following:

```
WIPECELL    {RECALC WIPECELL2}
WIPECELL2   {BLANK F1}
```

Note that the F1 in the {BLANK} instruction is a result of the formula, not a part of the instruction itself.

The {ENTER} subroutine must perform the remaining entry tasks: display an indicator showing what record is being entered, enter the data, and transfer the data to the Database range. Placing these operations in a routine separate from NEWRECORD allows these same instructions to enter changes as well as new records. To make the display indicate when data is being processed in the database rather than the the Criterion range, you can add another column to the REFTABLE range and use a VLOOKUP keyed by the range name in RANGE. The formula in the {LET} instruction that follows will display:

Entering DATABASE Record X

X is the record number for the new record.

This routine uses the /Range Input command to place data into the worksheet. When this command is invoked, control passes to the user, who can move the cell pointer and enter information. When the user presses Enter, control passes back to the program. The data can then be transferred from the form to the database or Criterion range.

```
ENTER       {LET POINTER,+"Entering "&@VLOOKUP(RANGE,REFTABLE,3)
            &" RECORD: "&@STRING(RECORDNO,0):VALUE}
            /riINPUTRANGE~
            {TRANSFERDATA}
```

The {TRANSFERDATA} routine sets up and calls a routine called COPYCELL. The first thing this routine must do is expand the range name to allow for the new record, but only if the data is a new record. Remember that you want to create a routine that can be used to transfer edited data in existing records as well as new data. The test for whether the data is new can reference the RECORDNO variable. If RECORDNO is larger than the current range size, the range will have to be expanded.

The expansion is a task that is best put in a separate routine. Keeping in mind that range contraction will also be necessary when records are deleted, you can assume that you will pass a parameter to a single routine that will either expand or contract the existing range name, as needed. The expansion and contraction can be accomplished by using the /Range Name Create command and either moving the cell pointer down or up to change the range size. Although you have just designed the routine to change the range size, you will save its code for a moment and finish the existing routine. You do know, however, that the parameter passed must move the cell pointer up or down. One easy way to accomplish this task is to pass the parameter directly. Remember that to be used as parameters, a command language instruction must be enclosed in quotation marks.

To be sure that no data is in the target area when you transfer, the program should erase the target area first. (An empty target area is important for editing.) The erase procedure can be accomplished in one instruction, again, with a dynamic {BLANK}. This formula uses the beginning and ending column letters calculated by the REFTABLE formulas that were described earlier.

```
TRANSFERDATA    {RECALC COPYCELL2}
                {IF RECORDNO>@ROWS(@@(RANGE))-1}{SIZECHANGE
                   "{DOWN}"}
                {RECALC TRANSFERDATA2}
TRANSFERDATA2   {BLANK I2..S2}
                {FOR i,0,@COLS(@@(RANGE))-1,1,COPYCELL}
```

Formula in TRANSFERDATA2:

```
+"{RECALC TRANSFERDATA2}{BLANK "&@VLOOKUP(RANGE,REFTABLE,1)
&@STRING(RECORDNO+1,0)&".."&@VLOOKUP(RANGE,REFTABLE,2)
&@STRING(RECORDNO+1,0)&"}"
```

The {COPYCELL} routine transfers the values from the Input range to the destination range, which can be either the Database or the Criterion range. The tests in the first and second lines keep the routine from transferring blank or null string data. Notice the use of the @@ function in the COPYCELL2 line. To make the cell address returned by the @INDEX function appear as a range address, the ! must be made a part of the argument.

```
COPYCELL    {IF @CELL("type",@@("!"&@INDEX(CELLLIST,0,i)))="b"}{RETURN}
            {IF @CELL("contents",@@("!"&@INDEX(CELLLIST,0,i)))=""}
               {RETURN}
COPYCELL2   {PUT DATABASE,i,RECORDNO,@CELL("contents",
               @@("!"&@INDEX(CELLLIST,0,i)))}
```

Formula in COPYCELL2:

```
+"{PUT "&RANGE&",i,RECORDNO,@CELL(""contents"",
@@(""!""&@INDEX(CELLLIST,0,i)))}"
```

This routine, described in the preceding text, alters the size of either the Database or Criterion range by calling the /Range Name Create command and adjusting the cell pointer up or down one row, as determined by the paramater passed into the MOVEMENT cell. (The MOVEMENT cell is initially blank.)

```
SIZECHANGE      {DEFINE MOVEMENT}
                {RECALC SIZECHANGE2}
                {WINDOWSOFF}
                /rnc
SIZECHANGE2     DATABASE
                ~
MOVEMENT
                ~
                {WINDOWSON}
```

Formula in SIZECHANGE2:

```
+RANGE
```

The next routine you will code handles the examination and editing of existing data. The first step is to copy the BROWSEFORM range described previously into the location of the input form. The formulas in BROWSEFORM are @INDEX functions tied to the current value of RECORDNO. When these formulas are in place in the input form, the input form will display the contents of the record specified by RECORDNO. Changing the value of RECORDNO causes all the formulas to change as well to display the new data. This method of displaying the database information allows rapid and easy changes from one record to the next (see fig. 10.5).

After copying the BROWSEFORM range, the program resets the value of RECORDNO to no more than the maximum number of records in the currently active range.

Finally, before calling a menu of editing operations, the routine calls a subroutine to display the current record number.

```
BROWSE  /cBROWSEFORM~INPUTRANGE~
        {LET RECORDNO,@MIN(RECORDNO,@ROWS(@@(RANGE))-1)}
        {DISPLAYPLACE}
        {MENUCALL EDITDB}
```

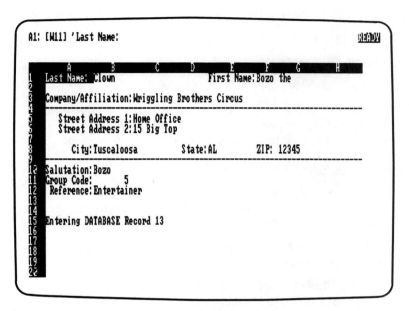

```
A1: [W11] 'Last Name:                                    READY

        A        B        C        D        E        F        G        H
1   Last Name: Clown                       First Name: Bozo the
2
3   Company/Affiliation: Wriggling Brothers Circus
4   ------------------------------------------------------------------
5       Street Address 1: Home Office
6       Street Address 2: 15 Big Top
7
8          City: Tuscaloosa        State: AL       ZIP: 12345
9   ------------------------------------------------------------------
10  Salutation: Bozo
11  Group Code:      5
12   Reference: Entertainer
13
14
15  Entering DATABASE Record 13
16
17
18
19
20
```

Fig. 10.5. The database contents displayed by the BROWSEFORM formulas.

The {DISPLAYPLACE} routine is similar to the first instruction in the {ENTER} routine, except that {DISPLAYPLACE} shows the total record count as well as the record number of the current record.

DISPLAYPLACE   {LET POINTER,+"Viewing "&@VLOOKUP(RANGE,REFTABLE,3)
             &" Record "&@STRING(RECORDNO,0)&" of "
             &@STRING(@ROWS(@@(RANGE))-1,0):VALUE}~

The EDIT menu contains the options for moving through the records, and for editing and deleting. This menu is structured in the same way as are all the other menus—that is, Long Prompt, Short Prompt, subroutine call, and {MENUBRANCH} back to the menu. You choose the prompts you want to use. See the section headed MENU DOCUMENTATION in the program listing (see fig. 10.4) for a full listing of all the menus.

    MENU:

    EditDB   Next   Previous   First   Last   RecordNumber   Edit   Delete   Quit

The following four routines control the display of the records. Each routine passes a value to the {CHANGERECORD} routine, which uses the passed value to set RECORDNO. The @MIN and @MAX functions prevent movement outside the currently existing range of records.

NEXT   {CHANGERECORD @MIN(@ROWS(@@(RANGE))-1,RECORDNO+1)}

PREVIOUS   {CHANGERECORD @MAX(1,RECORDNO-1)}

FIRST   {CHANGERECORD 1}

LAST   {CHANGERECORD @ROWS(@@(RANGE))-1}

The {VIEWNUMBER} routine is similar to the preceding routines, except that the record number is supplied by the user and is restricted by @MAX and @MIN functions at the same time. Note that this feature is a form of error control. In this case, no signal that an error has been made is given; the program simply refuses to go beyond the existing record limits.

VIEWNUMBER   {GETNUMBER "View which record number? : ",RECORDNO}
             {LET RECORDNO,@MAX(@MIN(RECORDNO,@ROWS(@@(RANGE))-1),1)}
             {CHANGERECORD RECORDNO}

The following routine passes the value from the calling routines directly into RECORDNO, then updates the displays.

CHANGERECORD   {DEFINE RECORDNO:VALUE}
               {RECALC INPUTRANGE}
               {DISPLAYPLACE}

Editing the current record turns out to be simple. The formulas in the input form, which are copied to that location from BROWSEFORM, are converted to their values by the /Range Value command. Then the existing {ENTER} routine handles all the work of updating the Database or Criterion range.

EDITRECORD   /rvINPUTRANGE~INPUTRANGE~
               {ENTER}
               /cBROWSEFORM~INPUTRANGE~

Deletion is more complicated than simple data entry. Because data entry always occurs at the end of the database, no existing data has to be shuffled around. With deletions, the gap created by the deleted record must be filled in. Before deleting, however, you should give the user a chance to change his or her mind, just as 1-2-3 is so good about doing anywhere data may be destroyed. The last chance comes in the form of a {MENUCALL}. By using a RESPONSE variable, you avoid the complicated branching that you would have to deal with otherwise.

DELETERECORD   {LET RESPONSE,0}
               {MENUCALL AREYOUSURE}
               {IF RESPONSE}{OKTODELETE}

MENU:

AREYOUSURE	No	Yes
	Delete the current . . .	Delete the current record and contract database
	{LET RESPONSE,0}	{LET RESPONSE,1}

The "heart" of the deletion routine is the formula in the OKTODELETE2 line. This dynamic instruction uses RECORDNO and the column information in REFTABLE to move a range of data. The range of data to be moved consists of the record below the record-to-be-deleted through to the end of the range. By moving this block up one row, the instruction deletes the selected record. The {SIZECHANGE} routine call before and after the /Move instruction allows this strategy to work for the last row in the database as well as for interior rows.

After the deletion, the routine cleans up the display.

```
OKTODELETE     {RECALC OKTODELETE2}
               {SIZECHANGE "{DOWN}"}
OKTODELETE2    /mI3..S16~I2~
               {SIZECHANGE "{UP}"}
               {IF RECORDNO<@ROWS(@@(RANGE))}{RETURN}
               {CHANGERECORD @MAX(1,RECORDNO-1)}
               {DISPLAYPLACE}
```

Formula in OKTODELETE2:

```
+"/m"&@VLOOKUP(RANGE,REFTABLE,1)&@STRING(RECORDNO+2,0)
&".."&@VLOOKUP(RANGE,REFTABLE,2)&@STRING(@ROWS(@@(RANGE))+2,0)
&"~"&@VLOOKUP(RANGE,REFTABLE,1)&@STRING(RECORDNO+1,0)&"~"
```

At this point, the coding for the record editing is complete. The next major section to code consists of sorting operations. These are fairly straightforward because they are simply adaptations of existing 1-2-3 commands. The menu of operations will look like the following. Also shown are the subroutine calls to KEYSET; these subroutines pass parameters to select either primary or secondary.

MENU:

Sort	Go	PrimaryKey	SecondaryKey	Reset	Quit
		{KEYSET p}	{KEYSET s}		

After the sort keys are specified, sorting the database is simply a matter of verifying the existence of a sort key, typing the database name, and sorting. Well, almost. If you enter the database name as the **Data-Range** for the sort, the top line of field names in your database will get mixed in with the data. To adjust the range that is sorted, you can take advantage of the fact that 1-2-3 remembers the range after it has been set. By calling up the **Data-Range** command a second time, your routine can adjust the range size to exclude the top row.

DOTHESORT	{IF @CELL("type",!KEY)="b"}{MENUCALL NOKEYS}{RETURN}
	{LET DOTHESORT2,@INDEX(REFTABLE,0,0):VALUE}
	{ESC}/dsd
DOTHESORT2	DATABASE
	~
	d..{DOWN}~
	g

The {KEYSET} routine uses a trick to display a custom prompt. The sequence is the following:

1. Turn off the windows.

2. {GOTO} a message cell. The message will appear in the control panel.

3. Turn off the control panel. The message will be "frozen" in place.

4. Turn on the windows.

When the windows come on after the prompt is frozen, the cell pointer is on the top line of the database. The user selects which column to use as a sort key by moving the cell pointer and pressing Enter.

The cell pointer's address at the time the Enter key is pressed is entered into KEYSET3. This address then becomes a part of the {KEYSET} routine and is subsequently entered into the /Sort command sequence. If the subroutine is being called to get a **Primary-Key**, the address is also saved in KEY, which is checked by the previous routine before the sort occurs. If KEY is blank, then no **Primary-Key** has been set.

After obtaining an address for the sort key, the program reactivates the panel, enters the sort key automatically, and lets the user enter the **Ascending** or **Descending** choice directly into the /Sort command.

The {CLEARKEYS} routine that follows simply resets all the sort information. Because the database name is always entered into the sorting operation before it is performed, resetting the **Data-Range** has no effect. The real purpose of this routine is to reset the sort keys.

KEYSET	{DEFINE WHICHKEY}
	{WINDOWSOFF}{GOTO}MESSAGE1~{PANELOFF}
	{LET KEYSET2,@INDEX(REFTABLE,0,0):VALUE}
	{GOTO}
KEYSET2	DATABASE

```
                        {WINDOWSON}{?}
                        {IF WHICHKEY="p"}{LET KEY,@CELLPOINTER("address")}
                        {LET KEYSET3,@CELLLPOINTER("address")}
                        {HOME}
                        {PANELON}
                        /ds
WHICHKEY                p
KEYSET3                 $J$1
                        ~
                        {?}~q

CLEARKEYS               /dsrq
                        {BLANK KEY}
```

The next major section to code is the routine for entering criteria into the Criterion range. The first instruction in the following routine changes the contents of RANGE. Recall that the contents of this range are used by the @@ functions that appear throughout this program to determine which range, the Database or Criterion, is referenced by the operations performed by the various routines. By changing the entry in RANGE, the inputs and outputs of all the routines that use @@ are changed from the Database to the Criterion range and back again. This routine, composed almost entirely of existing routines, illustrates the value of modular construction.

```
SPECIFY                 {LET RANGE,@INDEX(REFTABLE,0,1):VALUE}
                        {LET RECORDNO,1}
                        /cBROWSEFORM~INPUTRANGE~
                        {DISPLAYPLACE}
                        {BROWSE}
```

The {FIND} routine is the trickiest part of this program. Because of the {WINDOWSOFF} instruction, most of what this routine does is hidden to the user. You might want to omit this instruction initially so that you can view the steps throughout the routine and follow the logic of the its operation.

The {FIND} routine has two functions. The first is to manage the content and size of the RECORDLIST range. The routine first makes RECORDLIST very large because record numbers for matching records will be stored here, then makes RECORDLIST no larger than the number of entries it contains. This arrangement speeds the operation of the @VLOOKUP functions that use RECORDLIST as an argument.

After getting a list of record numbers, (see the {FIND} routine), this part of the program checks to see whether any matches have been found. The program signals if they have not been found; if they have, the program sets the display to the first matching record.

```
FIND        {WINDOWSOFF}
            {HOME}
            {BLANK RECORDLIST}
            /rncRECORDLIST~{ESC}.{END}{DOWN}~
FIND2       {RECALC FIND2}/dqiDATABASE~cDATABASE_CR~
            f
            {LET ADDRESSREF,"$A$1"}
            {GETLIST}
            ~q
            {RESETNAME}
            {IF @COUNT(RECORDLIST)=0}{MENUCALL NONEFOUND}{RETURN}
            {LET RECORDNO,@VALUE(@INDEX(RECORDLIST,0,0))}
            /cBROWSEFORM~INPUTRANGE~
            {DISPLAYMATCH}
            {WINDOWSON}
            {MENUCALL EDITMATCH}
```

Formula in FIND2:

```
+"{RECALC FIND2}/dqi"&@INDEX(REFTABLE,0,0)&"~c"&@INDEX(REFTABLE,0,1)&"~"
```

This routine uses {BRANCH} to create a DO-UNTIL loop. While the /Data Query Find operation is in effect, the routine tests the cell pointer's position in order to track the number of matching records found. If you were to operate the /Data Query Find operation manually, you would see that the cell pointer stays in its initial location if no matching records are found. By placing the cell pointer in A1 before calling the command and testing to see whether the cell pointer is still there after the command is called, you check for matches.

When multiple matches occur, pressing the down-arrow key moves the cell pointer to the next matching record. The last record match is signaled by the fact that the cell pointer doesn't move when the down-arrow key is pressed. By continually checking the current cell pointer location against that previous location, you test for when the last match is found.

The {PUT} instruction creates a growing list of entries. The list determines the placement of each new entry by counting the existing entries.

```
GETLIST     {IF @CELLPOINTER("address")=ADDRESSREF}{RETURN}
            {LET ADDRESSREF,@CELLPOINTER("address")}
            {PUT RECORDLIST,0,@COUNT(RECORDLIST),
               @STRING(@CELLPOINTER("row")-1,0)}
            {DOWN}
            {BRANCH GETLIST}
```

This last routine in the Find operations resets the size of the RECORDLIST range to cover the number of entries, or, at a minimum, two rows. If the range has only one row, 1-2-3 automatically converts that row to a cell address, which causes problems with the way some of the commands operate.

```
RESETNAME      /rncRECORDLIST~{ESC}.
               {DOWN @MAX(@COUNT(RECORDLIST),1)}~
```

The next menu, and the routines that follow, are adaptations of the browsing routines just described. The major modification is to the formulas in the subroutine calls. These formulas return the record numbers stored in RECORDLIST in sequence, rather than simple increments or decrements of record numbers.

```
MENU:

EditMatch   Next   Previous   First   Last   Edit   Output   Quit

NEXTMATCH          {CHANGERECORD @VALUE(@INDEX(RECORDLIST,0,
                       @MIN(@VLOOKUP(@STRING(RECORDNO,0),
                       RECORDLISTG,0)+1,
                       @COUNT(RECORDLIST)-1)))}
                   {DISPLAYMATCH}

PREVIOUSMATCH {CHANGERECORD @VALUE(@INDEX(RECORDLIST,0,
                       @MAX(@VLOOKUP(@STRING(RECORDNO,0),
                       RECORDLIST,0)-1,0)))}
                   {DISPLAYMATCH}

FIRSTMATCH         {CHANGERECORD @VALUE(@INDEX(RECORDLIST,0,1))}
                   {DISPLAYMATCH}

LASTMATCH          {CHANGERECORD @VALUE(@INDEX(RECORDLIST,0,
                       @COUNT(RECORDLIST)-1))}
                   {DISPLAYMATCH}
```

The following routine displays a second indicator in the input form. This indicator shows that the record being viewed is record X of Y total matches found.

```
DISPLAYMATCH   {LET POINTER2,+"Match "
                   &@STRING(@VLOOKUP(@STRING(RECORDNO,0),
                   RECORDLIST,0)+1,0)&" of
                   "&@STRING(@COUNT(RECORDLIST),0):VALUE}~
```

The last major section of code involves printing form letters. A sample of a form letter is shown in figure 10.3. The sentences in the form letter are actually string formulas that are tied to the input form. You can control the printing of the form letter by using the same routines that control the display of the selected records. You do this by placing the input form in BROWSE mode and tying the form letter string formulas to the input form. To print the entire database, you simply enter a blank criterion record, which will match all records.

The routine sets the PRINT range, then calls a loop that will do the actual printing.

OUTPUT	{IF @COUNT(RECORDLIST)=0}{NONEFOUND}{RETURN}
	{GETLABEL "What is the range name for the form
	letter: ",LETTERRANGE}
	{LET OUTPUT2,LETTERRANGE}
	{RECALC PRINT3}
	/ppcrr
OUTPUT2	FORMLETTER
	~q
	{FOR i,0,@COUNT(RECORDLIST),1,PRINT}
PRINT	{LET RECORDNO,@VALUE(@INDEX(RECORDLIST,0,i))}
	{RECALC INPUTRANGE}
PRINT3	{RECALC FORMLETTER}
	/ppagq

These last two routines are housekeeping routines. The first erases the second indicator in the input form when the matching mode is not in effect. The second resets the range name contained in RANGE to allow the operation of the various routines to affect the database instead of the Criterion range.

EXITFIND	{BLANK POINTER2}~
RETURNTODB	{LET RANGE,@INDEX(REFTABLE,0,0):VALUE}
	{DISPLAYPLACE}
	{CALC}

Finally, the next two routines are one-item menus that are used to display messages only.

NOKEYS	******* Unable to sort ********
	No Sort Keys set. Select Sort Keys and try again. Press Enter.
NONEFOUND	*********** No records matching criteria found ************
	Press Enter to continue.

Initial Testing

After you convert the program description into command language instructions, the next step is to execute the program. If all has gone according to plan, the program should work as intended. At this stage in the development of the program, however, you can expect problems. Human minds are too fuzzy and computers too literal for most first attempts at creating a program to succeed.

The basic goal of the testing phase is to put the program through its paces, trying it out with every possible condition. As mentioned at the beginning of this chapter, such testing isn't always possible because of the large number of possible pathways through most programs. The easiest way to test a program of the scope of this example is simply to begin using it. However, be sure that you back up your work frequently. You never know when the next step you try to execute will do something unexpected, which, you can be sure, will wipe out all the work you've done since the last save.

Debugging

If you find a problem in your program, you enter the phase of program development called debugging. Debugging is puzzle solving, detective work, and an art form, all of which makes the debugging process somewhat stimulating. Debugging can also be the most frustrating part of programming. Getting a program to run perfectly usually involves a series of successive approximations. The closer you think you are to getting rid of that last bug, and the more time you've spent finding the errors, the harder it is to give up and stop for the day. After all, the program *could* work on the next try. On more than one afternoon, I've sat down to eliminate that last bug in a program only to find that before I knew it, the sun was coming up. So, you've been warned.

You can proceed with the debugging process in several ways, and you can use a number of tricks to make things easier. The most helpful debugging aid, however, is not a trick. It is simply the use of good programming practices in writing the original program. If you created a carefully written, well-structured program, the entire process will move along smoothly (if not rapidly).

The first of the debugging tricks involves taking advantage of the modular structure of your program. By assigning a macro name to a routine in addition to its subroutine name, you can execute routines separately.

TRICK: Run each routine separately to be sure that all the routines work as intended.

Usually, the best time to test routines separately is as you are constructing them. If each routine works, then the problem has to do with the coupling between the routines.

TRICK: Use STEP mode to find programming problems.

The second debugging trick is to use STEP mode while you execute the program. In STEP mode, each program step is executed one at a time. Note, however, that a limitation to this procedure exists: command language instructions that have a repeat count execute all the counts as a single instruction. For example, {D 5} moves down 5 rows each time it is stepped.

Remember that 1-2-3 doesn't recalculate the worksheet with every step. When 1-2-3 does recalculate the worksheet, the software doesn't necessarily update the display.

TRICK: Use {RECALC}, {CALC}, and ~ instructions during debugging to update the worksheet.

If you suspect that formulas are not being calculated correctly, use a {CALC} or {RECALC} instruction wherever you think it might help. One of the most frequent programming errors in 1-2-3 involves using data that isn't updated. A strategically placed {CALC} instruction not only helps you find the problem but can fix it as well. You can use ~ to update the screen so that you can track the current condition of the variables during debugging. Be aware, however, that screen updating slows program execution.

TRICK: During debugging, create a split window to display crucial variables.

One problem you can encounter is that the variables you are interested in aren't always visible when you need to know their values. If you have followed the guidelines and placed all your reference variables in one place, you should be able to create a window that enables you to view all the variables simultaneously.

TRICK: Use the {BEEP} instruction to track program execution.

If you have a program that makes multiple branches or a program with multiple routines that produce no visible changes on the screen, you may have difficulty ascertaining where you are in a program when a problem occurs. You can solve this problem by using the {BEEP} instruction. Placing one or several {BEEP}s in your program can give you an auditory indication of how far the program has progressed before it stops. You can also use {BEEP}'s various pitches. By using differing numbers of beeps in various pitch combinations, you can create many unique indicators for program location. For example, two high-pitched beeps followed by a low-pitched beep could mean that the program is in a specific routine or that 1-2-3 has evaluated a specific {IF} instruction as TRUE or FALSE.

TRICK: During debugging, use the {?} instruction to make the program pause.

Having a program pause during debugging can be handy. You can use the cursor-movement keys to look at the condition of the worksheet, recalculate the worksheet, check values, switch windows, and so on. When you finish checking something, press the Enter key. The program then continues. (Be sure that you leave the cell pointer where you found it.) As a last resort, you can also take this opportunity to stop the program altogether.

Three Categories of Errors

Program errors generally fall into one of three categories: bad program design, incorrect use of the language, and dumb mistakes. The first of these categories is the most serious. Your program may be doing exactly what it was designed to do, but not what it is supposed to do. Such errors usually mean serious retrenchment (back to the drawing board).

When the other two kinds of errors occur, diligence and hard work will usually get the program up and running. If you write structured programs, you will have fewer errors, and you will be better able to find and fix any mistakes you do make. The following list of typical programming errors should help you if you get stuck. The list is abbreviated and is intended only to help you get an idea of where to look when you run into problems.

Design Errors

> Missing specifications
> Incorrect specifications
> Incorrect use of command language instruction
> Incorrect units (degrees versus radians)
> Incorrect data type (string versus numeric)
> Inadequate error trapping
> Inadequate user prompting
> No capability to handle exceptions

Typographical Errors

> Statement entered incorrectly
> Omitted { or }
> Parentheses substituted for braces
> Zero instead of the letter O
> @ omitted in function
> Misspelled instruction or range name
> Missing tilde (~)
> Function arguments in wrong order

Program Control

> Range name problems
>
>> Range not named
>> Range name duplicated
>> Call to unnamed subroutine
>> Subroutine name given to incorrect cell
>> Subroutine call to itself
>> Operation destroys range names

Boolean expression problems

Backward use of {IF} condition
Incomplete Boolean expression
Incorrect use of parentheses in Boolean expression
AND used instead of OR
Missing ELSE in IF-THEN-ELSE construct
Variable tested at wrong time (before recalculation)

Off-by-one error

Off-by-one is one of the famous computing errors. You can make this error in one of two ways. You can forget that offset numbering for 1-2-3 functions begins at zero instead of one. Or you can miscalculate the number of items between two numbers. For example, how many rows exist in the range A8..A18? If your answer is 10, you just committed the off-by-one error. The range includes both rows 8 and 18, so the number of rows in that range is 11.

Program flow problems

Stack error (using {BRANCH} instead of {RETURN})
Using {GOTO} instead of {BRANCH}
Infinite loops (no way to satisfy test or test omitted)
Spaghetti programming (untraceable [write only] code)

Parameter passing

Missing variable in {DEFINE}
Incorrect type specification in {DEFINE}
Incorrect order of parameters passed to subroutine

Instructions out of sequence

Data Manipulation and Control

Failure to initialize variables or counters
Failure to reinitialize variables or counters

Lookup errors

Table not defined
Table definition does not include all values
Table definition does not include area to be recalculated
Uppercase versus lowercase mismatch
Numeric versus string representation of numbers mismatch
Approximate numeric lookup
Out of range numeric lookup

Index errors

Off-by-one error
Out of range error

Missing validity check on input

If you run the sample program, you will find that it has a number of weak points. Some of the corrections are easy. For example, no way exists to call the {RETURNTODB} routine. To correct this, you need to add another menu item to the main menu, which is in operation in both the database and criterion EDIT modes. To get fancy, the final listing of the program uses string formulas to generate this last menu item. By referencing the current contents of RANGE, the menu option to return to the database appears only when the program is not in DATABASE mode.

At this stage in the program development process, while you are making program revisions, you can add a few embellishments as well as correct problems. One embellishment included in the final listing is a **Reset** option in the main menu. This option simply calls the {ERASE} routine to clear out the input form, should you desire to do this.

After you correct the obvious problems, you will have a program that works as intended most of the time. However, don't expect the program development process to end here. As you use the program yourself, you will probably uncover opportunities to add even more refinements.

Among your refinements, you could create a way to put formulas into the Criterion range. (Only labels can be inserted now.) You might also develop ways to incorporate automatically the appropriate formulas into form letters or insert a record at some location other than the end. This program is intended to illustrate programming techniques rather than to be a final product. Adding your own refinements is a good way to try out your programming wings.

Final Testing

After you debug any program you design, you should still test it rigorously, especially if other people will use it. For the example, you would need to exercise all the program's sections of code. To do so, you would have to create more than one database. Then you would actually have to use the program to print a series of form letters, using various selection criteria. In short, you should subject the program to as much real-world operation as possible.

Nygaard Testing

One of my earliest experiences with computers was designing automated machinery for an electronics manufacturing firm. My section of the firm designed machines and built and tested prototypes. My section head always insisted on conducting one final test on a new machine before it was sent to the manufacturing floor to be put into trial service. For the Nygaard test (named after my section head), he lined up along a wall everybody who had worked on the machine (so that nobody could touch anything), then proceeded to bang, poke, prod, and otherwise abuse the machine. He pushed every visible button in every conceivable order, pushed everything that could be pulled, turned switches on and off during the middle of a cycle, and loaded parts upside down or in the wrong slots. In other words, he deliberately tried to make the machine fail.

The purpose of the test was twofold: first, to subject the machine to the kind of treatment that the machine could be expected to receive on the manufacturing floor; and second, and most important, to keep the machine's designers from unconsciously nursing their "baby" over rough spots that represented weak points in the design.

Programmers are often guilty of this same kind of parenting behavior. Perhaps a program has a minor flaw that can be overcome by doing tasks in a certain order, avoiding the use of specific values, or, especially with 1-2-3, setting up special conditions ahead of time. Programmers tend to forget that other users won't know how to do these things or that people have limited memories. Programs that work flawlessly time after time in initial testing can fail consistently in the hands of a new user. If you find yourself saying such things as "You forgot to name the range" or "You started the program with the cell pointer in the wrong position," you are probably guilty of having "nursemaided" your program.

Nygaard testing can help find such problems. Giving a naive user what you think is a final version to try out (sometimes called *beta testing*) can be an excellent way to find the program's weak points. The objective behind Nygaard testing is to try to make the program fail. It is better that you discovery a flaw than a customer with half of his or her inventory tied up in your database routine.

Error-Trapping Provisions

Nygaard testing is most relevant when the program has error-trapping provisions and will be used by someone else. Be sure to test error traps thoroughly (try leaving both disk drive doors open instead of just one). This part of programming can be the most difficult, if for no other reason than that human beings are creative. No matter what you've tried, someone (probably the first user) will think of a new way to fool your program. In almost all programs of any size, the error-trapping provisions can require more programming than the primary task the program is designed to perform. Therefore, be prepared to put forth a great deal of effort. Error-trapping provisions are also the most time-consuming to test because so many error variations are possible.

A compromise is possible: instead of trying to create "bulletproof" error trapping, create clear documentation. In most settings, you can demand a little training for your users. If clear instructions are available, most people can learn to avoid doing the things that create the real disasters. Because training users and writing error-trapping code take time, you must make trade-off decisions. Just keep in mind that a simple cardboard template that fits over the function keys can save you days of code writing, testing, and debugging.

Programming for Speed

As explained in the beginning of this book, the command language is one of the world's slowest programming languages. The truth of that assertion, however, depends somewhat on how you program. If you transfer your programming techniques from BASIC to the command language, you will likely generate programs that work well, but run slowly. A programming language like no other, 1-2-3 has advantages over standard programming languages, but you have to learn what those advantages are and use them.

For instance, consider a simple list-processing problem. The task is to write various routines that delete 10 items from a list of 200. The list in this example is simply a series of cells in a column, each cell containing the word *Continue* . . . or the words *Erase this*.

    1 Continue . . .
    2 Continue . . .
    3 Continue . . .
    4 Erase this
    5 Continue . . .
    6 Continue . . .
    .
    .
    .
    200 Continue . . .

The timing routine that will be used to compare programming approaches is the \t module in figure 10.6. The module simply places the cell pointer at the beginning of the list, appropriately named LIST; starts and stops the timing; and clears the split window when the tested routine finishes.

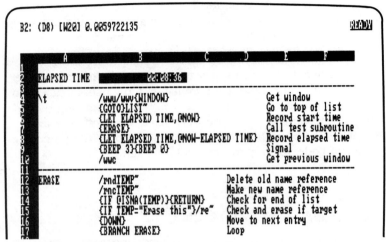

Fig. 10.6. A moving range name to process a list.

The first routine in the {ERASE} module uses the same strategy to scan a list that had to be used with 1-2-3 Release 1A's limited macro language. The routine tests successive cells in the list by creating and deleting a range name (TEMP) as the cell pointer moves downward a cell at a time. As you can see in the ELAPSED TIME listing, this routine is quite slow. It takes 8 minutes and 36 seconds (on an IBM PC equipped with an 8087 coprocessor) to scan the list completely and erase the 10 *Erase this* entries. 1-2-3 spends most of this time updating the screen and control panel.

You can improve the situation a great deal by adding {PANELOFF} and {WINDOWSOFF} instructions to the {ERASE} routine. By using {PANELOFF} alone, you decrease the time to 5 minutes and 55 seconds, a saving of about 30 percent. Be sure to keep {PANELOFF} outside the repeating loop. {PANELOFF} itself takes some time to execute and slows down the program if executed 200 times. By using only {WINDOWSOFF}, you decrease the time to 5 minutes and 19 seconds, an improvement of about 7 percent. If you use both {PANELOFF} and {WINDOWSOFF}, the elapsed time is 2 minutes and 29 seconds, for a total improvement of about 71 percent.

Using Advanced Features To Make a Program Run Faster

You can make a program run faster by using some of 1-2-3's more advanced functions. In figure 10.7, the /Range Name Create-/Range Name Delete sequence is replaced by the @CELLPOINTER("contents") instruction. This change eliminates all the activity associated with range naming and results in an elapsed time of 46 seconds (windows and panel on), a tenfold improvement over the range-naming method.

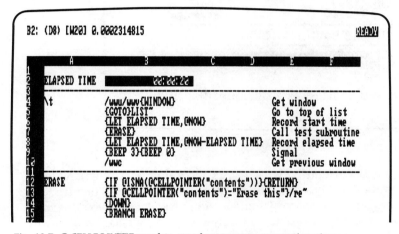

Fig. 10.7. @CELLPOINTER used to speed up program execution time.

You can also use a {FOR} loop to control the processing (see fig. 10.8). The subroutine operates on the defined range (LIST), rather than testing for the @NA value, and uses a dynamic instruction that incorporates the @CELLPOINTER("address") to test the contents of the current cell. This procedure eliminates one {IF} instruction and all the panel activity associated with the Erase command. As shown by the ELAPSED TIME, however, you lose more time than you gain because of the time 1-2-3 spends processing the {FOR} and {RECALC} instructions.

Eliminating Screen Activity

One way to gain more time in processing the list is to eliminate screen activity altogether. Figure 10.9 shows one way to accomplish this task. The general strategy during the improvements has been to perform more and more of the processing internally rather than use the same kinds of commands you would

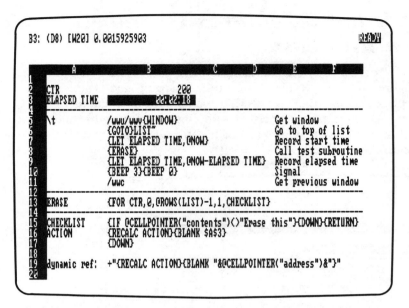

Fig. 10.8. A {FOR} loop to control the processing.

use to perform the task manually. What makes 1-2-3 slow as a programming language is the work 1-2-3 has to do to manage its complicated command structure and fancy screen displays. By eliminating these factors, you can make computation speeds more reasonable, but only if you are familiar enough with 1-2-3's commands and functions to create programs that don't require screen access.

Using Functions

You can achieve still another significant increase in speed by taking advantage of some special features of 1-2-3's functions. Figure 10.10 shows a routine in which @VLOOKUP locates the occurrences of the target string in the list. You may recall that @VLOOKUP returns a number that represents the position of a specific string in a vertical list. By combining that position information with the beginning row number of the LIST range, you can construct a string formula that returns the address of the target string's first occurrence in the list. You can then use {BLANK} to construct a dynamic instruction that erases that cell. After the cell is erased, @VLOOKUP returns the location of the next occurrence in the list of the target string, which is erased, and so on.

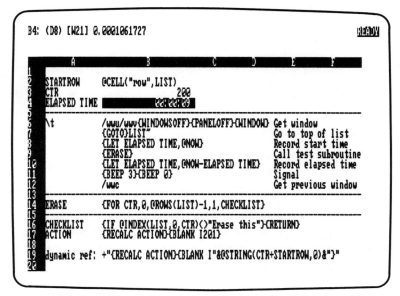

Fig. 10.9. @INDEX used to increase speed.

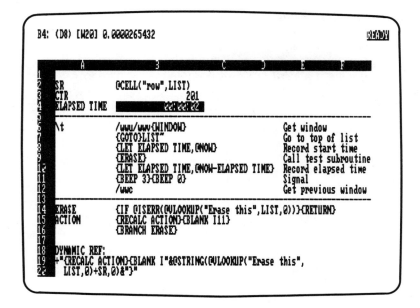

Fig. 10.10. The fast version using @VLOOKUP.

The @ISERR function traps the ERR condition that occurs when the last of the target entries is erased, then returns to the timing routine. This version of the routine operates in just 2 seconds—177 times faster than the first version.

To further increase speed, you can make one more modification to the program. You can eliminate the {IF} test and combine the {BLANK} dynamic instruction with the {BRANCH} instruction so that the {ERASE} routine consists of only one line:

    {RECALC ERASE}{BLANK I11}{BRANCH ERASE}

The routine consists of the following formula:

    +"{RECALC ERASE}{BLANK I"&@STRING(@VLOOKUP("Erase
    this",LIST,0))&"}{BRANCH ERASE}"

By using this method, you take advantage of the fact that @VLOOKUP returns an ERR value when all the entries have been erased. The entire dynamic instruction then converts to ERR. The ERR condition stops the execution of the {ERASE} loop, but makes the routine unusable as a subroutine because the program will be halted with an error message. Although this is a limitation, the program performs the task in less than 1 second, as near as I could time it. This time is somewhere between 300 and 400 times faster than the old version that uses /Range Name Create-/Range Name Delete.

The importance of the preceding examples is to underscore the necessity of approaching programming problems carefully. Remember that you aren't dealing with an ordinary programming language. 1-2-3 has so many features—and so many ways exist to program any task—that you will have to experiment to find the method best suited to your application. A speed difference of 30,000 percent can make the difference between a good program and one so slow that it is unusable.

11

Program Library

This chapter is the command language version of the macro library presented in Chapters 5 and 6. With the command language, even more than with macros, the possible applications are virtually unlimited. This library, then, does not present a complete coverage of everything you can do with the command language. The programs that are presented here are designed to stimulate your thinking and to present various programming concepts and construction techniques.

The chapter is divided into three major sections, according to the type of application described. The first section deals with the command language instructions that work with ASCII files. Moreso than any of the other command language instructions, this group of instructions must be mastered together. File operations require that a number of steps each be executed correctly and in a specific order. The examples presented show you how to use these instructions to create and manipulate ASCII file data.

The second section describes what I call super-macros. These short programs are like macros, in that their primary function is to perform a single task, usually associated with constructing or modifying worksheet data. These programs differ from macros, however, in that they use command language instructions to perform the task in ways that cannot be accomplished with macros.

Finally, the program library includes some longer programs that each perform a more sophisticated task than even the super-macros perform. When you try these programs, pay as much attention to how they are constructed as to what they do. As the section on "Programming for Speed" in Chapter 10 demonstrated, there usually are many ways to program a task, not all of which are equivalent. The last library programs contain many examples of how a programming task can be accomplished efficiently and elegantly, by adhering to good program design principles and by making effective use of the power of the spreadhseet as a programming environment.

One last word is in order about these sample programs. The relative quality of the programs—and I would not claim the programs are the best possible—is a reflection of careful planning and a lot of good old-fashioned work. Most of the programs have been rewritten several times, sometimes from the ground up, to take advantage of a better approach or technique. The Mapper program in this section is in its fifth major revision, the current version running some 100 times faster than the original version. When you create your own programs, don't be afraid of scrapping an old version and starting over from scratch. What you learn about programming by addressing the weak points of your program designs can be invaluable.

Finally, for those of you who are looking for sample routines to help you learn to program, be sure to go through the examples that accompany the command language references in Chapter 12. Many of the routines described there are usable programs in their own right.

Basic File Operations

One of 1-2-3's most convenient new features is its capability to read and write files directly. The instructions that perform these disk operations are far more flexible than 1-2-3's /Print File and /File Import commands, which handle only text files with a specific structure.

File operations are among the more difficult to learn in any system, because they are usually primitive and closely related to machine-level functioning. Therefore, instructions that deal with file operations usually contain a number of details that must be addressed in order for the system to work properly. These details often are related to file operations at a byte-by-byte level.

One of the most difficult things to understand about file operations is that the computer reads and writes information from and to a disk in large chunks, although what you do with the information appears to work a little at a time. The computer makes an interim copy of the information in a place in memory called a *buffer*. When you issue a {READ} or {WRITE} instruction, 1-2-3 reads data to or writes data from the buffer rather than directly to or from the disk file. When you read the last byte from the buffer or write into it until it is full, the operating system transfers another chunk of data to or from the disk.

Because 1-2-3 and DOS take care of buffer operations automatically, you don't have to worry about how they work. The buffers, however, are the reason that you must open and close a file. The {OPEN} instruction tells 1-2-3 that a buffer must be created, tells 1-2-3 what file you are going to process, and specifies whether you are going to read or write a file.

{CLOSE}, on the other hand, tells 1-2-3 that you are finished processing a file. If you have been writing to a file, {CLOSE} also tells 1-2-3 to "flush" the buffer to the disk. As mentioned before, 1-2-3 writes the buffer to disk only when the buffer is full. After you finish with a file, {CLOSE} makes sure that anything left in a half-buffer is also written to the disk. {CLOSE} also makes certain that the information about the new size of the file is written to the disk directory. If this information isn't current, the file may be unusable.

The Instruction Set

Brief descriptions of the instructions that handle file operations follow. For more information, see the alphabetical listing in Chapter 12.

{OPEN filename,mode}

This instruction creates input or output buffers and specifies the disk file to be processed and the kind of operation to be performed. The allowable operations are the following:

READ   For use with {READ} or {READLN}

WRITE   For use with {WRITE} or {WRITELN}. Information is written to the beginning of the file, unless the file pointer is altered with {SETPOS}. WRITE creates a new file if one doesn't exist.

APPEND For use with {WRITE} or {WRITELN}. 1-2-3 adds information to the end of the file, unless altered with {SETPOS}. APPEND doesn't create a new file.

MODIFY For use with all READ and WRITE instructions. This option enables you to perform both reading and writing operations on the same opened file. MODIFY doesn't create a new file.

Only the first character of the preceding "operations" words (*r, w, a,* and *m*) must be included in the braces of the {OPEN} instruction. If you use any other character, an error doesn't occur, but 1-2-3 treats the file in the same way as a file that was opened with the READ option.

Only one file can be opened at a time. If you open a new file before closing the current file, 1-2-3 abandons the originally opened file, and the subsequent file operations will apply to the new file.

TRAP: The instructions listed in this section have a special error-trapping feature that makes them different from almost all other command language instructions.

With almost all command language instructions except the file instructions listed in this chapter, you can place more than one instruction on a single line. When you put several instructions together this way, 1-2-3 executes them in order, from left to right. The exception to this rule is {IF}. With {IF}, instructions following on the same line are executed only when the condition in the {IF} instruction is evaluated as TRUE.

The file operation instructions behave in a similar fashion, except that they allow execution of instructions on the same line only when an error occurs in the file operation itself. This method of operation enables you to include provisions for error handling in your programs, without using the {ONERROR} instruction. You must be sure, however, not to include on the same line with the file instruction any operation that you want to perform when everything is working normally.

Error Conditions

Table 11.1 lists the types of errors that can occur in a file operation and the instructions that recognize an error and allow program execution to continue on the same line (ERROR mode). When an instruction invokes ERROR mode, the instruction itself is not executed.

Table 11.1
Error Conditions Using File Operations

Error Condition	Instructions Functioning in Error Mode	
Attempting to open a disk file that does not exist with READ, APPEND, or MODIFY options. (Opening a file that does not exist for WRITE operations causes a new file to be created.)	{READ} {WRITE} {GETPOS} {FILESIZE}	{READLN} {WRITELN} {SETPOS} {OPEN}
Attempting to READ from a file opened with the WRITE or APPEND options	{READ}	{READLN}

Attempting to READ from a file after using {SETPOS} to position the file pointer past the end of the file	{READ}	{READLN}
Attempting to WRITE to a file opened with the READ option	{WRITE}	{WRITELN}

{READ bytecount,location}

This instruction reads information from the file as a string of text and places the result in a specified cell. {READ} requires an additional argument that specifies the number of bytes to be read. You can use this instruction to read nontext files or text- processor-created files which contain lines that don't end with the Carriage Return/Line Feed (CR/LF) sequence 1-2-3 expects for use with {READLN}.

{READLN location}

This instruction reads information from a file, as does {READ}. Rather than reading a fixed number of bytes, {READLN} either reads until it finds a CR/LF sequence or reads a maximum of 240 characters.

{WRITE string}

This instruction transfers to the file the contents of its *string* argument or the string in the specified cell. The number of bytes written is equal to the length of the string.

{WRITELN string}

This instruction works like {WRITE}, but adds a CR/LF sequence to the contents of the string written. The number of bytes transferred to the file is therefore two more than the string length.

{CLOSE}

This instruction completes the file operations, as described previously.

{GETPOS location}

This instruction enters the file pointer's current position into the cell specified by the *location* argument. When the following conditions exist, 1-2-3 sets the file pointer automatically.

1. The file pointer is set to the beginning of the file, which is position zero, when a file is opened for READ or WRITE operations.

2. 1-2-3 sets the file pointer to the first position past the end of the file for APPEND operations, and subsequent WRITE operations add to the existing file.

3. The file pointer is set to the next READ or WRITE location when these operations are performed. 1-2-3 automatically repositions the file pointer after READ and WRITE operations. Therefore, repeated operations read or write to the file in sequential order.

{SETPOS file-position}

This instruction enables you to direct the file pointer to any position in an opened file. You can use {SETPOS} to position the file pointer past the end of the file for WRITE operations; 1-2-3 increases the size of the file to allow the WRITE operation to take place. Attempting to READ from a file after setting the file pointer past the end of the file causes the {READ} or {READLN} instruction to enter ERROR mode (see table 11.1).

{FILESIZE location}

This instruction returns the current size of the opened file. The result reflects the most recent write operations.

Performing File Operations

Creating routines that perform file operations involves knowing not only the various instructions that are involved, but how to put the pieces together. This section describes the more practical aspects of working with files.

Sequential Access Versus Random Access

The terms *sequential access* and *random access* refer to the way in which the system retrieves data from a file. With sequential access, data is read from a file in a continuous stream. To read something from the middle of a file, the system must first read all the preceding data. {READLN} performs this kind of file access. If the file to be read is constructed as most text files are, the data in the file has variable record lengths, and each record is separated by a CR/LF (ASCII 13/ASCII 10) sequence.

Storing data sequentially has two disadvantages: the data's relative inflexibility, and the time required to access records that aren't at the beginning of the file. Furthermore, if you want to change one record in a sequential access file, the system must read the entire file, change the desired record, and then write a new copy of the entire modified file.

The advantages to using sequential data storage are its simplicity and the compactness of the data files. For files you plan to use primarily for data storage, such as archive copies of text files, sequential access is preferable.

Unlike sequential access, random access enables you to access any part of a file anytime. You must, however, know the location of every record in the file so that the file pointer can be set to the appropriate position. You can usually accomplish this task by making all the records in the file a fixed length. By multiplying the record length by the record number, you can then compute the position in which the file pointer is set.

You can also generate very small files, or *key files*, to act as an *index*, which is a list of file pointers that refers to the positions of records in the file. You can then refer to a sorted key to list a file as if it were sorted in a specific order. Key files are usually much smaller and easier to use than data files. Having several key files enables you to list a file or a subset of the file in any order, without having to perform complex and time-consuming sorts on the data file.

The primary advantage of random-access files is the ease with which you can change any part of a file. Rather than reading and writing a whole file as you must do with sequential files, you can read a record, modify it, and then write it back to the file.

Random-access files have two disadvantages: the computational overhead involved with keeping track of the file pointer's position, and the storage overhead involved with keeping all records the same size. (The latter requirement frequently wastes disk space.)

Transferring Data to and from the Worksheet

READ and WRITE operations have two limitations. First, all the data must be in the form of a string. Therefore, you must convert numeric information by using the @STRING function or {CONTENTS} instruction. Only then can you transfer the information to disk. As 1-2-3 reads the information from disk, you must convert the information back to numeric form by using the @VALUE function or the /Data Parse command.

The second limitation is that the READ and WRITE operations can transfer data to and from only one cell. Therefore, you must combine multiple fields of data into one field by using string formulas or printing to a range. You must also use @INDEX or {PUT} to transfer multiple records to the cell on which the READ and WRITE instructions operate. The following sections provide examples of how to perform these tasks.

Writing to a Sequential File

The following example shows how to use {WRITELN} to create a sequential file. The data to be transferred to the file is in the form of a letter generated in Symphony's DOC environment. The range containing the letter is called TEXT, and the file that will store the data is named TEXTDATA.TXT (see fig. 11.1).

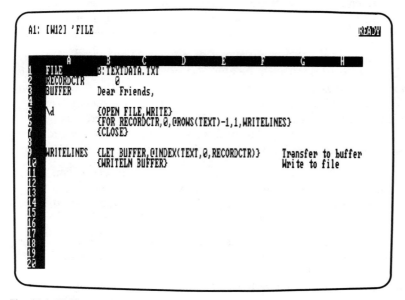

Fig. 11.1. Writing a sequential file.

You can read this file into 1-2-3 by using the /File Import Text command.

Adding to an Existing Sequential File

If you want to add to an existing file, use the program in figure 11.1, but change the operation in the {OPEN} instruction to APPEND.

TRAP: You can't APPEND a file that doesn't exist.

If you are working with a new file, you must use WRITE before you can use APPEND. Attempting to perform an APPEND to a file that doesn't exist causes the WRITE operation to enter ERROR mode.

Reading from a Sequential File

The program in figure 11.2 reads the file created in figure 11.1 back into the worksheet. As 1-2-3 reads the data into the worksheet, the program transfers the data from the buffer cell to the range called TEXT. That range must contain enough rows to accommodate all the lines 1-2-3 will read. The READ operations stop when the file pointer reaches the end of the file.

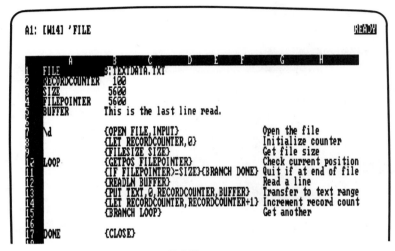

```
A1: [W14] 'FILE                                              READY

          A          B      C         D      E     F      G          H
1  FILE         B:TEXTDATA.TXT
2  RECORDCOUNTER    100
3  SIZE            5600
4  FILEPOINTER     5600
5  BUFFER       This is the last line read.
6
7  \d           {OPEN FILE,INPUT}              Open the file
8               {LET RECORDCOUNTER,0}          Initialize counter
9               {FILESIZE SIZE}                Get file size
10 LOOP         {GETPOS FILEPOINTER}           Check current position
11              {IF FILEPOINTER>=SIZE}{BRANCH DONE} Quit if at end of file
12              {READLN BUFFER}                Read a line
13              {PUT TEXT,0,RECORDCOUNTER,BUFFER} Transfer to text range
14              {LET RECORDCOUNTER,RECORDCOUNTER+1} Increment record count
15              {BRANCH LOOP}                  Get another
16
17 DONE         {CLOSE}
```

Fig. 11.2. Reading from a sequential file.

Writing to a Random-Access File

The program in figure 11.3 shows how to use {WRITE} to write to a random-access file. The program also demonstrates another way to construct fixed-length records.

The cell named BUFFER is written to the file; BUFFER contains a formula that concatenates the BUFFER1..BUFFER5 cells, which are intermediate buffers created with {CONTENTS}. Specifying a *width* argument in the {CONTENTS} instruction places in the destination cells a string with a fixed number of characters. Using the {CONTENTS} instruction's output guarantees that the final record created will have a fixed length.

The *width* argument in each of the {CONTENTS} instructions is equivalent to the field width of the corresponding data item. The total length of the record can be obtained by adding the various *width* arguments (20+4+12+12+12=60).

```
                    Intermediate buffers      Primary buffers      Cell formulas
RECORDCOUNTER    3
                    BUFFER1  Charlie Crabtree  BUFFER1A Charlie Crabtree  @INDEX(RECORDCOUNTER,0,DATARANGE)
                    BUFFER2    1               BUFFER2A   1               @INDEX(RECORDCOUNTER,1,DATARANGE)
FILE      B:DATA.DB BUFFER3    2500            BUFFER3A   2500            @INDEX(RECORDCOUNTER,2,DATARANGE)
                    BUFFER4    7500            BUFFER4A   7500            @INDEX(RECORDCOUNTER,3,DATARANGE)
                    BUFFER5    10000           BUFFER5A   10000          @INDEX(RECORDCOUNTER,4,DATARANGE)

------------------------------------------------------------------------------------------------

          Record structure as written to file

          --------------------|---|-----------|-----------|-----------|
BUFFER    Charlie Crabtree    1     2500         7500        10000
          --------------------|---|-----------|-----------|-----------|

          Cell formula for BUFFER

          +BUFFER1&BUFFER2&BUFFER3&BUFFER4&BUFFER5

------------------------------------------------------------------------------------------------

\d        {OPEN FILE,WRITE}                          Open file for writing
          {FOR RECORDCOUNTER,1,@ROWS(DATA_DB)-1,1,WRITELINES}  Write once for each record
          {CLOSE}                                    Finished


WRITELINES  {RECALC INDEXBUFFERS}                    Get current data into the @INDEX formulas
            {CONTENTS BUFFER1,BUFFER1A,20}           Transform the data to text form
            {CONTENTS BUFFER2,BUFFER2A,4,0}          "      "
            {CONTENTS BUFFER3,BUFFER3A,12,0}         "      "
            {CONTENTS BUFFER4,BUFFER4A,12,0}         "      "
            {CONTENTS BUFFER5,BUFFER5A,12,0}         "      "
            {RECALC BUFFER}                          Update formula that concatenates buffers
            {WRITE BUFFER}                           And write to disk
```

Fig. 11.3. Writing to a random-access file.

Constructing the Primary buffers BUFFER1A..BUFFER5A to use as a *source* argument in {CONTENTS} is necessary because the @INDEX function can't be entered directly into the {CONTENTS} instruction.

Reading from a Random-Access File

Figure 11.4 demonstrates how to read from a random-access file. 1-2-3 selects the record according to the user's response to {GETNUMBER}, emphasizing the random-access nature of this arrangement.

The formulas at the top of the listing show how to extract the numeric values from the text string that {READ} imports to the worksheet. Notice that the @MID function's *length* argument is equivalent to the field width for the corresponding data value.

```
                        Parsing formulas    Cell formulas

RECORDNUMBER      -1        BUFFER1  John Apples  @LEFT(B13,20)
                           BUFFER2             2  @VALUE(@MID(B13,20,4))
FILE          B:DATA.DB     BUFFER3         5,000  @VALUE(@MID(B13,24,12))
                           BUFFER4        15,000  @VALUE(@MID(B13,36,12))
RECORDLENGTH      60        BUFFER5        20,000  @VALUE(@MID(B13,48,12))


-----------------------------------------------------------------------------
              Record structure as read from file

              --------------------|---|-----------|-----------|-----------|
BUFFER        John Apples         2     5000        15000       20000
              --------------------|---|-----------|-----------|-----------|


-----------------------------------------------------------------------------
\d            {OPEN FILE,INPUT}                    Open file
LOOP          {GETNUMBER "Enter record number to read from file: ",RECORDNUMBER}
              {IF RECORDNUMBER=-1}{BRANCH DONE}    Minus 1 means quit
              {SETPOS RECORDLENGTH*RECORDNUMBER}   Set file pointer to selected record
              {READ RECORDLENGTH,BUFFER}           Read it in
              {RECALC PARSEBUFFERS}                Parse the record
              ~                                    Display it
              {BRANCH LOOP}                        Get another

DONE          {CLOSE}
```

Fig. 11.4. Reading from a random-access file.

Sending Output to the Printer

One of the tricks you can perform with file operation instructions is to send information directly to the printer, which you can open as if it were a file. DOS allows the designations PRN or LPT1 for a printer connected to parallel port 1, or LPT2 for a printer connected to parallel port 2. If you use a serial printer, you can still take advantage of this command language feature by using the DOS MODE command to redirect the output of the parallel port (see your DOS manual).

Figure 11.5 shows a short routine to print from a range directly to the printer. Unfortunately, 1-2-3 translates all control characters into spaces, and special ASCII codes into their LICS character equivalents. These are the same translations that are made during printing. Therefore, you can't send control codes and special characters to the printer, other than the characters in the predefined LICS set.

TRICK: Preview your printer output by sending it to the screen.

DOS enables you to specify CON as an input and output device in the same manner that you specify files and the printer. If you change the file name in the {OPEN} instruction to CON, the output will be typed directly on the screen instead of being directed to the printer. This operation usually makes a mess of the screen (see fig. 11.6), but it will "repair" itself if you press Enter. You can save youself a lot of wasted paper by using this trick. You can also do the same trick by using the standard **Print** commands and entering CON as a file name.

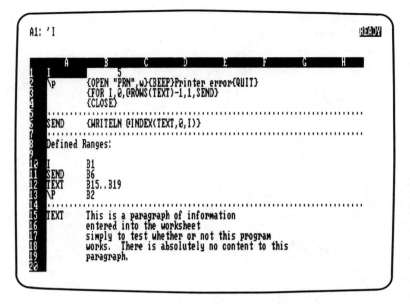

Fig. 11.5. Sending a range to the printer with the file commands.

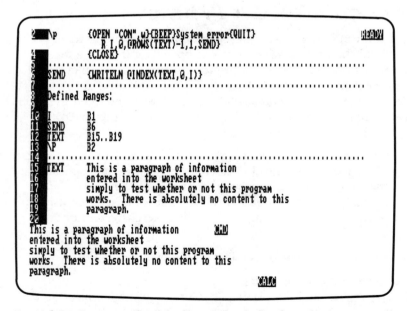

Fig. 11.6. Sending output from the file commands directly to the screen.

Searching a File

The program in figure 11.7 demonstrates how you can use the file instructions to search a text file for a specific string. In the example, the string FIG5_8 is entered as a search string. The @FIND function in the GETLINE routine serves as a test for the presence of the search string in the BUFFER cell. The BUFFER cell is loaded from the file, a line at a time by the {READLN} command in that same routine.

```
FILE     5LIST.PRN              LINECOUNT    9
SRCHSTR  FIG5_8                 MAXBYTES    393
BUFFER        FIG5_11  PIX  754 CURRENTPOS  270
I             1                 FOUND        1
--------------------------------------------------------------------
\x       {OPEN FILE,R}                          Open the file
         {FILESIZE MAXBYTES}                    How big is it?
         {LET LINECOUNT,0}{BLANK CONTEXT}       Initialize
         {FOR I,1,2,0,GETLINE}                  Loop forever
         {IF FOUND}{SHOW}                       Display if found
--------------------------------------------------------------------
GETLINE  {READLN BUFFER}                        Read a line
         {LET LINECOUNT,LINECOUNT+1}            Increment the line count
         {GETPOS CURRENTPOS}                    Get current file pointer
         {IF CURRENTPOS>=MAXBYTES}{FORBREAK}    End endless loop if past end
         {IF @ISERR(@FIND(SRCHSTR,BUFFER,0))=0}{LET FOUND,1}{FORBREAK}   ... or if found
--------------------------------------------------------------------
SHOW     {SETPOS @MAX(CURRENTPOS-200,0)}        Reposition file pointer
         {FOR I,1,2,0,REREAD}                   Endless loop again
--------------------------------------------------------------------
REREAD   {READLN BUFFER}                            Read lines before and after target
         {IF @ISERR(@FIND(SRCHSTR,BUFFER,0))=0}{LET BUFFER,+">>>>>"&BUFFER&"<<<<<"}
         {IF @ISERR(@FIND(SRCHSTR,BUFFER,0))}{LET BUFFER,+"     "&BUFFER}
         {PUT CONTEXT,0,@COUNT(CONTEXT),BUFFER}     Place line in output list
         {GETPOS MAXBYTES}                          Check current file pointer position
         {IF MAXBYTES>=CURRENTPOS+100}{FORBREAK}    Quit after listing 100 bytes past target
--------------------------------------------------------------------
Note: Range CONTEXT must be defined before the program will run.


     1   PIX     413   1-01-80  12:12a
      FIG5_3   PIX    1162   1-01-80  12:14a
      FIG5_18  PIX     522   1-01-80  12:06a
      FIG5_4   PIX     442   1-01-80  12:48a
>>>>>FIG5_8   PIX     696   1-01-80   4:03a<<<<<
      FIG5_9   PIX     388   1-01-80  12:35a
      FIG5_10  PIX     385   1-01-80  12:38a
      FIG5_11  PIX     754   1-01-80  12:41a
```

Fig. 11.7. Scanning a file for a string and showing the result in context.

In this sample program, when the search string is found, it is displayed in context. The program rereads the file, starting 200 bytes before the line containing the match and ending 100 bytes after. The buffer is tested and modified in the REREAD routine so that the line containing the match is flagged, as shown at the bottom of the figure. The listing containing the file information is assembled using a {PUT} instruction.

One notable aspect of this sample program is the use of {FOR} and {FORBREAK} to create a DO-UNTIL construction. DO-UNTIL is a programming term that refers to a section of program code that repeats indefinitely, until a specific test is satisfied. By setting the *step* value in the {FOR} instruction to zero, you create a condition that will never terminate as a result of the {FOR} operation, because the *counter* variable will never reach the *stop* value. The routine called by {FOR} therefore repeats until stopped by the {FORBREAK} instruction. This is an unorthodox use of the {FOR} instruction for all the programming purists who want to avoid a {BRANCH} instruction at all costs.

Super Macros

The following set of listings is included here to give you some ideas for using the command language to build utility macros. These macros are more powerful than those that you could create with ordinary macro keywords.

The first routine copies a cell the full width of a range that contains multiple columns. This program is similar to Macro 14 (described in Chapter 5), which uses the "grab and slide" technique to determine how far to the right the copies should extend.

This program improves on that macro in two ways. First, this routine "grabs and slides" even when the data doesn't exist in an immediately adjacent row. The program uses the {END}{UP} sequence to attach itself to any existing data in a row above, then returns to the original row before completing the Copy operation. When the routine moves up, it also tests whether it is in row 1. If so, the assumption is that the program has been activated improperly, and the Copy operation is aborted. A similar test is made to check for a righthand boundary beyond the 200th column. (Note that the ROWREF cell is initially blank.)

```
ROWREF

\r          {LET ROWREF,@CELLPOINTER("row")}
            /C~.{END}{UP}
            {IF @CELLPOINTER("row")=1}{BEEP 0}{ESC 6}{QUIT}
            {END}{RIGHT}
            {IF @CELLPOINTER("col")>200}{BEEP 3}{BEEP 3}{ESC 6}{QUIT}
            {DOWN ROWREF-@CELLPOINTER("row")}~
```

The following routine enters a label into the worksheet and invokes the equivalent of the /**R**ange **N**ame **L**abels **R**ight command to assign a range name in the worksheet. What makes this routine valuable is that it checks to see whether the range name you are attempting to enter into the worksheet is already assigned to another cell. The program makes this test by using the

/**Range Name Create** command and tracking the cell pointer to see whether it moves from its original location, as would be the case if the range name already existed in the worksheet. If a duplicate range name is found, the program gives you the option of either replacing the range name with the new specification or abandoning the whole operation.

```
\m              {GETLABEL "Enter macro or cell name: ",XMNAMEREF}
                {LET XMSAVEADD,@CELLPOINTER("Address")}
                /rnc

XMNAMEREF
                ~{IF @CELLPOINTER("address")<>XMSAVEADD}{XMEXISTS}
                {RIGHT}~{LET XMNAME2,XMNAMEREF}'

XMNAME2
                ~{RIGHT}{QUIT}

XMEXISTS        {BEEP 3}{BEEP 3}{GETLABEL "**** NAME ALREADY EXISTS **
                    ENTER to continue {BREAK} to QUIT, XMSAVEADD}
                {BS}
```

The next two programs are so simple that they would not be worth including here if not for the fact that they are so handy. If you write a lot of command language programs, you will eventually get tired of typing the following whenever you need to use this function:

@CELLPOINTER("contents")

Like anything else that is tedious in 1-2-3, the problem can be coded into a macro or program. In this case, the program is little more than a menu arranged to allow entry of the @CELL and @CELLPOINTER functions with a mere two keystrokes.

The @CELL menu, listed first, begins the entry and lets you specify the *range* argument.

The menu listings here have been "transposed" to make them readable. Short prompts are in the first column, long prompts are in the second, and program lines follow on a line-for-column basis.

TYPE @CELL("xxx",!

```
\c              @CELL{MENUBRANCH \cMENU}

\cMENU
Contents        @CELL("Contents")       ("Contents"      ,!
Address         @CELL("Address")        ("Address"       ,!
Type            @CELL("Type")           ("Type"          ,!
Width           @CELL("Width")          ("Width"         ,!
L(Col)          @CELL("Col")            ("Col"           ,!
```

| Row | @CELL("Row") | ("Row" | ,! |
| Format | @CELL("Format") | ("Format" | ,! |

TYPE @CELLPOINTER("xxx")

| \p | @CELLPOINTER{MENUBRANCH \pMENU} | |

\pMENU

Contents	@CELLPOINTER("Contents")	("Contents")
Address	@CELLPOINTER("Address")	("Address")
Type	@CELLPOINTER("Type")	("Type")
Width	@CELLPOINTER("Width")	("Width")
L(Col)	@CELLPOINTER("Col")	("Col")
Row	@CELLPOINTER("Row")	("Row")
Format	@CELLPOINTER("Format")	("Format")

The next routine is also simple and menu driven. Its function is to convert a string entered into the worksheet into uppercase, lowercase, or proper case. The operation requires two keystrokes and is invaluable, considering how prone users are to forgetting the Caps Lock effect.

The dynamic instruction used in this routine is a model for how to perform operations on the current cell pointer location. Each of the menu options has its own formula. The \w1 range encompasses all three dynamic formulas.

| \w | {MENUBRANCH \wMENU} |

\wMENU

Lower	Change current string to lowercase	{RECALC \w1}{LET A1, @LOWER(@CELLPOINTER("contents"))}
Upper	Change current string to uppercase	{RECALC \w1}{LET A1, @UPPER(@CELLPOINTER("contents"))}
Proper	Change current string to proper case	{RECALC \w1}{LET A1, @PROPER(@CELLPOINTER("contents"))}

The following formula documents the dynamic instructions in the first menu option (in the third column of the preceding):

```
+"{RECALC \w1}{LET
"&@CELLPOINTER("Address")&",
@LOWER(@CELLPOINTER(""Contents""))}"
```

This formula documents the second menu option:

```
+"{RECALC \w1}{LET
"&@CELLPOINTER("Address")&",
@UPPER(@CELLPOINTER(""Contents""))}"
```

This formula documents the third menu option:

+"{RECALC \w1}{LET
"&@CELLPOINTER("Address")&",
@PROPER(@CELLPOINTER(""Contents""))}"

Ever forget where a remote cell was located? Or lose track of a hidden cell in the far right part of your worksheet? If so, then the next routine is for you. It "sweeps" up and down worksheet columns, moving left a column at a time if the column is completely empty. If the program encounters a nonblank cell anywhere between rows 1 and 8,192, the program beeps and quits.

This following routine may seem frivolous, but it has proved valuable in a number of instances. If you want a better assessment of the state of your worksheet than you can get with this routine, see the Mapper program later in this chapter.

\d   {END}{DOWN}{IF @CELLPOINTER("row")<>8192}{BEEP}{QUIT}
       {LEFT}{END}{UP}{IF @CELLPOINTER("row")<>1}{BEEP}{QUIT}
       {LEFT}{BRANCH \d}

The following program is also simple, but provides a valuable service. This routine checks for cells that contain damaged formulas—that is, formulas containing a cell or range reference that has become ERR. The program takes advantage of the fact that you can't enter a formula containing ERR into the worksheet.

The heart of the program is a comparison of the cell pointer's location before and after the {EDIT}{DOWN} sequence. If the formula being checked doesn't contain any damaged ranges, it will enter normally when the {DOWN} keystroke is issued, and the cell pointer location will change. If the formula is damaged, the cell pointer won't move, and the program detects this and stops. Conveniently, an attempt to enter the bad formula (by moving down) causes 1-2-3 to beep. Therefore, when the routine discovers a problem, an audible indication is provided even though that feature isn't built into the program *per se*.

XMSAVEADD

\f   {IF @ISERR(@CELLPOINTER("contents"))=0}{DOWN}{BRANCH \f}
       {LET XMSAVEADD,@CELLPOINTER("address")}
       {EDIT}{DOWN}{IF @CELLPOINTER("address")=XMSAVEADD}{QUIT}
       {BRANCH \f}

Chapter 8 included the listing of a program that worked in conjunction with a technique to construct complex formulas. The formula construction technique involved placing each separate function in a multifunction formula in a separate cell. The final transformation or test desired from the formula was achieved by linking the various parts of the formula together using cell references. Building a complex formula in separate cells has the distinct advantage of allowing each part of the formula to be tested separately. The disadvantage of this construction technique is that converting the listings in their separate cells to one long formula is tedious and invites typographical errors.

The program listed in Chapter 8 and repeated in figure 11.8 is described in more detail here. The program constructs the formula with a search and replace operation created using @REPLACE. You must place the word *stop* two cells below the last entry in the formula list before running the program.

```
1    PROGRAM TO WRITE NESTED FORMULA FROM PARTS
2    ------------------------------------------------------------
3    SAVED                Copy of formula part
4    ADDR                 String version of cell reference
5    MODIFIED             String version of nested formula
6    ------------------------------------------------------------
7    \f         {CHECKSTRING}
8               {LET MODIFIED,@CELLPOINTER("contents")}
9    \f2        {DOWN 2}
10              {CHECKSTRING}
11              {LET SAVED,@CELLPOINTER("contents")}
12              {LET ADDR,@CHAR(@CELLPOINTER("col")+64)&@STRING(@CELLPOINTER("row"),0)}
13              {IF SAVED="stop"}{QUIT}
14   \f3        {LET MODIFIED,@REPLACE(MODIFIED,@FIND(ADDR,MODIFIED,0),@LENGTH(ADDR),SAVED)}
15              {IF @FIND(ADDR,MODIFIED,0+1){BRANCH \f3}
16              {BRANCH \f2}
17   ------------------------------------------------------------
18   CHECKSTRING  {IF @CELLPOINTER("type")<>"1"}{EDIT}{HOME}`~
```

Fig. 11.8. A program to write a nested formula from parts.

The line by line operation of the program is as follows:

Line 7, the first line in the program, is a call to the subroutine {CHECKSTRING}. The {CHECKSTRING} subroutine is actually a safety check that allows you to use the formula construction method described in Chapter 8 in two ways. To visualize the formula's operation during construction, you must be able to see the formula itself. The formula can be made visible either by converting a copy of the formula into a string, or by setting the format of the cell to Text. Because this program requires the formula to be present as a string, the {CHECKSTRING} routine checks the cell type and converts the contents to a string if necessary.

Line 8, {LET MODIFIED,@CELLPOINTER("contents")}, saves a copy of the string version of the formula in the cell MODIFIED.

Line 9, {DOWN 2}, moves to the next formula in the list.

Line 10 is a second call to {CHECKLIST}. The first time through the program, this subroutine call will do nothing, because it is redundant to the line 8. The call is included here so that the subroutine will be accessed when the program loops.

Line 11, {LET SAVED,@CELLPOINTER("contents")}, makes a copy of the formula at the current cell pointer position. This formula is referred to as a cell reference in the formula currently contained in MODIFIED.

Line 12,

{LET ADDR,@CHAR(@CELLPOINTER("col")+64)&@STRING(@CELLPOINTER("row"),0)}

constructs a string version of the current cell pointer address. This formula is used as an alternative to @CELLPOINTER("address"), because the latter returns an address that is in absolute reference form, and therefore unsuitable for this program.

Line 13, {IF SAVED="stop"}{QUIT}, tests to see whether the program has converted the last formula, and terminates program execution if this is the case.

Line 14,

{LET MODIFIED,@REPLACE(MODIFIED,@FIND(ADDR,MODIFIED,0).@LENGTH(ADDR),SAVED}

is the heart of the program. The operation this instruction performs is simple, despite its formidable appearance. The instruction simply replaces the first occurrence of the address contained in ADDR with the formula contained in SAVED. Because the address in the MODIFIED formula is a cell reference to the cell containing the SAVED formula, the function of the modified formula does not change.

Line 15, {IF @FIND(ADDR,MODIFIED,0)+1}{BRANCH \f3}, tests to see whether the cell address stored in ADDR is present in MODIFIED. Because the previous instruction removed the first occurrence of this address, this test will be TRUE only if there is more than one instance of the address in MODIFIED. If the test is TRUE, the program branches to \f3 to perform a second replacement operation. Conversely, if the test is FALSE, no more conversions are required and the program can proceed.

Line 16, {BRANCH \f2}, simply starts the process again. The reentry point is selected so that the cell pointer is advanced to the next set of formulas.

Larger Programs

This section contains a number of longer programs that perform sophisticated tasks. Programs include Timer, Mapper, Search and Replace, Goal Seeker, and Hangman. Each of these is described in turn.

Timer

This Timer program (see listing in fig. 11.9) emulates a stopwatch. When activated, the program prompts the user for a countdown time in hours, minutes, and seconds. The program then prompts the user to press Enter to start timing.

```
--------------------------------------------------------------------------
1 HRS           0
2 MIN           0
3 SEC           5
4 DUMMY       ^
5 DISP       07:19:59
6 TIMECHECK  ############
7
8 --------------------------------------------------------------------------
9 \g         {GETNUMBER "SET TIME:  Enter hours: ",HRS}      Enter countdown time
10           {GETNUMBER "SET TIME:  Enter minutes: ",MIN}
11           {GETNUMBER "SET TIME:  Enter seconds: ",SEC}
13           {INDICATE "TIMER"}                              Tell 'em what's happening
14           {GETLABEL "Press Enter to start",DUMMY}         Signal what to do
15           {LET DISP,@NOW+@TIME(HRS,MIN,SEC)}              Set the countdown time
16 TIMELOOP  {LET HRS,HRS}^                                  Update the display
17           {RECALC TIMECHECK}                              Check time remaining
18           {IF TIMECHECK>0}{BRANCH TIMELOOP}               Loop if not done
19 WAITHERE  {BEEP @INT(@RAND#3)+1}                          Make random beep tones
20           {LOOK DUMMY}{IF DUMMY=""}{BRANCH WAITHERE}      Keep beeping
21           {INDICATE}                                      Reset the indicator to normal
```

Fig. 11.9. The Timer program.

A number of special instructions are used to control the display. In particular, notice the instruction in line 16. This combination of a {LET} instruction followed by a tilde (~) causes the screen to be updated and thus lets you see the time count its way down to zero. Neither the {LET} nor the tilde by itself will update the screen correctly. Other methods of screen updating, such as {CALC} or {WINDOWSOFF}{WINDOWSON} operate more slowly and cause a distracting amount of screen activity. Also, the {LET} and tilde combination causes the screen to be updated more than once per second. If the time-remaining display is updated less than once per second, it will appear to count down erratically, missing some counts and displaying others twice.

The program emits a series of random beeps when the time runs out and continues to beep until the user presses any key.

Mapper

This program, listed in figure 11.10, creates a "map" of the worksheet, prompting the user for a range to map and a place in which to put the map. The program then checks each cell in the specified area, using the

@CELL("type") function. The strings returned by @CELL are translated into alternate characters by an @VLOOKUP function: blank cells are represented by spaces, labels by vertical bars, and value cells (numbers or formulas) by plus signs. These characters are concatenated into a long string representing one column of data. Thus, the resulting map reads as if the worksheet has been rotated 90 degrees clockwise.

```
Instructions: 1. File Combine this file into the worksheet
              2. Range Name Labels Right using labels in first column
              3. Press Alt-g

Area to be mapped can have no more than 240 active rows
 Map larger worksheets in segments
One clear row below starting position required for every column mapped
Five clear columns required from starting cell pointer location
-----------------------------------------------------------------------------
ROWCTR            0
COLCTR            8
REPCTR            -1
OLDCHAR
RIGHTEDGE         H
EDGEREF           @IF(@COLS(MAPRANGE)<27,@CHAR(@COLS(MAPRANGE)+64),
                      @CHAR(@INT((@COLS(MAPRANGE)-1)/26+64))
                           &@CHAR(@MOD(@COLS(MAPRANGE)-1,26)+65))
LEFTEDGE          A
EDGEREF2          @IF(@CELL("COL",!MAPRANGE)<27,@CHAR(@CELL("COL",!MAPRANGE)+64),
                      @CHAR(@INT((@CELL("COL",!MAPRANGE)-1)/26+64))
                           &@CHAR(@MOD(@CELL("COL",!MAPRANGE)-1,26)+65))
MESSAGE1          Specify the range to map (240 rows max) :
MESSAGE2          Indicate the location for the map :
CONVERT           B
                  V         +
                  L         !
-----------------------------------------------------------------------------
\g                {GETRANGE}
                  {LOCATE}
                  {MAKEFORMULAS}
                  {FOR ROWCTR,@CELL("ROW",MAPRANGE)+@ROWS(MAPRANGE)-1,@CELL("ROW",MAPRANGE),-1,MAPROW}
                  {LET OLDCHAR," "}
                  /cOLDCHAR~TYPECELLS~
                  {SUBROW}
                  /cCOLUMNHEADER~TYPECELLS~
                  {SUBROW}
                  {BLANK COLUMNHEADER}
                  {BLANK TYPECELLS}
                  {BLANK ACCUMULATE}
                  {GOTO}TARGET~
                  /RE{DOWN @COLS(MAPRANGE)}~
                  {GOTO}MAP~
-----------------------------------------------------------------------------
GETRANGE          {DISPMSG 1}
                  {HOME}
                  /rncMAPRANGE~{BS}
                  {?}~
                  {DISPMSG 2}
                  {?}{LET STARTPOINT,@CELLPOINTER("ADDRESS")}
                  {WINDOWSOFF}
                  {GOTO}RIGHTEDGE~
                  {LET RIGHTEDGE,EDGEREF:VALUE}
                  {EDIT}{HOME}{DELETE}~
                  {GOTO}LEFTEDGE~
                  {LET LEFTEDGE,EDGEREF2:VALUE}
                  {EDIT}{HOME}{DELETE}~
```

```
                /rncCONVERT~....{ESC}.{D 2}{R}~
                {WINDOWSON}
----------------------------------------------------------------------
DISPMSG         {DEFINE MSGNO:STRING}
                {PANELON}{WINDOWSOFF}{GOTO}MESSAGE
MSGNO           2
                ~{PANELOFF}
                {WINDOWSON}
----------------------------------------------------------------------
LOCATE          {GOTO}
STARTPOINT      $A$146
                ~{D 18}{U 17}
----------------------------------------------------------------------
MAKEFORMULAS    {MAKENAME COLUMNHEADER}{RIGHT}
                /rncTARGET~{BS}~{RIGHT}
                {MAKENAME TYPECELLS}{RIGHT}
                {MAKENAME ACCUMULATE}{RIGHT}
                {MAKENAME MAP}
                {FOR COLCTR,0,@COLS(MAPRANGE)-1,1,ENTERLETTER}
                {GOTO}TYPECELLS~
                @VLOOKUP(@CELL("TYPE",{LEFT}.),@CONVERT,1)~
                /c~TYPECELLS~
                {RIGHT}
                +{RIGHT}&{LEFT}~
                /c~ACCUMULATE~
                {RIGHT}'~
                /c~MAP~
                {UP}
                @REPEAT(" ",@MOD(@ROWS(MAPRANGE),10))&@REPEAT("!          ",@INT(@ROWS(MAPRANGE)/10))~
----------------------------------------------------------------------
MAKENAME        {DEFINE RANGENAME:STRING}
                /rnc
RANGENAME       MAP
                ~{BS}.
                {DOWN @COLS(MAPRANGE)-1}~
----------------------------------------------------------------------
ENTERLETTER     {PUT COLUMNHEADER,0,COLCTR,@IF(COLCTR<26,"",@CHAR(@INT(COLCTR/26)+64))&@CHAR(@MOD(COLCTR,26)+65)}
----------------------------------------------------------------------
MAPROW          {RECALC ADDRESS}
                /rt
ADDRESS         {RECALC ADDRESS}A1..H1~
                TARGET~
                {RECALC TYPECELLS}
SUBROW          {RECALC ACCUMULATE}
                /rvACCUMULATE~MAP~
                ~{IF @MOD(ROWCTR,@CELLPOINTER("WIDTH"))=0}{RIGHT}

DYNAMIC FORMULA IN ADDRESS
+"{RECALC ADDRESS}"&LEFTEDGE&@STRING(COLCTR,0)&".."&RIGHTEDGE&@STRING(COLCTR,0)&"~"
----------------------------------------------------------------------
```

Fig. 11.10. The Mapping program.

The Mapper program is designed to be imported as a utility into an existing
worksheet. After the program is imported, range names must be set with the
/Range Name Labels Right command. After this task is accomplished, the
program will run. The program begins by resetting some of its own ranges,
those that can't be named as required by the **/Range Name Labels Right**
command. The program then converts back into formulas some formulas stored
as labels. This *post hoc* conversion of formulas allows them to reference parts of
the worksheet into which the program is imported. Note that the formulas
contained in EDGEREF and EDGEREF2 must be entered into a single cell in

their entirely in order for the program to work. The split lines shown in figure 11.10 are used only to display the formula on the page.

This program exemplifies the way in which an imported program can be made to adapt to the ranges in an existing worksheet. Two examples of worksheet maps generated from the program listing in figure 11.10 are shown in figure 11.11. Notice in figure 11.11 that the groupings of the various sections of the worksheet are clearly visible. Notice also the method used to prompt the user for range specifications.

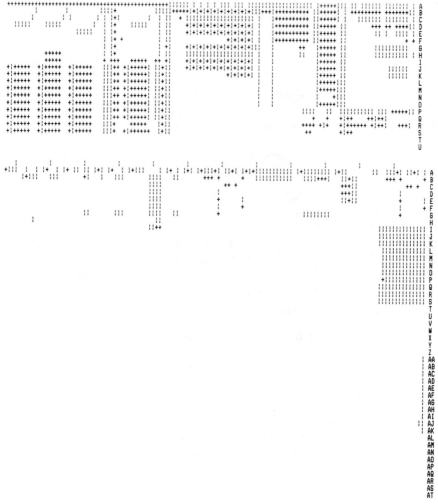

Fig. 11.11. Two worksheet maps.

Search and Replace

The Search and Replace program searches the contents of current cells in a specified range and replaces one string with a second string. Like the Mapper program, this program also prompts the user for a range on which to operate. The program is designed to be used only on labels. If you use it on string formulas, you may have a nasty surprise in store, because the program will process the cell's contents and replace a string formula with a label.

The Search and Replace program, like the Mapper program, can be imported into the worksheet and activated after the cells are named. The listing for the Search and Replace program is shown in figure 11.12.

Goal Seeker

The Goal Seeker program performs a kind of "what if" analysis which finds the value that must be entered into a given cell to cause the value in a second cell to reach a specific value. For example, if you had a complex model that calculated the return on investment for an investment in frog futures, you could use this program to determine the rate of appreciation required on frogs in order to give the investor a 35 percent annual return.

The Goal Seeker program, listed in figure 11.13, determines the value required to achieve the desired result the hard way: by trial and error. However, the trials are performed with a systematic method of reaching a desired value. This method, known as *binary search*, calculates the value that is either greater or smaller than the last value used, based on whether the test value is above or below the desired value. The source value is adjusted in increasingly finer increments until the test value converges on the final result.

The program requires you to enter seven pieces of information:

1. The target cell. This is the cell that is tested at each pass to see whether it has reached the goal value.

2. The adjusted cell. This is the cell whose contents are systematically varied to bring about the desired value in the target cell.

3. The goal value for the target cell.

4. and 5. Upper and lower limits for the adjusted value. These values give the program a range within which to work.

6. Accuracy value for how close to the goal the target cell must be before the search is terminated. The number is similar to the *places rounded to* argument in the @ROUND function. Positive numbers

```
 1 SRMESSAGE      Specify the range to scan by POINTING and press Enter
 2 CORNER1        A1
 3 CORNER2        B2
 4 SCANRANGE      A1..B2
 5 COLCTR                   1
 6 ROWCTR                   1
 7 SEARCHSTRING   B4
 8 REPSTRING      SCANRANGE
 9 -----------------------------------------------------------------------------
10 \r             {GETSTRINGS}
11                {SHOWMESSAGE}
12                {GETRANGE}
13                {SCANROWS}
14 -----------------------------------------------------------------------------
15 GETSTRINGS     {GETLABEL "Enter Search string: ",SEARCHSTRING}
16                {GETLABEL "Enter Replacement string: ",REPSTRING}
17 -----------------------------------------------------------------------------
18 SHOWMESSAGE    {WINDOWSOFF}{PANELOFF}
19                {DOWN 19}{UP}
20                /wwu
21                /wwh
22                {UP 17}
23                {WINDOW}
24                {GOTO}SRMESSAGE~
25                {PANELON}{PANELOFF}/wwc
26 -----------------------------------------------------------------------------
27 GETRANGE       +{UP}{DOWN}{WINDOWSON}{?}
28                {LET CORNER1,@CELLPOINTER("ADDRESS")}
29                ..{LET CORNER2,@CELLPOINTER("ADDRESS")}..
30                {LET SCANRANGE,+CORNER1&".."&CORNER2:VALUE}
31                {ESC 4}
32 -----------------------------------------------------------------------------
33 SCANROWS       {FOR ROWCTR,0,@ROWS(@@(SCANRANGE))-1,1,SCANCOLS}
34 -----------------------------------------------------------------------------
35 SCANCOLS       {FOR COLCTR,0,@COLS(@@(SCANRANGE))-1,1,CHECKCELL}
36 -----------------------------------------------------------------------------
37 CHECKCELL      {IF @ISERR(@FIND(SEARCHSTRING,@INDEX(@@(SCANRANGE),COLCTR,ROWCTR),0))}{RETURN}
38 CHANGECELL     {RECALC CHANGECELL}{PUT A1..B2,COLCTR,ROWCTR,
                    @REPLACE(@INDEX(@@(SCANRANGE),COLCTR,ROWCTR),
                      @FIND(SEARCHSTRING,@INDEX(@@(SCANRANGE),COLCTR,ROWCTR),0),
                        @LENGTH(SEARCHSTRING),REPSTRING)}
39
40                {BRANCH CHECKCELL}
41
42 Dynamic formula in CHANGECELL:
43 +"{RECALC CHANGECELL}{PUT "&SCANRANGE&",COLCTR,ROWCTR,
44     @REPLACE(@INDEX(@@(SCANRANGE),COLCTR,ROWCTR),
45         @FIND(SEARCHSTRING,@INDEX(@@(SCANRANGE),COLCTR,ROWCTR),0),
46             @LENGTH(SEARCHSTRING),REPSTRING)}"
47 -----------------------------------------------------------------------------
```

Fig. 11.12. The Search and Replace program.

```
 1 ------------------------------------------------------------------------------------
 2 RESULTS
 3 MESSAGE3
 4 $108,414.55 = FINAL VALUE OF ADJUSTED CELL
 5     $650.00 = FINAL VALUE OF TARGET CELL
 6 ------------------------------------------------------------------------------------
 7 GOAL              650
 8 HIGHLIMIT      200000
 9 LOWLIMIT   108414.4592
10 TOLERANCE          3
11 INCREMENT  0.095367431
12 ITERATIONS        50
13 COUNT             29
14 SAVECELL    $108,414.55
15 ------------------------------------------------------------------------------------
16 MESSAGE1    Point to the cell value to be TESTED -  press Enter
17 MESSAGE2    Point to the cell value to be ADJUSTED - press Enter
18 ------------------------------------------------------------------------------------
19 \g          {MAKEWINDOW}                                        Make a temporary window to work in
20            {BLANK MESSAGE3}
21            {GETCELLS}                                          Get the target and adjusted cells
22            {GETSPECS}                                          Get the parameters
23            {LET INCREMENT,(HIGHLIMIT-LOWLIMIT)/2}              Set initial value for adjusted cell
24            {FOR COUNT,1,ITERATIONS,1,ITERATE}                 Use {FOR} loop to control maximum iterations
25            {IF @ROUND(@@(CHECKADD),TOLERANCE)<>@ROUND(GOAL,TOLERANCE)}{FAILURE}
26            {DONE}                                              Delete window and restore values
27 ------------------------------------------------------------------------------------
28 MAKEWINDOW  /wwu                                                Hide the window activity
29            {D 18}{U}                                           Create a temporary window
30            /wwh{U 16}                                          Get the previous window
31            {WINDOWSON}                                         Turn the window on again
32 ------------------------------------------------------------------------------------
33 GETCELLS    {MESSAGE MESSAGE1}                                  Display a fixed message in control panel
34            /c{BS}{?}                                           Use the /Copy command...
35            {LET CHECKADD,@CELLPOINTER("ADDRESS")}                 get the address of this cell
36            {ESC 5}                                                and don't do any copying
37            {PANELON}                                           Turn the display back on
38            {MESSAGE MESSAGE2}                                  Display a message in control panel
39            /c{BS}{?}                                           Use the /Copy command...
40            {LET SAVEADD,@CELLPOINTER("ADDRESS")}                 get the address of this cell
41            ~SAVECELL~                                             and copy the contents for safe keeping
42            {PANELON}                                           Turn the display back on
43 ------------------------------------------------------------------------------------
44 MESSAGE     {DEFINE ADD:STRING}
45            {WINDOWSOFF}                                        Turn the window display off
46            {WINDOW}                                            Get the previous window
47            {GOTO}                                              Put cell pointer on message to be displayed
48 ADD         MESSAGE2                                            Message to be displayed
49            ~{PANELON}{PANELOFF}                                Make control panel show the message
50            {WINDOW}                                            Go back to the other window
51            {WINDOWSON}                                         And reactivate window (but not control panel)
52 ------------------------------------------------------------------------------------
53 GETSPECS    {GETNUMBER "Enter the goal value: ",GOAL}           Display prompts and get responses
54            {GETNUMBER "Enter the lower limit for the ADJUSTED cell: ",LOWLIMIT}
55            {GETNUMBER "Enter the upper limit for the ADJUSTED cell: ",HIGHLIMIT}
56            {GETNUMBER "Accuracy in decimal places: (-10..10) ",TOLERANCE}
57            {GETNUMBER "Enter the maximum number of iterations: ",ITERATIONS}
```

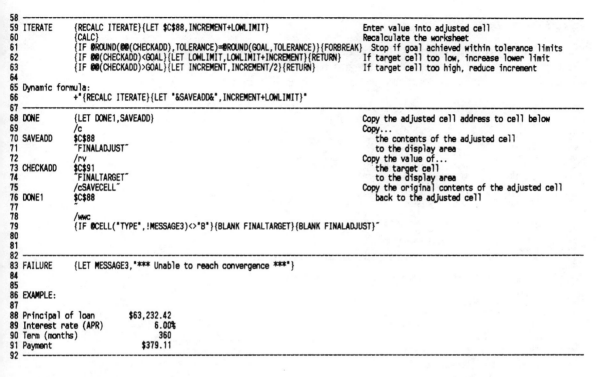

```
58 ------------------------------------------------------------------------------------------------------------------
59 ITERATE      {RECALC ITERATE}{LET $C$88,INCREMENT+LOWLIMIT}                    Enter value into adjusted cell
60              {CALC}                                                            Recalculate the worksheet
61              {IF @ROUND(@@(CHECKADD),TOLERANCE)=@ROUND(GOAL,TOLERANCE)}{FORBREAK}  Stop if goal achieved within tolerance limits
62              {IF @@(CHECKADD)<GOAL}{LET LOWLIMIT,LOWLIMIT+INCREMENT}{RETURN}   If target cell too low, increase lower limit
63              {IF @@(CHECKADD)>GOAL}{LET INCREMENT,INCREMENT/2}{RETURN}         If target cell too high, reduce increment
64
65 Dynamic formula:
66              +"{RECALC ITERATE}{LET "&SAVEADD&",INCREMENT+LOWLIMIT}"
67 ------------------------------------------------------------------------------------------------------------------
68 DONE         {LET DONE1,SAVEADD}                                               Copy the adjusted cell address to cell below
69              /c                                                                Copy...
70 SAVEADD      $C$88                                                             the contents of the adjusted cell
71              ~FINALADJUST~                                                     to the display area
72              /rv                                                              Copy the value of...
73 CHECKADD     $C$91                                                             the target cell
74              ~FINALTARGET~                                                    to the display area
75              /cSAVECELL~                                                      Copy the original contents of the adjusted cell
76 DONE1        $C$88                                                             back to the adjusted cell
77
78              /wwc
79              {IF @CELL("TYPE",!MESSAGE3)<>"B"}{BLANK FINALTARGET}{BLANK FINALADJUST}~
80
81
82 ------------------------------------------------------------------------------------------------------------------
83 FAILURE      {LET MESSAGE3,"*** Unable to reach convergence ***"}
84
85
86 EXAMPLE:
87
88 Principal of loan      $63,232.42
89 Interest rate (APR)         6.00%
90 Term (months)                 360
91 Payment                   $379.11
92 ------------------------------------------------------------------------------------------------------------------
```

Fig. 11.13. The Goal Seeker program.

represent the number of places to the right of the decimal point and, therefore, greater accuracy. Negative numbers represent tens, hundreds, thousands, and so on.

7. Iterations. This is the maximum number of times the program attempts to achieve the goal value. Some problems to which this program can be applied have no solution. When such a condition is encountered, this parameter serves as a safety device.

When the program stops—both when it has reached convergence on the desired value and when it has not—the original values of the target and adjusted cells will be restored. If the program was successful in achieving its final values, the final target and adjusted values will be displayed. If the program failed to achieve convergence, a message to that effect appears instead.

Hangman

The Hangman program, listed in figure 11.14, is just for fun, but contains a number of fairly sophisticated formulas and routines that make it worth a look-see, even if you aren't inclined toward electronic entertainment.

Word -->

```
NEWENTRY
SELECT      THIS IS A TEST    @UPPER(@INDEX(WORDS_DB,0,@RAND*@COUNT(WORDS_DB)))
WORD        COMPANIES
CHOICE      P
BLANKS                        @REPEAT("_",@LENGTH(WORD))
USED     - - - ERR - - - - -  @FIND(CHOICE,LETTERS,0)
FOUND            1
PLACE           9             LEVEL          2
WINNER         ERR            @FIND("_",TEST,0)
CTR             6
MESSAGE1    You can't use that letter - Press Enter to try again
MESSAGE2    Correct! - Choose another letter
MESSAGE3    That letter is not in the word - Try again
MESSAGE4    Press P to play again
MESSAGE5    ############################# YOU WIN!!! #############################
MESSAGE6    Choose a letter
MESSAGE7    Welcome to the game of 1-2-3 Hangman.          Press P to play.
```

```
\0          {BLANK LETTERS}
            {BLANK TEST}
            {BLANK MESSAGE}

            {MENUBRANCH MAINMENU}
```

```
MAINMENU    Play     Reset_scoName       Add_words
            Play a gaReset theEnter theAdd new words to the game database
            {BRANCH P{RESET}  {NEWNAME}{NEWWORDS}
                   {MENUBRAN{MENUBRANCH MAINMENU}
```

```
PLAY        {SETUP}
            {BRANCH CHOOSE}
```

SETUP	{WINDOWSOFF}/wwc	Hide the setup activities
	{HOME}{D 3}/wwu/wwh	Call up the display window
	{WINDOW}{GOTO}DISPLAY~	Call up the score window
	/wgc1~/wcs9~{R}/wcs9~	Call up the initial hangman window
REPLAY	{LET LEVEL,0}	Set the reference for the man picture to display
	{LET LETTERS," "}	Initialize the letters chosen display
NEWWORD	{IF SELECT=WORD}{RECALC SELECT}{BRANCH NEWWORD}	Make sure the new word is different from the last word
	{LET WORD,SELECT}	Place the new word in "word"
	{RECALC BLANKS}	Show how many letters in this word
	{LET TEST,BLANKS}	Copy blanks for later testing
	{REMOVESP}	Remove blanks if word has spaces
		Update the display
	{LET MESSAGE,MESSAGE6}	
	{CALC}{WINDOWSON}	Turn on the windows so the display shows

REMOVESP	{LET CHOICE," "}	Enter a space as the chosen letter
	{CHECKWORD}	Check the word for matches to CHOICE
	{LET FOUND,0}	Reset correct choice flag

CHECKWORD	{LET LETTERS,LETTERS&CHOICE}	Space as first letter (prevents choosing it again)
	{LET FOUND,0}	Reset the found flag
	{FOR PLACE,0,@LENGTH(WORD)-1,1,CHECKLETTER}	Check each letter in the word

---

CHECKLETTER	{IF @MID(WORD,PLACE,1)<>CHOICE}{RETURN}	Letter is not in word
	{LET TEST,@REPLACE(TEST,PLACE*2,1,CHOICE)}	Show the chosen letter in the display
	{LET FOUND,1}	Signal a correct choice

CHOOSE	`{GET CHOICE}`	Capture a single character input from the keyboard
	`{IF @LENGTH(CHOICE)>1}{GOOF}{BRANCH CHOOSE}`	Length > 1 means a non-alphanumeric character
	`{IF @UPPER(CHOICE)<" "#OR#@UPPER(CHOICE)>"Z"}{GOOF}{BRANCH CHOOSE}`	Illegal character
	`{LET CHOICE,@UPPER(CHOICE)}`	Display all caps
		Update the screen
	`{RECALC USED}`	Check if letter already used
	`{IF @IF(@ISERR(USED),0,USED)}{GOOF}{BRANCH CHOOSE}`	If letter has been used, it's a goof
	`{CHECKWORD}`	Check the response
	`{RECALC WINNER}`	Update winner test
	`{IF @ISERR(WINNER)}{BRANCH YOUWIN}`	Done!
	`{IF FOUND}{CORRECT}{BRANCH CHOOSE}`	One letter correct
	`{WRONG}{BRANCH CHOOSE}`	Letter not found
GOOF	`{BEEP 0}`	
	`{LET MESSAGE,MESSAGE1}`	Display goof message
		Update screen
	`{GET CHOICE}`	Wait for user to respond
	`{LET MESSAGE,MESSAGE6}`	Choose a letter
		Update screen
CORRECT	`{LET MESSAGE,MESSAGE2}`	One letter found
		Update the screen
	`{BEEP 3}`	Signal the user
WRONG	`{LET LEVEL,LEVEL+1}`	Add one to the window reference
	`{BEEP 1}`	Signal bad response
	`{RECALC FIGURE}~`	
	`{IF LEVEL=8}{BRANCH IWIN}`	End game - I win
	`{LET MESSAGE,MESSAGE3}`	Wrong letter
		Update screen
	`{WINDOWSON}`	Turn on the display
IWIN	`{LET MESSAGE,MESSAGE4}`	Repeat play message
	`{LET COMPUTER,COMPUTER+1}`	Update the score
	`{LET TEST,WORD}`	Show the word
	`{CALC}`	Update eveerything
	`{BEEP 0}{BEEP 0}`	Signal a loss
	`{BEEP 0}{BEEP 0}`	
	`{WINDOWSON}`	Turn display on
	`{MENUBRANCH MAINMENU}`	Start over
YOUWIN	`{LET MESSAGE,MESSAGE5}`	You win message
	`{LET YOU,YOU+1}`	Add to your score
		Update screen
	`{MAKENOISE}`	Make some beeps
	`{MENUBRANCH MAINMENU}`	Start over
MAKENOISE	`{FOR CTR,1,5,1,SOUND}`	
SOUND	`{BEEP 3}{BEEP 0}`	
RESET	`{LET COMPUTER,0}`	
	`{LET YOU,0}`	
	`{BEEP 3}`	
NEWNAME	`{GETLABEL "What is your name? ",YOURNAME}`	
	`{BEEP 3}`	
NEWWORDS	`{GETLABEL "Enter new words; [Enter] only to quit: ",NEWENTRY}`	
	`{IF NEWENTRY=""}{MENUBRANCH MAINMENU}`	
	`{IF @ISERR(@VLOOKUP(@UPPER(NEWENTRY),WORDS_DB,0))=0}{BRANCH OLDWORD}`	
	`{PUT WORDS_DB,0,@COUNT(WORDS_DB),@UPPER(NEWENTRY)}`	
	`{BRANCH NEWWORDS}`	
OLDWORD	`{BEEP 0}{GETLABEL "That word is already in the list, PRESS Enter",NEWENTRY}{BRANCH NEWWORDS}`	
\p	`{BRANCH PLAY}`	

```
MENU DOCUMENTATION:
MAINMENU    Play
            Play a game of HANGMAN
            {BRANCH PLAY}

            Reset_score
            Reset the score
            {RESET}
            {MENUBRANCH MAINMENU}

            Name
            Enter the name of a new player
            {NEWNAME}
            {MENUBRANCH MAINMENU}

            Add_Words
            Add new Words to the game database
            {NEWWORDS}
            {MENUBRANCH MAINMENU}
```

Fig. 11.14. The Hangman program.

Table 11.2 shows the formulas that create the display for the little man that appears in the figures 11.15–11.17.

Table 11.2
Cell Listing for Hangman Figure

```
AM304: U @CHAR(153)
AM305: U @CHAR(153)
AK306: U @IF($LEVEL>0, @CHAR(153), "")
AL306: U @IF($LEVEL>0, @CHAR(153), "")
AM306: U @IF($LEVEL>0, @CHAR(153), "")
AN306: U @IF($LEVEL>0, @CHAR(153), "")
AO306: U @IF($LEVEL>0, @CHAR(153), "")
AK307: U @IF($LEVEL>0, @CHAR(153), "")
AL307: U @IF($LEVEL<2, "", @IF($LEVEL>7, "-", @CHAR(176)))
AN307: U @IF($LEVEL<2, "", @IF($LEVEL>7, "-", @CHAR(176)))
AO307: U @IF($LEVEL>0, @CHAR(153), "")
AK308: U @IF($LEVEL>0, @CHAR(153), "")
AM308: U @IF($LEVEL<3, "", @IF($LEVEL>7, "-", "v"))
AO308: U @IF($LEVEL>0, @CHAR(153), "")
AP308: U @IF($LEVEL=7, "—-Help!!!", @IF($LEVEL>7, "—-Ugk!", ""))
AK309: U @IF($LEVEL>0, @CHAR(153), "")
AL309: U @IF($LEVEL>0, @CHAR(153), "")
AM309: U @IF($LEVEL>0, @CHAR(153), "")
```

```
AN3Ø9: U @IF($LEVEL>Ø, @CHAR(153), "")
AO3Ø9: U @IF($LEVEL>Ø, @CHAR(153), "")
AM31Ø: U @IF($LEVEL>1, @CHAR(153), "")
AJ311: U @IF($LEVEL>1, @CHAR(153), "")
AK311: U @IF($LEVEL>1, @CHAR(153), "")
AL311: U @IF($LEVEL>1, @CHAR(153), "")
AM311: U @IF($LEVEL>1, @CHAR(153), "")
AN311: U @IF($LEVEL>1, @CHAR(153), "")
AO311: U @IF($LEVEL>1, @CHAR(153), "")
AP311: U @IF($LEVEL>1, @CHAR(153), "")
AI312: U @IF($LEVEL>2#AND#$LEVEL<8, @CHAR(153), "")
AJ312: U @IF($LEVEL>7, @CHAR(153), "")
AM312: U @IF($LEVEL>4, @CHAR(153), "")
AP312: U @IF($LEVEL>7, @CHAR(153), "")
AQ312: U @IF($LEVEL>3#AND#$LEVEL<8, @CHAR(153), "")
AH313: U @IF($LEVEL>2#AND#$LEVEL<8, @CHAR(153), "")
AJ313: U @IF($LEVEL>7, @CHAR(153), "")
AM313: U @IF($LEVEL>4, @CHAR(153), "")
AP313: U @IF($LEVEL>7, @CHAR(153), "")
AR313: U @IF($LEVEL>3#AND#$LEVEL<8, @CHAR(153), "")
AG314: U @IF($LEVEL>2#AND#$LEVEL<8, @CHAR(153), "")
AJ314: U @IF($LEVEL>7, @CHAR(153), "")
AM314: U @IF($LEVEL>4, @CHAR(153), "")
AP314: U @IF($LEVEL>7, @CHAR(153), "")
AS314: U @IF($LEVEL>3#AND#$LEVEL<8, @CHAR(153), "")
AM315: U @IF($LEVEL>4, @CHAR(153), "")
AL316: U @IF($LEVEL>5, @CHAR(153), "")
AN316: U @IF($LEVEL>6, @CHAR(153), "")
AK317: U @IF($LEVEL>5#AND#$LEVEL<8, @CHAR(153), "")
AL317: U @IF($LEVEL>7, @CHAR(153), "")
AN317: U @IF($LEVEL>7, @CHAR(153), "")
AO317: U @IF($LEVEL>6#AND#$LEVEL<8, @CHAR(153), "")
AJ318: U @IF($LEVEL>5#AND#$LEVEL<8, @CHAR(153), "")
AL318: U @IF($LEVEL>7, @CHAR(153), "")
AN318: U @IF($LEVEL>7, @CHAR(153), "")
AP318: U @IF($LEVEL>6#AND#$LEVEL<8, @CHAR(153), "")
AI319: U @IF($LEVEL>5#AND#$LEVEL<8, @CHAR(153), "")
AL319: U @IF($LEVEL>7, @CHAR(153), "")
```

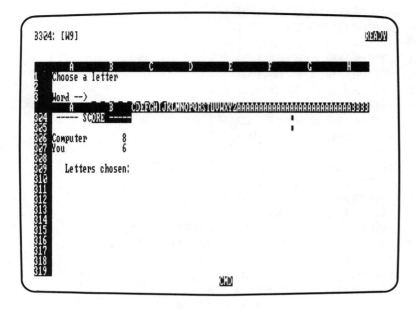

Fig. 11.15. Hangman: initial display.

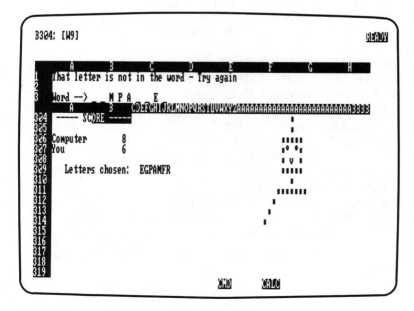

Fig. 11.16. Hangman: during the game.

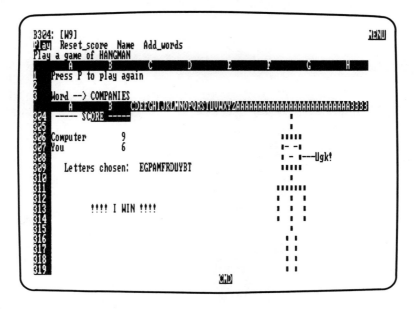

Fig. 11.17. Hung man.

12

Command Language
Instructions

This chapter contains a detailed description of each of 1-2-3's command language instructions. You will find an explanation of the arguments, required or optional, that each instruction uses and, after the description of each instruction's syntax, a detailed discussion of the instruction's operation. Also provided are one or more practical examples for using each instruction in a command language program.

This chapter provides a great deal of information about individual command language instructions—and command language programming in general. You should probably read through all the material at least once to familiarize yourself with the details. You will want to pay special attention to the examples included with the instructions. Wherever possible, I've attempted to demonstrate the use of each instruction with a practical application. Many of these examples contain routines or techniques (including some unorthodox, but useful applications of the instructions) that you can copy directly into your own programs.

Syntax

Command language instructions are a special form of keyword, like {UP} or {DOWN}. Most require one or more arguments, which are enclosed in braces along with the instruction name itself, as in the following:

{KEYWORD argument[,optional argument][,optional argument]}

For more information on instruction syntax, see Chapter 9.

String Formulas

As described in Chapter 9, command language instructions can be constructed from string formulas. Using string formulas enables you to create dynamic instructions that change with the worksheet. For example, the following instruction modifies the {LET} instruction so that the SOURCEDATA specified by {LET} is placed in the cell pointer's current location.

   +"{LET "&@CELLPOINTER("address")&",SOURCEDATA}"

If the cell pointer is in cell B15, the formula will appear in the worksheet as

   {LET B15,SOURCEDATA}

As a general rule, including a {RECALC} instruction, either within or immediately before any command language instruction constructed from a string formula, is a good idea. This ensures that the instruction is up-to-date when it is executed.

Screen Updating

To allow the command language instructions to execute as fast as possible, 1-2-3 does not update the screen to reflect operations performed by most instructions. The screen, in most cases, isn't updated even when the program is finished executing. Therefore, your program may appear to have functioned incorrectly.

To update the screen, all you need to do is press Enter. You can include a tilde (~) to update the screen from within an operating command language program. Because screen updating slows down programs substantially, you usually will want to force screen updating only when you want to monitor a program's progress.

Categories of Instructions

The command language listing in this chapter is organized alphabetically to make the instructions easy to find. Grouping the instructions according to their function, however, is possible, although many instructions and categories overlap substantially. For example, the {WRITE} instruction falls into the last four of the following six categories:

1. Instructions that modify the worksheet

2. Instructions that interact with the keyboard

3. Instructions that control program flow

4. Instructions that trap errors

5. Instructions that control output

6. Instructions that control file operations

In tables 12.1–12.6, each instruction's main function is indicated by an asterisk (*) placed next to the instruction in its primary category. {WRITE}, for instance, is primarily a file operation, although the instruction also controls program flow, traps errors, and controls output.

Table 12.1
Instructions That Modify the Worksheet

Instruction	Function of Instruction	Changes in Worksheet
{?}	Pauses program until Enter is pressed	Data or commands can be entered.
*{BLANK}	Erases specified range	Range is erased.
*{CONTENTS}	Enters formatted string into a cell	Destination cell has string result.
{DEFINE}	Places a passed parameter in a cell(s)	Specified cells contain data passed from subroutine.
{FILESIZE}	Places size of opened file in a cell	Specified cell contains a number.
{FOR}	Controls repetition of a subroutine	Counter variable changes with each iteration.
{GET}	Traps keyboard input	Keystroke is entered into specified cell.
{GETLABEL}	Prompts user input	String result is placed in target cell.
{GETNUMBER}	Prompts user input	Numeric result is placed in target cell.
{GETPOS}	Returns position of file pointer	Specified cell contains a number.
*{LET}	Places data directly into worksheet	Specified cell contains result of argument.
{LOOK}	Checks keyboard buffer for keystroke	Specified cell contains null string or keystroke.
{ONERROR}	Traps program errors	Specified cell contains error message (optional).

Table 12.1
Instructions That Modify the Worksheet

Instruction	Function of Instruction	Changes in Worksheet
*{PUT}	Places data directly into worksheet	Specified cell contains result of argument.
{READ}	Reads data from opened file	Specified cell contains string data from file.
{READLN}	Reads data from opened file	Specified cell contains string data from file.
*{RECALC}	Recalculates part of worksheet	Specified range of formulas is updated.
*{RECALCCOL}	Recalculates part of worksheet	Specified range of formulas is updated.

Note: * indicates that the primary function of the instruction is in this group.

Table 12.2
Instructions That Interact with the Keyboard

Instruction	Function of Instruction
*{?}	Pauses program for user response
*{BREAKOFF}	Disables the Ctrl-Break key
*{BREAKON}	Reenables the Ctrl-Break key
*{GET}	Traps keyboard input
*{GETLABEL}	Prompts user input
*{GETNUMBER}	Prompts user input
*{LOOK}	Checks keyboard buffer for keystroke
*{MENUBRANCH}	Displays a menu for user response and transfers program control
*{MENUCALL}	Displays a menu for user response and transfers program control

Note: * indicates that the primary function of the instruction is in this group.

Table 12.3
Instructions That Control Program Flow

Instruction	Function of Instruction
*{ }	Specifies no operation; allows program to continue
{?}	Causes program to pause until Enter is pressed
*{BRANCH}	Transfers program control directly to specified cell
*{DISPATCH}	Transfers program control indirectly to specified cell
{FILESIZE}	Executes instructions on same line when file error occurs
*{FOR}	Controls repetition of a subroutine
*{FORBREAK}	Interrupts execution of {FOR} instruction
{GETPOS}	Executes instructions on same line when file error occurs
*{IF}	Specifies conditional execution of instructions on same line
{MENUBRANCH}	Displays a menu for user response and transfers program control
{MENUCALL}	Displays a menu for user response and transfers program control
{ONERROR}	Transfers program control to specified routine when error occurs
{OPEN}	Executes instructions on same line when file error occurs
*{QUIT}	Stops program execution
{READ}	Executes instructions on same line when file error occurs
{READLN}	Executes instructions on same line when file error occurs
*{RESTART}	Clears subroutine return stack
*{RETURN}	Ends subroutine execution
{SETPOS}	Executes instructions on same line when file error occurs
*{WAIT}	Suspends program execution until a specified time
{WRITE}	Executes instructions on same line when file error occurs
{WRITELN}	Executes instructions on same line when file error occurs

Note: * indicates that the primary function of the instruction is in this group.

Table 12.4
Instructions That Trap Errors

Instruction	Function of Instruction
{FILESIZE}	Executes instructions on same line when file error occurs
{GETPOS}	Executes instructions on same line when file error occurs
*{ONERROR}	Transfers program control to specified routine when error occurs
{OPEN}	Executes instructions on same line when file error occurs
{READ}	Executes instructions on same line when file error occurs
{READLN}	Executes instructions on same line when file error occurs
{SETPOS}	Executes instructions on same line when file error occurs
{WRITE}	Executes instructions on same line when file error occurs
{WRITELN}	Executes instructions on same line when file error occurs

Note: * indicates that the primary function of the instruction is in this group.

Table 12.5
Instructions That Control Output

Instruction	*Function of Instruction*
*{BEEP}	Sounds the computer's speaker or bell
*{INDICATE}	Controls display of mode indicator
*{PANELOFF}	Suspends updating of control panel
*{PANELON}	Reenables updating of control panel
*{WINDOWSOFF}	Suspends updating of worksheet display
*{WINDOWSON}	Reenables updating of worksheet display
{WRITE}	Writes a specified string to a file
{WRITELN}	Writes a specified string and CR/LF to a file

Note: * indicates that the primary function of the instruction is in this group.

Table 12.6
Instructions That Control File Operations

Instruction	*Function of Instruction*
*{CLOSE}	Closes a file
*{FILESIZE}	Returns size of file in bytes
*{GETPOS}	Return file pointer's position in file
*{OPEN}	Opens a file for reading or writing
*{READ}	Reads a specified number of bytes from file
*{READLN}	Reads a line of text from file
*{SETPOS}	Sets file pointer's position in file
*{WRITE}	Writes a specified string to a file
*{WRITELN}	Writes a specified string and CR/LF to a file

Note: * indicates that the primary function of the instruction is in this group.

Glossary of Instructions

{BEEP}

FUNCTION: The {BEEP} instruction causes a computer to emit a tone from the computer's internal speaker.

SYNTAX: {BEEP}

or

{BEEP pitchnumber}

Argument types for *pitchnumber*:

Number
Numeric expression
Cell address or equivalent range name
@@ using cell address in pointer cell

DESCRIPTION: {BEEP} causes a computer's internal speaker to emit a brief "beep." Some older computers instead may have a bell that sounds.

You can use {BEEP} to signal error conditions or to tell the user that a response is required. This instruction is also useful for debugging a program (see the section on debugging in Chapter 10).

EXAMPLES: Figure 12.1 shows how {BEEP} signals an illegal response. In this example, the @FIND function screens for a valid response.

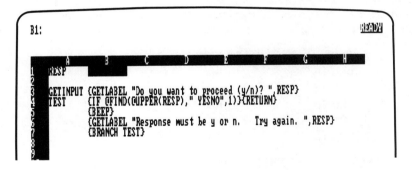

Fig. 12.1. {BEEP} *used to signal illegal responses.*

The one-line program in figure 12.2 can be used at the end of another program that takes some time to execute. The one-line program causes the computer to beep every five seconds until Ctrl-Break is pressed.

ARGUMENTS FOR {BEEP}: By using a number from 0 to 3 as an argument, you can change the beep's pitch and duration. Numbers not in the 0–3 range are treated as that number MOD 4. For example, 4 is equivalent to 0, 5 is equivalent to 1, and so on. Negative numbers are treated as (*pitchnumber* MOD

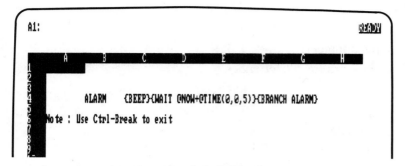

Fig. 12.2. {BEEP} used to signal the end of program execution.

4)+4. You can use a cell reference or numeric formula as an argument. If the result of the formula is not an integer, 1-2-3 truncates the fractional part of the number. 1-2-3 treats ERR and NA values as {BEEP 0}.

The pitch and duration figures for the various forms of {BEEP} follow. Notice that {BEEP} without an argument is equivalent to {BEEP 2}. These values were derived for the performance of 1-2-3 on a standard IBM PC. Your machine will have different pitch and duration values if you have a PC AT-type machine, an IBM PC compatible, a PC that uses an accelerator board, or any machine that doesn't use the 4.77 MHz clock speed of the standard PC.

Instruction	Pitch	Duration
{BEEP}	900 Hz	230 ms
{BEEP 0}	250 Hz	210 ms
{BEEP 1}	500 Hz	280 ms
{BEEP 2}	900 Hz	230 ms
{BEEP 3}	1000 Hz	120 ms

NOTES: Pitch is in hertz (cycles per second).

Duration is in milliseconds. The duration figure listed is actually the repetition rate for the various {BEEP}s and includes a brief pause that occurs between beeps.

All figures are approximate.

{BLANK}

FUNCTION: The {BLANK} instruction erases a cell or group of cells in a range.

SYNTAX: {BLANK location}

Argument types for *location*:

Cell address or equivalent range name
Range address or equivalent range name

{BLANK} is equivalent to the **/R**ange Erase command. Because {BLANK} doesn't force redrawing of the screen, this instruction has the advantage of being about 40 times faster than **/R**ange Erase. The time factor can be important if you want to erase many separate entries. Using {BLANK} instead of **/R**ange Erase also results in much less screen activity and, consequently, a cosmetically more appealing program.

EXAMPLES: The program in figure 12.3 flashes a message on the screen. The program causes the message and cell pointer to swap positions between cells DISPLAY and DISPLAY2.

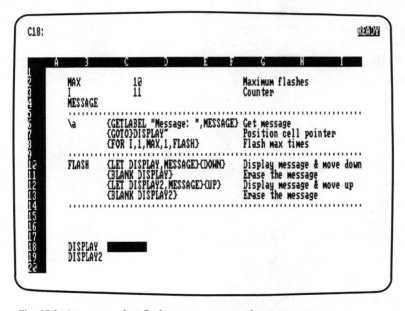

Fig. 12.3. A program that flashes a message on the screen.

Here is a detailed description of the program:

Line 6: {GETLABEL} gives the user a prompt and saves the response in MESSAGE.

Line 7: {GOTO} positions the cell pointer in the cell named DISPLAY. This positioning is required in order to achieve alternating effect.

Line 8: {FOR I,1,MAX,FLASH} calls the subroutine FLASH the number of times specified in MAX.

Line 10: {LET DISPLAY,MESSAGE} enters the stored message in the cell named DISPLAY. The {DOWN} following the {LET} instruction is necessary not only to reposition the cell pointer but to force redrawing of the screen. Neither the {LET} nor {BLANK} instructions redraw the screen when they are invoked. Without some deliberate action to make 1-2-3 update the screen, this program would run invisibly. If you want a screen update without cell pointer movement, you use a tilde (~) instead of a cursor-arrow key.

Line 11: {BLANK DISPLAY} erases the message just entered into DISPLAY by the {LET} instruction. Because {BLANK} by itself doesn't update the screen display, the erasure won't be evident immediately.

Line 12: {LET DISPLAY2,MESSAGE} enters a copy of the message into DISPLAY2. The {UP} after {LET} updates the screen, making the effect of {LET} and the previous {BLANK} visible at the same time. MESSAGE appears to "jump" from one cell to the next.

Line 13: {BLANK DISPLAY2} erases MESSAGE from DISPLAY2. The effect of this instruction isn't visible until the screen is updated.

{BRANCH}

FUNCTION: {BRANCH} transfers program control (the instruction pointer) to a specified location.

SYNTAX: {BRANCH location}

Argument types for *location*:

    Cell address or equivalent range name
    Range address or equivalent range name

The *location* argument can be in the form of a cell address, range address, or range name. If you specify a range address or an equivalent range name, 1-2-3 sets the instruction pointer to the range's upper left cell.

DESCRIPTION: {BRANCH}, which is also described in Chapter 4, transfers control of 1-2-3's internal instruction pointer to a specific cell. As you may recall, the instruction pointer indicates a location in a cell containing the next macro or command language instruction to be executed. Remember also that {BRANCH} differs from a {GOTO} instruction or command: {BRANCH} affects only the internal instruction pointer, whereas {GOTO} affects the cell pointer's location.

EXAMPLES: Previous chapters have shown numerous examples of the use of {BRANCH}. In figure 12.4, the {BRANCH} instructions generate a loop that terminates only when the user gives an acceptable response. This program checks the current date and runs special programs on the 1st and 15th of the month. Note that these {BRANCH} instructions don't create looping conditions, but guide program execution along one of several possible paths.

You would probably make this kind of program part of the autoexecute macro for a worksheet. For a similar example of an autoexecute macro, see "Macro 23: Date Stamp" in Chapter 5. Also, refer to Chapter 3 for an explanation of how to create an autoexecute macro.

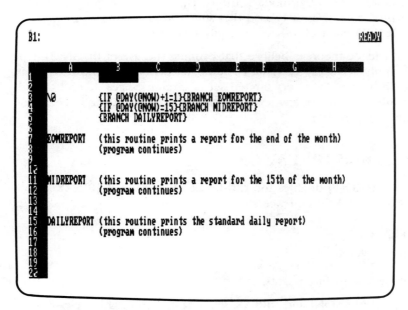

Fig. 12.4. {BRANCH} *used to select routines.*

Here is an explanation of the program:

Line 3: @DAY(@NOW) returns the current day of the month. If @DAY(@NOW) is the last day of the month, then @DAY(@NOW+1) will refer to the first day of the next month. Therefore, the test in the {IF} instruction is TRUE on the last day of the month, and program control passes to {BRANCH EOMREPORT}, which passes program control to the routine named EOMREPORT.

Line 4: The test in the {IF} instruction evaluates as TRUE on the 15th of the month. Program control then passes to the MIDREPORT routine.

Line 5: If neither of the preceding tests is TRUE, program control "falls through" the preceding {IF} tests and passes to the DAILYREPORT routine. Note that because of the way in which this example is programmed, the DAILYREPORT routine isn't executed if either of the other reports is run.

SPECIAL CONSIDERATIONS FOR USING {BRANCH}: {BRANCH} is an instruction you should be careful not to overuse. Overusing this instruction can easily generate "stream of consciousness" programs that hop from routine to routine in a disorganized fashion. This kind of programming is called *spaghetti programming* and is very bad practice. The {BRANCH} instruction is at the heart of the problem with spaghetti programs, which quickly become difficult or impossible to follow, debug, and modify. {BRANCH} is so tempting to use and generates such problems when it is used that some programming languages (most notably, Pascal) don't even have an equivalent instruction.

Many computer science theorists believe that banning the use of {BRANCH}-type instructions is an unnecessarily extreme position. Theorists agree, however, that {BRANCH} should be used in a very limited set of circumstances. Keep in mind that you can write programs of any level of complexity without such instructions (see Chapter 10).

{BREAKOFF} and {BREAKON}

FUNCTION: {BREAKOFF} disables the Ctrl-Break key sequence. {BREAKON} reenables the Ctrl-Break key sequence after {BREAKOFF}.

SYNTAX: {BREAKOFF}

{BREAKON}

Neither instruction accepts arguments.

DESCRIPTION: {BREAKON} and {BREAKOFF} enable and disable, respectively, the Ctrl-Break function during macro execution. With these instructions, you can create applications that users can't interrupt. While {BREAKOFF} is in effect, 1-2-3 ignores the Ctrl-Break key sequence. {BREAKOFF} remains in effect until the program ends, {BREAKON} is encountered, or an error occurs.

A special condition arises when you use {BREAKOFF} with {ONERROR}. Figure 12.5 shows a short routine that can be used to test the effects of {BREAKOFF} and {ONERROR} with and without an error condition. The heart of the program is line 5, which lists the files on a disk. By using a floppy disk drive as the default directory, you can easily create an error condition if you leave the disk drive door open.

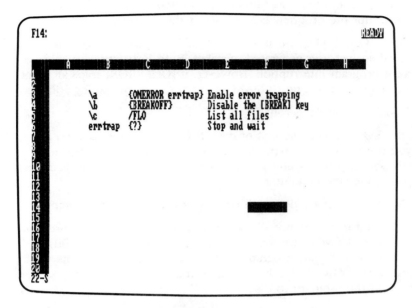

```
F14:                                                  READY

        A       B        C       D      E       F      G       H
  1
  2
  3     \a      {ONERROR errtrap} Enable error trapping
  4     \b      {BREAKOFF}        Disable the [BREAK] key
  5     \c      /FLO              List all files
  6     errtrap {?}               Stop and wait
  7
  8
  9
 10
 11
 12
 13
 14
 15
 16
 17
 18
 19
 20
 22-S
```

Fig. 12.5. A test program for {BREAKOFF}.

Here is an explanation of the program:

Line 3: {ONERROR ERRTRAP} puts 1-2-3 into error-trapping mode. If, during program operation, an error is encountered after {ONERROR}, the program doesn't stop, but instead branches to ERRTRAP.

Line 4: {BREAKOFF} disables the Break key.

Line 5: /flo lists other files.

Line 6: {?} stops and waits, leaving the program running.

If you use Alt-a to activate the program, both {ONERROR} and {BREAKOFF} are in effect. If the disk drive door is left open, an error is generated by the operation in line 5. {ONERROR} forces the program to branch to line 6, where the program pauses at the {?} instruction. Pressing Ctrl-Break at this point illustrates the way in which the error renables the Break function.

If you use Alt-b to activate the program, an error causes the program to stop, and 1-2-3 issues an error message. The Break function is also reenabled at this point.

Close the disk drive door so that no error occurs. Then notice how differently the program acts when you use Alt-b, as opposed to Alt-c, to start the program. If you press Alt-b to start the program, you can't stop it by pressing Ctrl-Break. But when you press Alt-c, the Break function isn't disabled, and you can press Ctrl-Break to interrupt the program as it pauses at the {?} instruction.

The interaction of {ONERROR} and {BREAKOFF} is important in programs designed to guard against user-generated mistakes. Both instructions would be in use to prevent program interruption. However, if {ONERROR} traps an error, you will have to include a second {BREAKOFF} in your error-handling routine.

TRAP: {BREAKOFF} can be dangerous.

Sometimes {BREAKOFF} can cause loss of data. If your programs have no exit points, or if you use the {GET} instruction to capture all keystrokes and leave yourself no exit points, you can find yourself working with a program you can't stop, unless you reboot the computer.

GUIDELINE: Don't use {BREAKOFF} until you finish and test your program.

You may save yourself from a minor disaster if you wait until you are sure that your program is perfect (well, reasonably tested, at least) before you add the {BREAKOFF} instruction. If your program locks up, and you can't stop its execution because {BREAKOFF} has been issued, you lose any changes you made since you last saved the program to disk.

TIP: In your program, put a {BREAKON} instruction where you plan to put your {BREAKOFF} instruction later.

This {BREAKON} instruction acts as a placeholder and reminder of where you will put the {BREAKOFF} instruction. {BREAKON} does nothing during normal operations. After you complete your program, you can replace {BREAKON} with {BREAKOFF}.

{CLOSE}

FUNCTION: {CLOSE} closes a file that has been opened with the {OPEN} instruction.

SYNTAX: {CLOSE} doesn't require any arguments.

DESCRIPTION: {CLOSE}, one of the nine command language instructions that have to do with file operations, closes the file that is currently open. Closing a file clears the file buffer, causing information in the buffer to be written to the file for APPEND, MODIFY, and WRITE files. Closing a file also makes data inaccessible to further READ operations.

For a more complete description of {CLOSE} and the other file commands, see "Basic File Operations" in Chapter 11.

{CONTENTS}

FUNCTION: The {CONTENTS} instruction creates a formatted string copy of *source* in *destination*.

SYNTAX: {CONTENTS destination,source[,width][,format]}

Argument types for *destination*:

Cell address or equivalent range name
Range address or equivalent range name (uses upper left corner only)

Argument types for *source*:

Cell address or equivalent range name
Range address or equivalent range name (uses upper left corner only)

Argument types for *width*:

Number
Numeric expression
Cell address or equivalent range name
Range address or equivalent range name referencing a single cell
@@ with cell address as pointer

Argument types for *format*:

Number
Numeric expression
Cell address or equivalent range name
Range address or equivalent range name referencing a single cell
@@ with cell address as pointer

{CONTENTS}'s syntax and result are rather complicated. You can use the instruction in any of three forms: with two, three, or four arguments. If you use a fourth argument, *format*, you must also include the third, *width*. {CONTENTS} takes one of the following forms:

{CONTENTS destination,source}

{CONTENTS destination,source,width}

{CONTENTS destination,source,width,format}

DESCRIPTION: Like {LET} and {PUT}, {CONTENTS} is an assignment instruction—that is, it takes a specific value (*source*) and assigns it to a specific cell (*destination*). In the process of assigning *source* to *destination*, {CONTENTS} turns the result into a string. The string looks just like what would appear in a cell if that cell contained the *width* and *format* settings specified by the optional arguments in {CONTENTS}.

If you omit the optional *width* or *format* arguments, {CONTENTS} uses the width and format settings of the *source* cell to create the *destination* string. {CONTENTS} uses the /Worksheet Global format if the *source* cell is not specifically formatted. If you have more than one window present on the screen, {CONTENTS} uses the /Worksheet Global format for the window that currently contains the cell pointer.

You can use 19 different formats, which correspond to the formats available in the worksheet with /Range Format. You can even specify the number of decimal places displayed for the formats that have that option. Table 12.7 lists the formats available.

EXAMPLES: {CONTENTS}'s primary function is to generate strings that appear to be numbers with specific numeric formats. You can also use {CONTENTS} to do some tricks with labels.

Figure 12.6 shows a program that generates the table of format examples shown in figure 12.7. In figure 12.6, {CONTENTS} modifies the five values on line 1 and places them in columns C–G of figure 12.7, according to the format description on the corresponding line in figure 12.7. Column A in figure 12.7 contains a written description of the format type. Neither the instruction nor the program uses the data in column A. The code number in column B is the argument that {CONTENTS} uses to generate the output shown in the remaining columns.

Here is a detailed description of the program in figure 12.6:

Line 1: Cells B1..F1 are the source data for the {CONTENTS} instruction.

Line 8: {FOR OFFSET,0,4,1,INNERLOOP} calls the INNERLOOP routine five times, each time incrementing the value of OFFSET by one.

Line 10: {RECALC INNERLOOP} is the first part of a dynamic instruction. This first part recalculates itself to be sure that the string formula that makes up the instruction is up-to-date.

/cg2~QUEUE2~ is the final part of the dynamic formula. This part copies one of the cells from line 1 into a cell that can be referenced by the {CONTENTS} instruction. The /Copy command is used, instead of {LET} in this application, to transfer the formula in cell C1 as a formula rather than a value.

Table 12.7
Format Codes for Use with {CONTENTS}

Code	Format
0..15	Fixed, 0 to 15 decimal places
16..32	Scientific, 0 to 15 decimal places
33..47	Currency, 0 to 15 decimal places
48..63	Percent, 0 to 15 decimal places
64..79	, (Comma), 0 to 15 decimal places
80..111	Unused (General)
112	+/– (Bar graph)
113	General
114	Date 1 (DD-MMM-YY)
115	Date 2 (DD-MMM)
116	Date 3 (MMM-YY)
117	Text
118	Hidden
119	Date 6 (Time 1 – HH:MM:SS AM/PM)
120	Date 7 (Time 2 – HH:MM AM/PM)
121	*Date 4 (Long Intn'l)
122	*Date 5 (Short Intn'l)
123	*Date 8 (Time 3; Long Intn'l)
124	*Date 9 (Time 4; Short Intn'l)
125..126	Unused (General)
127	/Worksheet Global format

*Note: The formats used for these codes are determined by the /Worksheet Global Default Other International Date and Time format settings.

/c"&@CHAR(66+B3)&"1~QUEUE2~", in line 16, is the formula that creates the dynamic instruction. @CHAR(66+B3) converts the value of CTR to a column letter.

Line 11: {FOR CTR,0,@ROWS(LIST)–1,1,SHOW} calls the SHOW routine once for each entry in LIST. Notice that the beginning value for CTR is 0, and the ending value is @ROWS(LIST)–1, to give CTR the correct values for use as an *offset* argument in @INDEX (line 13). This instruction creates a loop within a loop. The *offset* argument for the {FOR} instruction in line 8 acts as a pointer to each column in LIST, whereas CTR in this {FOR} instruction acts as a pointer to each row in LIST.

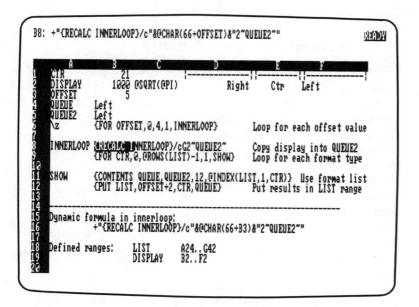

```
B8: +"{RECALC INNERLOOP}/c"&@CHAR(66+OFFSET)&"2~QUEUE2~"          READY

     A         B          C          D          E          F
1  CTR         21                   :-----------::----------::-----------:
2  DISPLAY   1000 @SQRT(@PI)           Right     Ctr   Left
3  OFFSET       5
4  QUEUE     Left
5  QUEUE2    Left
6  \z        {FOR OFFSET,0,4,1,INNERLOOP}         Loop for each offset value
7
8  INNERLOOP {RECALC INNERLOOP}/cG2~QUEUE2~        Copy display into QUEUE2
9            {FOR CTR,0,@ROWS(LIST)-1,1,SHOW}      Loop for each format type
10
11 SHOW      {CONTENTS QUEUE,QUEUE2,12,@INDEX(LIST,1,CTR)}  Use format list
12           {PUT LIST,OFFSET+2,CTR,QUEUE}        Put results in LIST range
13
14 ------------------------------------------------------------
15 Dynamic formula in innerloop:
16        +"{RECALC INNERLOOP}/c"&@CHAR(66+B3)&"2~QUEUE2~"
17
18 Defined ranges:    LIST     A24..G42
19                    DISPLAY  B2..F2
20
```

Fig. 12.6. A program to generate multiple {CONTENTS} formats.

```
C35: [W12] '                                                    READY

      A          B         C           D          E      F      G
24  FIXED)       0      1000           2         Right  Ctr   Left
25  SCIENTIFIC  16      1E+03       2E+00        Right  Ctr   Left
26  CURRENCY    32     $1,000          $2        Right  Ctr   Left
27  PERCENT     48    100000%        177%        Right  Ctr   Left
28  COMMA       64      1,000           2        Right  Ctr   Left
29  BAR GRAPH  112   ************+             Right  Ctr   Left
30  GENERAL    113      1000 1.772453850        Right  Ctr   Left
31  DATE 1     114   26-Sep-02 01-Jan-00        Right  Ctr   Left
32  DATE 2     115      26-Sep    01-Jan        Right  Ctr   Left
33  DATE 3     116      Sep-02    Jan-00        Right  Ctr   Left
34  TEXT       117      1000 @SQRT(@PI)        Right  Ctr   Left
35  HIDDEN     118
36  TIME 1     119   12:00:00 AM 06:32:20 PM    Right  Ctr   Left
37  TIME 2     120   12:00 AM    06:32 PM       Right  Ctr   Left
38  DATE 4     121   09/26/02    01/01/00       Right  Ctr   Left
39  DATE 5     122      09/26       01/01       Right  Ctr   Left
40  TIME 3     123   00:00:00    18:32:20       Right  Ctr   Left
41  TIME 4     124      00:00       18:32       Right  Ctr   Left
42  DEFAULT    127      1000 1.772453850        Right  Ctr   Left
43
```

Fig. 12.7. Possible output formats from {CONTENTS}.

Line 13: {CONTENTS QUEUE,QUEUE2,12,@INDEX(LIST,1,CTR)} takes the value placed in QUEUE2 by the copy operation in line 10 and places a string representation of the cell's appearance in QUEUE, using the format code indicated by @INDEX.

Line 14: {PUT LIST,OFFSET+2,CTR,QUEUE} takes the result of the {CONTENTS} instruction and places that result in the LIST range. The arguments used by {PUT} from the {FOR} loop counters cause the result to appear on the same row as the corresponding format code specified by @INDEX in the previous instruction, and in the same column order in which the original values appear in line 1.

To keep the output to a reasonable volume, only the 0-decimal-place format is shown for the first 5 format types. Each can be specified with 0–15 decimal places. The format numbers can be any number from 0 to 79, plus the numbers listed in the table. You can include a number other than those indicated, but {CONTENTS} uses format 113 (the General format) if the number isn't one of the predefined values. A number greater than 127 or less than 0 is treated as @MOD(number,128). You can think of the formats as going up to 127, then starting over, with 128 the same as 0.

TIP: Thinking in multiples of 16 makes remembering format numbers easy.

The first 5 formats, covering the numbers 0–79, appear in multiples of 16. These format types are the following:

0   **Fixed**
1   **Scientific**
2   **Currency**
3   **Percent**
4   **, (Comma)**

An easy way to find a specific format code is to assign to each format a number from 0 to 4, then multiply the assigned number by 16 and add the decimal places. For example, Currency format is number 2—(C2). To get a (C2) format, you multiply by 16 and add 2.

Format Type * 16 + Decimal Places = Code

(2 = Currency)

2 * 16 + 2 = 34

{CONTENTS} is very complicated, primarily because of the number of arguments the instruction takes and the variety of outputs possible. Any result of {CONTENTS} can be influenced by the contents, label prefix, format, and width of the *source* cell; the /Worksheet Global format; and the presence and values of the optional *width* and *format* arguments.

To add to its complexity, {CONTENTS} does some strange things to long labels with right-justified or centered label prefixes. Figure 12.8 shows a short program, similar to the one shown in figure 12.6, that places the results of {CONTENTS} in a series of columns in the LIST range, varying the *width* argument in {CONTENTS} from 1 to 20.

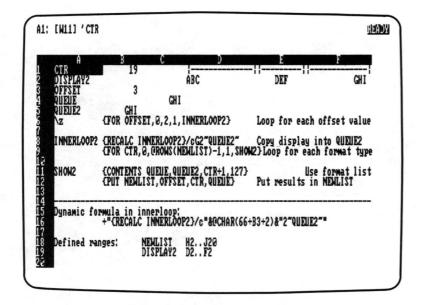

Fig. 12.8. A program to generate labels.

Figure 12.9 shows the output produced by this program. The LIST range contains only left-justified labels, but the labels are padded with spaces to make them appear as they would in cells of increasing width. As you can see, the labels are truncated to the specified column width when the width is narrower than the label. As the width specification becomes wider, the centering and right-justification become apparent.

Figures 12.10 and 12.11 show slightly different outputs from the program in figure 12.8 as it is run with the labels Left, Centered label, and Right label in cells D2, E2, and F2, respectively. Figure 12.10 shows the result of the program in figure 12.8 as it is run with a column width of 9 for column B, which is the *source* cell for {CONTENTS}. In figure 12.11, the source cell has been narrowed to a width of 4.

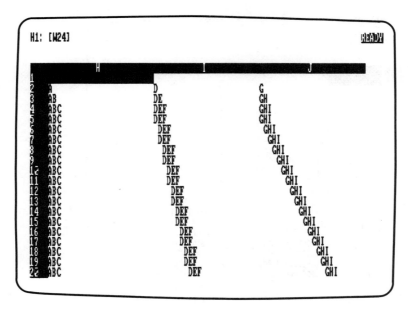

Fig. 12.9. Labels produced by {CONTENTS}.

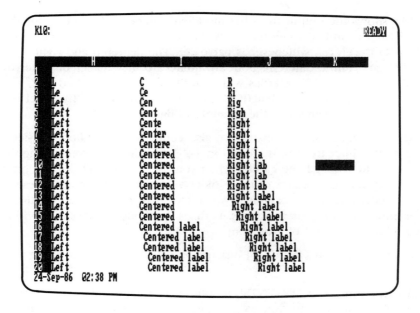

Fig. 12.10. Longer labels produced by {CONTENTS}, *using a column width of 9.*

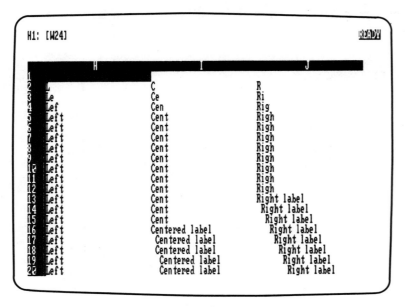

Fig. 12.11. Longer labels produced by {CONTENTS}, using a column width of 4.

Figure 12.11 shows the output from the modified program. The output for the left-justified label is limited to either the width of the *source* cell or the width specified in {CONTENTS}, whichever is narrower. The centered and right-justified labels are a little different. Both are limited to the smaller of either the source cell's width or {CONTENTS}'s width, until the width specified in {CONTENTS} is longer than the length of the label. At that point, the label is formatted in the same manner as the example in figure 12.9.

In Symphony, the {CONTENTS} instruction also contains subtle idiosyncrasies, but the problems differ from those found in 1-2-3 and differ between Symphony Release 1.0 and Release 1.1. Be careful when you use {CONTENTS} in programs that will be transferred to either of these older versions of Symphony. These obscure differences between versions of what appear to be identical functions can create horrible debugging problems. Perhaps these incompatibilities will be eliminated with Release 1.2 of Symphony.

TRAP: The result of the {CONTENTS} instruction usually contains invisible spaces.

Be careful when you use {CONTENTS}. Its output is a left-justified label that always contains as many characters as specified by either the default width (the default column width of the current window) or the *width* argument. The instruction's output is *exactly* what would appear in a cell with the indicated format. Therefore, the results usually contain extra spaces.

For example, the number 1000 in cell C24 of figure 12.7 contains 7 spaces to the left of the numerals and *an additional space to the right*. Although this arrangement may seem odd, remember that numbers appear with a one-space margin to the right of the cell. If you are going to use {CONTENTS} to process numbers, you may need to use the @TRIM function to delete these extra spaces. For instance, suppose that you use {CONTENTS} to create in cell A21 the number 13 with a width of 4. Then the following formula

    +"Friday the "&A21&"th"

would yield

    Friday the   13 th

To eliminate the unwanted spaces, you enter the formula

    +"Friday the "&@TRIM(A21)&"th"

And the result is

    Friday the 13th

Remember that the one-space margin also applies to cell formulas in the **Text** format. If the *width* argument is 12, a 12-character formula will be missing the rightmost character.

The only output results that don't contain righthand spaces are the **Percent** formats (48–63) and any format too wide for the width specification.

Notice that when you specify format 118 (**Hidden**), the result is a label with nothing but spaces. {CONTENTS} produces such labels for numeric as well as string *source* specifications.

If the *source* cell displays ERR or NA, the program creates a label that contains the characters ERR or NA, respectively.

TRAP: If the width specification is too narrow for the formatted result, {CONTENTS} generates a row of asterisks.

When you specify the format and width, you must take into consideration the potential width of the output. If the output field you specify isn't wide enough, 1-2-3 produces a row of asterisks. This display of asterisks is not temporary (as is that which appears when a column is too narrow for a given numeric format) and is entered into the cell as a label. You can't convert the asterisks into the source number by expanding the column width after the program produces such a label; labels aren't affected by the width of the current column. Therefore, whatever number {CONTENTS} would have displayed is *lost*, and to achieve a readable result, you must adjust the width setting and *rerun your program*. If you are working with a program that takes several hours to process, you might want to add a few extra spaces to the width specification, just in case.

GUIDELINE: Unless you have good reason to do otherwise, use the *width* and *format* arguments in a {CONTENTS} instruction.

The width and format settings use the current /Worksheet Global specifications as defaults. Therefore, you must include these arguments in order to ensure control of your output format. If the global settings aren't what you think they are when you invoke your program, and you don't specify the *width* and *format* arguments in {CONTENTS}, you could end up with junk for output.

TRAP: {CONTENTS} accepts only addresses and range names as its *source* and *destination* arguments.

Most command language instructions don't accept @ functions as *destination* arguments, but do accept @ functions as *source* arguments. The following, for example, is a legal construction for the {LET} instruction:

{LET QUEUE,@DATE(85,DATECTR,1)}

However, if you try to use the following instruction,

{CONTENTS QUEUE,@DATE(85,DATEREF,1)}

1-2-3 displays the error message

`Macro: Illegal range in CONTENTS`

To make the preceding instruction work, you must establish reference cells containing the desired formulas and use {CONTENTS} to refer to those cells.

Despite the limitations described, {CONTENTS} can be very useful. Without it, you couldn't access the display format, a task I've sometimes wished an @ function could perform. {CONTENTS} enables you to access everything that can be displayed in a cell.

The program in figure 12.12 uses {CONTENTS} to produce a series of month abbreviations. In this case, format 116 is the MMM-YY format. The {PUT} instruction places in a range array the three leftmost characters of the result of the @TRIM function. Notice that the DATEREF cell contains a formula that must be recalculated during program execution. To see the results, you press the Calc key (F9) or the Enter key at the end of the program.

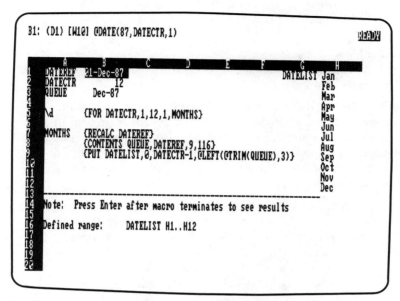

Fig. 12.12. {CONTENTS} *used to generate date labels.*

{DEFINE}

FUNCTION: The {DEFINE} instruction reserves space for variables passed to a subroutine and (optionally) defines the type of data the variable will contain.

SYNTAX: {DEFINE address1[:type1][,address2[:type2]] . . . }

Argument types for *address* arguments:

Cell address or equivalent range name
Range address or equivalent range name

Argument types for optional *type* arguments:

:string (default)
:value

{DEFINE} accepts as many arguments as you can enter, within the 240-character limit on label length. This instruction must have at least one argument, as specified by *address1*. The *type* specifications are optional and can follow any or all of the *address* specifications. The *type* specifications must be either *:value* or *:string*. If you don't specify the *type* argument, *:string* is assumed.

The following are all valid {DEFINE} instructions:

    {DEFINE B1}
    {DEFINE B1:value}
    {DEFINE refcell:string,counter,queue:string}
    {DEFINE B1,B2,B3,B4}

If you omit the {DEFINE} statement from a subroutine, 1-2-3 ignores the arguments in the subroutine call. If the {DEFINE} statement is present in a subroutine, the number of arguments in {DEFINE} must match the number of parameters passed to the subroutine by the instruction containing the subroutine call. If the number of parameters does not match, an error occurs when you run the program.

DESCRIPTION: {DEFINE} is used only at the beginning of subroutines which accept arguments from the instruction that calls the subroutine. {DEFINE} is unique in that it doesn't do anything by itself—that is, nothing happens when the instruction executes. Rather, {DEFINE} reserves space for storing the parameter values that are passed to this instruction in the subroutine call. {DEFINE} also determines the way in which those values are stored.

RESERVING SPACE FOR PARAMETERS: A command language program can call a subroutine and send specific values to it at the same time—a procedure known as *parameter passing*. This capability is powerful, allowing a program to call the same subroutine from several places in the main program and give that subroutine different values to process each time. With each set of new values it receives, the subroutine can perform different functions. Therefore, you can use one subroutine where numerous subroutines usually would be required. By making one subroutine perform multiple tasks, you can write programs that are both powerful and short.

In keeping with 1-2-3's general design philosophy, parameters passed to a subroutine are stored in the worksheet. {DEFINE}'s first function is to reserve cells in which to store the values. The examples that follow demonstrate ways in which you can use these parameters in a subroutine.

DEFINING THE PARAMETER TYPE: As mentioned previously, each cell indicated in the {DEFINE} instruction can be specified as a string or value. If the type is not explicitly declared, the {DEFINE} instruction uses string as the default. If the type of the argument is a string, the parameter is passed exactly as it appears in the calling statement. If the type of the argument is a value, 1-2-3 tries to evaluate the argument before passing the parameter. The difference between a string and a value is most evident when the parameter passed to the subroutine is a formula. For example, the subroutine call to a routine called MONTHS might look like this:

    {MONTHS 3*12}

Here are the results for both kinds of parameter definition:

{DEFINE} Statement	What Is Stored in refcell
{DEFINE refcell}	3*12 (a label)
{DEFINE refcell:string}	3*12 (a label)
{DEFINE refcell:value}	36 (a number)

String formulas generate the same kind of output. If the type is not declared to be a value, what appears in the defined cell is a copy of the string formula. If the type is declared to be a value, the result of the string formula appears instead (as a label, not as a formula).

The range name appears in the defined cell if the parameter passed is a range name and the type is a string. If the type is declared to be a value, the contents of the cell specified by that range name appears. The same holds true for cell addresses. If you don't explicitly specify the argument as a value, the cell address (or range name) itself—not the contents of that cell—appears in the reserved cell.

EXAMPLES: You can use {DEFINE} in several different ways in a subroutine. Each will be examined in turn.

Figure 12.13 shows a subroutine with no parameters. It is called from the program called \d, which appears at the top of the screen. The subroutine uses the /Data Fill command to create a column of date headings. Starting at the cell pointer's current location, the subroutine specifies a 12-row range, fills it with numbers representing months (starting with Jan-87), and formats the range to Date format 3.

This subroutine can be called from anywhere within the program, but isn't very flexible. The subroutine always generates a 12-row range, starts with the same date, and uses Date format 3. If you wanted to generate headings containing variable numbers of months without parameters, you would need a separate routine for each heading. (You could use {LET} instructions and /Range Value commands to simulate the {DEFINE} instruction's function, but that process is cumbersome compared to using {DEFINE}.)

Figure 12.14 shows the same program, but modified with a {DEFINE} statement. This example illustrates the most basic use of {DEFINE}, which is to specify a storage cell for a value that the subroutine will use. In this case, the cell contains a value that {DOWN} uses to specify the size of the range to be filled. Notice that the parameter type is defined as a value, the subroutine call contains a formula that is evaluated to the final value, and {DOWN} has been modified to include as its *repetition* argument the defined cell. This example assumes that a range already exists and that the number of date labels created must match the range (which is not shown).

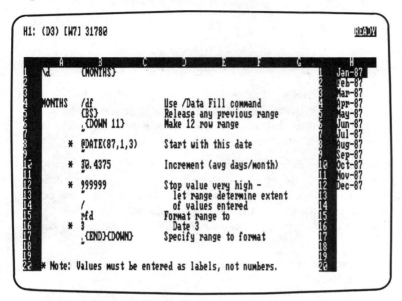

Fig. 12.13. A subroutine with no parameters.

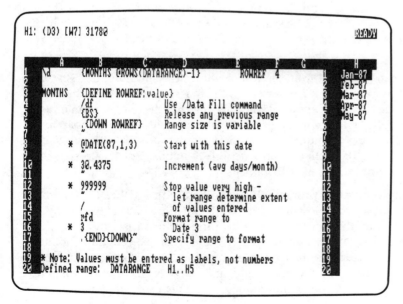

Fig. 12.14. A reference parameter passed to a subroutine.

Figure 12.15, which uses {DEFINE} a little differently, shows a further modification of the program. A second parameter, representing the beginning month of the list, is passed to the subroutine. {DEFINE} specifies the parameter type as a string. The reference cell for the new parameter (MONTHREF) is in the body of the subroutine. Placing the reference cell for the parameter in the body of the subroutine is a powerful way to generate flexible subroutines. You can even pass new keywords or command language instructions as parameters so that the subroutine modifies its own instruction set.

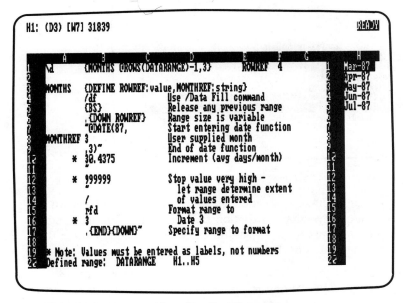

Fig. 12.15. A parameter passed into the subroutine code.

Figure 12.16 demonstrates how you can make the subroutine modify its own instruction set. You must enter the new instruction as a string formula and enclose the instruction in quotation marks, as shown in the subroutine call in line 2. {DEFINE} must then declare this parameter to be a value. When the program calls the subroutine with the arguments shown, {DEFINE} automatically inserts the new instruction into the code. The subroutine generates a row of date labels rather than a column.

The example in figure 12.16 also demonstrates how to pass the instruction to two locations at once. Notice that when the orientation of the list of date labels is changed from vertical to horizontal, the instructions that format this range in line 13 must be changed in a corresponding fashion. The straightforward way to perform this task is to add another parameter that is identical to the last

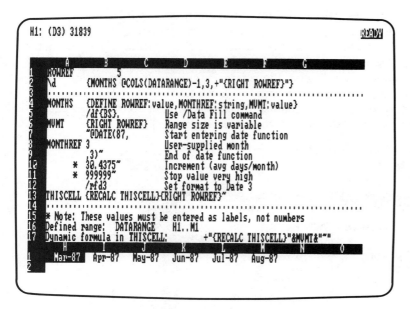

Fig. 12.16. A command language instruction passed as a parameter.

parameter shown, but at a different location. An alternative method, shown in the example, is to create a dynamic instruction that references the instruction that was modified. The formula used appears in the control panel. Notice that the instruction first recalculates itself.

You can also use {DEFINE} to store information not directly related to the subroutine's operation. The subroutine in figure 12.17 shows how to use {?} to display a prompt and enter data into the correct cell. This is a macro function that ordinarily can be accomplished only with the /xl and /xn commands. The usual syntax for /xl and /xn requires a prompt and a cell address, each followed by a tilde, as in the following:

/xlEnter the new data here~CELLADDRESS~

Whatever the user enters is placed into the cell specified by the range name CELLADDRESS. One of the nice features of /xl and /xn is that they enable you to omit the cell address so that you can enter the data directly into the current cell, as in the following:

/xlEnter the new data here~~

Short of some complex string formula constructions, the {GETLABEL} and {GETNUMBER} instructions lack this capability. Sometimes, however, you may want an alternative to /xl and /xn—for instance, when your prompt exceeds the

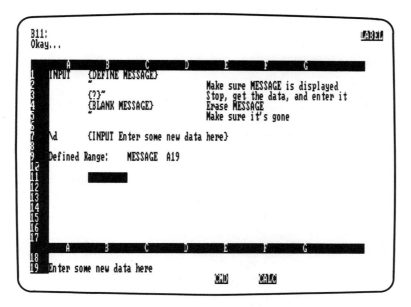

Fig. 12.17. {DEFINE} *used to place messages in the worksheet.*

40-character limit of the /x commands. Ordinary use of the {?} command does enable you to place data into the current cell, but without the benefit of a prompt. By using {DEFINE}, however, you can use {?} to create a routine that allows you to enter data directly into the current cell, with a prompt and without the limitations imposed by /xl and /xn (see fig. 12.17).

To display a prompt, the program in figure 12.17 uses a remotely located cell that appears in a second window. The program then uses {?} to enter into the current cell whatever is typed. The instruction in line 7, whose only parameter is the prompt, calls the INPUT subroutine. The ~ macro instructions are necessary in order to force 1-2-3 to update and display the prompt, when entered, and to display a blank screen after {BLANK} erases the cell.

To guide users through a sequence of operations, you could use a similar method to display an entire series of prompts.

{DISPATCH}

FUNCTION: The {DISPATCH} instruction performs an indirect branch to the location specified by its argument.

SYNTAX: {DISPATCH location}

    or

    {DISPATCH string-formula}

Argument types for *location*:

    Cell address or equivalent range name
    Range address or equivalent range name

Argument types for *string-formula*:

    Any formula or function that returns a valid cell address or equivalent
        range name

DESCRIPTION: A variant of the {BRANCH} instruction, {DISPATCH} controls the instruction pointer and therefore determines which instructions in a program are executed. {DISPATCH} can be thought of as a {BRANCH} instruction whose argument must be evaluated before branching occurs. The argument in {DISPATCH} is, in essence, a cell formula. The transfer of program control occurs as if the instruction were a {BRANCH} to the *contents* of that cell formula (see fig. 12.18).

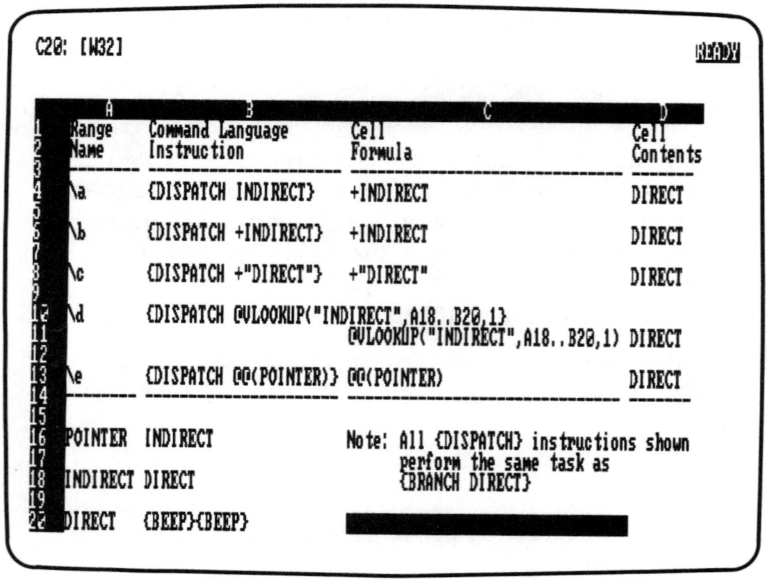

Fig. 12.18. Five examples of using {DISPATCH}.

Figure 12.18 contains five examples of {DISPATCH}. For comparison, columns C
and D contain, as cell formulas, the same arguments that appear in the various
examples of {DISPATCH}. Column C is formatted to Text to show the formula,
and column D displays the contents of the cell. Notice that in all cases the
content of the cell is the label DIRECT. Likewise, in all cases, the {DISPATCH}
instruction performs the same action as would a {BRANCH DIRECT} instruction.
The label result of the argument could also be B20, which is the cell-address
equivalent of the range name DIRECT; all the instructions shown would work
the same. The example shown in \b helps emphasize the fact that the argument
to {DISPATCH} is indeed a cell formula. The \b example is equivalent to the \a
example.

Notice that the final example, \e, uses the @@ function, which provides
indirect addressing capabilities. When @@ is used in this manner with
{DISPATCH}, the result is *doubly* indirect. Technically, {DISPATCH} tells the
program to "branch to the address specified by the address indicated by the
address in the @@ function." This example of {DISPATCH} is related to
{BRANCH} in the same way that your second cousin is related to your sister.

Figure 12.19 further illustrates indirect branching. The program is an infinite
loop: \d contains a {DISPATCH} instruction that makes the program branch to
the location specified by POINTER. And that location is \d.

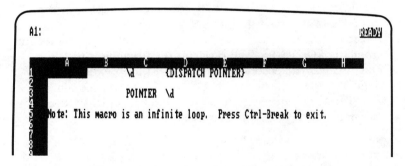

Fig. 12.19. {DISPATCH} *used to create an infinite loop.*

USING A FORMULA OR A FUNCTION AS AN ADDRESS: {DISPATCH}
enables you to specify the branch location by using a formula or an @ function
as the address argument (see fig. 12.20). Used this way, {DISPATCH} is similar
to the opposite of a subroutine called with parameters. Whereas parameter
passing enables you to call a single subroutine from various locations in a
program, {DISPATCH} allows you to branch to different parts of a program from
a single instruction.

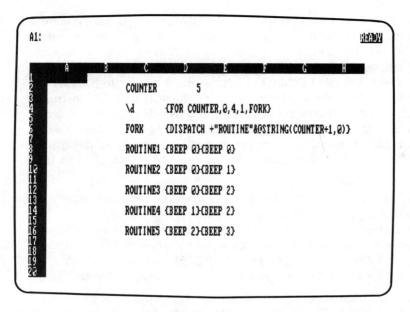

Fig. 12.20. Formula addressing with {DISPATCH}.

{DISPATCH}'s argument in figure 12.20 is a string formula. It starts with the string "ROUTINE" and adds to it the string value of the counter variable (plus 1) used by the {FOR} instruction. Therefore, the first time the {FOR} loop executes, the value of the formula is ROUTINE1. The program then branches to D8, which bears that range name. The second time the {FOR} loop executes, the counter value is 1, the formula evaluates to ROUTINE2, and the program branches to cell D10. These routines are "dummies," but, in actual practice, they could be subprograms anywhere in the worksheet.

EXAMPLES: Figure 12.21 is a more elaborate version of figure 12.20. {DISPATCH}'s *location* argument is an @INDEX function. That function finds the branch location in a two-dimensional table of names by referencing both the counter that the {FOR} loop uses and another variable named OFFSET. Changing OFFSET's value causes the routines to execute in a different order and some routines to repeat, according to the list specified in POINTERLIST. Because the list includes a "dummy" routine that does nothing, the list of routines executed does not always have to number five. OFFSET could refer to a specific day of the week or to another indicator that determined which set of routines were to be executed. If you wanted to make this arrangement even more complex, you could make one of the routines alter OFFSET so that the order of execution varies, depending on the action of the program.

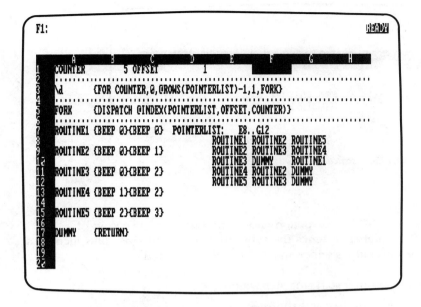

Fig. 12.21. {DISPATCH} *used to execute routines in varying orders.*

{FILESIZE}

FUNCTION: {FILESIZE} returns the size in bytes of the currently opened file.

SYNTAX: {FILESIZE location}

Argument types for *location*:

> Cell address or equivalent range name
> Range address or equivalent range name

If the range specified by *location* contains more than one cell, only the cell in the upper left corner of the range is used.

DESCRIPTION: {FILESIZE}, another of 1-2-3's file-handling instructions, returns the size in bytes of the currently opened file in the location which that address specifies. As occurs with 1-2-3's other file-handling instructions, if {FILESIZE} can't return the file size (for example, when no {OPEN} instruction precedes the {FILESIZE} instruction), an error condition results, and 1-2-3 executes instructions following {FILESIZE} on the same line. Figure 12.22 illustrates the use of this instruction. (See Chapter 10 for a more complete description of file operations.)

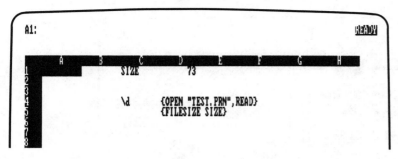

Fig. 12.22. The {FILESIZE} *instruction.*

{FOR}

FUNCTION: The {FOR} instruction allows the repeated execution of a subroutine. The number of times the subroutine is executed is controlled by a variable that is continuously incremented (or decremented).

SYNTAX: {FOR counter,start,stop,step,routine}

Argument types for *counter* and *routine*:

Cell address or equivalent range name
Range address or equivalent range name

If the range specified by *counter* or *macro* contains more than one cell, only the cell in the upper left corner of the range is used.

Argument types for *start, stop,* and *step*:

Cell address or equivalent range name
@@ (cell address or equivalent range name)
Number or numeric expression (integers or real values)

Note about using @@: When you use the @@ function to supply indirect cell references for *start, stop,* and *step*, {FOR} may not work normally, depending on the argument specified in @@. The @@ function's *pointer* argument must be a cell address or range address referring to a single cell; otherwise, @@ evaluates to ERR (see the discussion on ERR and NA, following). Although the target address for @@ can be a cell address or range address, {FOR} works properly only when cell addresses are used. If range addresses (even single cell range addresses) are used for the target cell specifications for *start* or *stop*, {FOR} operates as if these values had been set to zero, regardless of their actual values. If you use a range address for the *step* argument, {FOR} doesn't call the specified subroutine, but neither does it give any error indications.

Note about ERR and NA values for *start, stop*, and *step*: {FOR} doesn't operate normally if *start, stop*, or *step* evaluate to NA or ERR. The number of times the specified subroutine is called, however, depends on which argument takes on the NA or ERR value. Table 12.8 shows the number of times the subroutine specified as the argument to {FOR} will be called, according to various argument values.

Table 12.8
The Number of Times a {FOR} Subroutine Executes
with Various Argument Values

	Argument Value		
	ERR	NA	0 (zero)
Argument			
start	0	Infinite	Normal
stop	Infinite	0	Normal
step	1	Infinite	Infinite

DESCRIPTION: {FOR}'s syntax looks formidable, but will become clearer after you understand how the instruction works.

You can think of {FOR} as a kind of subroutine call, although {FOR} can't pass parameters directly. This kind of instruction is found in almost all high-level programming languages—for example, the FOR..NEXT loop in BASIC and FOR..DO in Pascal. The *start, stop*, and *step* arguments determine how many times the instructions which that routine specifies are called.

The term *loop* refers to the way {FOR} works in other languages. In its usual configuration, a loop has two parts: one that specifies the beginning of a series of instructions to be repeated and another that marks the end of the series. If you were to trace the flow of instructions in such a program, you would move down to the "end" marker, then "loop" back to the beginning marker and repeat this process the specified number of times.

1-2-3 marks the beginning and end of its instruction series by placing all the instructions in a subroutine, which {FOR} references.

Regardless of the syntax of this kind of instruction in various languages, the instruction's operation is basically the same:

1. A *counter* variable is assigned an initial value, as specified by *start*.

2. The *counter* variable is tested against the value specified by the *stop* argument (the *stop* value). If *counter* is less than or equal to the value of *stop*, the program calls the subroutine. Otherwise, the subroutine is not called, and program control is passed to the next instruction in the program.

3. The *counter* variable is incremented by the value of the *step* argument, and the test described in #2 is repeated. The test is repeated until *counter* is equal to or greater than *stop*. If *counter* never reaches the value of *stop*, {FOR} keeps on running.

When the test is made before any instructions are executed, the loop is sometimes called a *top-tested* loop. It can execute zero times (not at all).

In a *bottom-tested loop*, the instructions are executed once before the test is made and are repeated only if the test is passed. In 1-2-3, if the *counter* variable is greater than the *stop* value when the program encounters {FOR}, the program does not call the specified routine. In this case, {FOR} operates like a *top-tested* loop.

Other factors that can affect the operation of a loop are whether *counter* is incremented before or after it is tested, and whether *counter* must be greater than or merely equal to the *stop* value in order for the loop to terminate. In 1-2-3, *counter* is incremented before it is tested and must be greater than the *stop* value in order to terminate the loop. Because {FOR} operates this way, *counter* will always be incremented beyond the *stop* value when the {FOR} instruction is finished. If your program uses *counter* as an argument to @ functions, the extra increment may cause them to return ERR when the program terminates. The program should operate normally as long as the values between the *start* and *stop* values in {FOR} are legal as arguments to your function. When designing your programs, however, you should take into account the final value that will be assigned to *counter*.

To understand {FOR}, you may find helpful the concept that *counter* variables work the same way as the numbers generated by the /Data Fill command. That command takes all the resulting numbers and arranges them in a row or column of cells, whereas {FOR} generates the sequence of numbers in the counter cell, one at a time. Both /Data Fill and {FOR} stop executing when they reach the *stop* value.

Many programming languages restrict the kind of numbers that can be used as arguments; the numbers have to be integers or positive numbers. In 1-2-3, however, the *start, stop,* and *step* variables can be positive or negative (counting backward), can be formulas or functions, can refer to each other, and can even be changed during program execution. The following construction, for example, is legal:

{FOR counter,counter+1,counter*3,@SIN(counter),routine}

When the {FOR} instruction executes, 1-2-3 makes internal copies of the values of the loop control arguments and uses those copies to control the loop's execution. Therefore, the values 1-2-3 uses when it executes the {FOR} instruction are the values of the variables *when the instruction is first accessed*. The values don't change during execution. Therefore, the *step* value is always an even increment. In the preceding example, the values used would depend on the value of *counter* at the time the instruction was executed. If the *counter* value was 2 when the program called the {FOR} instruction, the *start* value would be 3, the *stop* value would be 6, and the *step* value would be @SIN(2) (or about .90930).

TRAP: If *step* is a negative number, 1-2-3 evaluates *stop* as if the program were counting backward.

1-2-3 automatically adjusts its *stop* test according to the direction in which the loop counts. If *step* is a negative number, 1-2-3 assumes that you are counting backward. Therefore, the program calls the routine in the {FOR} instruction only if *counter* is *greater than or equal to* the *stop* value.

In the preceding example, if *counter* is 4 when the program executes the {FOR} instruction, the program does not execute the routine that {FOR} references, because @SIN(4) equals −.71 (approximately). For a negative *step* value, 1-2-3's *stop* test determines whether the *stop* value is *less than* the *start* value. Because the *stop* value is not less than the *start* value, the *stop* condition has already been met.

The *counter* is updated when {FOR} is executed. Therefore, functions and formulas can be updated automatically to reflect the number of times the referenced routine has been executed. The *counter*, then, can be used not only as a counter but as an argument for functions that are part of the routine that {FOR} calls. The routine in figure 12.23, for instance, rearranges the characters in a string vertically. The @LENGTH function determines the number of times the loop is executed, and the @MID function extracts each character in turn.

In this example, notice that the ending value of COUNTER that is displayed is one greater than the upper limit {FOR} specifies. This is because 1-2-3 terminates the {FOR} loop when this value is *greater than* the *stop* value.

EXAMPLES: In figure 12.24, two {FOR} loops are nested one within the other. The program takes the contents of the source range (SCE) and performs a 180-degree transposition, placing the contents in a destination range (DEST). The

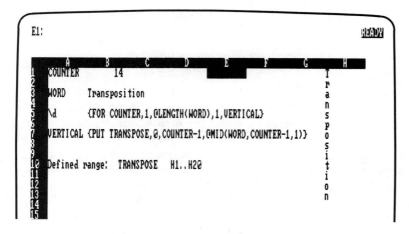

Fig. 12.23. The {FOR} loop counter used as an argument for a function.

first {FOR} loop calls the second {FOR} loop, which calls the transposition routine (TRP). {PUT} uses the counters used by the {FOR} loops to control the selection and placement of the range contents.

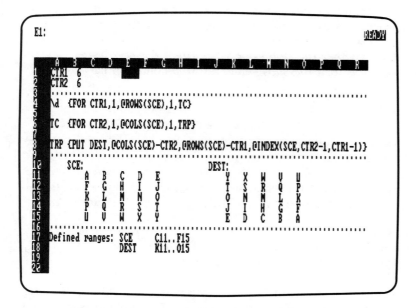

Fig. 12.24. Nested {FOR} loops using counters as arguments for functions.

TRAP: If you assign the same *counter* variable to two {FOR} instructions, 1-2-3 displays only the most recent value for that variable.

The program runs normally if you assign the same *counter* variable to two {FOR} instructions at the same time. 1-2-3 makes an internal copy of the variable before executing the {FOR} loop and uses the copy to control the loop.

Programs get complicated, however, if you use the *counter* variable as an argument for functions, as in figures 12.23 and 12.24. Both the {FOR} loops reset the value of the *counter* variable. Therefore, the *counter* variable's current *displayed* value is the value assigned by the last executed {FOR} instruction. This "competition" for the value of the *counter* variable doesn't affect the operation of the {FOR} loops themselves. (That's done with internal copies of the initial values.) The competition does affect the operation of any functions that use the *counter* variable as an argument. These functions use the most recent value.

In figure 12.25, the string that the program assembles displays every value of COUNTER as it changes. The first {FOR} instruction assigns COUNTER a value of 10 and increments it by 10 in order to distinguish it from the values the other loop assigns. As you can see, each {FOR} loop changes COUNTER's value.

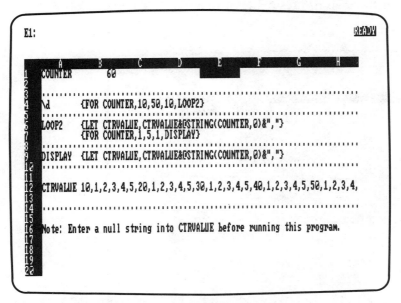

Fig. 12.25. Shared counter variables with multiple {FOR} loops.

Shared *counter* variables can be useful in unusual programming situations, but are more likely to be a source of problems. This description of how 1-2-3 works with shared counters is included here to help you spot errors that arise when a *counter* variable is inadvertently duplicated. I don't recommend that you use this feature unless you really know what you are doing.

{FORBREAK}

FUNCTION: This instruction terminates execution of a {FOR} loop before the *stop* value is reached (also see {FOR}).

SYNTAX: {FORBREAK}

{FORBREAK} requires no arguments.

DESCRIPTION: 1-2-3's {FOR} instruction is difficult to use in situations in which a loop may be forced to stop early—a common occurrence in programming. You may want a loop to terminate early if a specific condition is encountered during the execution of the loop. For example, the program shown in figure 12.26 prompts the user for data entries and places them in a range called ENTRIES. Because the program "assumes" that the user will enter the entire range of data, the entry process is coded into a {FOR} loop. The user, however, can exit the loop by pressing Q in response to the Enter value prompt.

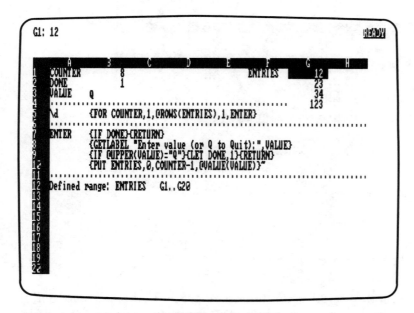

Fig. 12.26. A {FOR} loop with optional early termination.

To exit the loop, you have to allow {FOR} to cycle through its entire range (note the value of COUNTER in the example). This task is accomplished by setting a variable—DONE in this example—to 1 and testing for this value at the beginning of each loop. If the variable is set after the second {IF} instruction, the program, on the next and all subsequent passes through the loop, exits the subroutine at the first {IF} statement.

This procedure handles the job done, but is cumbersome. {FORBREAK} was designed for just such situations. Figure 12.27 shows the figure 12.26 program modified with {FORBREAK}. When the modified program encounters {FORBREAK}, the program terminates the {FOR} loop immediately. Setting DONE to 1 and testing for this value at the beginning of each loop is now unnecessary.

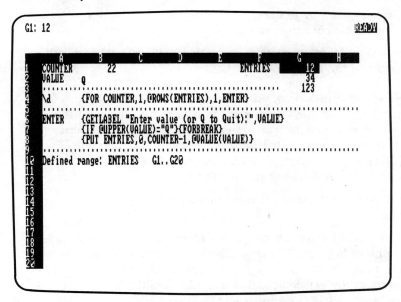

Fig. 12.27. {FORBREAK} *used to terminate a* {FOR} *loop.*

The two programs, one using {FOR} and the other using {FORBREAK}, perform the same function but differ in three important ways:

1. The program with {FORBREAK} is shorter and requires fewer cells for variable storage.

2. The program with {FORBREAK} runs faster. This program has one fewer {IF} test while operating and does not require that COUNTER in the {FOR} instruction be incremented all the way to the *stop* value.

3. After the program containing the {FOR} loop finishes executing, COUNTER displays the number of times the {FOR} loop was executed. This information can be important if you have to keep track of the number of such loops.

{GET}

FUNCTION: {GET} captures keystrokes from the keyboard and places the keystroke (or equivalent keyword) in the cell specified by *location*.

SYNTAX: {GET location}

Argument types for *location*:

Cell address or equivalent range name
Range address or equivalent range name

If the range specified by *location* contains more than one cell, only the cell in the upper left corner of the range is used.

DESCRIPTION: {GET} causes program execution to pause and accept one keystroke from the keyboard. {GET} puts the result of the keystroke in the cell specified by the *location* argument. For example, when you type the letter A, {GET} places that letter in the cell that *location* specifies. The difference between using {GET} and the standard input from the keyboard is that {GET} *intercepts* the keystrokes but does not *execute* them.

For those of you familiar with BASIC, this instruction is similar to BASIC's INKEY$ instruction.

One of {GET}'s most useful aspects is that it intercepts the special keys as well as the standard alphabet keys. {GET} follows the same convention for naming special keys as the macro keywords. For example, when you press the Edit key (F2), {EDIT} appears in the cell indicated. Table 12.9 lists the labels that appear in the *location* cells when {GET} captures special keystrokes.

Missing from this list are {HELP}, {STEP}, {COMPOSE}, and {BREAK} (available in Symphony), none of which {GET} can capture. Also missing from this list are the {APP1} through {APP4} keys (Alt-F7 through Alt-F10), which will be used by application programs when that support becomes available. These keys may become active when an application program is attached. Notice alo that {GET} captures the Tab and Backtab keys as {BIGRIGHT} and {BIGLEFT} respectively.

When {GET} intercepts a numeric key (0–9), {GET} enters that keystroke into the capture cell *as a label* rather than as a number.

Table 12.9

The Labels in *Location* Cells
Corresponding to Captured Keystrokes

Function Keys	Labels
F2	{EDIT}
F3	{NAME}
F4	{ABS}
F5	{GOTO}
F6	{WINDOW}
F7	{QUERY}
F8	{TABLE}
F9	{CALC}
F10	{GRAPH}

Direction Keys	Labels
↑	{UP}
↓	{DOWN}
←	{LEFT}
→	{RIGHT}
PgUp	{PGUP}
PgDn	{PGDN}
Ctrl-← or Backtab	{BIGLEFT}
Ctrl-→ or Tab	{BIGRIGHT}

Other Keys	Labels
Esc	{ESCAPE}
Backspace	{BACKSPACE}
Ins	{INSERT}
Del	{DELETE}

To get a better idea of how {GET} works, you might want to type the short program in figure 12.28. The loop in this program places the keystroke captured by {GET} into the cell called VALUE. You must press Ctrl-Break to exit the loop. The tilde (~) causes 1-2-3 to display the results of the {GET} operation; {GET} by itself does not force 1-2-3 to update the screen.

EXAMPLES: If you run the program in figure 12.28, you will notice that the keystrokes that {GET} captures are not executed. {GET} merely displays in VALUE the representation of the keystroke. Although the keystrokes are in

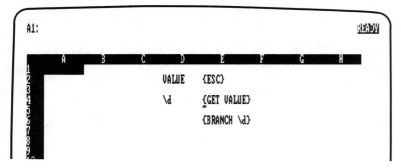

Fig. 12.28. The {GET} instruction used to capture keystrokes.

executable form, to make the program execute them as they are captured, you must call VALUE as a subroutine.

Figure 12.29 shows the routine modified to accomplish this task. This routine doesn't have a tilde (~). Therefore, you won't see the keystrokes entered into VALUE unless a keystroke entered updates the screen. For the program to operate properly, the tilde must be omitted. Because the program executes each keystroke as you press the keys, you can enter conditions where the tilde would not be allowed or would change the intended operation of the program.

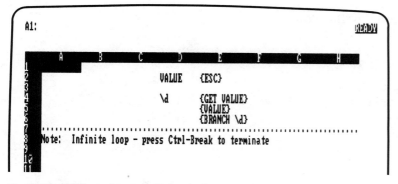

Fig. 12.29. {GET} used to execute keystrokes.

You can modify this program further to create what is known as a fixed-field data entry program, which is similar to Macro 22 in Chapter 5. You use a *fixed-field* program when you are entering data in which each entry has the same number of characters or digits. An example is a column of four-digit numbers. The fixed-field data entry program saves additional keystrokes by automatically issuing the cell pointer movement command (and its implied Enter) after you type the correct number of digits (see fig. 12.30).

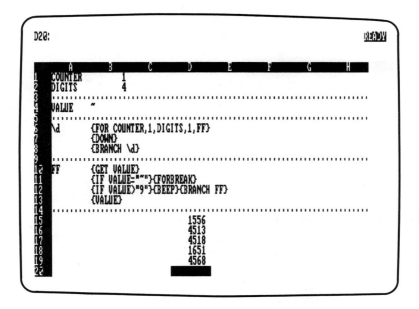

Fig. 12.30. {GET} *used for fixed-field data entry.*

In figure 12.30, the {FOR} loop in line 6 controls the number of digits entered. You can easily vary the width of the fixed field by simply changing the DIGITS entry. The {FOR} loop calls the FF routine the number of times that DIGITS specifies. When the program exits the loop, the cell pointer moves down, entering the number in the current cell. The program then branches back to \d to get another number.

To give you some idea of what {GET} can do, a couple of extra features have been added to the FF routine. The first feature is a check for the tilde (~); remember that this character appears in VALUE whenever you press Enter. If the tilde is encountered, the program executes the {FORBREAK} instruction, which ends the loop and enables you to enter numbers with fewer than four digits. The program automatically moves down one cell after you enter the fourth consecutive digit. If you enter a number with fewer than four digits, the program moves down one cell after you press Enter.

The second {IF} tests the value of each digit entered to make sure that it is indeed a digit. Note that because {GET} enters digits into VALUE as labels, the test compares an ASCII value, not a numeric value. The left-brace character has an ASCII value greater than nine, so this instruction also prevents entry of anything beginning with a left brace, including any of the special keystrokes. Therefore, only digits and the tilde are acceptable characters.

If you set the field width to 1, you can create a nonnumeric version of this subroutine, which you can use as a module in other programs. The module would accept only single-key responses. In response to a yes/no question, the user could then type Y or N without having to press Enter afterward.

You can also use {GET} to screen for the special key indicators. The example in figure 12.31 uses a VLOOKUP table to rearrange the function keys. The Edit key, which is usually F2, is swapped with the Calc key, which is usually F9; and the Abs key (F4) is swapped with the Table key (F8). The GoTo (F5) and Window (F6) keys are disabled.

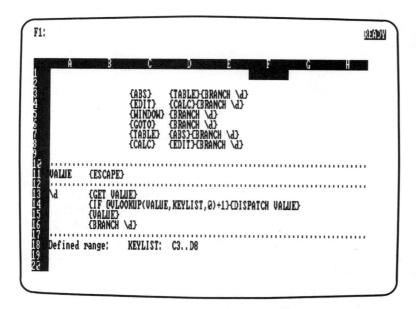

Fig. 12.31. {GET} used to rearrange the function keys.

By pairing the {GET} instruction with a VLOOKUP table, you can create sophisticated keyboard-handling routines that are simple to write. The routine in figure 12.31 is only four lines long. The {IF} and {DISPATCH} instructions, however, are a little complex and deserve a few words of explanation.

The statement

    {IF @VLOOKUP(VALUE,KEYLIST,0)+1}

screens for a specific set of keystrokes by comparing the result of the {GET} instruction with the values in a VLOOKUP table. If the value is not in the table, @VLOOKUP returns an ERR value, which {IF} interprets as FALSE. You must add a 1 to the result of the @VLOOKUP instruction in the {IF} test. @VLOOKUP returns a 0 value if the @VLOOKUP argument is the first item in the lookup table. Therefore, if you don't add the 1, {IF} interprets a lookup to the first item in the table as FALSE.

{DISPATCH} uses a trick to reassign the function keys. The trick is that the /Range Name Labels Right command has been used on the label entries in column C to assign the cells in column D range names equivalent to the keys being reassigned. Therefore, cell D4 has the range name {EDIT}—braces and all. The effect of the {DISPATCH} instruction can be interpreted as "Transfer program control to the cell with the range name contained in VALUE." When VALUE contains the keyword {EDIT}, VALUE's content is interpreted as a range name, and program control is passed to cell D4. Cell D4 contains the {CALC} keyword and a branch back into the \d loop.

This procedure is a little complicated. If you follow the logic step-by-step, however, you will see that pressing the Edit key (F2) causes the program to execute the Calc key (F9) instead. In the case of GoTo (F5) and Window (F6), the program simply branches back to \d. Nothing is executed, and the keys are disabled.

When this program is operating, a slight lag occurs between the time you press the key and the time the result appears. If you type characters too fast, 1-2-3 stops updating the screen, and the character cursor leaves a trail of blanks when it moves. When you pause in your typing, 1-2-3 catches up, and the blanks turn into the characters you typed. Unless you are a very fast typist, you probably won't find this lag too objectionable. The lag, however, can last longer if you put more {IF} statements in the loop.

TRAP: {GET} can't capture all the characters you can type in 1-2-3.

A few limitations apply to using {GET} to capture keystrokes. These limitations relate to what 1-2-3 does or does not execute when the VALUE cell is called as a subroutine. The following keywords are not executable:

  {HELP}

  {STEP}

  {COMPOSE}

The left-brace character ({) is not executable either. 1-2-3 interprets that character as the beginning of a macro keyword. If you press this key in the sample program, an error occurs. You *can* capture a tilde (~) with the {GET} instruction, but the keystroke is executed as if it were an Enter.

You also can't execute any macros, including the Alt-[character] macros.

TRAP: Using {BREAKOFF} with the {GET} instruction can put your program in a loop that the program can't exit.

To stop the execution of all the programs in this section, you must press Ctrl-Break. If you issue a {BREAKOFF} instruction before entering the {GET} loop, you have no way of turning off the program, unless you include a specific test that enables you to escape from the loop. In some cases, you may be able to create deliberately an error that interrupts program execution. For example, you could issue a /File List command and intentionally leave the disk drive door open.

However, you can also write the program so that an error can't be generated. If your program traps the slash (/) and less-than (<) keys, you won't be able to access the command menu and create such an error. Therefore, you may have to turn off the computer to get out of the loop. This situation may be desirable in applications in which you don't want users to access anything outside of specific predefined operations. Such programs, however, can also result in lost data if everything doesn't go as planned. So be careful.

{GETLABEL}, {GETNUMBER}, /xl, and /xn

FUNCTION: The {GETLABEL}, {GETNUMBER}, /xl, and /xn instructions pause program execution, display a prompt, and place the user's response in a specified location.

SYNTAX: {GETLABEL prompt,location}

{GETNUMBER prompt,location}

/xlprompt~location~

/xnprompt~location~

Argument types for *prompt* in {GETLABEL} and {GETNUMBER}:

String, 0 to 73 characters long, entered into the instruction. If the string contains any of the following characters, it must be enclosed in quotation marks:

, ; : }

You can include quotation marks within a string that is set off by quotation marks by using two quotation marks in sequence. For example, suppose that you type the following prompt:

"Type the word ""Hello"" now"

When the instruction executes, the prompt will appear as the following:

Type the word "hello" now

Argument types for *location* in {GETLABEL} and {GETNUMBER}:

Cell address or equivalent range name
Range address or equivalent range name

If the range specified by *location* contains more than one cell, only the cell in the upper left corner of the range is used.

Argument types for *prompt* in /xl and /xn:

String, 0 to 39 characters long, entered into the instruction. The string can't contain either of the following characters:

~

{

All other characters, including quotation marks, will appear in the prompt exactly as they are entered.

Argument types for *location* in /xl and /xn:

Cell address or equivalent range name
Range address or equivalent range name
{?}

If the range specified by *location* contains more than one cell, only the cell in the upper left corner of the range is used.

The *location* argument can be omitted with /xl and /xn, in which case the user's response will be placed in the cell pointer's current location.

DESCRIPTION: All four of these instructions display a prompt in the control panel, pause for you to type something (and press Enter), and place the input into the cell specified by the *location* argument. If *location* is a range, the result is placed in the upper left corner of that range.

The /xl command is the approximate equivalent of the {GETLABEL} instruction, and the /xn command is the approximate equivalent of the {GETNUMBER} instruction. The /xl and /xn commands are carryovers from 1-2-3 Version 1A's macro language and differ from their more modern {GET . . . } counterparts in minor ways, as described in table 12.10.

The basic difference between {GETLABEL} and /xl on the one hand and {GETNUMBER} and /xn on the other is that the former interpret all entries as labels, whereas the latter accept only numeric input. Therefore, if you type a number in response to {GETLABEL} or /xl, the instruction puts the number into the address cell as a left-justisfied label. All label entries created by {GETLABEL} and /xl are left-justified labels. If you type nonnumeric characters in response to

Table 12.10
The /xl and /xn Commands and Their {GET . . . } Counterparts

{GETLABEL} and {GETNUMBER}	/xl and /xn
Entire instruction must appear on one line	Instruction can be on more than one line
Prompt can be 0 to 73 characters	Prompt can be 0 to 37 characters
Quotes included in prompt by using two quote characters in a row	Quotes appear in prompt exactly as entered
Prompt can include any characters (but must be enclosed in quotes for some characters—see text)	Prompt cannot contain ~ or {
Response cannot be entered into current cell pointer location	Response can be entered into current cell pointer location
Maximum length of string response for {GETLABEL} is 80 characters	Maximum length of string response for /xl is 240 characters
{GETNUMBER} enters ERR into *location* cell if response is a string or range name referring to a range address	/xl does not accept string responses or range name referring to a range address
	/xl and /xn can contain embedded command language instructions

{GETNUMBER}, it enters an ERR value in the address cell. If you type nonnumeric characters in response to /xn, you get an Invalid number input error message, and you can make a second entry attempt after you press Esc.

You *can* type a range name in response to {GETNUMBER} or /xn. If the range name refers to a cell address *and* if the range name contains a value, {GETNUMBER} and /xn enter that value into the *location* cell. If the range name specifies a cell that contains a numeric formula, {GETNUMBER} and /xn enter the *value* of that formula into the *location* cell. The result is zero if the named cell is blank. In this sense, {GETNUMBER} and /xn work like the /Range Value command. If the named cell contains a string or string formula, the instructions enter the ERR value into the *location* cell. If the range name entered refers to a range address, {GETNUMBER} enters ERR into the *location* cell, whereas /xn returns an Invalid number input error message.

In response to {GETNUMBER} or /xn, you can also enter a function whose result is numeric—for example, the @DATE function. {GETNUMBER} and /xn put the result rather than the formula into the specific cell. String formulas cause the instruction to enter the ERR result.

According to the 1-2-3 *Reference Manual*, the prompt strings in {GETLABEL} and {GETNUMBER} can't be cell references or formulas. However, as described in Chapter 9, this restriction can be circumvented by making the entire instruction a string formula.

INPUT SCROLLING: The control panel space that these instructions can use is 73 characters wide for {GETLABEL} and {GETNUMBER} and 79 characters wide for /xl and /xn. What space the prompt doesn't use is left for displaying the user's response. If the prompt to {GETLABEL} or {GETNUMBER] occupies 72 of the maximum 73 characters, no space is available for the response, and it won't appear as it's typed. If the prompt is 71 characters long or less, and the response is longer than the space available, the response scrolls to the left as it is entered. Note that the response scrolls across the space remaining after the prompt. If you have a 71-character prompt, your response will show only one character at a time.

If you are a veteran 1-2-3 (Release 1A) programmer, you probably have used /xl and /xn as a form of {?}. With /xl and /xn, you can enter data into the current cell by omitting the *location* argument. Often, this procedure is convenient because the user can relate the control panel prompt to the placement of the cell pointer and make the nature of the requested data more obvious.

With the {GET . . . } instructions, however, you can't use this little trick so easily. Both {GETLABEL} and {GETNUMBER} require *both* their arguments. You can keep a prompt from being displayed by entering the null string (*""*) or simply a comma (,) as the prompt, but you must place the user's response in the cell specified by *location*. To make a {GET . . . } instruction enter the data into the current cell, you must use an intermediate cell as the *location* argument, then give the /**R**ange Value command to copy the data from that cell to the current cell. The sequence of instructions would look something like the following:

```
{GETLABEL "Enter the data",REFCELL}
/rvREFCELL~~
```

You can also use string formula instructions to perform this task—a much more complicated but faster method that is described in the first example in the EXAMPLES section that follows.

GUIDELINE: To make the screen more readable, leave a space and/or a colon after a prompt.

When any of these four instructions displays its prompt and accepts input, no space appears between the prompt and response when they appear in the control panel. The display can therefore look a little cluttered, as you can see in figure 12.32.

You can remedy this situation somewhat if you always end your prompt with a colon. You achieve an even better effect by using a colon and a space. Figure 12.33 shows the {GETLABEL} instruction with a colon and a space added.

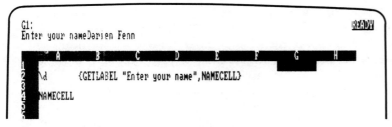

Fig. 12.32. No spaces between the prompt and response.

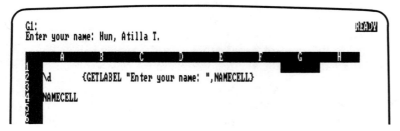

Fig. 12.33. A colon added to help make the response more readable.

GUIDELINE: Anything that can reduce input errors is worth doing.

The space between the prompt and response helps users see what they are entering. The easier inputting data is for the user, the fewer input errors you will have to process.

EXAMPLES: Figure 12.34 shows a complicated {GETNUMBER} application. A long string formula generates a {GETNUMBER} instruction. That instruction places its results into the current cell and uses the data entry range's row and column headings to create a prompt that changes with each entry. The result is a kind of miniature database form.

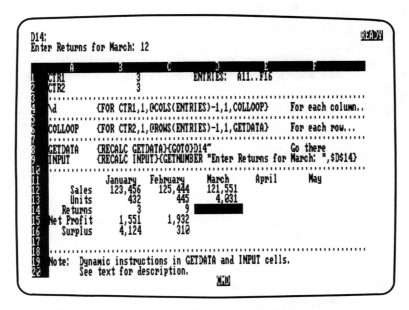

Fig. 12.34. Dynamic prompts and addresses in {GETNUMBER}.

Figure 12.34 also shows the program in action. The ENTRIES range into which the data is being entered includes cells A11..F17. Both instructions that appear in the GETDATA subroutine are the result of string formulas, which are described in the following text. Notice that each instruction begins with a self-recalculation instruction.

Here is a description of the way the program works:

Line 4: {FOR CTR1,1,@COLS(ENTRIES)−1,1,COLLOOP} repeats COLLOOP for each column in ENTRIES, minus the column that contains the headings on the left. Notice that the loop begins by setting CTR1 to one rather than zero, which is the first column in ENTRIES.

Line 6: {FOR CTR2,1,@ROWS(ENTRIES)−1,1,GETDATA} calls the GETDATA subroutine once for each row in ENTRIES—again, minus one to allow for the row containing the headings. The combination of these loop instructions moves through the ENTRIES range, down one column, then up to the top of the next column and down, and so on.

The first instruction in GETDATA is a string formula:

```
+"{RECALC GETDATA}{GOTO}"&@CHAR(CTR1+65)
&@STRING(@CELL("row",ENTRIES)+CTR2,0)&"~"
```

Notice that the address for the {GOTO} instruction is composed of modifications of the CTR1 and CTR2 variables used by the two {FOR} loop instructions. In the second instance, the @CELL function is used to avoid tying the formula to a specific worksheet location. By constructing the ENTRIES range this way, you can move ENTRIES anywhere in the worksheet, and the program will work as intended.

The instruction in INPUT (cell B9) is another string formula:

```
+"{RECALC INPUT}{GETNUMBER ""Enter "
&@INDEX(ENTRIES,0,CTR2)&" for "
&@INDEX(ENTRIES,CTR1,0)&": ""","
&@CELLPOINTER("address")&"}"
```

The prompt in this instruction is constructed from the row and column headings of the ENTRIES range. The prompt begins as follows:

Enter ____ for ____ :

The instruction uses @INDEX functions, which reference the {FOR} loop counters, to insert the headings for the blanks.

The @CELLPOINTER("address") function deposits the data at the cell pointer's current location. Although this part of the formula could have been constructed like the corresponding section in GETDATA, this version is shorter.

By using the @@ function instead of the range name ENTRIES, you could use this module to enter data in any range. You could therefore use such a module, without modification, in any program (for details on using the @@ function, see Chapter 8).

The {GETLABEL} and {GETNUMBER} instructions can be useful for prompting data entry in nonprogram applications. For example, figure 12.35 shows an amortization schedule set up in a worksheet. This short program does nothing more than enter the values used by the formulas in the table. One advantage to entering data by using {GETLABEL} instructions is that more elaborate prompts can be used than might be feasible as worksheet labels. Also, including the variables in a program ensures that users don't overlook any variables during the data entry process. This arrangement can be especially helpful when you go back to a complex worksheet after some time.

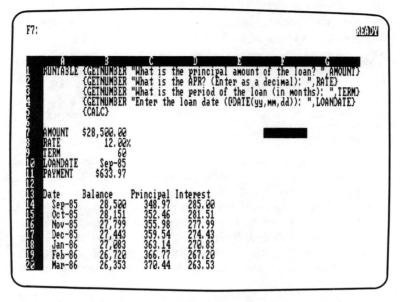

Fig. 12.35. {GETNUMBER} *used to enter data into a worksheet table.*

USING {?} WITH /xl AND /xn: One of the more unusual tricks you can perform with the command language is to combine the {?} instruction with /xl and /xn. Because 1-2-3 treats /xl and /xn as if they were commands entered from the keyboard, you can embed command language instructions in /xl and /xn. When you put {?} inside an /xl or /xn command, 1-2-3 stops and waits for you to specify the prompt that /xl or /xn will use, the destination cell, or both. The order in which the various actions occur when you use this trick can be a little confusing. For instance, the following command enables you to enter the prompt that will be displayed:

/xl{?}~A1~

When this instruction executes, no prompt appears. If you watch the screen closely, however, you will see that the CMD indicator at the bottom of the screen lights up, and 1-2-3 enters EDIT mode. The {?} instruction waits to accept your input. Whatever you type (up to 39 characters) is entered into the system as the prompt that will be displayed. When you press Enter, nothing seems to happen; the EDIT and CMD indicators remain unchanged. But program control is transferred from the {?} instruction to the /xl command, which waits for your response. The prompt you typed is redisplayed exactly where you entered it, so no indication is provided that any change has taken place. Typing data and pressing Enter at this point results in that data being placed in A1.

You can also include {?} with a specified prompt. For example, the following command displays Enter your name: , pauses for you to add to the prompt, and enters the remainder of the prompt when you press Enter.

   /xlEnter your name: {?} Thanks.~A1~

When you use the {?} in place of the *location* specification in /xl or /xn, the sequence of events is even more confusing. For example, if you use the following command, the prompt is not displayed first, as you might expect.

   /xlEnter something: ~{?}~

Rather, the first thing that happens when the command executes is that it stops to get the *location* from your input. The on-screen clues which tell you that this process is taking place are the word POINT in the mode indicator and the appearance of the current cell address in the command line (see fig. 12.36). At this point, you can use the cursor-arrow keys to point to a destination address, or you can type a cell address, range address, or equivalent range name. Whatever you specify becomes the repository for the data you are about to enter. When you press Enter, the prompt appears, and the command operates normally.

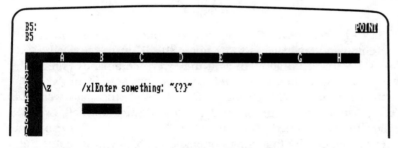

Fig. 12.36. {?} used to enter a destination address in /xl.

If you use {?} instructions in both the *prompt* and *location* arguments, the /xl or /xn command stops first for the prompt, then for the location, and then displays the prompt and stops for input.

Using {?} with /xn or /xl gives you both the flexibility of the {?} instruction and prompts. Although this combination is useful, the way these instructions interact isn't intuitive; users aren't given a clear indication of the steps they are supposed to take at each point along the way. I would advise against using this combination of instructions unless you really have to. In every situation I can think of, you can use other, better command language techniques to achieve the same ends.

{IF} and /xi

FUNCTION: {IF} and /xi control program flow based on the result of a specified test.

SYNTAX: {IF condition}

/xi condition~statement~

Argument types for *condition*:

Boolean expression

The *condition* argument can be either a comparative test or anything that generates a numeric result. The test is FALSE if the result is zero; TRUE, if the result is not zero. If the result is NA or ERR, the {IF} instruction may produce unexpected results (see the following).

DESCRIPTION: {IF}'s syntax always strikes me as a bit odd in appearance. IF condition, then what? The instruction has no second part. In most other computer languages, the consequence of the IF test is also part of the instruction. In the command language, however, the result of the test affects the instruction pointer, which, as you may recall, determines the sequence in which instructions are executed. Usually, 1-2-3 executes all the instructions in a cell, then continues downward until encountering a nonlabel cell. With {IF}, you can divert the regular flow of program execution. The following describes how {IF} works.

{IF the-test-that-appears-here-is-true} then-do-whatever-is-here otherwise-continue-in-this-direction

In other words, {IF} acts as a "gatekeeper" for the instruction pointer when more than one executable function appears on one line. If the result of the test is TRUE, then the "gate" opens, and program flow continues on the same line as the {IF} instruction. If the test is FALSE, the gate does not open, 1-2-3 ignores the instructions following {IF}, and the program continues executing in the cell below the {IF} instruction.

The /xi command (from Release 1A) has a syntax similar to {IF}, as shown here:

/xi<condition>~ do if true otherwise-continue-here

The exact condition for /xi is somewhat more relaxed than for {IF}. The command itself, the conditional test, and the one required tilde may all be on one line or spread among several lines. For example, both of the following equivalent constructions are permissible:

```
/xiA1=1~{BEEP}
/
x
i
A
1
=
1
~{BEEP}
```

Your only syntax restriction is that the statement(s) to be executed if the conditional test is TRUE must be on the same line as the tilde, as shown in the preceding example.

Although there may be special circumstances under which /xi may prove more convenient to use than {IF}, /xi is more difficult to read in a program listing than {IF}, is prone to syntax errors from omitted tildes, and is nine times slower than {IF}. You old Release 1A macro pros will be better off in the long run using {IF}, even if /xi is more familiar initially.

You can use {IF} to construct IF-THEN-ELSE tests. The IF part of this kind of test is usually called the *test*, and the THEN and ELSE parts, each of which can contain numerous instructions, are called *clauses*.

Figure 12.37 demonstrates an IF-THEN-ELSE construction. The program asks the user to specify the drive to be used in a /File Save operation. If the user specifies the A drive, program flow continues on the same line as the {IF} instruction, and the /File Directory is set to A:\, which is equivalent to the THEN clause in IF-THEN-ELSE.

The instruction below the {IF} instruction represents the ELSE clause. Because of the way the test condition is specified, the ELSE clause is executed if the user enters something that does not begin with the letter A. If the user presses Enter or Q, for example, 1-2-3 executes the test condition. This test is actually a test for A vs. anything else, rather than a test of A vs. B, as the prompt suggests. Be careful when you set up such conditions. Make sure that your application can tolerate an "anything else" response. If your application cannot, you should make a more elaborate test or use either the {MENUBRANCH} or {MENUCALL} instruction.

Notice that the THEN clause in this instruction must contain a {BRANCH} instruction. Otherwise, 1-2-3 executes the ELSE clause after the THEN clause.

Depending on the nature of the THEN and ELSE clauses, you can condense the IF-THEN-ELSE construction. For instance, figure 12.38 shows a complete IF-THEN-ELSE on one line. Calling this construction an ELSE-IF-THEN would

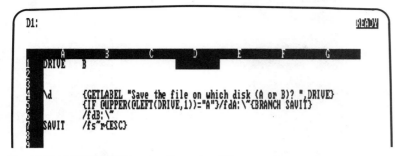

Fig. 12.37. IF-THEN-ELSE construction using {IF}.

probably be more accurate, because 1-2-3 first sets the variable to the value that applies to a FALSE test. 1-2-3 resets the variable to the new value only when the {IF} test is TRUE. This procedure works only for variable assignments or other simple functions. For branching to specific routines or executing commands, use the structure outlined in figure 12.37.

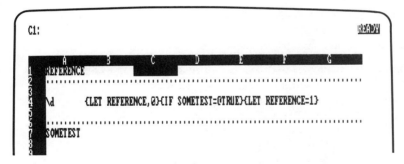

Fig. 12.38. ELSE-IF-THEN construction using {IF}.

MULTIPLE {IF} STATEMENTS: You can use multiple {IF} instructions to generate the equivalent of the logical operations AND and OR. When the {IF} instructions appear on the same line, all the tests that the {IF} instructions contain must be passed (evaluated as TRUE) before 1-2-3 can execute the instructions that follow on that line. This arrangement is equivalent to an AND condition. If you put multiple {IF} instructions on succeeding lines, and any one instruction is passed, then 1-2-3 can execute the conditional instructions. This arrangement is equivalent to an OR condition. Figure 12.39 demonstrates both these situations.

Using AND and OR combinations as the argument of the {IF} instruction is probably easier than using multiple {IF} instructions. Sometimes, however,

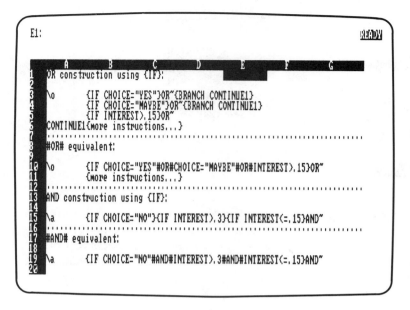

```
E1:                                                          READY

       A      B      C      D      E      F      G
1 OR construction using {IF}:
2
3 \o      {IF CHOICE="YES"}OR~{BRANCH CONTINUE1}
4         {IF CHOICE="MAYBE"}OR~{BRANCH CONTINUE1}
5         {IF INTEREST>.15}OR~
6 CONTINUE1{more instructions...}
7 ..................................................................
8 #OR# equivalent:
9
10 \o      {IF CHOICE="YES"#OR#CHOICE="MAYBE"#OR#INTEREST>.15}OR~
11         {more instructions...}
12 ..................................................................
13 AND construction using {IF}:
14
15 \a      {IF CHOICE="NO"}{IF INTEREST>.3}{IF INTEREST<=.15}AND~
16 ..................................................................
17 #AND# equivalent:
18
19 \a      {IF CHOICE="NO"#AND#INTEREST>.3#AND#INTEREST<=.15}AND~
20
```

Fig. 12.39. AND and OR arrangements of multiple {IF} instructions.

complex logical tests are easier to follow when they are separate instructions. Conversely, the logic of a program with many {IF} instructions is easier to follow when statements on the same line are thought of as representing AND, and sequential statements are thought of as representing OR. (However, the sequential {IF}s are equivalent to OR only if they are followed by the same set of conditional instructions.)

EXAMPLES: You can use {IF} to create some programming constructs that are not supported by built-in 1-2-3 command language instructions. The only kind of loop the command language supports is the {FOR} loop. {FOR} can count and stop the execution of the loop (really a subroutine in 1-2-3) when the count reaches a predetermined high or low value.

Two other kinds of loop exist and are sometimes referred to as DO-WHILE and DO-UNTIL loops. Like {FOR} loops, these loops cause a program to execute series of instructions repeatedly until a specific condition is achieved. The difference between these two loops and the {FOR} instruction is that DO-WHILE and DO-UNTIL don't necessarily use {FOR}'s incremental strategy. Instead, they simply test to see whether a specific condition exists. This procedure is most useful when you don't know in advance the exact number of repetitions required for the loop. If the specified condition is not found, such a loop could run forever.

The only difference between DO-WHILE and DO-UNTIL is what happens when they perform the test that terminates a loop. DO-WHILE makes the test *before* any instructions are executed. If the condition that terminates the DO-WHILE exists when the program first enters the loop, the program doesn't execute the loop at all. DO-UNTIL, on the other hand, performs a test *at the end of the loop*. Therefore, the loop is always executed at least once. DO-WHILE and DO-UNTIL are also known as *top-tested* and *bottom-tested* loops, respectively.

Figure 12.40 shows examples of both loops. This program takes advantage of a feature, new with Release 2, which assigns the value ERR to any range name that has been damaged (by deleting rows, overwriting with the /Move command, and so forth). The /Range Name Table command lists currently assigned range names, and the program counts the number of names *not* labeled as ERR in the list.

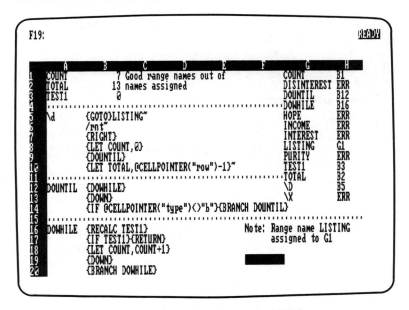

Fig. 12.40. DO-WHILE and DO-UNTIL implemented with {IF}.

Here is an explanation of how the program works:

1. The \d portion of the program sets up the table and calls the DOUNTIL loop.

2. The DOUNTIL loop first calls the DOWHILE loop. (Remember that the DOUNTIL loop always executes at least once.) When the program exits the DOWHILE loop, the program moves the cell pointer down one row and tests for a blank cell, which defines the end of the list.

The program stops if it finds a blank cell; otherwise, the program executes the loop again.

3. The DOWHILE loop first tests to see whether the entry in the current cell is ERR. If the entry is ERR, which indicates that it isn't an active range name, the program exits the loop and doesn't execute the remaining instructions. If the entry is not ERR, the COUNT variable is incremented, the cell pointer is moved down one row, and the loop is repeated. Notice that the test in this loop is in a separate cell (TEST1). This test could easily have been included in the {IF} instruction but was listed this way in order to improve the readability of the program.

TRAP: Beware of the ERR result in formulas used by {IF}.

This program won't work if the test in TEST1 is reversed (to count bad range names instead of good). If the last entry in the list has a value of ERR, as in this example, the program will be in the {DOWHILE} loop. To exit this loop, TEST1 must evaluate to TRUE. However, as the cell pointer drops below the last entry on the list, the cell pointer encounters a blank cell. The comparison in TEST1, @CELLPOINTER("contents")="ERR", is a string formula. If the cell pointer is in a blank cell, the formula tries to compare a string (in the formula) with a numeric cell (as 1-2-3 considers blanks to be), and the result will be ERR rather than TRUE or FALSE. Because ERR within {IF} always evaluates as FALSE, the test can never be satisfied, and no way exists to exit the DOWHILE loop. The program, therefore, runs forever.

{INDICATE}

FUNCTION: The {INDICATE} instruction displays a message in the mode indicator at the top right of the screen. (The *mode indicator* is the five-character reverse-field block in the upper right corner of the screen.)

SYNTAX: {INDICATE [string]}

Argument types for *string*:

String entered into the instruction

The *string* argument can be any character string up to five characters long. If *string* is longer than five characters, 1-2-3 uses only the first five.

The *string* argument does not have to be enclosed in quotation marks unless it contains commas, colons, or semicolons. Figure 12.41 shows how to use quotation marks in the *string* argument to center one character (a quotation mark) in the five-character field. Figure 12.42 shows how to use quotation marks to center a three-character *string* in a five-character field. The quotation marks are necessary in this case because the *string* contains a colon.

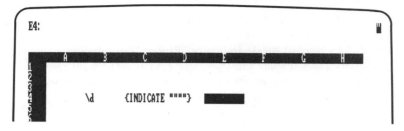

Fig. 12.41. The string *arguments for* {INDICATE}.

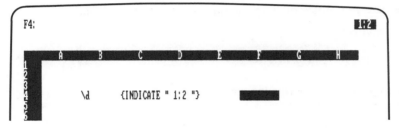

Fig. 12.42. A centered indicator display.

If a comma or semicolon appears in a *string* argument that is not enclosed in quotation marks, only the part of the argument to the left of the delimiter is used. By omitting the *string* argument, you return control of the indicator to 1-2-3's standard display messages. You can also achieve this effect by including in a *string* argument a colon that is not enclosed in quotation marks. You can do so even when the *string* is longer than five characters. A colon anywhere in the *string* returns the indicator to its default (normal) functioning.

You can turn off the indicator by specifying the null string as an argument, as in the following:

   {INDICATE ""}

or

   {INDICATE }

Notice that the second example contains one space between the end of the word INDICATE and the closing brace. Any additional spaces would appear as reverse-field spaces in the indicator.

According to the 1-2-3 *Reference Manual*, you must type the *string* argument in the instruction. You can, however, avoid this limitation by making the entire instruction a string formula, as described in Chapter 9.

DESCRIPTION: You can use {INDICATE} to control what 1-2-3 displays in the mode indicator. When you invoke {INDICATE}, whatever you specify as the argument replaces 1-2-3's normal mode indicator display. Your display continues to override the standard 1-2-3 display until you use {INDICATE} with no argument or with a colon in an argument not enclosed in quotation marks. Control then returns to 1-2-3.

The indicator does not update automatically each time you use the {INDICATE} instruction. Updating takes place the first time the instruction is encountered, when the screen (or, more accurately, the control panel) is updated, or when the program encounters a {PANELON} instruction after a {PANELOFF}. The most rapid way to update the indicator is to include the following in your program:

{PANELOFF}{PANELON}

EXAMPLES:

GUIDELINE: In subroutines that run longer than a minute or two, include some indication of program progress.

{INDICATE} can be useful to customize display presentations and to monitor the progress of a program. Figure 12.43 shows one way to use {INDICATE} to accomplish the latter task.

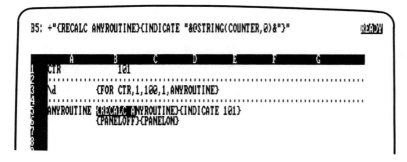

Fig. 12.43. {INDICATE} *used to monitor program progress.*

The program uses the indicator to display the current iteration number of the {FOR} loop that calls the subroutine. This procedure can be useful for programs that run for more than one or two minutes. The user knows that the program is running and can get some idea of how much longer the program will run.

Suppose that you substitute the following for the string formula in the {INDICATE} instruction:

@STRING(100–CTR,0)

The indicator performs a countdown to zero rather than counting up to the upper limit of the count. In general, the longer a program runs, the more important it is to give users an indication that the program is running.

To update the indicator, you can use {CALC}—or, in many cases, the tilde (~)—as an alternative to the {PANELOFF}{PANELON} used in this example. {PANELOFF}{PANELON}, however, is faster for most applications. {RECALC} does not update the display for {INDICATE}.

You can also use {INDICATE} to monitor a program's progress through its various subroutines and main instructions. Used this way, {INDICATE} can be an important debugging tool. See the section on debugging in Chapter 10 for more ideas along these lines.

{LET}

FUNCTION: The {LET} instruction enters values into the worksheet.

SYNTAX: {LET location,expression[:type]}

Argument types for *location*:

Cell address or equivalent range name
Range address or equivalent range name

Argument types for *expression*:

Cell address or equivalent range name
Numeric value or expression
String or string formula
Function
Boolean expression
Combinations of the preceding

Argument types for *type*:

:string
:value

DESCRIPTION: With {LET}, you can enter data into a cell from within a command language program. This instruction is analogous to the LET instruction in BASIC or the := operator in Pascal. You can enter either string or numeric data. By specifying a cell address or cell name as the *expression* argument, you can transfer the value of one cell into another. You can also enter the result of formulas into the cell specified by *location*. In this sense, {LET} acts like the **/R**ange Value command.

One of the most useful applications for formula arguments is to increment variables. By specifying the same cell as the address and as part of a formula in the *expression* argument, you can modify a variable's contents. The following {LET} instruction, for example, increments by 1 the value in the cell named COUNTER:

    {LET COUNTER,COUNTER+1}

If COUNTER had a value of five before this instruction was executed, COUNTER would have the value of six after the instruction was executed.

ARGUMENT TYPES: {LET} acts with what appears to be a certain amount of "intelligence." When you specify an argument for {LET}, either string or numeric, 1-2-3 tries to evaluate the argument as if it were a value. If you use a string or string formula as the *expression* argument, 1-2-3 places a string in the address cell. If you use a number or numeric formula as the *expression*, the result is a number.

TRAP: If 1-2-3 can't evaluate the *expression* argument, the program treats the argument as a string instead of a value.

You can get some unexpected results if you don't enter a formula correctly as the *expression* argument. The result in the DEMO1 cell (G7) in figure 12.44 is the intended result of the {LET} instruction's formula. In row 8, 1-2-3 does not recognize the range name specified in the @SUM statement; and in row 9, the function name is misspelled. Therefore, in both rows 8 and 9, 1-2-3 enters the *expression* argument as a string. This result is, in general, what you can expect from formula errors in a {LET} statement. Sometimes, however, 1-2-3 can recognize a syntax error, as the program does with the last {LET} instruction. When 1-2-3 encounters this instruction, the program generates the error that appears at the bottom of the screen.

My experience with {LET} suggests that you are as likely to get one error result as you are another. When some errors occur, 1-2-3 converts the formula containing the mistake into a string and enters it into the address cell. When other errors occur, 1-2-3 stops executing the command language program and displays an error message.

Sometimes, 1-2-3's automatic evaluation of the *expression* argument doesn't produce the desired result. For example, you may want {LET} to enter the string equivalent of a number rather than the numeric value. In such cases, the optional *type* argument can make 1-2-3 evaluate the *expression* argument as a value or string. Figure 12.45 shows how *type* affects the way {LET} works.

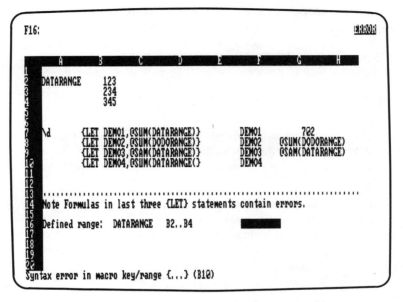

Fig. 12.44. Improper formulas evaluated with {LET}.

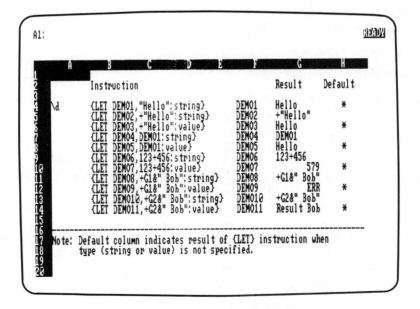

Fig. 12.45. The type argument in a {LET} instruction.

The example shows numerous variations of *expression* and *type* arguments in
{LET} instructions. The result of each instruction appears in column G. Each
expression argument is shown with the *type* specified first as *:string*, then as
:value. Column H indicates which of these results would occur if no *type*
argument were specified and if 1-2-3's default evaluation were used instead.

TRAP: {LET} doesn't accept as an *expression* argument a name assigned to a
range address.

{LET} is tolerant of range names in the *location* argument. The instruction
accepts names assigned to cell addresses, or range addresses. If the range named
contains more than one cell, 1-2-3 deposits {LET}'s result in the upper left
corner of the range.

For the *expression* argument, however, you can use only range names that are
assigned to cell addresses. If you use a name assigned to a range, 1-2-3 does not
evaluate that range's contents and instead treats the range name as a string. The
following examples describes this procedure in more detail. Assume that
DEMO1 contains the label *Hello*.

Instruction:	{LET DEMO2,DEMO1}
Range assigned to DEMO1:	G4
Result placed in DEMO2:	Hello
Instruction:	{LET DEMO2,DEMO1}
Range assigned to DEMO1:	G4..G5
Result placed in DEMO2:	DEMO1

If you try to use the instruction

{LET DEMO2,DEMO1:value}

to make 1-2-3 evaluate the second example as a value, the screen displays the
error message

`Macro: Invalid string in LET ( )`

EXAMPLES: You can use @@ with {LET} to assign values contained in
different cells. The example in figure 12.46 shows {LET} and the @@ function
used with a {FOR} loop.

{LET} uses @@ to specify an "indirect reference" as the *value* argument. With
each pass through the {FOR} loop, 1-2-3 recalculates REFCELL's value. The result
of the formula in REFCELL (shown in the control panel) is a range name, which
{LET} uses as the source for {LET}'s *value* argument. During the last pass
through the loop, the result is placed in the destination cell.

At a less exotic level of programming, you can use the {LET} instruction to
display messages or operator prompts (see fig. 12.47). You can use variations of

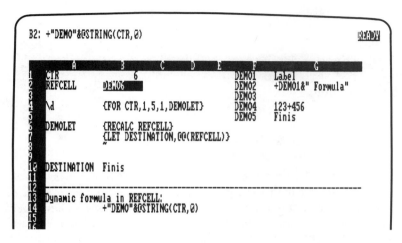

Fig. 12.46. {LET} *using @@ as a* value *argument.*

this program as a program module to provide detailed operator feedback. This level of prompting can be useful for users with little or no computer experience.

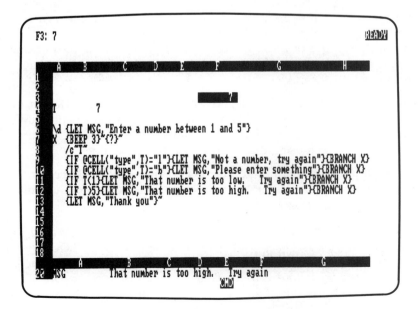

Fig. 12.47. A user-friendly prompting system using {LET}.

{LOOK}

FUNCTION: The {LOOK} instruction checks the status of the keyboard buffer and places the first character the instruction finds in the *location* cell.

SYNTAX: {LOOK location}

Argument types for *location*:

    Cell address or equivalent range name
    Range address or equivalent range name

DESCRIPTION: {LOOK} checks the status of the keyboard buffer. The *keyboard buffer*, sometimes called the *typeahead* buffer, is a limited amount of computer memory (16 characters on a standard IBM PC) that stores keystrokes while the computer is busy doing something else. When the computer is ready, it empties the keystrokes out of the buffer, one at a time, in the same order in which you typed them.

TRAP: Contrary to what is stated in the 1-2-3 *Reference Manual*, {LOOK} doesn't "erase" its target cell.

When 1-2-3 encounters the {LOOK} instruction, the program checks the keyboard buffer to see whether it contains any keystrokes that haven't been processed. If the buffer is empty, {LOOK} enters the null string into its target cell, as specified in the *location* argument. This procedure has the effect of blanking the cell *display*, which is *not* the same as erasing the cell. The null string is a label with a length of zero. A cell containing a null string *looks* blank but is not. If your program is "expecting" this cell to be blank, you could wind up with a hard-to-find error.

If the buffer isn't empty, {LOOK} makes a copy of the keystroke and places it in the target cell. The procedure that {LOOK} uses to store keystrokes is the same procedure that {GET} uses—that is, numbers are stored as label entries, and special keystrokes are entered using the macro keyword conventions.

{LOOK} is similar to {GET}, but has some differences. Figure 12.48 describes what happens before, during, and after 1-2-3 executes each instruction. (Assume that Enter is pressed during program execution.)

If you follow the flow of the example, you will see that {LOOK} can be used to determine whether anything has happened at the keyboard. Usually, {LOOK} is placed inside a loop that repeatedly checks the keyboard. If something *is* typed, any of a number of specific actions can be taken: a branch to another part of the program, a signal to break out of an (otherwise) infinite loop, or a signal to terminate the program.

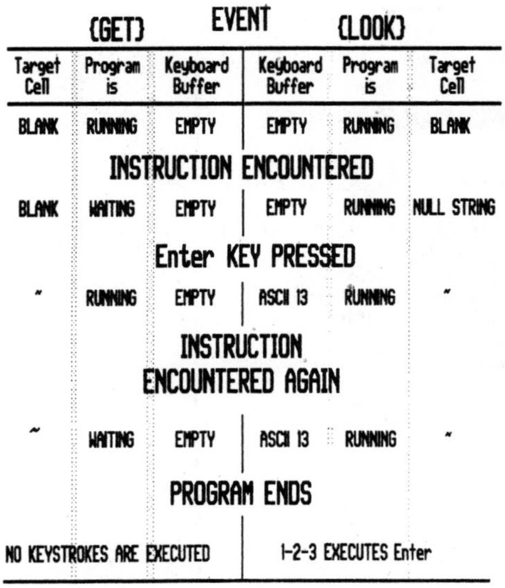

	{GET}		EVENT	{LOOK}		
Target Cell	Program is	Keyboard Buffer	Keyboard Buffer	Program is	Target Cell	
BLANK	RUNNING	EMPTY	EMPTY	RUNNING	BLANK	
			INSTRUCTION ENCOUNTERED			
BLANK	WAITING	EMPTY	EMPTY	RUNNING	NULL STRING	
			Enter KEY PRESSED			
~	RUNNING	EMPTY	ASCII 13	RUNNING	~	
			INSTRUCTION ENCOUNTERED AGAIN			
~	WAITING	EMPTY	ASCII 13	RUNNING	~	
			PROGRAM ENDS			
NO KEYSTROKES ARE EXECUTED			1-2-3 EXECUTES Enter			

Fig. 12.48. Comparison of {LOOK} and {GET}.

Unlike {GET}, {LOOK} does not empty the keyboard buffer. This action makes {LOOK} and {GET} different in two important ways. First, when {GET} empties the keyboard buffer, the instruction "uses up" the keystroke and is no longer available to the system. {LOOK}, on the other hand, leaves the keystroke in the buffer. Therefore, as soon as the program stops or as soon as 1-2-3 encounters any instruction that reads the keyboard, the keystroke is passed through.

Second, because {LOOK} doesn't empty the keystroke from the buffer, additional keystrokes can't be detected. Instead, they are placed in line in the keyboard buffer behind the first keystroke. You must therefore test the target cell from {LOOK} and base subsequent program activity on the results of that test.

EXAMPLES: The example in figure 12.49 uses {LOOK} to break out of an infinite loop. The ALERT subroutine beeps periodically while checking the keyboard. This capability enables you to use your $4,000 computer system to simulate the $5 timer built into your kitchen stove. If you put this subroutine at the end of a long program, the subroutine beeps to tell you that the program is through. You can then turn off the alert signal by pressing any key on the keyboard.

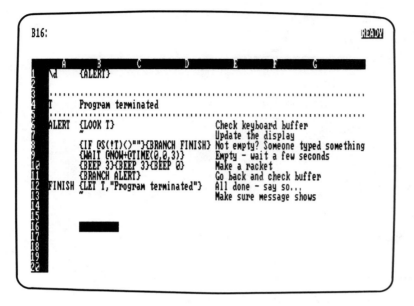

Fig. 12.49. {LOOK} *used to branch out of an infinite loop.*

{MENU}

Undocumented 1-2-3 Release 2 Feature

FUNCTION: {MENU} is an alternative to using the backslash key (\) to invoke the command menu.

SYNTAX: {MENU}

This instruction requires no arguments.

DESCRIPTION: Like the backslash key (\), {MENU} enables you to invoke the command menu from within a command language program or macro. This instruction is completely redundant in the standard form of 1-2-3. {MENU} was likely included, however, for use with add-in programs that will become available later or for compatibility with command language programs written for Symphony.

Although this is pure speculation, some clue to the potential use of this instruction can be derived by looking at how the instruction is used in Symphony. For example, in Symphony's word-processing environment, you can't use the backslash (\) to invoke the command menu, because you need to be able to type the backslash in documents from time to time. Instead, {MENU} is available to call the command menu. If a word-processing add-in is in the works for 1-2-3, {MENU} may provide the means for creating macros or command language programs that can access the command menu.

If you are familiar with Symphony's use of {MENU}, you should be aware of two important differences in using {MENU} in 1-2-3. First, you can't abbreviate {MENU} as {M}, as is possible in Symphony. Second, in Symphony, {MENU} can also take a special form of argument that enables you to control the lists of range names you can use with many commands (equivalent to using the {NAME} key in 1-2-3). With 1-2-3, you can't use {MENU} to perform this special selection function. You can give {MENU} repeat counts as an argument—for example, {MENU 3}—although I know of no constructive use for this feature, other than to make beeps. 1-2-3 considers multiple calls of the command menu to be invalid keystrokes.

{MENUBRANCH}, {MENUCALL}, and /xm

FUNCTION: The {MENUBRANCH}, {MENUCALL}, and /xm instructions create user-defined menus that look and work like standard 1-2-3 menus.

SYNTAX: {MENUBRANCH location}

{MENUCALL location}

/xmlocation~

Argument types for *location*:

Cell address or equivalent range name
Range address or equivalent range name

If you omit the *location* argument with /xm, 1-2-3 will use the current cell pointer address as *location*.

DESCRIPTION: Of all 1-2-3's command language instructions, {MENUBRANCH} and {MENUCALL} (and the release 1A equivalent, /xm) are the most powerful and probably the most useful. You can use them to create your own menus, using the same menu system that 1-2-3 uses for its commands. These custom-made menus follow all the conventions that 1-2-3 uses for its internal menus:

1. The system displays the menu on the top two lines of the control panel and waits for the user to make a selection.

2. The top line of the menu in the control panel contains the short prompt entries for the menu.

3. The second line of the menu contains a long prompt that changes with the corresponding short prompt as the user moves the menu pointer.

4. The user can choose menu items by using the right-arrow and left-arrow keys to change selections, then pressing Enter.

5. The user also can select menu items by pressing the letter corresponding to the first character in the short prompt. Upper- and lowercase keystrokes are equivalent.

6. The Home key moves the pointer to the first menu item. The End key moves the pointer to the last item. The space bar, like the right-arrow key, moves the pointer to the right.

7. Pressing Esc exits the menu.

SETTING UP A MENU: When 1-2-3 encounters a {MENUBRANCH} or {MENUCALL} instruction, the program transfers the instruction pointer to the address indicated (or the upper left corner of the specified range). The structure of the menu which must be at that location differs from other forms of command language instructions.

Figure 12.50 illustrates the form a menu must take. The first line of the menu must be a series of short prompts, and the second line of the menu must contain the long prompts. When you select a menu item, 1-2-3 begins executing instructions in the cell below the long prompt of the selected entry.

The following restrictions apply to menu creation:

1. You must use a {MENUBRANCH} or {MENUCALL} instruction to call the menu. If you {BRANCH} to the location specified by the *location* argument, the strings you entered as short and long prompts are interpreted by 1-2-3 as characters to be typed.

2. You must include a short prompt for each menu entry. If you omit the prompt for the first entry, the screen displays the error message

   `Invalid use of Menu macro command`

   If you omit the short prompt for any entry after the first column of entries, 1-2-3 truncates your menu. For example, if you omit the short prompt on the third menu entry, the menu will have only two selections.

3. When using {MENUBRANCH} or {MENUCALL}, you can't have a number or numeric formula as either the long or short prompt. Blank cells are permitted on the second line; the long prompt is simply omitted when that menu selection is displayed. Any type of numeric

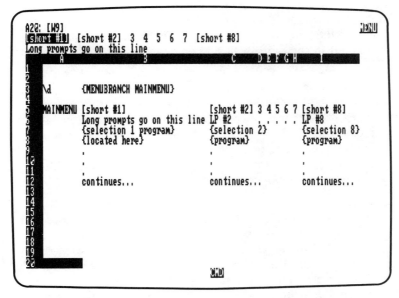

```
A20: [W9]                                                    MENU
[short #1] [short #2] 3 4 5 6 7 [short #8]
Long prompts go on this line
       A            B            C    D E F G H    I
 1
 2
 3  \d       {MENUBRANCH MAINMENU}
 4
 5  MAINMENU [short #1]              [short #2] 3 4 5 6 7 [short #8]
 6           Long prompts go on this line LP #2 . . . . . . LP #8
 7           {selection 1 program}   {selection 2}       {selection 8}
 8           {located here}          {program}           {program}
 9              .                       .                   .
10              .                       .                   .
11              .                       .                   .
12           continues...            continues...         continues...
13
14
15
16
17
18
19
20
                                CMD
```

Fig. 12.50. A menu structure.

entry (including @ERR or @NA) in either the long or short prompt positions causes the menu to be truncated. This restriction, however, doesn't apply to /xm. That command not only uses numbers, formulas, @ERR, or @NA as menu choices, but displays the cell contents formatted with any of the formats except Hidden.

4. A menu can have a maximum of eight menu selections. If you try to include more selections, 1-2-3 ignores them. If you have fewer than eight entries, the cell to the right of the last short prompt entry must be a nonlabel cell (or, in the case of /xm, blank) that identifies the end of the menu list.

5. The long prompt can display a maximum of 80 characters. 1-2-3 ignores additional characters.

6. The short prompts can be of variable length. 1-2-3 automatically places two spaces between the short prompts in the display. As long as the short prompts, plus the additional spaces, don't exceed 80 characters (77 for /xm), 1-2-3 allows any mixture of short prompt lengths, from one to the specified maximum. However, if the total exceeds the 80-character limit, 1-2-3 issues an error message.

7. The short prompts can be any set of characters. With {MENUBRANCH} and {MENUCALL}, however, if you want to be able to select the menu

option by pressing the first letter of the short prompt, you must capitalize the first character in the short prompt. The /xm command capitalizes the first letter in the short prompt automatically, regardless of what you entered in the worksheet.

Any of the other keyboard characters except the space are valid menu selection characters; you can even use compose characters. When you use nonlabel entries as short prompts with /xm, however, the prompt that appears when the menu is activated determines the selection character. For example, if you use a function such as @SUM as a short prompt, the first number displayed in the result will be the selection character. If you change the format to Currency, the dollar sign will be the selection character; if you format to Text, the leading @ sign will be the selection character.

Also applicable to the {MENUBRANCH}, {MENUCALL}, and /xm instructions is a second restriction, which you must observe when constructing your menu in order to take full advantage of the single-character selection feature. Each short prompt must begin with a unique first character. You can repeat first characters, but 1-2-3 always selects the first menu selection that matches the letter entered on the keyboard. You can still select entries with duplicate first characters by pointing to the short prompt and pressing Enter.

Menus present a slight documentation problem. They are in some sense self-documenting because of the detail provided by short and long prompts. Putting a comment line above the menu listing, however, can help you keep track of the menu's function. The problem lies in the fact that the long prompts are usually longer than the column widths of the cells in which the long prompts are placed. Therefore, the entries obscure each other. This arrangement does not affect the macro's operation but does make the entries difficult to read.

One easy way to get a readable listing of the menu prompts is to use the /Range Transpose command to copy the long and short prompts to an area near the actual menu. The short prompts will appear in the left of the two transposed columns, and the long prompts will appear immediately to their right. Figure 12.51 shows the menu from figure 12.50 transposed in this manner.

GUIDELINE: Don't place program code under a menu entry.

The documentation problem becomes more serious when the program code is entered directly under the menu. And because each menu selection must be in a column next to the previous entry, no columns are available for comments and program descriptions. Because program code also can easily overlap adjacent columns, code, too, may be obscured.

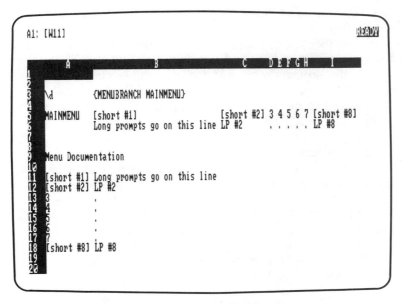

Fig. 12.51. The structure for documenting the prompts in a menu.

A possible solution to this problem is to use very wide column widths in your macro window. Wide columns mean that program code is less likely to be obscured. However, you have no room for comments and have difficulty seeing the whole menu and therefore following its operation.

A better solution is to make the first line of program code under a menu option a {BRANCH} instruction to a named routine. Then each option in your menu is three lines deep, and the menu as a whole is more readable. The program code for each selection (as specified by the {BRANCH} instructions) can be organized in the same fashion as other program modules, with one column each for the routine name, program code, and comments. An example of such organization appears in figure 12.52 in the section on basic menus.

{MENUBRANCH} VERSUS {MENUCALL}: {MENUBRANCH} and {MENUCALL} process menus in the same way. The difference between the instructions involves the flow of the program when the menu or subroutines called by the menu stop processing.

{MENUBRANCH} and /xm are a kind of {BRANCH} instruction. They transfer program control to the menu, then to the routines specified in the menu. The program ends if a menu selection contains no program instructions after the long prompt or when the routine specified by the menu selection ends.

If you use {MENUCALL} instead of {MENUBRANCH}, and either of the these conditions occurs, program execution resumes immediately after the {MENUCALL} instruction (see the "Examples" section). {MENUCALL} is like a call to a named subroutine; when 1-2-3 encounters the end of a subroutine *or* a {RETURN} instruction, the program returns to the instruction immediately after {MENUCALL}. But {MENUCALL} is unlike a named subroutine call in that parameters can't be passed to the subroutine using {MENUCALL} (see {DEFINE} and { . . . subroutine . . . }).

NESTING MENUS: Sometimes, you may want to have menus within menus, as 1-2-3 has in its command structure. You can branch to other menus simply by using a {MENUBRANCH} or {MENUCALL} instruction rather than using the {BRANCH} instruction that follows the long prompt. By carefully arranging {MENUBRANCH} and {MENUCALL} instructions, you can create a hierarchy of menus. Then you can move to a successive level in the menu structure by pressing a specific key or move backward to previous menus by pressing Esc or selecting a quit option. The example in the section on nested menus shows how to construct such a menu hierarchy.

Basic Menus

With the {MENUBRANCH} and {MENUCALL} instructions, you can set up a system of prompts that guides users in program usage. The example in figure 12.52 shows a simple three-option menu that helps users perform the basic tasks associated with entering data into a database.

The menu program shown in figure 12.52 has three basic options. The \m range name that invokes the menu can also be named \0 to make it an autoexecute macro. Then when you load the program, the menu appears automatically. Notice the use of the {BRANCH} instructions and the vertical alignment of the routines, which make the example more readable.

Nested Menus

Figure 12.53 is an extended example of a menu structure. A number of things about this listing are important.

Lines 1–3: These lines list assumptions about the range names and file names used in the program.

Line 5: This instruction starts the program. The instruction's construction is similar to that used in figure 12.52.

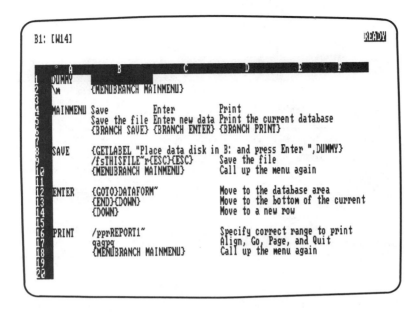

Fig. 12.52. A basic user menu.

Line 6: {BRANCH \m} traps an Esc that is pressed when MAINMENU is active. Including a {BRANCH} instruction in this location forces the user to choose one of the menu selections. The program can exit the routine if the user presses Ctrl-Break. You can trap this possibility by issuing the {BREAKOFF} instruction prior to the {MENUBRANCH}; then the user can't exit the menu system without selecting a menu option. Use this technique if you are setting up a system in which you want to limit possible user responses.

Lines 8–11: These lines comprise the MAINMENU, which is identical to that in figure 12.52 except for the addition of the fourth option and the use of {MENUCALL} in line 10. {MENUCALL} makes the program easier to follow. For example, when you look at the {MENUCALL} instruction in the SAVE selection, you know immediately that the program processes the SAVE routine, then returns to this menu. This arrangement is better than giving control to the routine and having a {BRANCH} or {MENUBRANCH} at the end of that routine, because you don't have to look all over the page to locate the routine and find out how it stops. Another reason for making the program flow this way is that you create a situation in which exiting the menu by pressing Esc returns you to the same place as pressing Enter does. This arrangement also makes the program easier to follow.

```
 1 Assumptions:  Database name is DATA_DB
 2               File name is THISFILE
 3               The line immediately above DATA_DB is empty
 4 --------------------------------------------------------------------------------
 5 \m            {MENUBRANCH MAINMENU}
 6               {BRANCH \m}
 7 --------------------------------------------------------------------------------
 8 MAINMENU      Save              Enter            Print            Initialize
 9               Save the file     Enter new data   Print the current Erase all records
10               {MENUCALL SAVE}   {BRANCH ENTER}   {MENUCALL PRINT} {MENUCALL INITIALIZE}
11               {BRANCH \m}                        {BRANCH \m}      {BRANCH \m}
12 --------------------------------------------------------------------------------
13 SAVE          Place a data disk in drive B: and  Use a menu
14               Press Enter                          as a prompt
15               /fsTHISFILE~r{ESC}{ESC}            Save the file
16 --------------------------------------------------------------------------------
17 ENTER         {GOTO}DATA_DB~                      Move to the database area
18               {END}{DOWN}                         Move to the bottom of the current entries
19               {DOWN}                              Move to a new row
20 --------------------------------------------------------------------------------
21 PRINT         Listing           Summary          Assumptions      Quit
22               Print the data base Print the listing Print the assumptiReturn to the main menu
23               {PSUB REPORT1}    {PSUB SUMMARY}   {PSUB ASSUMPTIONS}
24               {MENUBRANCH PRINT} {MENUBRANCH PRINT} {MENUBRANCH PRINT}
25 --------------------------------------------------------------------------------
26
27 PSUB          {DEFINE RNAME}                     Parameter storage cell
28               /ppcrr                             Clear range and
29 RNAME                                              enter new range
30               ~
31               qagpq                              Align, Go, Page, and Quit
32
33 --------------------------------------------------------------------------------
34 INITIALIZE    No                      Yes
35               ARE YOU SURE? THIS OARE YOU SURE? THIS OPTION DELETES ALL DATA IN DATABASE!!!
36               {RETURN}                {ERASEIT}
37 --------------------------------------------------------------------------------
38 ERASEIT       {GOTO}DATA_DB~                     Goto the database range
39               /c{END}{RIGHT}~{UP}~               Save the database header
40               {BLANK DATA_DB}                    Erase the database range
41               {UP}
42               /c{END}{RIGHT}~{DOWN}~             Copy range names from above range
43               /rncDATA_DB~                       Adjust the size of the named database range
44               {END}{UP}~                           by moving the bottom to the top
45 --------------------------------------------------------------------------------
46 MENU DOCUMENTATION
47
48 MAINMENU
49 Save          Save the file
50 Enter         Enter new data
51 Print         Print the current database listing
52 Initialize    Erase all records
53
54 PRINT
55 Listing       Print the database
56 Summary       Print the listing
57 Assumptions   Print the assumptions
58 Quit          Return to the main menu
59
60 INITIALIZE
61 No            ARE YOU SURE?  THIS OPTION DELETES ALL DATA IN DATABASE!!!
62 Yes           ARE YOU SURE?  THIS OPTION DELETES ALL DATA IN DATABASE!!!
63 --------------------------------------------------------------------------------
```

Fig. 12.53. A program that uses {MENUCALL}, {MENUBRANCH}, nested menus, and message menus, and enables you to press Esc to move backward through the menu hierarchy.

When a routine terminates, the program loops back to MAINMENU. In line 11, the {BRANCH \m} instruction is used rather than {MENUBRANCH MAINMENU} to trap the Esc response. With {MENUBRANCH} in this location, a second Esc would cause the program to try to execute the cell below the {MENUBRANCH} instruction. Because the cell is blank, the program would then stop instead of looping back to MAINMENU.

Line 13: The menu here is simply a prompt (see fig. 12.54 for another example). The menu offers only one choice, so the only executable instructions immediately follow the menu. This method is slightly shorter than that used in figure 12.52 because no dummy cell is required to intercept the response from {GETLABEL}. Also, the user can press Esc to abort the save operation. If the user pressed Esc in the previous example, 1-2-3 would save the file anyway.

Line 17: The ENTER routine is the same as that in figure 12.52.

TIP: A menu that branches back to itself enables you to select several options in a row by typing a string of characters.

Lines 21–24: The PRINT routine in figure 12.52 has been replaced with a menu that enables the user to select a specific area to print. Notice that all the print option sections end with a {MENUBRANCH} back to the Print menu. Therefore, the user can select combinations of print areas simply by typing a sequence of characters. For example, if, at this menu level, you type ASL, 1-2-3 first prints the Assumptions portion of the worksheet. Then the routine branches back to the menu, where the S waiting in the keyboard buffer selects the Summary option for printing; after that section prints, the final L waiting in the keyboard buffer actuates the Listing option in the print menu and prints the database listing.

Because the print routines loop back to the Print menu, the Quit option was added. This selection has no program instructions. Because a {MENUCALL} instruction calls the Print menu, the entire process runs as a subroutine. When the user selects Quit, the program encounters the blank cell, which is equivalent to {RETURN} in a routine. The program then "returns" to the instruction following the {MENUCALL PRINT} instruction in line 10. Pressing Esc at this menu would have the same effect.

TIP: To minimize program code, use subroutines whenever possible.

Line 23: Notice here that all the print options use the same subroutine. The parameter passed with the subroutine call specifies the area to be printed (see the description for line 27).

Lines 27–31: You can use the PRINT subroutine as a module in almost any program. The {DEFINE} instruction loads the name parameter into RNAME, where 1-2-3 uses the name parameter as a range specification. When this subroutine stops, it returns program control to the instruction immediately following the subroutine call, which in all cases is the {MENUBRANCH} to the Print menu.

TIP: Include a "last chance" menu whenever an option can destroy data.

TIP: Always put the No option (or the option that enables users to change their minds) first.

Lines 34–36: The menu here acts as a "last chance to change your mind menu," like the menu that 1-2-3 uses when you save files and erase the worksheet. The first option is No rather than Yes. Making No the first option is a safety feature—that is, if you inadvertently press Enter, the process aborts. Notice also the use of capital letters in the long prompt. Uppercase is another way to emphasize the danger that exists here. The long prompt is the same for both options (see the documentation of the menus in lines 46–62).

TRICK: You can make users select a menu option by pointing instead of using the single-character selection method.

Line 34: The Yes option in this line is not exactly aligned with the prompt below it, because the Yes option was entered with a leading space. Therefore, because 1-2-3 interprets a space as a right-arrow keystroke, you can't use the letter-selection method. When you want to take all measures possible to guard against users accidentally deleting data when using a menu, use this arrangement to add one more level of deliberate decision-making to the process.

Unfortunately, a user who is expecting the first-character method to work may become confused. If you are going to use this method with new users, you should probably include in the long prompt a notation which states that the point method must be used.

Line 36: The {RETURN} instruction is optional here. A blank cell would serve the same purpose. You can include the {RETURN} to emphasize what happens when this option is selected.

Lines 38–44: The fairly self-explanatory routine here erases the database range.

A reminder: The lines separating the subroutines in this program are the result of @REPEAT("–",110) placed in the same column as the range name headers. The cell to the right of each of these entries is blank and *must* be blank. Otherwise, the execution of the subroutines will run together. Visually marking off routines helps readability. Be sure, however, that you don't attempt to separate the routines with a repeating label (\–) copied across all columns; if you forget and use the repeating label this way, your routines will not return or quit properly, and your program may type dashes into your worksheet.

Lines 46-62: This area of the listing is not an executing part of the program, but is documentation for the menus. You should always create a secondary listing of menus such as this, so that all of the menu is readable. The listing is created by using the **Range Transpose** command to make a copy of each menu that is rotated 90°. With the rotated listing, none of the entries, especially the long prompts, overlap.

Message Menus

The previous program contained an example of a "message menu" (see line 13), which is simply a way to use 1-2-3's menu facility to display a prominent message in the control panel. This example is being repeated here to demonstrate the striking messages that you can create.

Figure 12.54 shows a message menu and the result of executing the menu. This example is constructed using a subroutine call that allows the menu to display messages from a list. The message string is passed as a parameter by the subroutine call. This parameter contains an @INDEX instruction, which selects a message from a range that contains a list of messages. The MNUMBER variable determines which message 1-2-3 displays from the MESSAGELIST range. Notice that the emphasized message, which appears highlighted on the screen, is actually the short prompt.

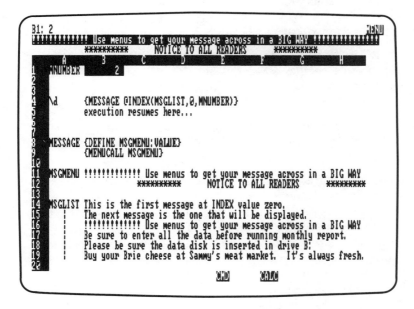

Fig. 12.54. A message menu module with variable message content.

{ONERROR}

FUNCTION: The {ONERROR} instruction causes a program branch to a specified location if an error occurs.

SYNTAX: {[ONERROR branch,message]}

>   or

>   {ONERROR}

Argument types for *branch*:

> Cell address or equivalent range name
> Range address or equivalent range name

Argument types for *message*:

> Cell address or equivalent range name
> Range address or equivalent range name

DESCRIPTION: {ONERROR} causes program execution to transfer to the address specified by *branch* when an error occurs during program execution. An *error* in this sense is defined as any condition that causes 1-2-3 to interrupt its command processing and display an error message in the bottom left corner of the screen. Such conditions include manual interruption of a program or command by pressing Ctrl-Break. They don't include formula errors that generate an ERR result in the worksheet.

With {ONERROR}, you can create programs that tolerate user mistakes and unexpected system problems, such as a disk-full situation. If you couldn't use {ONERROR} to trap errors, you might be forced to start a program over from the beginning and lose whatever work you had done before the error occurred.

Error trapping is essential when a system is being created for inexperienced users. Nothing is more frustrating for new users than trying to operate a "black box" program that doesn't do what users think it is supposed to do.

The optional *message* argument is a location in which 1-2-3 stores the message generated by the error. You probably will want to include this parameter when you use {ONERROR}. When {ONERROR} is in effect, the error messages don't appear in the bottom left corner of the screen. Therefore, if you don't specify the *message* parameter, you have no way of knowing what error has occurred. Also, if you want a program to take specific actions for specific errors, you must use the message string returned by 1-2-3 so that the program can determine what action to take.

EFFECTS OF PRESSING CTRL-BREAK: If you press Ctrl-Break during program execution, a Break error message appears. If, however, you issue the {BREAKOFF} instruction in a program, pressing Ctrl-Break no longer generates an error; 1-2-3 ignores the Ctrl-Break keystroke.

{ONERROR}'S LIMITATIONS: After the {ONERROR} instruction is issued, it remains in effect until one of three things occurs:

1. The program terminates.

2. 1-2-3 encounters another {ONERROR} instruction, in which case, the new {ONERROR} overrides the old {ONERROR}. Only one {ONERROR} instruction can be in effect at a time.

3. An error occurs. After an error occurs, {ONERROR} is "used up," and 1-2-3 does not trap subsequent errors. If you want to continue trapping errors, you must reissue an {ONERROR} instruction. A good way to begin error trapping again is to put an {ONERROR} instruction in the error-handling subroutine.

{ONERROR} performs a branch rather than a subroutine call. This limitation is serious. BASIC, which has a similar statement, has a companion instruction called RESUME that restarts the program at or just after the place in the program in which the error occurred. With 1-2-3, if you want to return to the place where the error happened, you must insert extra program code to keep track of where the problem occurred. This procedure can be tricky from a programming point of view because you have to be sure that the program reenters at the right place, neither skipping any essential program steps nor repeating any steps that shouldn't be duplicated. Trying to duplicate every possible error condition to test the error-handling subroutines is difficult and time-consuming. Therefore, these subroutines often will be a source of program failure. You may be tempted simply to leave them out of the program.

Keeping track of the error locations is possible, at least for the most predictable kinds of error. The example that follows includes some suggestions on ways to accomplish this task.

TURNING OFF ERROR TRAPPING: You can disable (turn off) the {ONERROR} condition, even if an error has not occurred, by placing the following, with no argument, in your program:

{ONERROR}

To turn error trapping back on, you must include in your program another {ONERROR} statement (with arguments).

EXAMPLE: Figure 12.55 shows how to set up an error-trapping system. The example system includes two routines that could be called as subroutines from a main program. The system assumes that the various databases are being loaded one at a time into one worksheet.

The two routines in figure 12.55 perform a /File Xtract (FSAVE) and a /File Combine (FCOM) to move the database information into and out of the worksheet. Each subroutine uses the same error-trapping routine (DISKERROR) to trap the possible errors. Because both file subroutines use only one error-trapping routine, each calling subroutine must set up a return address that 1-2-3 can use after an error condition has been corrected. To accomplish this task, both FSAVE and FCOM use a {LET} instruction to store their subroutine names in the cell named, naturally enough, ROUTINE. Because the original subroutine name is used as a reentry address, 1-2-3 reexecutes the entire subroutine after an error has occurred and has been corrected in the error-trapping routine. You may choose, however, not to use this strategy to handle errors. You can specify a different reentry point by using a different routine name.

The heart of the error-trapping routine is the table in lines 4–12, which has the range name ERRORLIST. In the left column of the table is a list of error messages that disk operations can generate. These messages appear *exactly* as 1-2-3 issues them. They must be exact copies so that @VLOOKUP in line 54 can use them. (Recall that the LOOKUP functions must have exact string matches.)

In the next column of the table are responses that appear when an error occurs. These responses prompt the user about correcting the error. A one-item menu displays both the error and the user prompt. The whole point of having an error-trapping routine is to keep the program from crashing (terminating prematurely) when something unexpected occurs. Some error conditions can be detected and corrected automatically, but other error conditions, such as those this program traps, must be manually corrected by the user. Therefore, detailed prompts that guide the fix-up efforts are desirable.

Lines 4–12: These lines show a list of possible error messages and responses that appear when an error is encountered. See the preceding section for more information.

Line 16: The cell called ROUTINE is a reference cell for the two disk operation subroutines. As 1-2-3 executes each of these subroutines, the program places that subroutine's name in this cell. The {DISPATCH} instruction in line 58 uses the name as a return address at the end of the error-handling subroutine.

Line 17: The cell called MESSAGE is used in the *message* argument for the {ONERROR} instructions in lines 25 and 38.

```
1  -------------------------------------------------------------------------------------------
2            Error                        Response
3
4  ERRORLIST File does not exist         Possible reasons: Misspelled name; Wrong directory; Wrong disk
5      !     Disk drive not ready        Possible reasons: Disk drive door open; Disk inserted incorrectly
6      !     Disk error                  Could be system error.  Try again (be sure you are using a formatted disk).
7      !     Illegal file format         Probably not a worksheet file, or file has been damaged.
8      !     Directory does not exist    Possible reasons: Misspelled directory name; Wrong disk; Directory not created
9      !     Disk is write-protected     Please remove write protect tab and try again.
10     !     Invalid character in file name Punctuation not allowed.  Begin name with A..Z, numbers okay thereafter.
11     !     Disk full                   NOTE!! File has not been saved.  Insert a new, formatted disk and try again.
12     !     Cannot create file          Possible reasons: Subdirectory not found; Wrong disk; Illegal file name
13
14
15
16 ROUTINE   FCOM                                                    Name of routine generating error
17 MESSAGE   Disk drive not ready                                    Error message from 1-2-3
18 DBREF     DATA_DB                                                 Database name used
19
20
21 -------------------------------------------------------------------------------------------
22 Note:  This routine saves only the database range specified in DBREF
23
24 FSAVE     {LET ROUTINE,"FSAVE"}                                   Store name for return from error routine
25         {ONERROR DISKERROR,MESSAGE}                              Set error trap
26         {LET DBNAME,DBREF}                                       Make sure database name is current
27         {GETLABEL "Enter the file name to use for saving the database: ",FNAME}   /File Xtract command
28         /fxv                                                     File name entered from {GETLABEL}, above (initially blank)
29 FNAME                                                            File name entered from {GETLABEL}, above (initially blank)
30         ~                                                        Enter name into command
31 DBNAME                                                           Extract range (initially blank)
32         ~                                                        Complete command
33
34 -------------------------------------------------------------------------------------------
35 Note: This routine combines a file into the database range specified by DBREF
36
37 FCOM      {LET ROUTINE,"FCOM"}                                    Store name for return from error routine
38         {ONERROR DISKERROR,MESSAGE}                              Set error trap
39         {RECALC NAMEREF}                                         Update string formula commands
39         {GETLABEL "Enter the name of the database file to edit: ",FNAME2}
41         {DOWN 19}{UP}/wwu/wwh                                    Split window temporarily
42         {UP 17}{WINDOW}                                          Restore curser position & switch windows
43 NAMEREF  {GOTO}DATA_DB~          +"{GOTO}"&DBREF&"~"             Dynamic instructions: locate load point
44 NAMEREF  /reDATA_DB~             +"/re"&DBREF&"~"                Clear current data
45         /fcce                                                    /File Combine command
46 FNAME2                                                           File name from {GETLABEL}, above (initially blank)
47         ~                                                        Enter name into command
48         /wwc                                                     Return to original window
49
50 -------------------------------------------------------------------------------------------
51 This is the error-handling routine for disk operations
52
53 DISKERROR {BEEP 3}{BEEP 0}                                       Signal
54         {LET ERRMSG2,@VLOOKUP(MESSAGE,ERRORLIST,1)}             These two lines set an error message
55         {LET ERRMSG,+"### ERROR ### ("&MESSAGE&") Correct and press Enter":value}
56         {IF @ISERR(ERRMSG)}{LET ERRMSG,"Non-Disk Error"}       If the message is not in list, give another message
57         {MENUCALL ERRMSG}                                       Display the error message
58         {DISPATCH ROUTINE}                                      Return to the calling routine
59 -------------------------------------------------------------------------------------------
60 The following two lines are a menu used to display a Message
61
62 ERRMSG    ### ERROR ### (Disk drive not ready) Correct and press Enter
63 ERRMSG2   Possible reasons: Subdirectory not found; Wrong disk; Illegal file name
```

Fig. 12.55. An error-trapping system that uses {ONERROR}.

Line 18: The DBREF cell is used as a reference for the disk subroutines. This cell names the database range used in the /File Combine and /File Xtract operations. You could type the database name into the program instructions, but your program will be more flexible if you use named references such as this.

You can change the entry in this cell either manually or with the program. 1-2-3 then alters all the listed subroutines accordingly.

Lines 24–28: The FSAVE routine is fairly well-documented by the comments in the listing. Notice the use of the {GETLABEL} instruction to enter directly into the FSAVE routine the name of the file to be saved.

Lines 37–45: The FCOM routine is similar to FSAVE, except that FCOM must reference the name of the database in two locations. Rather than use two {LET} instructions, as was done in the FSAVE routine, 1-2-3 enters the database references into the program as string formula dynamic instructions in lines 43 and 44. The string formulas in the left column are shown to the right of that column. You can't use the /Range Name Labels Right command to create the range name NAMEREF, because the range name encompasses two cells. The names in the far left column are for reference only.

Line 53: The two {BEEP} instructions tell the user that an error has occurred.

Line 54: The {LET} instruction copies the response from the ERRORLIST table in lines 4–12 to the menu location where this response will be displayed. Note that the @VLOOKUP formula could be entered directly into the menu area, in which case you would need to replace the {LET} instruction in line 54 with {RECALC ERRMSG2}.

Line 55: The {LET} instruction assembles the short prompt that will appear in the first line of the message menu. Note that the short prompt that results includes a listing of the actual error message, as referenced by the MESSAGE cell in line 17.

Line 56: This line enters something into the menu area when the trapped error does not appear in the ERRORLIST table. Without this line, the program would halt and display the error message

    Invalid use of Menu macro command

Line 57: The instruction here calls the menu set up by the previous instructions. The menu displays the error message and response prompt, and halts program execution until the user presses Enter.

Line 58: The {DISPATCH} instruction returns the program to the beginning of the subroutine in which the error occurred, allowing the program to continue.

{OPEN}

FUNCTION: The {OPEN} instruction opens a DOS file for subsequent operations.

SYNTAX: {OPEN filename,mode}

Argument types for *filename*:

Literal string
String formula
Cell address or equivalent range name

The literal string must be enclosed in quotation marks if it contains the following delimiters:

, ;

The *filename* argument must conform to the operating system's name conventions. If you include a drive or path specification in the *filename* and enter it directly into the {OPEN} instruction, you must enclose the *filename* in quotation marks—for example,

{OPEN "A:TESTFILE.TXT",W}

Argument types for *mode*:

READ
WRITE
APPEND   *(Undocumented Release 2 Feature)*
MODIFY

Because 1-2-3 uses only the first character of each argument, you can specify the argument by using one character, either lower- or uppercase. Although you can enclose the argument in quotation marks, this procedure is not required. If characters other than R, W, A, or M are specified, 1-2-3 treats those other characters as R (READ). You can't use cell references or formulas for the *mode* argument.

WRITE sets up the operating system interface so that data can be output to a disk file, using {WRITE} or {WRITELN}. When 1-2-3 executes this instruction, the program checks to see whether the file exists on the disk. If the file is not on the disk, 1-2-3 creates a file with a length of zero bytes. Because the WRITE option usually positions the file pointer at the beginning of the file, any data output is entered starting at the beginning of the file. (You can change the file pointer's position in the file by using the {SETPOS} instruction.) Note that you must use {CLOSE} to close the file; 1-2-3 is then forced to write to disk all the data in the file buffer and enter the file information into the disk directory.

APPEND opens an existing file and positions the file pointer at the end of the file. If the file does not exist on the disk, an error occurs. Usually, APPEND is used to add to an existing file and is otherwise identical to the WRITE option.

READ opens an existing file to allow 1-2-3 to read data into the worksheet, using subsequent {READ} or {READLN} instructions. If the file does not exist, an error occurs. After a file is opened for READ, the file pointer is positioned at the beginning of the file.

MODIFY opens an existing file for reading and writing purposes. If the file does not exist, an error occurs. After a file is opened for the MODIFY operation, the file pointer is positioned at the beginning of the file.

For more detailed information on file operations, see Chapter 11.

SPECIAL OPERATIONS: The {OPEN} command works with standard DOS files. Therefore, you also can use the standard output device names—CON, PRN, LPT1, COM1, and so on—instead of file names. When you use these device names, subsequent {READ}, {READLN}, {WRITE}, and {WRITELN} instructions can receive input from the keyboard (CON) or a serial port (COMx), or send output to the screen (CON), printer (PRN or LPTx), or serial port (COMx).

ERROR HANDLING: Errors encountered during command language file operations don't generate a 1-2-3 error. 1-2-3 enables you to manage in a special way any errors arising from the use of the command language file instructions. For instance, if an error occurs during an {OPEN} operation—as happens when you try to READ a file that doesn't exist—program execution continues in the same line as the {OPEN} instruction. When the {OPEN} operation is successful, program execution continues on the line immediately following {OPEN}. This error-trapping scheme therefore requires that the {OPEN} instruction be the last instruction (except for the error-handling instructions associated with {OPEN}) on a line that contains multiple instructions.

{PANELOFF} and {PANELON}

FUNCTION: {PANELOFF} and {PANELON} disable and enable the updating of the control panel, respectively.

SYNTAX: {PANELOFF}

{PANELON}

Neither instruction requires arguments.

DESCRIPTION: {PANELOFF} and {PANELON} switch off and on, respectively, the display that usually appears in 1-2-3's control panel (the uppermost three lines of the screen and the bottom line of the screen). A {PANELOFF} condition is in effect only during program execution. As soon as the program terminates, the control panel is automatically reactivated. When 1-2-3 executes a {PANELOFF} instruction, the control panel display "freezes."

When program execution or a {PANELON} condition reactivates the display, it may not accurately reflect 1-2-3's current status. 1-2-3 updates only the parts of the control panel that change as the program executes commands. Therefore, any updating that takes place may leave the control panel in a partially updated state, as shown in figure 12.56.

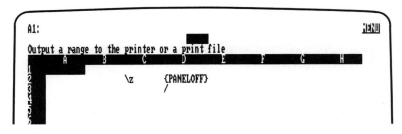

Fig. 12.56. The control panel left in a partially updated state by {PANELOFF}.

{PUT}

FUNCTION: The {PUT} instruction enters information into a specified row and column location of a range.

SYNTAX: {PUT range,column,row,contents[:type]}

Argument types for *range*:

　Cell address or equivalent range name
　Range address or equivalent range name

Argument types for *column*:

　Number or numeric expression
　Cell address or equivalent range name
　@@

Argument types for *row*:

　Number or numeric expression
　Cell address or equivalent range name
　@@

Argument types for *contents*:

Number or numeric expression
String or string formula
Cell address or equivalent range name
@@

Argument types for *type*:

:string
:value

The target address for the @@ function, as specified by @@'s *pointer* argument, should be in the form of a cell address or equivalent range name. Although specifying a range address or equivalent range name doesn't necessarily cause an error, @@ returns a zero instead of the value contained in the target cell.

The *column* and *row* arguments refer to the column and row offsets of a particular cell within a range. Offsets, as with all other 1-2-3 functions, begin numbering with zero. Therefore, the upper left corner of the range has an offset of 0,0. The offsets can be entered as constants into the instruction or referenced with a cell address or equivalent range name that refers to a cell address. Any form of range address for these arguments causes the error

`Invalid integer in PUT`

If the *range* argument is a single cell, both *column* and *row* must be zero. If either argument is larger than the corresponding number of columns or rows in the specified range, the following error occurs:

`Invalid offset in PUT`

As with the {LET} instruction, you can specify *contents* as a string or numeric value by adding the optional *type* suffix. The syntax for *type* is identical to that for {LET}.

DESCRIPTION: With the exception of the *column* and *row* arguments, {PUT} is exactly like {LET}. The *column* and *row* arguments enable you to place the value of the *contents* argument in any cell within a range. For more details, see {LET}.

{PUT} is a companion to the @INDEX function. @INDEX can extract the contents of a specific cell within a range, whereas {PUT} can place values in any of those cells. Using @INDEX as the argument for {PUT} enables you to increment any cell within a range. This procedure is similar to the method used with {LET} to increment the values in cells. For example, the {LET} instruction that adds 1 to the value in REFCELL would be

{LET REFCELL,REFCELL+1}

The equivalent {PUT} instruction is more complex. To add 1 to the value in the third column (offset 2), fifth row (offset 4) of the range DATARANGE, you would use

{PUT DATARANGE,2,4,@INDEX(DATARANGE,2,4)+1}

EXAMPLE: {PUT} has the potential to be one of the most powerful command language instructions because you can use it with @INDEX to manipulate any cell in a worksheet. By using cell references as *offset* arguments in {PUT} and @INDEX, and by using those same cell references as *counter* arguments in a {FOR} instruction, you can make {FOR} loops and other numeric expressions manipulate the worksheet cells.

The program in figure 12.57 performs a search-and-replace operation on a specified range. Performing without regard to the original cell's label prefix, the program searches for all occurrences of the string *1986* and replaces each with the string *1987*. To perform the operation on the entire worksheet, you simply define the W range to be equal to the area of the worksheet.

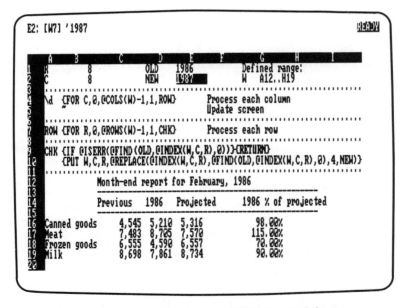

Fig. 12.57. {PUT} *used to search and replace values in a worksheet.*

In figure 12.57, the range names have been abbreviated to one or two characters so that the rather complicated instruction in line 10 can fit on the screen. You will probably want to use more readable range names.

If you plan to use this method of searching and replacing cell entries, you should keep its two limitations in mind. First, {PUT} can create only left-justified label entries. If you have used centered label prefixes for cosmetic alignment purposes, that arrangement would be altered.

Second, this method is very slow. On a standard IBM PC, the program can process in about 0.2 seconds a cell that does not contain the search string and can take as long as 0.6 seconds to process a cell that contains a long string. If you use the program on a worksheet with 60 columns and 300 rows, and if only 1 percent of the label cells requires replacement, the procedure would take

$$(60 * 300 * .01 * .6) + (60 * 300 * .99 * .2) = 3672 \text{ seconds} =$$
1 hour, 1.2 minutes

As slow as this method is, it may be preferable to changing 180 labels by hand. I run programs this long (or longer) during lunch or overnight. If you have a math coprocessor chip installed, the time should be reduced by about 20 percent. Machines based on the 80286 processor, such as the IBM PC AT or COMPAQ Deskpro 286®, run 3 to 4 1/2 times faster than the times stated.

{QUIT} and /xq

FUNCTION: The {QUIT} and /xq instructions terminate execution of a command language program or macro.

SYNTAX: {QUIT}

       /xq~

These instructions require no arguments.

DESCRIPTION: {QUIT} halts program execution. Don't confuse {QUIT} with {RETURN}, which terminates subroutine execution. When 1-2-3 encounters the {RETURN} instruction, program execution resumes at the point just beyond the instruction that called the subroutine. {QUIT} stops all execution, even if the instruction is encountered in the middle of a subroutine.

The vestigial /xq command performs the same function as the {QUIT} instruction. The /xq command is probably the most frequent source of macro coding errors due to omitted tildes. Compared to {QUIT}, /xq is harder to read, more prone to syntax errors, and slower—although this last limitation hardly matters, given the function of the instruction. The only reason to use /xq instead of {QUIT} is if you have existing programs written for Release 1A and don't want to take the time to change each entry.

EXAMPLES: {QUIT} is most useful when you want to stop program execution in the middle of a routine, usually after an {IF} statement.

Figure 12.58 shows a program that removes all blank lines from a block of double-spaced text. The cell pointer moves through the text a line at a time, and the program tests the "type" of the cell in column A to determine whether the cell is blank. If the cell is blank, the program deletes the row. To stop the process when the end of the text is reached, an @NA value is inserted in the cell below the text. An {IF} instruction in the loop that processes the file tests for this condition, and when the @NA value is found, stops the program with a {QUIT} instruction.

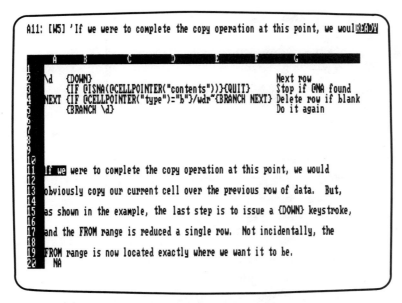

Fig. 12.58. {QUIT} *used to stop a looping program.*

You can also use {QUIT} to stack macros close together when space is at a premium (see fig. 12.59). Each macro ends with a {QUIT} instruction. Therefore, inserting blank lines between the macros is unnecessary.

{READ} and {READLN}

FUNCTION: The {READ} and {READLN} instructions read from a currently opened DOS file and place the results in the worksheet.

SYNTAX: {READ bytecount,location}

{READLN location}

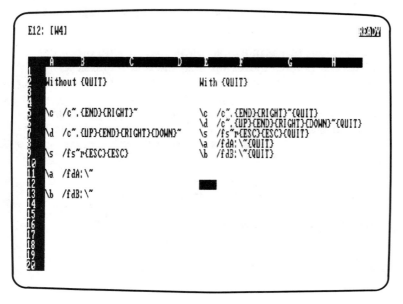

Fig. 12.59. {QUIT} used to make a macro stack.

Argument types for *bytecount*:

Number or numeric expression
Cell address or equivalent range name

Argument types for *location*:

Cell address or equivalent range name
Range address or equivalent range name

The value of *bytecount* determines how many characters of data 1-2-3 reads
from an input file and places in the cell specified by the *location* argument.
Because a cell can hold a maximum of 240 characters, the practical limits for
bytecount are 0–240. 1-2-3 does accept values outside this range, but interprets
negative values and values larger than 240 as 240. The program truncates any
fractional portion of *bytecount*.

DESCRIPTION: {READ} and {READLN} read information from a file specified
in a previously executed {OPEN} instruction. This information is placed, in the
form of a label string, in the cell specified by the *location* argument. {READ}
and {READLN} use an internal counter called a *file pointer*, which indicates the
position in the opened file from which characters will be read. Both
instructions also reposition the file pointer to the character position

immediately following the last character read. Therefore, subsequent {READ} and {READLN} instructions read the file in contiguous segments.

{READLN} reads one line of text that ends with a Carriage Return/Line Feed sequence (CR/LF). Most ASCII text files are stored in this format, including the PRN files generated by 1-2-3's /Print File commands. The string placed in the *location* cell does not contain the CR/LF sequence. {READLN} recognizes as a line terminator only the CR/LF sequence. Single CRs and single LFs are read into the *location* cell as part of the string, but are not recognized as terminators.

TRAP: Some word processors use a LF/CR sequence that {READLN} does not recognize as a line terminator.

If {READLN} does not encounter a CR/LF sequence, the instruction reads up to 240 characters each time it is executed.

{READ} reads the number of characters specified in the *bytecount* argument—up to 240 characters. All characters, including CR/LF sequences, are placed in the string that appears at the *location* cell.

Each time they are executed, {READ} and {READLN} read data from a file. When a command language program stops executing, it doesn't close the file or reset the file pointer. Therefore, a file can be opened by one program and read by another program later. {READ} and {READLN} stop reading when they reach the end of the file, as defined by the size specified in the DOS disk directory.

CONVERTING NONTEXT CHARACTERS: The characters that {READ} and {READLN} read into the worksheet are converted from ASCII to LICS codes, according to 1-2-3's internal translation protocol. 1-2-3 can read all the control characters (those with values of less than ASCII 32) except ASCII 0, and all the standard ASCII codes less than ASCII 128. 1-2-3 translates ASCII codes that are greater than 127 into their equivalent LICS codes. ASCII codes that have no LICS equivalent are converted to LICS 153. When you write to DOS files, a different set of translations is used.

This automatic translation limits the use of command language file operations to the manipulation of text files, even though the @CHAR and @CODE functions enable you to read or construct strings containing all the ASCII codes (except ASCII 0). Assume, for example, that the input string has been placed in the cell named BUFFER. The following formula converts the character specified by PTR into the character's ASCII code equivalent.

    @CODE(@MID(BUFFER,PTR,1))

By using the following formula, you can convert a code into its character equivalent and place the code in a string that {WRITE} or {WRITELN} can write to a file.

@REPLACE(BUFFER,PTR,1,@CHAR(ASCIIVALUE))

TRAP: Other command language instructions cannot follow {READ} and {READLN} on the same line.

Like other file operation instructions, {READ} or {READLN} will only execute instructions on the same line as the {READ} or {READLN} instruction when an error occurs in file operations. Therefore, during normal operation, {READ} or {READLN} must be the last instruction in a cell.

EXAMPLES: For more information on the use of {READ} and {READLN}, see the section on file operations in Chapter 11.

{RECALC} and {RECALCCOL}

FUNCTION: The {RECALC} and {RECALCCOL} instructions recalculate a range of cells.

SYNTAX: {RECALC location[,condition[,iteration]]}

{RECALCCOL location[,condition[,iteration]]}

Argument types for *location*:

Cell address or equivalent range name
Range address or equivalent range name

Argument types for *condition*:

Boolean expression
Number or numeric expression
Cell address or equivalent range name

Argument types for *iteration*:

Number or numeric expression
Cell address or equivalent range name

DESCRIPTION: With {RECALC} and {RECALCCOL}, you can recalculate part of a worksheet. These instructions become especially valuable when you run programs in large worksheets. If a program alters values in cells referenced by other cells, you usually must update the worksheet calculations to reflect the changes. If the worksheet is large, the time required to perform a complete recalculation can make program run-time unacceptably long. By using {RECALC} and {RECALCCOL} to update only those cells affected by the changes, you can make the program run significantly faster.

When you use {RECALC} or {RECALCCOL}, you lose the "natural order" recalculation for which the Lotus programs area famous. Natural order recalculation is foolproof only when the whole worksheet is recalculated. {RECALC} and {RECALCCOL} recalculate the cells specified in the *location* argument in a particular order, which is unrelated to the relationships between the variables that determine natural order. {RECALC} recalculates a range by moving from left to right, then down a row at a time. {RECALCCOL} moves down a cell at a time in a column, then from left to right a column at a time.

Whether you use {RECALC} or {RECALCCOL} depends on the physical layout of the cells you are recalculating. With a chain of references, where a first cell refers to a second that refers to a third and so on, you should calculate the third cell first and the first cell last (see fig. 12.60).

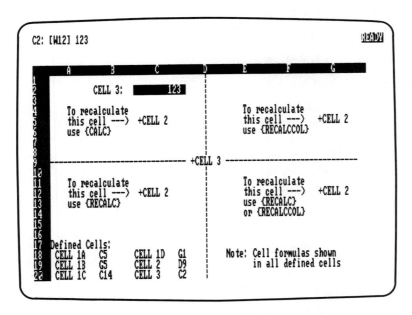

Fig. 12.60. When to use {RECALC} or {RECALCCOL}.

The example in figure 12.60 assumes that the value in the cell labeled CELL 3 is altered first. The value in CELL 2 depends on the value in CELL 3, and the value in all versions of CELL 1 depends on CELL 2. The form of recalculation to use to update the CELL 1 and CELL 2 entries appears as marked in the quadrants. In each case, the specified recalculation range should include CELL 1 *and* CELL 2.

When CELL 1 is above and to the left of CELL 2, neither {RECALC} nor {RECALCCOL} can recalculate CELL 2 before recalculating CELL 1. If the cells are arranged this way, you might want to use {CALC} to be sure that all cell values are up-to-date. However, using {RECALC} or {RECALCCOL} *twice* might be faster, depending on the application. Eventually, unless you have circular references, any cell arrangement will be up-to-date after repeated applications of {RECALC} or {RECALCCOL}.

SPECIFYING THE CONDITION AND ITERATION ARGUMENTS: Both the {RECALC} instructions enable you to specify two optional arguments to control the number of times the specified range is recalculated. The first of these arguments, *condition*, provides a test for stopping the calculations. When you execute a {RECALC} with a *condition* argument, the instruction recalculates the specified range and checks the value of *condition*. If the value is equal to zero, the recalculation is repeated, and *condition* is checked again. If the value is equal to anything but zero, program control passes to the next instruction. For example, the following instruction would recalculate the range named PART1 until the cell called INCOME was greater than zero.

    {RECALC PART1,INCOME>0}

You can also specify the maximum number of recalculations that can take place, in case the *condition* never becomes satisfied. You accomplish this task by adding the *iteration* argument after the *condition*. For example, the following instruction performs the same recalculation specified in the preceding example but stops the process if INCOME is not greater than 0 after 100 attempts.

    {RECALC PART1,INCOME>0,100}

If you want to force recalculation a specified number of times and not relate the process to a condition, you set *condition* to zero and include the *iteration* count. The following examples illustrate how this task is accomplished:

    {RECALC PART1,0,100}

    {RECALC PART1,@FALSE,100}

The *iteration* argument can be a formula or a cell reference that is part of the recalculated range. The initial value of *iteration* determines the number of recalculations. Changes in this value as a result of recalculations don't have any effect on the recalculation process.

DETERMINING RECALCULATION SPEED: {RECALC} and {RECALCCOL} work staggeringly fast. The time needed for recalculation depends, of course, on the number of cells in the recalculation range and the formula in each cell. The time per cell also depends on the number of iterations; whether the recalculation range is long and thin or more nearly square; and some other things you wouldn't expect, such as which column the recalculation range is in and how much other information is in the worksheet.

The following rough benchmarks were run on a COMPAQ Deskpro 286 with an 80287 math coprocessor and probably represent the best performance you are likely to see. For a standard IBM PC, multiply the times shown here by 3.54 and increase the times another 15 percent if you don't have a coprocessor. The calculations were performed on a 100-row-by-10-column range in an otherwise empty worksheet.

Overhead time to call the {RECALC} instruction:

0.01 second

Time to recalculate a blank cell:

0.00005 seconds/cell or 20,000 cells/second

Time to recalculate a simple cell reference (+A1):

0.00038 seconds/cell or 2,631 cells/second

Time to recalculate a very complex string formula:

0.0108 seconds/cell or 93 cells/second

EXAMPLES: You can use {RECALC} with the @CELLPOINTER function to make temporary copies of the contents of various cells (see fig. 12.61).

This method examines a list of range names, created by using the /Range Name Table command. When a /Worksheet Delete or Move command damages a named range, the address assigned to that name becomes ERR. The program examines the ranges assigned to each name in the list and deletes any such damaged range names.

You can also use {RECALC}—not as part of an operating program but as an alternative to using {CALC}—to update part of a large worksheet. If the sections of the worksheet are independent, you can specify each section with a separate range name and include each section in a utility macro which recalculates only that section. For example, if a section of your worksheet is dedicated to an income statement, you could give that section the range name INCOME. The following macro would then recalculate only that section:

\r   {RECALC INCOME,0,2}

If you set up such a macro, you probably will want to recalculate more than once to be sure that all cells are up-to-date. To test the effectiveness of your macro in recalculating a particular area of the worksheet, press the Calc key

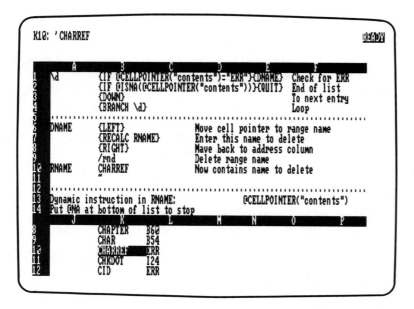

Fig. 12.61. {RECALC} and @CELLPOINTER used to clean up a list of range names.

(F9) after using your recalculation macro. If no changes appear in the calculations, then your macro works. If changes do occur, add another iteration to {RECALC}.

{RESTART}

FUNCTION: The {RESTART} instruction clears all return addresses from the subroutine stack.

SYNTAX: {RESTART}

No arguments are required for this instruction.

DESCRIPTION: {RESTART} clears the subroutine return address stack. A *stack* is a list of addresses that grows as subroutines are called and addresses are added. To understand {RESTART}'s function, you have to know something about subroutine calls. If a program has no subroutines, 1-2-3 moves the instruction pointer from cell to cell as the program executes. When 1-2-3 encounters a subroutine, however, the program moves the instruction pointer to the location of the subroutine. The instruction pointer must return to the cell following the subroutine call when the subroutine finishes executing. For this to happen,

1-2-3 must keep a record of that cell's position, or a *return address*. 1-2-3 must keep in order two return addresses if the program encounters a subroutine within a subroutine.

1-2-3 (and other programming systems) keeps track of return addresses by keeping them in a stack. The stack shrinks as the subroutines finish executing and the corresponding return address is removed from the list. Figure 12.62 shows a program that contains two levels of nested subroutine calls. If you could see the stack for this program, the stack would change as shown in table 12.11.

Table 12.11
The Operation of the Subroutine Return Address Stack

Program Event	Stack
Line 1	none
Line 2: call routine {load}	Line 3
{load} routine executes then:	Line 3
blank cell encountered in line 8:	Line 3
Program branches to address on stack	Line 3
Address removed from stack	none
Line 3: call routine {process}	Line 4
Line 9: call routine {format}	Line 4, Line 10
{format} routine executes then:	Line 4, Line 10
blank cell encountered in line 20:	Line 4, Line 10
Program branches to address on stack	Line 4, Line 10
Address removed from stack	Line 4
Line 11: call routine {format}	Line 4, Line 12
{format} routine executes then:	Line 4, Line 12
blank cell encountered in line 20:	Line 4, Line 12
Program branches to address on stack	Line 4, Line 12
Address removed from stack	Line 4
Line 13: call routine {format}	Line 4, Line 14
{format} routine executes then:	Line 4, Line 14
blank cell encountered in line 20:	Line 4, Line 14
Program branches to address on stack	Line 4, Line 14
Address removed from stack	Line 4
blank cell encountered in line 14:	Line 4
Program branches to address on stack	Line 4
Address removed from stack	none
blank cell encountered in line 5:	none
Stack is empty; program terminates	none

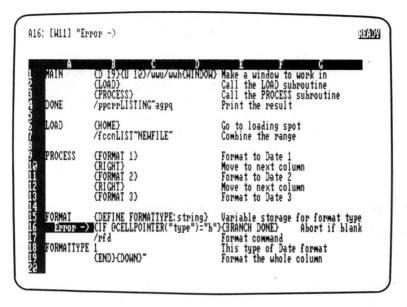

Fig. 12.62. A sample program that contains an error.

Although this process is rather tedious to follow, sometimes we need to understand what is going on inside a program. Notice in table 12.11 that whenever the program encounters a blank cell, the program checks the stack to see where to branch, using the address most recently added. Program execution stops if the stack is empty.

The program in figure 12.62 has a deliberate error in line 16. If the {BRANCH} instruction were executed, the program would process the last part of the MAIN routine and print as intended. However, return addresses have been left in the stack. When the program encounters the blank cell in line 5, the program peels the top address from the stack and continues execution somewhere in the {PROCESS} subroutine. Eventually the program stops, but only after printing two copies of the specified print output.

Admittedly, this example has been simplified. Several ways exist to program around this problem (see the example accompanying the {RETURN} instruction). Sometimes you need to be able to branch out of a subroutine when return addresses are still in the stack. To keep the program from running away with itself when it encounters these leftover addresses, 1-2-3 has the {RESTART} instruction, which clears stacks. The program would run as intended if you inserted {RESTART} before the {BRANCH DONE} instruction.

{RETURN} and /xr

FUNCTION: {RETURN} specifies the end of a subroutine.

SYNTAX: {RETURN}

/xr~

These instructions require no arguments.

DESCRIPTION: {RETURN} causes the executing program to return from a subroutine. {RETURN} is analogous to {QUIT}, except that {RETURN} stops a subroutine from executing and returns program control to the instruction immediately after the subroutine call (see the description of the return address stack under {RESTART}). {QUIT}, by comparison, stops *all* processing.

1-2-3 automatically executes a return from a subroutine when the program encounters a blank or numeric cell. Therefore, considerations for using {RETURN} are the same as those for using {QUIT}. You will use {RETURN} most frequently following an {IF} instruction to make the subroutine stop at a location other than the end.

Those of you who are familiar with Release 1A's macro language will recognize that {RETURN} performs the same function as /xr. Like all the other /xr commands, /xr is difficult to read, prone to encoding errors from omitted tildes, and much slower than its command language equivalent. You should probably avoid using /xr entirely. In fact, because a blank cell forces a subroutine return, you can in most cases omit the {RETURN} instruction. The only time a {RETURN} is required is when you want to terminate a subroutine after an {IF} test.

EXAMPLE: The subroutine in figure 12.63 sets the format of a column of numbers to one of the Date formats (1–5), as determined by the parameter specified in the {DEFINE} instruction. The second line of the subroutine contains an {IF} instruction that checks for a blank cell. If the cell is blank, the {RETURN} instruction is issued, and the subroutine is not executed.

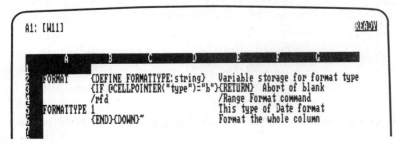

Fig. 12.63. {RETURN} *used to stop a subroutine conditionally.*

{SETPOS}

FUNCTION: The {SETPOS} instruction sets the position of the file pointer in files opened with {OPEN}.

SYNTAX: {SETPOS file-position}

Argument types for *file-position*:

Number or numeric expression
Cell address or equivalent range name

DESCRIPTION: {SETPOS} enables you to position the file pointer in an opened file. The file pointer specifies in bytes the offset from the beginning of the file, where reading and writing operations take place using one of the {READ} or {WRITE} instructions. {SETPOS} is a companion instruction to {GETPOS}, which returns the file pointer's current position.

When you first open a file for READ, WRITE, or MODIFY operations, the file pointer is set to the beginning of the file, which is offset zero. For APPEND operations, the file pointer is set to the end of the file, which is equivalent to the file size. Specifying a negative value for the *file-position* argument is equivalent to setting it to zero. For READ operations, the file pointer can't be positioned beyond the end of the file, as specified by the file size information in the DOS disk directory (the value returned by the {FILESIZE} instruction). You can specify an argument larger than the file size, but then subsequent {READ} instructions won't work. If you position the file pointer beyond the end of the file for WRITE operations, the file will be enlarged to place the data at the position you specify.

EXAMPLES: You can use {SETPOS} to read and write to any location in a file. One of the most common uses for this kind of operation is to manipulate database files with fixed record lengths. If you know the standard record length, you can access any record in the file by setting the file pointer to a number you obtain by multiplying the record length by the record number. For instance, if you are working in a data file with fixed record lengths of 80 bytes, and you want to read the data from record 20, you set the file pointer to 1600. (The first record in the file is assumed to be numbered 0.)

By extending this idea, you can create index files that reference the database file. This technique is common for handling large database files. Rather than sort the database itself, you create a *key file* that lists the record numbers in the sorted order. Then an output routine can list the database in sorted order by accessing the records in the order in which they appear in the key file. Using multiple key files, you can list a database in any order without rearranging the database. If you add records to the database, you need only to re-sort the key file, which is usually much smaller and easier to sort than the database file.

The example in figure 12.64 is an output routine that lists records in the order specified by the range named KEY. The numbers in the KEY range are record numbers rather than file position numbers. Therefore, KEY is independent of the record length. Listed with the program are two sample outputs from the program, shown in figures 12.65 and 12.66, as well as the KEY range for that listing.

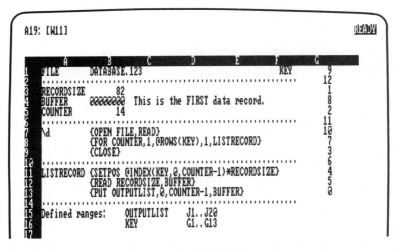

Fig. 12.64. Random record access using {SETPOS}.

```
00000009   This is the TENTH data record.
00000012   This is the THIRTEENTH data record.
00000001   This is the SECOND data record.
00000008   This is the NINTH data record.
00000002   This is the THIRD data record.
00000011   This is the TWELFTH data record.
00000010   This is the ELEVENTH data record.
00000007   This is the EIGHTH data record.
00000003   This is the FOURTH data record.
00000006   This is the SEVENTH data record.
00000004   This is the FIFTH data record.
00000005   This is the SIXTH data record.
00000000   This is the FIRST data record.
```

Fig. 12.65. Sample output from program using {SETPOS}. *The KEY range specifies the order of the listed records.*

```
00000000   This is the FIRST data record.
00000001   This is the SECOND data record.
00000002   This is the THIRD data record.
00000003   This is the FOURTH data record.
00000004   This is the FIFTH data record.
00000005   This is the SIXTH data record.
00000006   This is the SEVENTH data record.
00000007   This is the EIGHTH data record.
00000008   This is the NINTH data record.
00000009   This is the TENTH data record.
00000010   This is the ELEVENTH data record.
00000011   This is the TWELFTH data record.
00000012   This is the THIRTEENTH data record.
```

Fig. 12.66. Second sample output from the program using {SETPOS}. The KEY range was sorted using /Data Sort prior to running the program.

{ . . . subroutine . . . }

FUNCTION: { . . . subroutine . . . } performs a subroutine call to a named subroutine.

SYNTAX: {routine-name}

>   or

>   {routine-name parameter1[,parameter2]..[,parameter*n*]}

Argument types for *routine-name*:

Any valid range name

Argument types for optional *parameters*:

Number or numeric expression
String or string formula
Cell address or equivalent range name
Range address or equivalent range name

If the range name contains spaces, it must be enclosed in quotation marks—for example,

{SUBROUTINE}

{"SUB ROUTINE"}

Cell addresses and range addresses can't be used for subroutine calls.

If you include parameters in a subroutine call, the subroutine must contain a {DEFINE} statement. Whether a *parameter* is interpreted as a string or formula depends on the corresponding *type* specification in the {DEFINE} statement (see {DEFINE}).

TRAP: Range names that duplicate macro keywords or command language instruction names take precedence over standard names.

If you create a range name that has the same name as a macro keyword or command language instruction, 1-2-3 tries to execute what is in that range as a subroutine instead of the keyword or command language function the range name duplicates. Therefore, you can write subroutines that replace the standard functions.

However, if you inadvertently create a range name that duplicates a standard name, strange things happen when you run a program which tries to use that function. The range name doesn't have to be assigned to a macro or program in order for this problem to occur. Suppose, for instance, that you are creating a reference cell to store the name of the window to be used in printing. If you name that cell WINDOW and later try to execute a {WINDOW} command from within a program, the program reads WINDOW as a subroutine name—not as the {WINDOW} keyword—and sends the instruction pointer to that location. Then your program attempts to execute that cell's contents as a macro.

DESCRIPTION: { . . . subroutine . . . } is a call to a subroutine. The subroutine name is enclosed in braces and included in the program as if it were another instruction. When 1-2-3 encounters a subroutine call, 1-2-3 sets the instruction pointer to the upper left corner of the range named within the braces. 1-2-3 also makes a record of the instruction pointer's position before the subroutine call is made (see {RESTART} for a description of the stack). When the subroutine finishes executing, 1-2-3 sets the instruction pointer to the address following the subroutine call.

You use a subroutine exactly like you use any of 1-2-3's built-in keywords or instructions. 1-2-3 executes a subroutine as a separate unit, then passes control to the next instruction. In designing programs, you may want to think of subroutines as new command language instructions that you have created. You simply build your new instructions from existing instructions.

The ability to create new instructions enables you to organize programs by assembling into modules groups of instruction that perform a specific task. For example, you could have a subroutine named {LOADFILE} that loads a file into your worksheet; a routine named {SORTFILE} that uses 1-2-3's sorting functions to rearrange the file; a routine named {PRINTOUT} that prints the new listing; and a routine named {SAVEFILE} that uses /**File Xtract** to extract out the new, sorted file to disk. Your entire program, then, could consist of the four subroutine calls in the following order:

{LOADFILE}

{SORTFILE}

{PRINTOUT}

{SAVEFILE}

The main program becomes short and virtually self-documenting because the routines' names describe what they do. You can temporarily assign a macro name to each routine so that you can develop and test each module separately.

A subroutine can contain a call to another subroutine, an arrangement called *nesting*. 1-2-3 allows nesting up to 32 levels.

You can pass parameters to subroutines. A *parameter*, in this sense, is simply a value that a subroutine can use. This capability is powerful because it enables you to write "generic" subroutines that you can use in more than one place. Figure 12.53 shows an example of such a routine in the description of {MENUCALL}.

EXAMPLE: Figure 12.67 shows another example of a subroutine that uses passed parameters. I used this subroutine to extract various ranges from the worksheet I used in writing a book on Symphony. The subroutine asks for the current chapter ID (each chapter was written in segments of about 20 pages each) and saves the response in the range called CID. This range is then passed as the second parameter in the subroutine call. Notice that the corresponding entry in the {DEFINE} statement identifies this parameter as a value. Without this definition, the three characters c, i, and d would have been used instead. When the subroutine executes, it constructs a file name from the first two parameters and saves the range named in the third parameter in that file.

{WAIT}

FUNCTION: The {WAIT} instruction causes program execution to pause and wait until the computer's system clock registers a specific date and time.

SYNTAX: {WAIT date-timevalue}

Argument types for *date-timevalue*:

Number or numeric expression
Cell address or equivalent range name

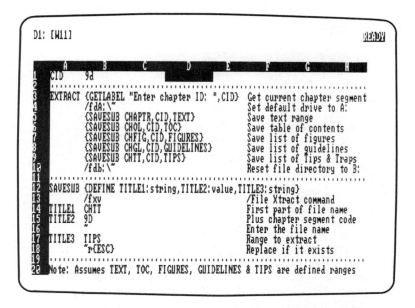

Fig. 12.67. A subroutine with passed parameters to extract a series of ranges.

The *date-timevalue* argument is a number representing the date and time in 1-2-3's standard date and time format. You can also use the @NOW, @DATE, @TIME, @DATEVALUE, and @TIMEVALUE functions to create arguments for this instruction.

DESCRIPTION: {WAIT} halts program execution until the computer's internal clock (as shown in the lower left corner of the screen) reaches the specified value. When setting the {WAIT} instruction for a particular time setting, you must enter both the date and time as a single argument.

When the {WAIT} instruction is in effect, the program retains control over the system, and the WAIT indicator appears in the upper right corner of the screen.

EXAMPLES: Figure 12.68 shows two ways to use the {WAIT} instruction. The first subroutine (WAIT) makes 1-2-3 wait until the specified time and date are reached. This subroutine could come in handy should you ever find yourself somewhere with a computer but without an alarm clock. You could also use {WAIT} to wake you up after a quick lunch-hour nap.

The second routine (PAUSE) makes 1-2-3 wait for the amount of time specified in the @TIME function. {WAIT} is used differently in these subroutines. In the first subroutine, the program waits for a specific time to be reached. In the

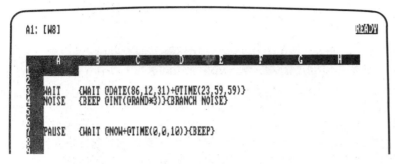

```
A1: [W8]                                                    READY

          A      B      C      D      E      F      G      H
1
2
3     WAIT     {WAIT @DATE(86,12,31)+@TIME(23,59,59)}
4     NOISE    {BEEP @INT((@RAND*3))}{BRANCH NOISE}
5
6
7     PAUSE    {WAIT @NOW+@TIME(0,0,10)}{BEEP}
8
9
```

Fig. 12.68. Two subroutines that use {WAIT}.

second subroutine, the program waits for a particular amount of time, starting from the time {WAIT} is first executed.

{WINDOWSON} and {WINDOWSOFF}

FUNCTION: {WINDOWSON} and {WINDOWSOFF} enable and disable, respectively, the updating of the worksheet screen during program execution.

SYNTAX: {WINDOWSOFF}

{WINDOWSON}

Neither instruction requires an argument.

DESCRIPTION: {WINDOWSOFF}, a companion instruction to the {PANELOFF} and {PANELON} instructions that control the control panel display, suspends the updating of the screen until program execution stops or 1-2-3 encounters a {WINDOWSON} instruction. {WINDOWSOFF} is used primarily for cosmetic purposes. It hides the flashing and movement of the display while a program is running.

TIP: {WINDOWSOFF} can speed program operation.

If you have used Symphony's Command Language, you are probably aware of what little effect the {WINDOWSOFF} command has on program execution time. With Symphony, apparently all the calculations to generate the display are made, even with the windows off; therefore, the speed advantage from {WINDOWSOFF} is in the range of 3 to 5 percent. Things are different with 1-2-3. Using {WINDOWSOFF} can save you 30 to 40 percent in execution time. By combining {WINDOWSOFF} with {PANELOFF}, you can double your program's speed.

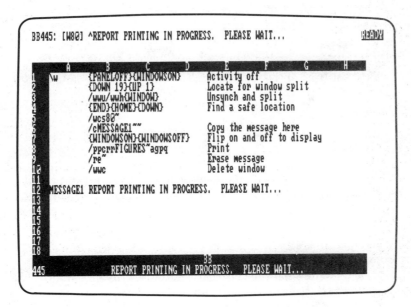

Fig. 12.69. {WINDOWSOFF} *used to display messages while the program is running.*

EXAMPLE: You can use the program in figure 12.69 to display a message whenever you want to hide the action on the screen. Notice both that the {PANELOFF} instruction was issued before the program switched windows and that the {WINDOWSOFF} instruction was issued after switching windows. This procedure keeps the control panel from echoing the display on the screen. The highlighting effect was created by setting the column width in the second window to 80.

By extending this procedure, you can create messages that change as the hidden program runs. To replace the message displayed, you can use a {LET} instruction or the {DEFINE} portion of a subroutine. After changing the message, you must switch to the message window and issue {WINDOWSON}{WINDOWSOFF} to be sure that the message is displayed.

{WRITE} and {WRITELN}

FUNCTION: The {WRITE} and {WRITELN} instructions send the string contents of a specified worksheet cell to a DOS file opened with {OPEN}.

SYNTAX: {WRITE bytes,output-string}

{WRITELN output-string}

Argument types for *bytes*:

Number or numeric expression
Cell address or equivalent range name

Argument types for *output-string*:

String or string formula
Cell address or equivalent range name

If you use a range name as the *output-string*, it must use as its reference a cell address. If *output-string* doesn't evaluate to a cell address, 1-2-3 writes the range name as if it were a string argument enclosed in quotation marks rather than the contents of the named range.

The *output-string* argument must be a string. Before you can write numbers to a file, you must convert the numbers to a string. The output also must be a single cell. If you want to write multiple-cell data, you must create a string formula to concatenate all the values into one cell and use that as the output cell.

DESCRIPTION: Both {WRITE} and {WRITELN} write string information to a file that has been opened for WRITE, APPEND, or MODIFY operations (see {OPEN}). Both instructions transfer the contents of the *output-string* argument to the file, using 1-2-3's internal translation scheme. Both instructions also write the number of characters contained in *output-string*.

If you want to write a fixed number of characters in a WRITE operation, as you would with fixed-length records, you must pad short entries with spaces. For example, if you were using a cell named BUFFER as the source of your *output-string* and wanted to write fixed-length, 80-character records, you could make all records that length by including the following {LET} instruction before the {WRITE} or {WRITELN}:

{LET BUFFER,BUFFER&@REPEAT(" ",80−@LENGTH(BUFFER))}

The difference between the two instructions is that {WRITELN} adds a CR/LF sequence (ASCII 10/ASCII 13) at the end of each WRITE operation, whereas {WRITE} does not. Therefore, you can import records written with {WRITELN} by using 1-2-3's /File Import Text command. This command can't read records written with {WRITE} unless CR/LF sequences occur to break the records into groups of 240 characters or less.

TRAP: {WRITELN} adds two characters to the length of every line.

When you use {WRITELN}, keep in mind that {WRITELN} adds the CR/LF to the string you specify. Therefore, if you are writing 80-character records, the records will be 82 characters long when the records appear in the file. This is important if you are using {SETPOS} to position the file pointer for reading or writing purposes.

CLOSING FILES: When writing data to a file, you must complete the writing process by using {CLOSE} to close the file. When a {WRITE} instruction is executed, the information written isn't immediately written to the disk. In fact, as the program runs, you will probably notice that the disk drive light comes on intermittently. It does so because 1-2-3 writes data to the disk a sector (512 bytes) at a time. As 1-2-3 executes the {WRITE} or {WRITELN} instruction, the data goes into an internal buffer in the computer's memory until 512 bytes have been accumulated. Only when the buffer is full does 1-2-3 write the buffer's entire contents to the file.

When your program finishes processing, chances are that some data in the buffer hasn't been written to the disk. {CLOSE} forces the buffer's contents to be written, even if the buffer isn't full, and ensures that all the data gets to the disk file. {CLOSE} also updates the information in the disk directory that describes the file. If this information isn't updated, your data probably will be inaccessible. For more information, see Chapter 11.

EXAMPLE: The program in figure 12.70 writes a series of records to a file called DATABASE.SYM. Each record is 82 characters long and consists of an 8-character record number, 2 spaces, and a 70-character data field that is entered through a {GETLABEL} instruction. Notice the formula used to construct the record number with leading zeros.

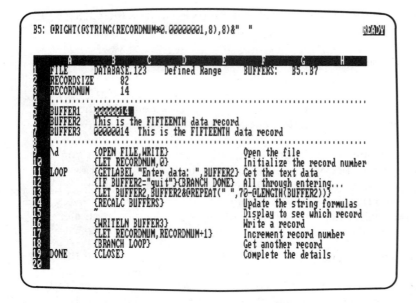

Fig. 12.70. A program to create a fixed-record-length data file.

Glossary

Command Language Programming Terms

Address

An *address* refers to the location of data or program instructions. Unless you are brand new to spreadsheets, the term *address* should be familiar to you, because it is the basis of most spreadsheet work.

You may be less familiar with indirect addressing, a powerful programming concept that, when used correctly, can perform complicated operations with just a few instructions. You can think of an *indirect address* as the address where you find the address in which you are interested. For example, I can give you directions to Bob's house by telling you where Jerry lives. You take Jerry's address, go there, and Jerry gives you Bob's address so that you can go there. Jerry's address is the indirect address. The @@ function and {DISPATCH} instruction both provide indirect addressing in 1-2-3.

Array

An *array* is a set of data, usually arranged in a specific order. In most programming languages, an array is a single name assigned to more than one data element. To refer to a specific data element in an array, you use the element's name and a number, which is frequently enclosed in parentheses following the name and called a *subscript*. For instance, to refer to the third data element in the array called *ARC* (an arbitrary name), you specify *ARC(3)*. This is usually read aloud as "ARC sub three." The subscript specifies the order and position of the data elements in the array.

A single subscript refers to a list of information, but arrays can contain more than one list. Arrays that contain two lists are said to have two *dimensions*, analogous to rows and columns. You use two subscripts in a two-dimensionsal array—for example, *ARC(3,5)*. One subscript number is a row number; the other, a column number. In 1-2-3, the @INDEX function and the {PUT} instruction manipulate numbers in a range in the same way other programming languages use two-dimensional arrays.

Branch

Branch refers to the transfer of control in an operating computer program. Usually, the computer executes a sequence of instructions in the same order they would be read: left to right, top to bottom. The usual order of execution, however, can be violated by "branching" to another location. Some computer languages have an instruction called GOTO that performs the branching function. Because GOTO in 1-2-3 usually refers to the F5 function key, I've tried to avoid using the word *GOTO* when I mean *branch*. This distinction is frequently confusing for new users. Just remember that GOTO is something that happens to the cell pointer, the effect of which is usually visible on the screen. Branching, on the other hand, is something that happens to 1-2-3's internal command language instruction pointer, and the results are never directly visible.

Bug

A *bug* is something wrong with a program. There are many stories regarding the origin of the term, and they are probably all apocryphal. One version holds that in the early days of the telephone, poor connections sometimes generated a buzzing sound in the telephone—hence, "bugs" in the system. Today, the term is invoked whenever a program doesn't perform as intended and is usually a euphemism for a *stupid mistake*.

Call

Call refers to the process of invoking a subroutine in a program. A *subroutine* is a set of instructions, just like any other set of program instructions. Two features make instructions a subroutine: (1) the way in which program control is transferred to the first of the subroutine instructions, and (2) what happens to program control when the subroutine is finished executing. When a subroutine is *called* from inside a program, the instruction pointer is transferred to the subroutine. This is the same thing that happens when you use a

{BRANCH} instruction. With a subroutine, however, the instruction pointer returns to where it left off in the original program. This procedure is similar to giving someone instructions to "stop doing this, go do that, then come back here and continue doing this again."

Code

Code is a generic term for program instructions. If you are new to programming, this term may seem especially appropriate.

Constant

A *constant* is a value that doesn't change during program execution. In 1-2-3, a number or label entered into a cell is a constant. The value 3.3 is a constant in the following {IF} statement:

    {IF SOMEVALUE=3.3}

A formula can also be a constant. What matters is not so much how the value is derived but whether it changes during or as the result of program operation.

Dynamic Variables

Dynamic variables, or simply *variables*, are values that change during program operation. With the command language, you can use variables within string formulas to create program instructions that change as the program runs. This type of instruction is referred to as a dynamic instruction.

END

END can have two different connotations in programming, depending on the programming language used. In Pascal, BEGIN and END define sections of code that work as a unit, ranging from a single instruction to an entire program. If you are a BASIC programmer, you know that the END statement occurs only once, as the last statement encountered by a normally operating program. This use of END at the end of a program is a holdover from FORTRAN, which required that an END statement be the last statement in the listing of a program or subprogram.

The use of END in both BASIC and FORTRAN differs from the use of the STOP instruction. STOP causes a program to stop running at something other than its natural end-point—for instance, when an error is encountered. The difference between the two instructions is that END does some computer housekeeping, such as making sure that all files are properly saved, whereas STOP just stops, leaving unfinished business unfinished. If the distinction seems a little fuzzy, compare the terminology with traveling in a car: you can *stop* at the store, but you haven't reached the *end* of your journey until you get home.

Programmers like myself, whose first language was FORTRAN, tend to use the terms *stop* and *end* to imply the different types of endings just described. Although the distinction is subtle, it is useful, and I use it throughout this book. Because both *stop* and *end* have special connotations, many computer programmers have adopted *terminate* as the more general term to describe the process of ending or stopping. I also use *terminate* in this way. Thus, a program can *end* normally or *stop* prematurely. A subroutine can *end*, or a loop can *terminate* execution; in both cases, the program hasn't *stopped*. These distinctions aren't critical for programming with the command language, but may help clarify some of the program descriptions in this book.

Literal

Literal, which can sometimes be a synonym for *constant*, most frequently refers to the characters enclosed in quotation marks in a string formula.

Module

A *module* is a subroutine or group of subroutines that performs some well-defined program function. At the lowest level of definition, any subroutine can be a module. A group of subroutines, however, can also function as a module. A program might have an *input module, a processing module*, and a *printing module*, each composed of one or multiple subroutines.

Nesting

Nesting is the action of including a subroutine in another subroutine or including a function in another function. Subroutines can contain subroutines that contain subroutines, and so forth. A subroutine inside a subroutine is said to be *nested one level deep*. If the inside subroutine contains still another subroutine, this latter subroutine is said to be *nested two levels deep*. The first of these subroutines is sometimes called the *parent*; the nested subroutine, the *child*. The *child* subroutine becomes a *parent* if it contains another level of nested subroutine.

Return

Return has two distinct meanings in computerese: the word refers to the Enter (or Return) key on the keyboard as well as to the action taken by 1-2-3 when it reaches the end of a subroutine (when program execution "returns" to where it left off when the subroutine was called). 1-2-3 has a special instruction, {RETURN}, that marks the end of a subroutine. Unfortunately, because of the way in which keywords are listed in 1-2-3, this instruction looks like the keyword equivalent of the Enter (or Return) key. As you know from the macro chapters of this book, the keyword for the Enter key is the tilde (~). To differentiate between the two uses of the word *return*, I use Enter to refer to the keystroke, and {RETURN} or just *return* to refer to what happens when a subroutine terminates.

Routine

Routine is a more general term for *subroutine*. Whereas a *sub*routine, strictly speaking, is a subpart of something larger, a routine can stand on its own. My usage of the term, however, isn't so formal. I use the word *routine* as a synonym for *module*, with the same broad definition.

Index

More Computer Knowledge from Que

FOLD HERE

———————————————————

———————————————————

———————————————————

———————————————————

Place
Stamp
Here

Que Corporation
P. O. Box 50507
Indianapolis, IN 46250

LEARN MORE ABOUT 1-2-3
WITH THESE QUE TITLES

Using 1-2-3, 2nd Edition
by Douglas Cobb and Geoffrey LeBlond

Nationally acclaimed, *Using 1-2-3* is "the book"
for every 1-2-3 user. Whether you are using
Release 1A or 2, you will find *Using 1-2-3*, 2nd
Edition, your most valuable source of information.
Spreadsheet, database, graphics, and macro
capabilities common to both Releases 1A and 2
or new to Release 2 are all covered in depth.
Notations in the text and a tear-out command
chart help you locate quickly the differences
between Releases 1A and 2. Like thousands of
other 1-2-3 users, you will consider this book
indispensable.

1-2-3 Business Formula Handbook
by Ron Person

The *1-2-3 Business Formula Handbook*, a
convenient desktop reference, helps you create
the formulas you need for building your 1-2-3
models. More than 30 models show you how to
create 1-2-3 formulas for financial analysis,
business forecasts, investment analysis, and
statistical and survey analysis. Each section
explains thoroughly the 1-2-3 model, formulas
used, and assumptions. You can easily duplicate
the model or modify it for your applications. The
1-2-3 Business Formula Handbook will save you
time while you develop your skill in using
complex 1-2-3 formulas. A companion disk is
available.

1-2-3 Financial Macros
by Thomas W. Carlton

1-2-3 Fianancial Macros is for 1-2-3 users who want
to learn to use the full power of 1-2-3 macros. This
book will show how to develop complex
spreadsheets and database models controlled by
macros. Expanding on the applications introduced in
1-2-3 Macro Library, this book contains macro
applications for accounting, budgeting, forecasting,
and analysis. Other sophisticated applications in
1-2-3 Financial Macros are macros for a stock
portfolio model and project management. A
companion disk is available.

1-2-3 Macro Library, 2nd Edition
by David P. Ewing

Take advantage of 1-2-3, Release 2's macro
capability, including its powerful command
language, with *1-2-3 Macro Library*, 2nd Edition.
This easy-to-use reference teaches the user how to
create more than 100 macros for 1-2-3 spreadsheet,
data management, and graphics applications.
Readers will learn how to develop file management
and print macros and design macros for special
applications, such as using 1-2-3 to develop mail
merge capabilities. And for 1-2-3, Release 1A users,
references throughout the book and an appendix
help create Release 1A macros. For those just
getting started or looking for help with advanced
macro applications, this comprehensive library
provides all of the necessary information.

Mail to: Que Corporation • P. O. Box 50507 • Indianapolis, IN 46250

Item	Title	Price	Quantity	Extension
130	Using 1-2-3, 2nd Edition	$21.95		
196	1-2-3 Business Formula Handbook	$19.95		
187	1-2-3 Financial Macros	$19.95		
44	1-2-3 Macro Library, 2nd Edition	$19.95		

Book Subtotal

Shipping & Handling ($2.50 per item)

Indiana Residents Add 5% Sales Tax

GRAND TOTAL

Method of Payment:

☐ Check   ☐ VISA   ☐ MasterCard   ☐ American Express

Card Number _____ Exp. Date _____

Cardholder's Name _____

Ship to _____

Address _____

City _____ State _____ ZIP _____

If you can't wait, call **1-800-428-5331** and order TODAY.

All prices subject to change without notice.

REGISTER YOUR COPY OF
1-2-3® *COMMAND LANGUAGE*

Register your copy of *1-2-3 Command Language* and receive information about Que's newest products relating to integrated programs. Complete this registration card and return it to Que Corporation, P.O. Box 50507, Indianapolis, IN 46250.

Name _____

Address _____

City _____ State _____ ZIP _____

Phone _____

Where did you buy your copy of *1-2-3 Command Language*?

_____

How do you plan to use the programs in this book?

_____

_____

_____

What other kinds of publications about integrated software would you be interested in?

_____

_____

Which operating system do you use? _____

THANK YOU!

123CL-869